The ICSA

Corporate Governance *Handbook*

The ICSA

Corporate Governance *Handbook*

BRIAN COYLE

Published by ICSA Publishing Ltd
16 Park Crescent
London W1B 1AH

Designed and typeset in 9.75 on 13 pt Goudy by Paul Barrett Book Production, Cambridge
Printed and bound in Great Britain by TJ International Ltd, Padstow, Cornwall

British Library Cataloguing in Publication Data

A catalogue record for this book is available from the British Library

ISBN 1 86072 248 2

Contents

Preface

The ICSA Corporate Governance Handbook has been developed as a single-source reference manual for professionals engaged in this increasingly important aspect of corporate life.

The aim is to provide a reliable and accessible tool for readers. Each chapter is a self-contained unit in its own right, covering a particular aspect of the field and divided into numbered, fully cross-referenced sections. The commentary is accompanied by a comprehensive set of appendices, which provide the full text of a wide range of codes of practice and best practice guidelines from the key authorities. A comprehensive index aids navigation, together with a table outlining coverage of all Combined Code Principles and Provisions. A Directory section brings together further reading and other useful sources of information, including a web-site listing.

Corporate governance is a fast-moving field, which is defined and developed by regular new developments, ongoing consultations and emerging best practice. To reflect this, purchasers of the printed *Handbook* also receive free access to ICSA Publishing's *Corporate Governance Briefing* service, a bi-monthly news digest accessed either via the ICSA Publishing web-site or, on request, via e-mail. To access this service, readers should:

- go to www.icsapublishing.co.uk
- select Online Briefings, then Corporate Governance Briefing
- enter the current username and password: cghand1
- register to receive Briefings via e-mail and/or browse the current edition/archive.

The *Corporate Governance Briefing* homepage also offers access to electronic versions of the appendices included in the book, and any revised or new guidance issued since the publication of the current print edition.

Brian Coyle
January 2005

Acknowledgements

ICSA Publishing would like to thank the following for permission to reproduce material in this Handbook:

The Association of British Insurers (ABI) for Appendix 15, ABI Principles on Executive Remuneration, © ABI, 2004, and Appendix 23, Disclosure Guidelines on Socially Responsible Investment, © ABI, 2001.

Financial Reporting Council for The Combined Code on Corporate Governance 2003. © Financial Reporting Council, 2003. Reproduced with permission.

Linklaters for Appendix 25, The Matrix, reproduced with the kind permission of Linklaters. © Linklaters. All Rights reserved 2004.

National Association of Pension Funds (NAPF) for Appendix 18, NAPF Corporate Governance Policy 2005. © NAPF, 2005.

Abbreviations

ABI	Association of British Insurers
AGM	annual general meeting
APB	Auditing Practices Board
ASB	Accounting Standards Board
CDDA	Company Directors Disqualification Act 1986
CEO	chief executive officer
COSO	Committee of Sponsoring Organisations
CRE	Corporate Responsibility Exchange
CSR	corporate social responsibility
D&O	directors' and officers'
EBITDA	earnings before interest, taxation, depreciation and amortisation
ES	Ethical Standards
Excom	executive committee
FRC	Financial Reporting Council
FRRP	Financial Reporting Review Panel
FSA	Financial Services Authority
GRI	Global Reporting Initiative
ICAEW	Institute of Chartered Accountants in England and Wales
ICGN	International Corporate Governance Network
IFAC	International Federation of Accountants
IoD	Institute of Directors
IPC	Investor Protection Committee
IPPR	Institute for Public Policy Research
ISC	Institutional Shareholders' Committee
ISS	Institutional Shareholder Services
NAPF	National Association of Pension Funds
NED	non-executive director
OECD	Organisation for Economic Cooperation and Development
OFR	Operating and Financial Review
PBIT	profit before interest and taxation
PIRC	Pensions and Investment Research Consultant Ltd
RREV	Research Recommendations and Electronic Voting
SEC	Securities and Exchange Commission
SEE	social, environmental and ethical
SID	senior independent director
SOX	Sarbanes–Oxley Act 2004
TSR	total shareholder return

CHAPTER

The Scope of Corporate Governance 1

1 Defining corporate governance
2 A corporate governance framework
3 Approaches to corporate governance
4 Issues in corporate governance
5 The development of the corporate governance framework

1 Defining corporate governance

'Governance' refers to the way in which something is governed, and can be defined as government, control or direction. *Corporate* governance refers to the way in which companies are governed, and to what purpose. 'Corporate governance is the system by which companies are directed and controlled' (Cadbury Report 1992).

The corporate governance structure specifies the distribution of rights and responsibilities among different participants in the corporation, such as the board, managers, shareholders and other stakeholders, and spells out the rules and procedures for making decisions on corporate affairs. By doing this, it also provides the structure through which the company objectives are set, and the means of attaining those objectives and monitoring performance (OECD Principles).

It is concerned with practices and procedures for trying to ensure that a company is run in such a way that it achieves its objectives. Institutional investors might take the view that *good practice* in corporate governance increases the long-term value of a company, and is therefore highly desirable.

A distinction must be made between governance and management. Whereas management is concerned with operational matters and running businesses, governance is concerned with ensuring that businesses are run properly.

2 A corporate governance framework

Best practice in corporate governance is determined by a combination of:

- legislation
- regulation
- voluntary codes of practice and institutional guidelines.

The relative significance of each varies between countries. In the UK, key elements of the corporate governance framework include the Companies Act 1985, the UK Listing Rules, the Combined Code on Corporate Governance (including its annexes), and guidelines issued for members by the institutional investor organisations.

Broad guidelines are also provided on an international level, notably the OECD Principles of Corporate Governance and the internal control framework of the Committee of Sponsoring Organisations (COSO).

2.1 Stakeholder groups

Corporate governance issues arise because a company is a legal entity, separate from its owners, the equity shareholders. Large companies are run by their directors and management, rather than their shareholders, giving rise to a *principal–agent problem*. Corporate governance issues are concerned largely with the balance of power in a company, and the respective rights and interests of its owners, its managers and other interest groups.

Each interest group in a company is referred to as a *stakeholder group*, and good corporate governance should be concerned with finding a suitable balance between the interests and rights of the different groups. The nature of stakeholder groups will vary from one company to another, but it is useful to make the following distinctions.

The board of directors

- The chairman of the board (leader of the board)
- The chief executive officer (CEO) (leader of the executive management team)
- Executive directors (reporting to the CEO on management issues)
- Non-executive directors, who can be either independent or 'non-independent'.

The unitary board system, in which executive and non-executive directors sit on the same board and share decision-making responsibilities, contrasts with the two-tier board system, operated in some European countries, in which there is a lower-tier management board of executive directors and a higher-tier supervisory board of non-executives.

Employees

- Senior management, reporting to an executive director or the CEO: some senior managers might be influential in running an entity without being on its governing board
- Other employees.

Equity shareholders

- Institutional investors. The interests of institutional investors are represented by associations such as the Association of British Insurers (ABI), the National Association

of Pension Funds (NAPF), and for institutional shareholders with international investment portfolios, the International Corporate Governance Network (ICGN). The main associations of UK investment institutions also issue collective guidance to their members through the Institutional Shareholders' Committee (ISC).
- Private shareholders.

Other groups

- Customers
- Other investors (e.g. bond investors) and lenders
- Suppliers
- The general public, represented perhaps by a government or by pressure groups.

There are differing views about the extent to which good practice in corporate governance should recognise the interests of employees and other groups, and not focus exclusively on the relationship between shareholders, directors and senior management.

2.2 Powers and rights

Corporate governance is concerned with:

- who has the power within companies to make decisions
- in whose interests the powers are exercised and the decisions taken
- whether those powers are properly exercised
- the rights of the various stakeholder groups
- how those rights can be, or should be, protected.

The key issues in corporate governance are generally seen as focusing on the relationship between the directors, who are entrusted with most of the powers, and the equity shareholders, in whose interests a company should be governed. Concerns about governance have arisen where individual directors, or groups of directors, have run companies more in their own interests than in the interests of shareholders.

2.3 Potential conflicts of interest

A major concern with corporate governance is the conflict of interests between the board of directors (and its individual directors) and other stakeholder groups, particularly the shareholders and employees. When the directors take decisions that are in their personal best interests, and regardless of the interests of other stakeholders, should this be allowed or how can it be prevented? The directors, particularly executive directors, have greater access to the information systems of their company and thus know more about what is going on. They are also often in a position to control or manipulate the information that is released to the shareholders or employees.

Shareholders have to rely on the board of directors to govern their company competently and in their best interests. They are able to monitor the performance of the company (and, by implication, its directors), primarily through the company's annual report and accounts. They make their decisions to invest in the company's shares and hold on to them, largely on the basis of information supplied by the directors in the company's name. Their only assurance that the information they are supplied is correct is the honesty of the directors and the assertion by the company's auditors that the published accounts give a true and fair view of the company's profitability and financial position.

The problem has been well expressed by the OECD, as follows:

> *What makes corporate governance necessary? Put simply, the interests of those who have effective control over a firm can differ from the interests of those who supply the firm with external finance. The problem, commonly referred to as a principal–agent problem, grows out of the separation of ownership and control and of corporate outsiders and insiders. In the absence of the protections that good governance supplies, asymmetries of information and difficulties of monitoring mean that capital providers who lack control over the corporation will find it risky and costly to protect themselves from the opportunistic behaviour of managers and controlling shareholders.*

The relationship between the shareholders and the board of directors is at the centre of many of the problems that arise in corporate governance. Many of the guidelines in the codes of conduct for corporate governance and codes of best practice are directed towards reducing the potential for conflict, by seeking to put some restraints on individual directors, particularly the CEO and other executive directors, and by trying to reconcile the interests of the two stakeholder groups.

3 Alternative approaches to corporate governance

There has been some debate about what the objectives of sound corporate governance should be. The different views can be divided into three broad approaches:

- the shareholder value approach
- the stakeholder or pluralist approach, and
- the enlightened shareholder approach.

3.1 Shareholder value approach

A well-established view, supported by company law in advanced economies, is that the board of directors should govern their company in the best interests of its owners, the shareholders. This could mean that the main objective of a company should be to maximise the wealth of its shareholders, in the form of share price growth and dividend payments, subject to conforming with the rules of society as embodied in laws and customs. The directors should be accountable to their shareholders, who should have the power to remove them from office if their performance is inadequate. The OECD, in the introduction to its principles of corporate governance, states that, from a company's perspective, corporate governance is about:

> *maximising value subject to meeting the corporation's financial and other legal and contractual obligations. This inclusive definition stresses the need for boards of directors to balance the interests of shareholders with those of other stakeholders – employees, customers, suppliers, investors, communities – in order to achieve long-term sustained value.*

The strength of this approach to corporate governance is its general acceptance. Many people hold the view that public companies are in business to earn profits for the benefit of their shareholders. Successful companies are perceived as those paying dividends to shareholders and whose share price goes up. Within the broad objective of maximising shareholder values, the board of directors will also act fairly in the interests of employees, customers, suppliers and others with an interest in the company's affairs. Institutional shareholders supporting good corporate governance practices argue that the best-run companies will deliver higher value for shareholders over the long term.

3.2 The stakeholder approach (pluralist approach)

An alternative view is that the aim of sound corporate governance is not just to meet the objectives of shareholders, but also to have regard for the interests of other individuals and groups with a stake in the company, including the public at large. The OECD argues that there is a public policy perspective towards corporate governance, as well as a corporate perspective:

> *From a public policy perspective, corporate governance is about nurturing enterprise while ensuring accountability in the exercise of power and patronage by firms. The role of public policy is to provide firms with the incentives and discipline to minimize the divergence between private and social returns and to protect the interests of stakeholders.*

From a 'stakeholder view', corporate governance is concerned with achieving a balance between economic and social goals, and between individual and communal goals. Sound corporate governance should recognise the economic imperatives companies face in competitive markets and should encourage the efficient use of resources through sound investment. It should also require accountability from the board of directors to the shareholders for the stewardship of those resources. Within this framework, the aim should be to recognise the interests of other individuals, companies and society at large in the decisions and activities of the company.

A problem with the stakeholder approach is that company law gives certain rights to shareholders, and there are some legal duties on the board of directors towards their company. The interests of other stakeholders, however, are not reinforced by company law. In the UK, there is currently a requirement that the directors should 'have regard in the performance of their functions' to the interests of the company's employees in general as well as to the interests of the shareholders (Section 309 of the Companies Act 1985). In practice, however, this provision of the Act has had little, if any, effect, because it is not specific and is presumably open to wide interpretation.

Supporters of a stakeholder approach (or pluralist approach) to corporate governance argue that there would have to be company legislation giving it support. A pluralist approach is that co-operative and productive relationships will be optimised only if the directors are permitted or required to balance shareholder interests with the interests of other stakeholders who are committed to the company.

It is important to remember that although employee interests are not well protected by company law, extensive protection is provided by other aspects of law such as employment law, health and safety legislation and environmental law.

3.3 The enlightened shareholder approach

The enlightened shareholder approach to corporate governance is that the directors of a company should pursue the interests of their shareholders, but in an enlightened and inclusive way. The directors should look to the long term, not just to the short term, and they should also have regard to the interests of other stakeholders in the company, not just the shareholders. Managers should be aware of the need to create and maintain productive relationships with a range of stakeholders having an interest in their company.

A UK Company Law Review Steering Group issued a consultative document in 1998, in which it commented that UK company law currently does not embrace the enlightened shareholder approach, and if this approach was deemed desirable, suitable changes in the law would need to be considered. Enlightened change, it felt, would not come voluntarily, but (like a pluralist approach) would need the backing of the law.

3.4 The King Reports: an integrated approach to corporate governance

The King Reports, published in South Africa, take an integrated approach to corporate governance. In 1992, the Institute of Directors in South Africa established the King Committee, which produced its first report in 1994. This was followed by a second report in 2002 (King Report on Corporate Governance for South Africa). The report took the view that in developing countries in particular, companies should consider the interests of the communities in which they operate. It made a distinction between the accountability and responsibility of the board of directors:

- Accountability is the liability to render account to someone else. A director is accountable to the shareholders, at common law or by statute, and the company's annual report and accounts, for example, should be presented to the shareholders for approval. The King Committee rejected the stakeholder concept that the board of directors should be accountable to other stakeholder groups, arguing that if a board of directors is accountable to everyone, the result would be accountability to no one. Accountability to all stakeholder groups would also restrict enterprise.

- Responsibility is the liability of a person to be called to account when that person is responsible. The King Committee suggested that a board of directors, whilst being accountable to the shareholders only, should be responsible to other stakeholder groups as well as the shareholders.

The 2002 Report comments:

> *The inclusive approach recognises that stakeholders such as the community in which the company operates, its customers, its employees and its suppliers, need to be considered when developing the strategy of a company. The relationship between a company and these stakeholders is either contractual or non-contractual. The inclusive approach requires that the purpose of the company should be defined, and the values by which the company will carry on its daily life should be identified and communicated to all stakeholders. The stakeholders relevant to the company's business should also be identified. These three factors must be combined in developing the strategies to achieve the company's goals. The relationship between the company and its stakeholders should be mutually beneficial. A wealth of evidence has established that this inclusive approach is the way to create sustained business success and steady long-term growth in shareholder value.*

The King Report argued in favour of a balance in corporate governance between allowing the directors to run the company in the way they considered best for the stakeholders, while providing stakeholders with some protection against a board of directors that ignores its responsibilities and is not held properly accountable.

There are three 'corporate sins': sloth, greed and fear:

1. *Sloth* is the unwillingness to take risks and initiatives. It results in a loss of flair and enterprise, and the creation of a slow-moving bureaucracy to manage the company.
2. *Greed* is the desire of executive managers to get the best for themselves out of their company. It leads to short-term decision-making, without proper regard for the long-term future. Decisions are often based on the wish to drive up the share price and so the value of the directors' own share options.
3. *Fear* arises when executives worry about what their shareholders (or the investment community) will say or do, so that decisions are taken that will keep shareholders content. Fear, like sloth, leads to an erosion of enterprise.

The Report suggested that concerns about corporate governance arose out of investor concerns about excessive powers in the hands of greedy professional executive managers. However, protecting investors against greed runs the risks of sloth and fear. Hence the need for a proper balance within a sound system of governance.

3.5 Which approach is likely to apply?

In practice, the shareholder value approach to corporate governance is the generally accepted view, but questions about the merits of the other approaches were raised in a consultation document published by the UK Company Law Review Steering Group in 1998. In discussing the interests that a company should be required to serve, the document stated that: 'A case is recognised for ensuring that company managers have regard, where appropriate, to the need to ensure productive relationships with a range of interested parties and have regard to the longer term.' The relative merits of the enlightened shareholder concept and the pluralist concept should therefore be considered.

4 Issues in corporate governance

Concerns about the quality of corporate governance have often arisen out of a 'scandal' or adverse media publicity. Whenever something goes wrong, the reasons can vary, and the finger of blame can point in different directions. At the heart of much of the debate about corporate governance lie the conflicts of interest, or potential conflicts of interest, between shareholders and either the board of directors as a whole or individual board members. The directors may be tempted to take risks and make decisions aimed at boosting short-term performance. Many shareholders are more concerned about the longer term, the continuing survival of their company and the value of their investment. If a company gets into financial difficulties, professional managers can move on to another company to start all over again, whereas shareholders suffer a financial loss.

The main issues in corporate governance are:

- the powers of the directors and the rights of the shareholders
- the role and responsibility of the board of directors
- the structure of the board of directors, and decision-making by the board in the interests of the shareholders and/or other stakeholders
- directors' remuneration and its relationship with performance (or not)
- financial reporting and auditing
- internal control and risk management
- the role of the shareholders and the relationship between the board of directors and the shareholders
- ethical and social issues, and corporate social responsibility (CSR).

4.1 Directors' powers and shareholders' rights

Company law provides a framework for directors' powers and duties, and shareholders' rights:

- The powers of directors are extensive, granted to them by the Articles of Association. There are legal restrictions on these powers, and directors can be made liable for their actions.
- The law also provides certain rights to shareholders, which can be exercised if they consider that the company is not being properly run.

This legal background is discussed in detail in Chapter 2. Director–shareholder relations are covered in Chapter 7.

4.2 Structure of the board of directors

In a well-governed company, the board of directors acts collectively in the best interests of the company, bringing collective experience and judgement to its decision-making. It should not be dominated by one or two powerful individuals, because of the risk that the all-powerful individual will run the company to suit his (or her) personal interests. Checks and balances can be established by separating the roles of board chairman and chief executive officer, and by including a strong element of independent non-executive directors on the board.

Objectivity should be introduced into important aspects of the board's responsibilities, particularly appointing new directors, negotiating the remuneration of individual directors, supervision of the external audit and the company's relationship with its external auditors. Good corporate governance practice is that responsibilities for new appointments, remuneration and audit should be delegated to committees of the board.

If good corporate governance relies on the contributions of independent non-executive directors, problems can arise in recruiting individuals of sufficient calibre to the board, and giving them training and induction to make them more effective more quickly.

Chapters 3–5 look at the issues surrounding board roles, structures and balance.

4.3 Directors' remuneration

Concerns about directors' remuneration have possibly been greater in the UK than in other countries. Directors may reward themselves with excessive salaries and other rewards, such as bonuses, a generous pension scheme, share options and other benefits. Although there are public concerns about the rewards for 'fat cat' executives, the main concern about corporate governance is not high remuneration. The problem is that reward schemes do not provide sufficient incentive for directors to achieve performances that are in the best interests of shareholders. The main complaint about 'fat cat' directors' remuneration is that when the company does well, the directors are rewarded well, which is fair enough, but when the company does badly, the directors continue to be paid just as well.

Another issue has been the large pay-offs for chief executives and other directors who are dismissed for failing to perform to the standard expected. Such high payments on leaving have been described as 'rewards for failure'. The contract of employment for an executive director often fails to consider the possibility that the director will eventually be dismissed, and the terms of employment allow the director to claim large payments on dismissal under the terms of the contract. To some extent, the problem is reduced by rolling one-year contracts, which might limit the compensation for loss of earnings to one year's salary, provided there are no entitlements due under bonus pay arrangements or share option schemes. Institutional investor associations have issued extensive guidelines to members on directors' remuneration (see Chapter 7). The issues surrounding directors' remuneration are looked at in full in Chapter 6.

4.4 Financial reporting and auditing

The directors may try to disguise the true financial performance of their company by 'dressing up' the published accounts and giving less than honest statements. 'Window-dressed' accounts make it difficult for investors to reach a reasoned judgement about the financial position of the company. Concerns about misleading published accounts provided an early impetus in the 1980s and early 1990s to the movement for better corporate governance in the UK. Accounting irregularities in a number of companies led to a tightening of accounting standards, although the problems of window dressing are unlikely ever to disappear completely. Although the UK has avoided major financial reporting scandals in recent years, the risks remain.

Concerns about financial reporting in the US emerged with the collapse of the energy corporation Enron in 2001, which filed for bankruptcy after 'adjusting' its accounts. This was followed by similar problems at other US companies, such as the telecommunications group WorldCom (which admitted to fraud in its accounting), Global Crossing and Rank Xerox. A corporate governance issue is the question of the extent to which the directors were aware in each case of the impending collapse of their company, and if they knew about the problems, why shareholders were not informed much sooner.

The implications of false or misleading financial reporting for the relationship between investors and companies was well expressed by Arthur Levitt, former chairman of the Securities and Exchange Commission, in a speech in 2001:

> *If a country does not have a reputation for strong corporate governance practice, capital will flow elsewhere. If investors are not confident with the level of disclosure, capital will flow elsewhere. If a country opts for lax accounting and reporting standards, capital will flow elsewhere. All enterprises in that country, regardless of how steadfast a particular company's practices, may suffer the consequences. Markets must now honour what they perhaps too often have failed to recognise. Markets exist by the grace of investors. And it is today's more empowered investors who will determine which companies and*

which markets will stand the test of time and endure the weight of greater competition. It serves us well to remember that no market has a divine right to investors' capital.

When the annual financial statements of a company prove to have been misleading, questions are inevitably raised about the effectiveness of the external auditors. There are two main issues relating to the external audit of a company:

- One is whether it should be the job of the auditors to discover financial fraud and material errors. (For example, in December 2003, the Bank of America claimed that a document, apparently issued by the bank to the auditors of a subsidiary of Parmalat and confirming the existence of an account containing €3.95 billion, was a forgery. In this case, the auditors argued that they were knowingly misled, and could not have been expected to spot the fraud.)
- The second is the problem of the relationship between a client company and its auditors, and the extent to which the auditors are independent and free from the influence of the company's management. If auditors are subject to influence from a client company, they might be persuaded to agree with a controversial method of accounting for particular transactions, which shows the company's performance or financial position in a better light.

Financial reporting and external audit – and the trend towards more detailed non-financial reporting – are covered in Chapter 8.

4.5 Corporate governance and risk management

As a general rule, investors expect higher rewards to compensate them for taking higher business risks. If a company makes decisions that increase the scale of the risks it faces, profits and dividends should be expected to go up. Another issue in corporate governance is that the directors of companies might take decisions intended to increase profits, without giving due regard to the risks. In some cases, companies may continue to operate without regard to the changing risk profile of their existing businesses.

When investors buy shares in a company, they have an idea of the type of company they are buying into, the nature of its business, the probable returns it will provide for shareholders, and the financial risks involved. To shareholders, investment risk is important, as well as high returns. Directors, on the other hand, are rewarded on the basis of the returns the company achieves, linked to profits or dividend growth, and their remuneration is not linked in any direct way to the risk aspects of their business. Risk management is now recognised, particularly in the UK, as an ingredient of sound corporate governance.

A common denominator in past corporate failures has been a lack of effective control over the company and the absence of risk management procedures and systems. The problem with corporate collapse could be dishonest management finally being exposed, but is much more likely to be the consequence of a well-intentioned board of directors failing to carry out its duties adequately. The duties of the board of directors must include ensuring that there is an operative and effective internal control system, and system of risk management. Shareholders should feel confident that suitable controls are in place, that the board is aware of the risks faced by the company, and that a system for monitoring and controlling them operates effectively.

The significance of risk and risk management to corporate governance debates is analysed in Chapter 10.

4.6 Role of shareholders

There are two aspects to the role of shareholders in the governance of their company:

- Shareholders should normally expect to be supportive of the company's management, but they should be entitled to know what the directors are doing on their behalf. Shareholders, particularly those with a large financial investment in the company, should be able to voice their concerns to the directors and expect to have their opinions listened to. Small shareholders should at least be informed about the company, its financial position and its intentions for the future, even if their opinions carry comparatively little weight.
- If they accept the view that good corporate governance will increase the long-term value of a company, shareholders should use the powers and rights they have to promote good governance. In particular, they should be able to express their opinions to the company and they should exercise their right to vote at general meetings.

The responsibility for improving communications rests with the companies themselves and their main institutional shareholders. Companies can make better use of the annual report and accounts to report to shareholders on a range of issues and the policies of the company for dealing with them. The annual report and accounts should not be simply a brief directors' report and a set of financial statements. The company should explain its operations and financial position (in an Operational and Financial Review) and report on a range of governance issues, such as directors' remuneration, internal controls and risk management, and policies on health, safety and the environment. Many companies now use their web-site to report on such matters. A company can also try to encourage greater shareholder attendance and participation at annual general meetings as a method of improving communications and dialogue. Electronic communications, including electronic voting, should also be considered. On their part, institutional investors should develop voting policies, and apply these in general meetings. Where necessary, they can vote against the board to alert the directors to the strength of their views. Shareholders are looked at in more detail in Chapter 7.

4.7 Ethics and social issues

A widely held view is that companies have a responsibility to society as a whole and should act in an ethical manner. In the Committee of Sponsoring Organisations (COSO) Framework, a code of corporate ethics is regarded as an important element in a system of effective internal control:

- The board of directors should set the standards for behaviour (the 'tone at the top').
- Companies should encourage employees to report unethical behaviour, and if they are unable to do so through normal reporting channels within the organisation, they should be encouraged to 'blow the whistle' on the offenders, without fear of reprisal.
- Companies should also consider their social responsibilities to the environment and to the communities in which they operate.

More on corporate social responsibility is provided in Chapter 11.

5 The development of the corporate governance framework

Concerns about corporate governance have grown over time. In recent years, the recognition of a need for changes in the way that public companies are governed began with a number of spectacular and well-publicised corporate failures. In the US, many organisations in the savings and thrift industry had to be rescued from financial collapse in the 1980s. In the UK, a number of companies collapsed unexpectedly in the 1980s and 1990s. These included Polly Peck International, the Bank of Credit and Commerce International, British and Commonwealth, the Mirror Group News International and Barings Bank. In each case, there appeared to be serious accounting or financial reporting irregularities and inadequate internal controls and risk management. In some cases, 'creative accounting' and inadequate financial regulation were seen as the cause of the corporate failure. In other cases, such as the collapse of Barings Bank due to the losses of a rogue trader, inadequate controls were a key factor.

When questions were asked about how the corporate collapse could happen to such well-established companies without warning, some common themes emerged. Investors were not kept informed about what was really going on in the company and the published financial statements were misleading. External auditors were accused of failing to spot the warning signs, but much of the blame was heaped on the self-seeking activities of powerful company chiefs, their apparent lack of personal and business ethics, and the inability of their colleagues on the board to restrain them from acting improperly. In addition, it was recognised that the risk of financial collapse can be prevented by adequate risk management, and that in the case of all the companies concerned, the financial controls had been inadequate or ineffective.

This Handbook is concerned mainly with corporate governance in the UK, but events in other countries have influenced thinking in the UK, most notably the collapse of corporations such as Enron and WorldCom in the US (2001–2002), the world-wide collapse of auditors Andersens and the problems in 2003 of Europe-based corporations Ahold (Netherlands) and Parmalat (Italy).

UK companies with a listing in the US are now required to comply with the statutory and regulatory requirements of the Sarbanes–Oxley Act 2002 (SOX). Comparisons of UK best practice and regulatory requirements under SOX are given throughout the text.

5.1 Corporate governance in the UK: a brief history

The Cadbury Report

The main impetus for better practices in corporate governance began in the UK in the late 1980s and early 1990s. The Report of the Committee on the Financial Aspects of Corporate Governance (the 'Cadbury Report') was published in 1992, and was later described as 'a landmark in thinking on corporate governance'. The Report included a Code of Best Practice, and UK listed companies came under pressure from City institutions to comply with the requirements of the Code.

The Greenbury Report

On the recommendation of the Cadbury Committee, another committee was set up to review progress on corporate governance in UK listed companies. This committee issued the Greenbury Report in 1995, which focused mainly on directors' remuneration. At the time, the UK press was condemning 'fat cat' directors, particularly those in newly privatised companies. The Greenbury Report issued a Code of Best Practice on establishing remuneration committees, for disclosures of much more information about the remuneration of directors and remuneration policy, and for more control over notice periods in directors' service contracts and compensation payments in the event of early termination of contracts.

The Myners Report

In 1995, a working group was set up to look into the relationship between companies and institutional investors. It was chaired by Mr Paul Myners, then chairman of Gartmore plc, and produced the Myners Report, which made a variety of recommendations about how the relationship between institutional investors and company managements should be conducted. The Report included suggestions for improving the communications between companies and institutional investors, and for the conduct of annual general meetings. The significance of the Myners Report is that it urged institutional investors to reassess their role as shareholders and their responsibilities for ensuring good corporate governance and the success of the companies in which they invested. Today, the various institutional shareholders groups publish guidance for their members, and encourage 'activism' where this is cost-effective (see Chapter 7).

Hampel and the Combined Code

A Committee on Corporate Governance, chaired by Sir Ronald Hampel, was set up in 1995 to review the recommendations of the Cadbury and Greenbury Committees. The final report of the Hampel Committee was published in 1998. Its Report covered a number of governance issues, such as the composition of the board and role of directors, directors' remuneration, the role of shareholders (particularly institutional shareholders), communications between the company and its shareholders, and financial reporting, auditing and internal controls. The Hampel Report also suggested that its recommendations should be combined with those of the Cadbury and Greenbury Committees into a single code of corporate governance. This suggestion led to the publication of a Combined Code, which was attached to the UK Listing Rules and became recommended practice for listed companies (Appendix 1). Listed companies were required to include a report on corporate governance within their annual report and accounts, explaining how they had complied with the Combined Code, or explaining any non-compliance.

Public Interest Disclosure Act 1998

A largely separate, although interconnected, development has been a growing awareness on the part of large companies of the potential risks to their reputation and long-term success from failures to comply with laws and regulations or to act in an ethical way. Many companies have also claimed to recognise the potential long-term benefits from acting in a socially responsible manner. In the UK, the Public Interest Disclosure Act 1998 seeks to protect employees who act as 'whistleblowers' on the activities of their employer. Whistleblowing is looked at in more detail in Chapter 12.

The Turnbull Report 1999

An element of the first Combined Code was a requirement for the board of directors to review risk management, and to produce an annual statement. Guidance for company boards on their risk management responsibilities was produced by a committee of the Institute of Chartered Accountants in England and Wales as the Turnbull Report (see Chapter 10).

Directors' Remuneration Report Regulations 2002

The Listing Rules also included requirements for extensive disclosure of details about directors' remuneration, but these were subsequently superseded by a change to the Companies Act 1985, introduced by the Directors' Remuneration Report Regulations 2002. UK quoted companies are now required to prepare a directors' remuneration report, some of which must be audited, and which must be put to the shareholders for approval at the annual general meeting of the company. This report must include both extensive disclosures about the remuneration of individual directors and also a statement about the company's remuneration policy.

Higgs, Smith and the 2003 Combined Code

Concerns over the role and effectiveness of non-executive directors and about the role of the audit committee and the independence of the external auditors continued. In January 2003, two reports were produced: the Higgs Report on non-executive directors (which had been commissioned by the Department of Trade and Industry) and the Smith Report on audit committees (which had been commissioned by the Financial Reporting Council). The Financial Reporting Council has responsibility for the Combined Code, and in July 2003 published a revised Combined Code, incorporating most of the Higgs and Smith recommendations. The revised Combined Code includes, as appendices, related guidance and good practice suggestions from the Turnbull, Smith and Higgs reports. The Combined Code remains voluntary, but listed companies are required to comply with its provisions or explain any non-compliance. The full text of the 2003 Code is reproduced in Appendix 1.

Modernising company law

The UK government has also considered changes to company law to improve corporate governance. A company law review was initiated in 1998. Some amendments to the Companies Act 1985 have been introduced by the Companies (Audit Investigations and Community Interest) Act, which came into force in November 2004 (see Chapter 9). Other changes are planned, including a requirement for quoted companies to include an Operating and Financial Review (OFR) in their published annual report and accounts (see Chapter 8) and a proposal to provide a statutory codification of the general duties of the company directors (see Chapter 2).

5.2 The 2003 Combined Code

The *Combined Code on Corporate Governance* (2003) consists of:

- Main Principles
- Supporting Principles, and
- more detailed Code provisions.

There are also three annexes, which do not form a part of the Code itself:

- Guidance on Internal Control (the Turnbull Guidance)
- Guidance on Audit Committees (the Smith Guidance)
- Suggestions for Good Practice from the Higgs Report (Higgs Suggestions for Good Practice).

The Combined Code is voluntary, but has regulatory backing from the UK Listing Rules. Under the Listing Rules (Rule 12.43A), listed companies are required to make a disclosure in the annual report and accounts in two parts:

- in the first part, the company must report in a narrative statement how it applies the principles in the Code (both the main and Supporting Principles), giving sufficient explanations to enable shareholders to evaluate how the principles have been applied, and
- in the second part, the company has either to confirm that it has complied with all the Code provisions or, where it does not, give a reason for the non-compliance. This is known as the 'comply or explain approach'.

The preamble to the Code states that although listed companies will be expected to comply with the Code provisions, non-compliance may be justifiable in particular circumstances. Smaller listed companies in particular might find some of the Code provisions less relevant to their circumstances. The preamble urges shareholders to use common sense in judging any non-compliance with the Code, give proper consideration to the company's reasons for non-compliance, and be prepared to enter into a dialogue with the company if they do not agree with its position.

In the chapters that follow, the principles and the provisions of the Code will be explained in detail. Principles have a code number (reference number), and each Code provision also has a unique reference number.

5.3 Responsibility for the Combined Code

In April 2004, the Financial Reporting Council (FRC), an independent regulator, took over the responsibilities of the Accounting Foundation. The FRC, whose subsidiary boards include the Accounting Standards Board (ASB) and the Auditing Practices Board (APB), is responsible for:

- setting and enforcing accounting standards and auditing standards in the UK
- oversight of the regulatory activities of the professional accountancy bodies
- certain statutory responsibilities with regard to the regulation of audit
- promoting high standards of corporate governance.

A specific responsibility in connection with corporate governance is to monitor and, where appropriate, amend the Combined Code. Note the following:

- The FRC is not responsible for enforcing the Combined Code. This is considered a responsibility of company shareholders.
- However, the FRC will continue to monitor the effectiveness of the Combined Code, and may propose and implement changes as circumstances seem to require.

In reviewing the implementation of the Combined Code, the FRC intends to rely on the findings of bodies such as PIRC and RREV, whose main tasks include monitoring corporate governance in listed companies.

Reviewing Turnbull

In December 2004, the FRC group charged with reviewing the Turnbull Guidance, chaired by Douglas Flint, issued a consultation aimed at assessing how well the current guidance has worked, and ways in which it might be improved. This is expected to result in a second consultation on revised draft guidance in mid-2005, with any revised guidance taking effect for accounting periods commencing on or after 1 January 2006.

CHAPTER

Directors in UK Law

2

Until the introduction of a code of best practice for corporate governance and various regulations for the improvement of corporate governance in large companies, the basic corporate governance framework was provided by law. The legal framework for corporate governance, consisting of a combination of common law and statutory provisions, is still in place, although its adequacy in providing protection and transparency for shareholders has been called into question. Increasingly, company law is being amended to clarify areas relevant to corporate governance, such as the 2002 Directors' Remuneration Report Regulations and the introduction of the statutory OFR.

This chapter describes the legal framework of corporate governance in the UK, and in particular the powers and duties of the board of directors. This should indicate:

- the extent to which the law fosters good corporate governance in the UK, and
- the limitations of the legal framwork for good corporate governance.

1 The powers of directors

The powers of the board of directors are set out in a company's Articles of Association. The powers are given to the board of directors as a whole, but Table A (Article 72) states that they may be delegated:

- The board may delegate powers to a *board committee* consisting of one or more directors.
- The board may also delegate to *any executive director*, such as a chief executive officer or managing director, such of its powers that it considers desirable for that director to exercise.

A distinction should be made between:

- the powers and duties of executive directors as members of the board, and
- their responsibilities as managers of the company.

Under the Articles of Association, managers have neither powers nor duties. The relationship they have with the company (including their authority and responsibilities) is established by their contract of employment and by the law of agency.

1.1 Borrowing powers of directors

There is no restriction in law on how much the directors can borrow on behalf of their company. As far as the law is concerned, the borrowing powers of companies are limited only by what lenders are prepared to allow them. Conceivably, the directors could therefore put the investment of their shareholders at risk by borrowing more than the company can safely afford.

The National Association of Pension Funds (NAPF) has recommended that, to reduce this risk, there should be a reasonable limit in the company's Articles of Association on the directors' powers to borrow. This should relate to the borrowings of the entire group of companies, not just individual companies within the group.

2 The duties of directors to their company

The directors act as agents of their company. Their duties are to the company itself, not to its shareholders, nor its employees or any person external to the company. They include a fiduciary duty and a duty of skill and care to their company.

2.1 Fiduciary duty of directors

In common law, the directors have a fiduciary duty to their company. 'Fiduciary' means given in trust, and the concept of a trustee, as established in US and UK law, is applicable. The directors hold a position of trust because they make contracts on behalf of the company and also control the company's property.

If a director were to act in breach of his or her fiduciary duties, legal action could be brought against him or her by the company. In such a situation, 'the company' might be represented by a majority of the board of directors, or a majority of the shareholders.

Presumably, an accusation of breach of fiduciary duty would focus on a particular action or series of actions by the director concerned. If the court were to find a director in breach of his or her fiduciary duties, it might order him or her to compensate the company for any loss it has suffered and account to the company for any personal profit he or she has made from his or her actions.

Tests for breach of fiduciary duty

There are three key tests of whether a director is in breach of his or her fiduciary duties in carrying out a particular transaction or series of transactions:

1. A transaction should be reasonably incidental to the business of the company. If a transaction initiated by a director is not related to the business of the company in any way, it would be a breach of fiduciary duty.
2. The transaction should have been carried out 'bona fide' (in good faith); otherwise it would be a breach of fiduciary duty.
3. The transaction should have been made for the benefit of the company, and not for the personal benefit of the director. A director has a fiduciary duty to avoid a conflict of interest between himself personally and the company, and must not obtain any personal benefit or 'secret profit' from a transaction without the consent of the company.

2.2 A director's duty of skill and care

A director also has a duty of skill and care to the company: this arises in common law. A director should not act negligently in carrying out his or her duties, and could be personally liable for losses suffered by the company as a consequence of his or her negligence.

The standard of skill and care expected of a director is the higher of the skill that he has or the skill that would objectively be expected of a director of the particular company. In the case *Re D'Jan of London [1993]*, the judge ruled that the common law duty of care was the equivalent to the statutory test applied by Section 214 of the Insolvency Act 1986. This statutory test refers to what would be expected of:

> *a reasonably diligent person having both:*
> *(a) the general knowledge, skill and experience that may reasonably be expected of a person carrying out the same functions as are carried out by that director in relation to the company, and*
> *(b) the general knowledge, skill and experience that that director has.*

A director's duty of skill and care was given clearer definition in a case concerning the disqualification of the former deputy chairman of Barings plc. Mr Justice Parker stated that directors, both individually and collectively, have a duty to acquire and maintain an understanding and knowledge of their company, sufficient for them to discharge their duties properly. This suggests that directors must ensure that they are kept properly and sufficiently informed, and possibly also must question the reliability of the information that is provided to them.

Spending time in the company

The duty of skill and care does not extend to spending time in the company. A director should attend board meetings if possible, but at other times is not required to be concerned with the affairs of the company. This requirement is perhaps best understood with NEDs, who might visit the company only for board or committee meetings. The duties of a director are intermittent in nature and arise from time to time only, such as when the board meets.

If a director holds an executive position in the company, a different situation arises, because he is an employee of the company with a contract of service. This contract might call for full-time attendance at the company or on its business. However, this requirement arises out of his or her job as a manager, not out of his or her position as a director.

Supervising management activities

It is also not a part of the duty of skill and care to watch closely over the activities of the company's management. Unless there are particular grounds for suspecting dishonesty or incompetence, a director is entitled to leave the routine conduct of the company's affairs to the management. If the management appears honest, the directors may rely on the information they provide. It is not part of their duty of skill and care to question whether the information is reliable, or whether important information is being withheld.

Ill-judged decisions

A board of directors might make a decision that appears ill-judged or careless. However, the courts are generally reluctant to condemn business decisions made by the board that appear, in hindsight, to show errors of judgement. Directors can exercise reasonable skill and care, but still make bad decisions.

2.3 Case examples: fiduciary duty and duty of skill and care

Case example

Industrial Development Consultants Ltd v Cooley [1972]

Cooley, an architect, was the managing director of a firm of consultants which advised clients on construction projects in the gas industry. A potential client was planning a new construction project, but had made it clear that it would not use the firm's consultancy services. Cooley was aware that although the client had objections to using the firm, it might award the work to him personally. He informed the board of his company that he was seriously ill and obtained release from his contract of employment. Having been released, he then succeeded in negotiating a contract with the client to provide a consultancy service personally. His former company took him to court, claiming that he was in breach of his fiduciary duty and must account for his profits. The court agreed, even though the company would not have been awarded the work, and ordered Cooley to account to the company for the profits he had made from the work.

Case example

Dorchester Finance Co. Ltd v Stebbing [1989]

A company brought an action against its three directors for alleged negligence and misappropriation of the company's property. The company (Dorchester Finance) was in the money lending business and it had three directors, S, H and P. Only one (S) was involved full-time with the company; the other two were non-executives who made only rare appearances. There were no board meetings. S and P were qualified accountants and H, although not an accountant, had a large amount of accountancy experience. S arranged for the company to make some loans to persons with whom he appears to have had dealings. In the loan-making process he had persuaded P and H to sign blank cheques that were subsequently used to make the loans. The loans did not comply with the Moneylenders Acts and they were inadequately secured. When the loans turned out to be irrecoverable, the company brought its action against the directors.

It was held that all three directors were liable to damages. S, as an executive director, was held to be grossly negligent. P and H, as non-executives, were held to have failed to show the necessary level of skill and care in performing their duties as non-executives, even though it was accepted that they had acted in good faith at all times.

Case example

Re D'Jan of London [1993]

An insurance broker completed an insurance proposal form on behalf of a client. The completed form contained an incorrect answer, but a director of the client company signed the form. The company's premises burned down, but on discovering the mistake on the proposal form, the insurance company repudiated all liability under the policy. The company went into insolvent liquidation.

The liquidator brought an action against the director who had signed the proposal form, alleging a failure to exercise reasonable care. The court found that although it would be unreasonable to expect a director to read every word of every document that he signed, in this case the form consisted of a few simple questions that the director was the best person to answer. The director was therefore guilty of a breach of duty of care. (In this case, the director was exonerated on other grounds.)

Case example

Neptune (Vehicle Washing Equipment) Ltd v Fitzgerald [1995]

A sole director (who was not a shareholder of the company) decided to terminate his own contract of employment and pay himself over £108,000 in compensation for loss of office. He was held to be in breach of his fiduciary duty and was required to repay the money to the company. The court found that he had put his own interests first and had not acted in the *bona fide* interests of the company. Furthermore, he had not acted reasonably and so was not entitled to relief from liability under Section 727 of the Companies Act 1985. (Table A, Article 94 states that a director cannot vote on any matter in which he has a material interest; therefore in this case the court also ruled that he did not have the authority to vote himself a compensation payment.)

Case example

Bairstow and others v Queen's Moat Houses plc [1994]

Queen's Moat Houses plc paid dividends to its shareholders on the basis of its accounts in 1990 and 1991. However, the dividend payments exceeded the company's distributable reserves, and so were in breach of Sections 263 and 264 of the Companies Act 1985, which make it unlawful for dividends to be paid except out of profits available for that purpose. The directors did not benefit from the dividend payments themselves.

It was claimed that the 1991 accounts were misleading, because they included some unlawful transactions, adopted some inappropriate accounting treatments and involved significant non-disclosure of information.

QMH brought an action seeking repayment of the unlawful dividends from the directors, claiming that they were in breach of their duties by authorising the dividend payments when they should have known that there were insufficient distributable reserves.

The directors argued that the breach was only technical, because there were sufficient distributable reserves within the group even if not within QMH itself, so no loss was suffered. They also asked the court to use discretionary powers available under Section 727 of the Companies Act 1985 to relieve them from liability, on the grounds that they had acted honestly and reasonably.

The judgment had three main aspects, and the court ruled as follows:

- A reasonably diligent director should know that dividends cannot be paid from capital, and so should know that any dividend paid on the basis of accounts showing insufficient distributable reserves would be unlawful. Any director not aware of this would be in breach of his or her duty of skill and care.

continued

- *The 1990 accounts*. The directors had placed too much reliance on their auditors, and had overlooked their responsibilities to ensure that the distributable reserves were sufficient. However, they had acted honestly and reasonably, therefore the court relieved them of liability (under s727 CA1985).
- *The 1991 accounts*. The directors had knowledge that the 1991 accounts did not give a true and fair view. Dividends paid on the basis of inaccurate accounts are unlawful, because the distributable profits cannot be properly established. The authorisation of the dividend payments by the directors, on the basis of accounts they knew to be misleading, amounted to a breach of trust and fiduciary duty, because it was not in the best interests of the company. The conduct of the directors was not honest; therefore they were not entitled to relief under Section 727 and were liable to repay the dividends (of £26.7 million).

This case went to the Court of Appeal in 2000, but the breach of fiduciary duty was not an issue in the appeal. In 2004 John Bairstow, the former chairman of Queen's Moat Houses, was disqualified from acting as a director for six years by the High Court, following an application for his disqualification from the Secretary of State under the Company Directors Disqualification Act 1986.

Proposals to write directors' duties into statutory law

A government White Paper, *Modernising Company Law*, was published in 2002. This included a proposal to codify in statute the common law duties of directors, but without significantly changing the nature of those duties. These proposed changes were concerned with the *duties* of directors, not with the way that directors take their decisions (which is a matter for the company's constitution and common law).

Another White Paper on company law reform was published in March 2005. This included a proposal that the general duties of directors should be specified in the amended Companies Act. These duties are:

- to act within their powers
- to promote the success of the company for the benefit of its members
- to exercise independent judgement
- to exercise reasonable care, skill and diligence
- to avoid conflicts of interest
- not to accept benefits from third parties
- to declare any interest in a proposed transaction with the company.

Comments in the explanatory material to the White Paper make interesting reading:

- The statement of directors' duties 'makes it clear that, as in the existing law, the general duties are owed by a director to the company. It follows that, as now, only the company can enforce them.'

- The effect of the duties is cumulative and directors should comply with every duty that applies in any given case. 'This is important because many of the general duties will frequently overlap. Taking a bribe from a third party would, for example, clearly fall within the duty not to accept benefits from third parties ... but could also, depending on the facts, be characterised as a failure to promote the success of the company for the benefit of its members ... or as an aspect of failing to exercise independent judgement.'
- The statutory duties do not in general change the law. However, they make changes to the law on directors' conflicts of interest, by allowing the other directors to authorise a conflict. 'Any common law rule or equitable principle requiring shareholder consent in this situation is abolished. Companies may still require such consent in their constitutions.'
- The proposed statutory duties are based on the existing common law rules and equity principles. The civil consequences for a breach of these duties would be the same as if the corresponding common law rule or equity principle applied. These include:
  - damages or compensation where the company has suffered loss;
  - restoration of the company's property;
  - an account of profits made by the director; and
  - rescission of a contract where the director failed to disclose an interest.

The full text of the relevant section of the White Paper is given in Appendix 2.

2.4 Duties of directors and delegation

The duties of a director with regard to functions he has delegated were summarised as follows by Mr Justice Parker, in a case concerning the disqualification of Mr T, a former deputy chairman of Barings plc.

- Directors, both individually and collectively, have a duty to acquire and maintain sufficient understanding of the company's business to enable them to discharge their duties properly.
- Subject to the Articles of Association, directors are allowed to delegate particular functions to individuals beneath them in the management chain. Within reason, they are also entitled to have trust in the competence and integrity of these individuals. However, delegation of authority does not remove from the director a duty to supervise the exercise of that delegated authority by the subordinate.
- There is not a universal rule for establishing whether a director is in breach of his or her duty to supervise the discharge of delegated functions by subordinates. The extent of the duty, and whether it has been properly discharged, should be decided on the facts of each case.

Matters that could be an issue in any particular case include:

- whether the authority was delegated to the appropriate person
- whether the individual should have checked how the subordinate was discharging the delegated functions
- whether the system itself, within which the failure occurred, was itself inadequate (for which the person with overall responsibility must accept criticism)
- what was the extent of the director's duties and responsibilities in this case.

When there is a question about the extent of the director's duties and responsibilities, a significant factor could be the level of reward that the director was entitled to receive from the company. *Prima facie*, the higher the rewards, the greater the responsibilities should be expected.

In the Barings case, Mr Justice Parker concluded that Mr T had failed in his duties because he did not have a sufficient knowledge and understanding of the nature of the derivatives markets and the risks involved in derivatives dealing (which led to the collapse of Barings). He was therefore unable to consider properly matters referred to the committee of which he was chairman.

2.5 Duty of skill and care for non-executive directors

All board members have the same duty of skill and care to the company. However, non-executive directors are likely to spend significantly less time on the affairs of the company than their executive director colleagues. The knowledge and experience they have of the company's affairs will therefore be much less.

The Combined Code includes a supporting Schedule that gives some guidance on what might be required from a non-executive director to comply with the requirement to exercise skill, care and diligence. It comments:

> *It is up to each non-executive director to reach a view as to what is necessary in particular circumstances to comply with the duty of skill, care and diligence they owe as a director of the company. In considering whether or not a person is in breach of that duty, a court would take into account all relevant circumstances.*

In its guidance, the Code suggests that relevant considerations might be as follows:

- The letter of appointment for a non-executive director should set out the expected time commitment for the role. This can be compared with the actual time commitment the director has given.
- The Combined Code requires that directors should be supplied in a timely manner with all the information they need to discharge their duties, and the information should be in a suitable form and of an appropriate quality. A check can be made to establish whether the information provided to the director met these requirements.

- Non-executive directors are expected to seek clarification of information from management, and additional information if required, and also to take and follow professional advice where appropriate.
- Non-executive directors are required by the Code to undertake an induction on first becoming a director, and to update and refresh their skills, knowledge and familiarity with the company.
- Where a director has concerns about a particular matter, he/she must ensure that these are considered by the board, and to the extent that the matter is not resolved, make sure that the concerns are minuted in the minutes of the board meeting at which they are discussed.
- On resignation, a director should give a written statement to the chairman if there are any unresolved concerns.

3 Fair dealing by directors

Certain responsibilities are placed on directors by statute, which restrict the extent to which directors could seek to gain unfairly at the expense of the company or its shareholders. Some of the restrictions on directors are contained in the Companies Act 1985 (Sections 311–347) under the broad heading of enforcement of fair dealing by directors.

3.1 Prohibition on loans to directors and connected persons

Section 330 of the Companies Act 1985 prohibits loans and quasi-loans by a company to any of its directors. In the case of public limited companies, this prohibition extends to connected persons of a director. The spouse of a director, child or stepchild under the age of 18 and companies in which the director has an equity interest of 20 per cent or more are all classified as connected persons.

A quasi-loan would occur if the company agrees to pay a sum of money on behalf of a director to a third party, on terms that the director will at some time in the future reimburse the company.

There are some exceptions to the Section 330 prohibition on loans and quasi-loans:

- A company can make a loan or quasi-loan to a director provided it does not exceed £5,000 and in the case of a quasi-loan is repayable within two months.
- A company may enter into a transaction for a director if the total of the relevant amounts does not exceed £10,000.
- A company may lend money to a director to assist him or her in the performance of his or her duties. For example, if the director has to move home from one part of the country to another, the company can assist with a bridging loan. However, in the case of a public company, such financial assistance cannot exceed a certain limit (currently £20,000) and must also be approved by the shareholders at or before the next AGM.

Case example

> In the case of Tait Consibee (Oxford) Limited v Tait (1997), a company made a loan of £10,000 to the defendant, Tait, who was at the time a director. Later in the same year (1994), Tait left the company and ceased to be a director. In January 1995, the company demanded repayment of the loan. Tait refused, arguing that it had been agreed that the loan would be repaid out of dividends, and the company had not made any dividend payments since the loan was made. The company disputed this. However, it also argued that the loan was illegal, having been made to a director, and so was recoverable immediately. The court agreed, and ordered Tait to pay back the loan with interest.

- Loans may be made by the company on proper commercial terms in the ordinary course of its business. For example, a bank can lend money to a director in a normal lending transaction.

In most circumstances, a loan contravening the provisions of the Companies Act is voidable (i.e. it is not automatically void but can be made void if desired) at the instance of the company (Section 341) and the company can demand immediate repayment. There is also criminal liability for any director who, with full knowledge, authorises or permits any such illegal loan.

3.2 Interests in contracts with the company

Section 317 of the Companies Act 1985 requires a director who has a direct or indirect interest in a contract (or proposed contract) with the company to declare the nature of that interest to the board of directors. Typically, a director might be a shareholder in another company which is or is about to enter into a supply contract with the company. In this case:

- The interest should be disclosed as soon as possible – when the individual first becomes a director, or when the possibility of entering into a contract is first proposed or as soon as the director acquires an interest.
- The Act allows a director to make a blanket declaration, by informing the board that he/she is a shareholder in another company with which the company is or might be about to enter into a contract.
- Article 94 of Table A provides that a director shall not vote at a board meeting on any matter in which he/she has a material conflict of interest. (In practice, the director might be asked to leave the meeting whilst the matter is being discussed.)

Failure to make a disclosure as required by Section 317 will make the director liable to a fine.

If a director has an interest in a contract with the company and has failed to disclose it, and has received a payment under the contract, he or she will be regarded as holding the money in the capacity of constructive trustee for the company (and so is bound to repay the money).

3.3 Substantial property transactions

Under Section 320 of the Companies Act 1985, shareholder approval is required for any transaction between a director and the company in which the director receives from or transfers to the company any non-cash asset (e.g. land and buildings) worth the lesser of £100,000 and 10 per cent of the company's net assets (and subject to a minimum value of £2,000). This is to prevent a director from selling non-cash assets to the company for more than they are worth, or buying non-cash assets at less than their market value, without the shareholders having the opportunity to say no.

When a company enters into a contract in contravention of Section 320, the contract is voidable at the instance of the company, unless one of three conditions applies:

- restitution of the money or other asset is no longer possible
- a third party has acquired rights *bona fide* and for value, without being aware of the contravention of Section 320, or
- the arrangement is, within a reasonable period, affirmed by the company at a general meeting.

If a director or connected person is in breach of Section 320, that director and any other director who authorised the transaction shall be liable to account to the company for any profit from the transaction, and indemnify the company for any loss or damage arising from the transaction.

3.4 Related party transactions and the UK Listing Rules

For companies whose shares are listed and traded on the London Stock Exchange, legal requirements are further reinforced by the UK Listing Rules, which include a section on related party transactions. In broad terms, a 'related party' means a substantial shareholder of the company, a director of the company, a member of a director's family or a company in which a director or family member holds 30 per cent or more of the shares. A related party transaction is a transaction between a company and a related party, other than in the normal course of business.

For most related party transactions above a minimum size, a listed company is required to do the following:

- make an announcement to the stock market giving details of the transaction
- send a circular to shareholders giving more details, and
- obtain the prior approval of the shareholders for the transaction.

The effect of the Listing Rules should be to prevent directors or major shareholders of UK listed companies from obtaining a personal benefit from any non-business transaction with their company, unless the shareholders have given their approval.

3.5 Directors' contracts

Section 318 of the Companies Act 1985 requires companies to keep (at an 'appropriate place') a copy of directors' service contracts, which should be open to inspection by members without charge.

Section 319 of the Companies Act 1985 requires prior shareholder approval to be given for any contract of service with a director where the term of employment exceeds five years. (The Combined Code seeks to limit contracts to a notice period of twelve months, therefore Section 319 should not be relevant in the case of listed companies.)

3.6 Compensation to a director for loss of office

Section 312 states that a payment to a director by way of 'compensation' for loss of office is not lawful unless particulars of the proposed payment are disclosed to and approved by the shareholders. However, Section 316 states that such payments do not include *bona fide* payments by way of damages for breach of contract, or by way of pension payments in respect of past services. The governance issue of severance payments to former directors on termination of office is therefore essentially a matter of contract of employment terms (see Chapter 6).

4 Directors' share interests and share dealings

Directors usually own some shares in their company. As directors, they will have access to price-sensitive information before it is announced to the stock market. A number of laws and regulations are intended to prevent directors from carrying on dealing in shares without the knowledge of the other shareholders, or in such a way as to benefit from inside information. These include:

- a duty to notify the company of interests in shares and transactions in shares of the company
- a law against insider dealing
- a law against market abuse
- the Model Code on share dealings by directors and certain other employees.

4.1 Director's duty to notify the company

On appointment, a director must notify the company of any shares, debentures or other interests that he or she holds in the company, and as an ongoing obligation must notify the company of any purchases or disposals that he or she subsequently makes.

Section 324 of the 324 Companies Act 1985 requires a director to notify the company in writing of the number of shares/debentures he or she currently holds in either the company or its parent company. Any subsequent transactions must also be notified. (Directors of a subsidiary company must notify the companies of their interests in shares in the parent, including any share options.) This requirement to notify extends to interests held by spouses and infant children of the director. (An infant child is defined as one under 18, including step-children.)

The director has five days to notify the company (from the date of entering the transaction to buy or sell/dispose), excluding weekends and bank holidays. Thus, if a director buys shares in his or her company on a Wednesday, and there is no intervening bank holiday, he or she must notify the company by the following Wednesday evening.

4.2 Register of directors' interests

Section 325 of the Companies Act 1985 requires a company to enter the information provided by directors under Section 324 in a register of directors' interests. This register must also record:

- the grant to a director of rights to subscribe for shares or debentures, giving details of the date of the grant, the period of exercise, number of options granted, and consideration
- on exercise, details of the date, the number exercised and the person in whose name the shares are registered.

Notification to the stock market

Section 329 of the 329 Companies Act 1985 requires a company whose shares are quoted on a Recognised Investment Exchange in the UK to notify the Exchange by the end of the next business day following receipt of a notification from a director. The Act requires disclosure of any item that should be entered in the Register of Directors' Interests.

The UK Listing Rules require that this information should be notified to the Exchange together with additional details, such as the price of the securities and the date and nature of the transaction.

4.3 Insider dealing

Part V of the Criminal Justice Act 1993 makes it a criminal offence for anyone to make use of 'inside information' to buy or sell shares in a company in a regulated stock market. Inside information is defined as information that is specific or precise, has not yet been made public, and if it were made public, would be likely to have a significant effect on the price of the company's shares.

In practice, however, there have been relatively few successful prosecutions of individuals for insider dealing, because the guilt of an alleged 'insider dealer' has been difficult to prove in specific cases. Insider dealing is a criminal offence, with offenders liable to a fine, imprisonment or both.

4.4 Market abuse

The Financial Services and Markets Act 2000 (Section 118) introduced a civil offence of 'market abuse'. Market abuse is a civil offence, not a crime, and the burden of proof is less than for insider dealing. It relates to behaviour by one or more individuals in relation to 'qualifying investments' that are traded on a market and include shares in companies that are traded on a stock market. For market abuse to occur in relation to a company's shares, the behaviour of the individual or individuals concerned must satisfy one or more of three conditions:

1. The behaviour is based on information not generally available to the market, but if the information were available generally, it would be likely to influence investment decisions by regular users of the market.
2. The behaviour is likely to give a regular user of the market a false or misleading impression about the supply or demand for the shares, or the price or value of the shares.
3. A regular user of the market would regard the behaviour as something that would be likely to distort the market in the shares.

The Financial Services Authority has the power to impose penalties for market abuse, including fines. The offence of market abuse applies generally, not just to company directors.

This Handbook does not go into the details of what constitutes market abuse or insider dealing. Essentially, however, individuals, including company directors, must not trade in shares of their company when aware of price-sensitive information that is not available to the market generally. Otherwise, they could be criminally liable for insider dealing or liable for market abuse (a civil offence, and so more easily proved than insider dealing).

4.5 The Model Code and directors' dealings

The law on dealing in shares by directors is supplemented by a requirement in the UK Listing Rules that listed companies should have rules for share dealings by their directors that are no less stringent than the rules in a 'Model Code' provided as an appendix to the chapter in the Rules on directors. The purpose of the restrictions is to try to ensure that directors 'do not abuse, and do not place themselves under suspicion of abusing, price-sensitive information that they may have or be thought to have, especially in periods leading up to an announcement of results'.

The Model Code in the Listing Rules applies to share dealing by directors and 'relevant employees'. Compliance with the Code should ensure that directors (and other individuals with access to key unpublished financial information about the company) do not breach the rules on either insider dealing or market abuse.

The main provisions within the Model Code are as follows:

- Directors must not deal in shares of their company during a 'close period' – the two months before the announcement of the company's interim and final results, or between the end of the financial year and the announcement of the annual results. (If the company produces quarterly results, the non-trading period is just one month before publication, in the case of the three interim quarterly results, but the same rules apply to the final results.)
- A director must not deal at any time that he or she is privy to price-sensitive information. Information is 'price-sensitive' if its publication could have a significant effect on the share price.
- A director must seek clearance from the chairman (or another designated director) prior to dealing in the company's shares, and must not deal without having obtained clearance. Clearance must not be given during a 'prohibited period'. A prohibited period is a close period and any period during which there is unpublished price-sensitive information which is reasonably likely to result in an announcement being made.
- In exceptional circumstances, clearance to deal can be given during a prohibited period where the director has a pressing financial commitment or would suffer financial hardship if unable to deal.
- A director must ensure that none of his or her connected persons deals during a prohibited period, nor any investment manager acting on his or her behalf or on behalf of a connected person. Connected persons include spouse and infant children, and companies in which the director controls over 20 per cent of the equity.

5 Disqualification of directors

A director may be disqualified from holding office as a director. On disqualification, he or she would have to step down from office immediately. Table A (Article 81) provide for the disqualification of a director who is:

- bankrupt
- suffering from mental disorder, or
- disqualified by the rest of the board for being absent from board meetings for more than a certain period of time without their permission.

A director may also be disqualified from office by the court. Examples of offences for which UK directors have been disqualified from office by the court include insider dealing in the shares of the company, a failure to keep proper accounting records, and making a loan to an associated company on uncommercial terms. Directors can also be disqualified for either fraudulent trading or wrongful trading, when their company is insolvent.

The main statute dealing with the disqualification of directors is the Company Directors Disqualification Act 1986 (CDDA), as amended by the Insolvency Act 2000 and the Enterprise Act 2002. The court may make a disqualification order against an individual under different sections of the Act:

- When a company has failed, the official receiver or insolvency practitioner should send a report to the Secretary of State on the conduct of directors who were in office during the last three years of trading by the company. The Secretary of State should then decide whether it is in the public interest to seek a disqualification order from the court. Reasons for seeking a disqualification order would include continuing to trade to the detriment of creditors when the company was insolvent, failure to keep proper accounting records and failure to prepare and file financial statements.
- The procedure above is a civil proceeding. There are also provisions in the Act for criminal proceedings in cases where the individual has already been disqualified from acting as a director, or where fraudulent trading or the misappropriation of company funds has occurred.
- The Insolvency Act 2000 introduced a disqualification undertaking, as an alternative to a disqualification order. The individual director gives an undertaking to the Secretary of State not to act as a director for an agreed length of time. If the Secretary of State accepts the undertaking, this has the same effect as a disqualification order, but court proceedings are avoided.
- The Enterprise Act 2002 introduced new sections into the CDDA 1986, to enable the court to disqualify a director who has been involved in a breach of competition law.

5.1 Disqualification by the court with personal liability

UK law makes a distinction between the crime of fraudulent trading (criminal law) and the personal liability of individual directors for fraudulent or wrongful trading (civil law). A court has the power to disqualify a director who has been involved in either fraudulent trading or wrongful trading when the company is insolvent. In these circumstances, the disqualified director could also be held personally liable for the debts of the company. Only the liquidator of the company, not the company's shareholders or other directors, can apply to the court for a declaration of civil liability.

Fraudulent trading during the course of winding up a company means carrying on business with the intent of defrauding creditors 'or for any fraudulent purpose' (Insolvency Act 1986). Examples of fraudulent trading are falsifying the company's accounting records, omitting a material fact from a formal statement about the company's affairs, or making a false representation to creditors with the intention of persuading them to come to a financial settlement with the company.

To disqualify the director and hold him or her personally liable for the company's debts, a court would need to be satisfied that fraud has occurred, and this could be difficult. A lower burden of proof is required for wrongful trading. A court will disqualify a director and hold him or her liable for wrongful trading if negligence, rather than criminal conduct (fraud), is proved. Wrongful trading occurs when a director knew, or should have known, before the start of the official winding up procedures, that the company would be insolvent and go into liquidation but did not do enough to minimise the potential losses for the company's creditors.

6 Other statutory obligations on directors

6.1 Accounts and audit

Although not directly related to corporate governance, the directors have a duty to prepare:

- the annual financial accounts (ss226–227 of the Companies Act 1985)
- a directors' report (s234), and
- deliver a copy of the company's report and accounts to the Registrar of Companies.

Directors' remuneration report and OFR

More directly relevant to corporate governance is the requirement for the directors of quoted companies to produce a directors' remuneration report (s234B of the Companies Act 1985) (see Chapter 6), and also an Operating and Financial Review (OFR) with the annual report and accounts (see Chapter 8).

6.2 Directors' legal responsibilities to employees

The fiduciary duty of directors to their company includes a requirement to have regard to the interests of the company's employees. Section 309 of the Companies Act 1985 states:

> *The matters to which the directors of a company are to have regard in the performance of their functions include the interests of the company's employees in general, as well as the interests of its [shareholders]. Accordingly, the duty imposed ... on the directors is owed by them to the company (and the company alone) and is enforceable in the same way as any other fiduciary duty owed to a company by its directors.*

This means that although the directors should have some regard to the interests of employees, the employees themselves do not have the right to enforce this requirement, because the duty of the directors is to the company. In practice, therefore, this 'duty' to employees would appear to have little practical value.

6.3 Directors' responsibilities to company outsiders

Although the duty of directors is to their company, a breach of that duty could affect outsiders of the company. When the directors make a contract with an outsider, the contract is binding on the company when it is in accordance with its Articles of

Association. However, the directors might exceed their powers in making the contract, for example, because they should have obtained shareholder approval first, but failed to do so. Contracts entered into without proper authority are known as 'irregular contracts':

- An outsider making a contract in good faith with the directors, when the contract is irregular, would be unable to enforce the contract if it is void.
- On the other hand, if an irregular contract is not void and is enforceable, a company has no protection against the consequences of unauthorised actions by its directors.

Company law provides that an irregular contract is binding on a company when an outsider, acting in good faith, enters into the contract and the contract has been approved by the board of directors, The directors will be liable to the company for any loss suffered. This rule means that irregular contracts do not affect third parties (outsiders).

7 Shadow directors and *de facto* directors

The duties, responsibilities and potential liabilities of directors extend to shadow directors and *de facto* directors.

7.1 Shadow directors

A shadow director is a person who is not on the board of directors, but who is able to give instructions and directions to the directors with which the directors will comply. Section 741 of the Companies Act 1985 defines a shadow director as follows: 'In relation to a company, a "shadow director" means a person in accordance with whose directions or instructions the directors of a company are accustomed to act.' A shadow director exists if just a majority of directors follow his or her instructions, rather than all the board directors. (Individuals giving professional advice, such as accountants or solicitors acting in a professional advisory capacity, are excluded from this definition. For the purposes of various company law matters, holding companies are also exempted from being shadow directors of their subsidiary companies.)

Shadow directors are not common. But where they do exist, shareholders ought to be informed about them. For example, an individual who has been disqualified as a director might be the effective controller of the board of a company (probably a private company) without being a director.

Deciding whether an individual is or is not a shadow director will vary according to the circumstances of the case.

Proof that an individual is a shadow director requires specific evidence that instructions have been given by the individual that were acted on by the company. The case *Re Hydrodan (Corby) Ltd* illustrates the very restrictive definition applied by the courts to the definition of a shadow director. The judge in this case ruled that for a person to be a shadow director, there has to be clear evidence that he had interfered in the

Case example

> In 2000, 'shadow directors' of Euro Express, a West Sussex travel agency owing creditors £4.6 million, were disqualified by the court from future involvement in giving instructions to companies, for periods of up to sixteen years. This decision by the Court of Appeal was seen as a legal milestone in attempts by the authorities to prevent 'unfit' individuals from controlling companies.
>
> In this case, two individuals controlled Euro Express without being directors. The company sold 'bucket shop' holiday flights between Gatwick and Nice, and in 1991 had diversified into the schools ski holiday market. To operate in the schools market, the company's directors had to assure the Civil Aviation Authority and the association of travel operators (ATOL) that it could pay a compulsory bond of £472,000. It was shown that the two 'shadow directors' had been prime movers in deceiving the CAA about this matter. A High Court had ruled that the individuals could not be considered shadow directors, but on appeal, the Court of Appeal overturned this ruling and decided that they were. Euro Express went into voluntary liquidation in 1993.

company's affairs to such an extent that the company's appointed directors simply substituted the shadow director's decisions for their own.

When a company does have a shadow director, various statutory and governance issues arise:

- Shadow directors, as well as ordinary directors, are subject to the provisions of the Companies Act 1985 with respect to long-term service contracts, loans from the company, interests in contracts made with the company, and so on. Shadow directors can be found guilty of wrongful trading. They must also disclose their shareholdings to the companies.
- The issue of transparency also arises. Companies should inform shareholders about the existence of any shadow director, so that the shareholders are aware of how board decisions might be influenced.

7.2 *De facto* directors

De facto directors are more common than shadow directors, and similar governance issues apply to them. A *de facto* director was defined by Mr Justice O'Neill in *Re Lynrowan Enterprises Ltd [2002]* as someone who:

- is the sole person directing the company's affairs, or
- conducts the company's affairs equally with other individuals who have not been validly appointed as directors, or
- conducts the company's affairs equally with other individuals who have been validly appointed as directors.

CHAPTER

The Role of the Board 3

1 The Combined Code and the role of the board

Table A gives all powers to the directors, and states that the directors can delegate these powers to committees or individual directors (Articles 70 and 72). The articles do not state what the responsibilities of the board of directors collectively should be, or what decisions the board should take for itself. In theory, the board could delegate virtually all its decision-making responsibilities to the executive management.

In this respect company law could be seen as being weak in promoting good corporate governance. The articles do not state what the responsibilities of the board of directors collectively should be. An important aspect of corporate governance is the view that the board of directors has certain responsibilities that it should exercise collectively, and should not delegate. Principles and provisions on this issue are included in the Combined Code, and further practical guidance has been published by the ICSA.

The Combined Code begins with the role of the board. Main Principle A1 states that

> *every company should be headed by an effective board, which is collectively responsible for the success of the company.*

A Supporting Principle spells this out in more detail, stating that the role of the board is to do the following:

- provide entrepreneurial leadership for the company within a framework of prudent and effective risk management
- set the company's strategic aims

- make sure that the necessary resources (financial and human) are in place for the company to meet its objectives
- review management performance
- set the company's values and standards
- make sure that the company's obligations to its shareholders are understood and met.

2 The board and decision-making

The main decision-making powers in a company belong to the board of directors. Although the board delegates many of the operational decision-making responsibilities to executive management, it should:

- retain the most significant decisions; and
- monitor the performance of the executive management.

An important aspect of corporate governance is therefore the nature of the decisions that the board reserves to itself (rather than delegating them to executive management) and the way in which the board reaches its decisions. The board needs to be able to reach decisions that are well considered and in the interests of the company.

The board of directors therefore needs:

- a clear set of decision-making responsibilities
- access to information to enable the directors to arrive at well-judged opinions
- a suitable balance of power amongst board members, so that the views of a single individual or group of individuals do not dominate decision-making.

The need for a suitable balance of power on the board was emphasised by the Cadbury Committee, which recommended (in the Cadbury Code) that control over the company should be exercised by the board of directors as a whole, and not by an individual executive director or chairman, nor by a small group of executive directors. It made a number of detailed recommendations about decision-making by the board:

- The board should meet regularly and retain full and effective control over the company.
- It should monitor the performance of the executive management.
- Some important decisions should be referred to the board for a decision, and should not be taken by executive managers. Decisions by the board should include, for example, decisions on major new investments or divestments, and decisions about large mergers and takeovers.
- A formal schedule should specify matters about which decisions must be taken by the board and not by executive managers. A clear schedule of decision-making responsibilities should make it difficult for a powerful chief executive to usurp

decision-making powers and ensure that the ultimate control of the company remains firmly in the hands of the board (see Section 4 below).

It has to be recognised that the individual board members might not have the technical knowledge to make some important decisions unaided. The Cadbury Code, recognising that occasions will arise when a director needs professional advice in order to form an opinion, recommended that there should be an agreed procedure enabling him or her to obtain professional advice at the company's expense. This principle has prevailed and is currently specified by Combined Code Provision A.5.2.

3 Good boardroom practice

Boardroom practice refers to the way in which a board conducts its procedures and reaches its decisions. The ICSA has argued that it is not sufficient to rely on unwritten boardroom procedures and practices, and has issued a Code for Directors and Company Secretaries on Good Boardroom Practice. This also contains guidance on matters that the board should consider and, where applicable, formally adopt.

The ICSA's Code includes the following provisions:

- There should be written procedures for the conduct of board business. Compliance should be monitored, preferably by an audit committee.
- Each director, on first appointment, should be given sufficient information to enable him or her to carry out the duties of a director properly, and this should include details of procedures for obtaining information about the company and requisitioning a board meeting.
- In conducting board business, each director should receive the same information at the same time, and should be given sufficient time in which to read it and consider it.
- The board should identify matters that require the prior approval of the board. As a general rule, all material contracts should be subject to prior approval by the board before the company commits itself to them. (Procedures should be established for reaching decisions reserved for the board, where a decision is required before the next board meeting.)
- Decisions about the agenda for a board meeting should be taken by the company chairman, in consultation with the company secretary.
- The company secretary should be responsible to the chairman for the proper administration of board meetings, the meetings of board committees and general meetings of the company. To carry out these responsibilities, the company secretary should be entitled to be present at and prepare the minutes for all such meetings. The minutes of meetings should record all decisions that were taken, and procedures should be established for the approval and circulation of minutes.

- The board should give its prior approval for the membership, terms of reference and powers of any committee of the board that is established. Minutes of board committees should be circulated to all board directors prior to the next board meeting, to give them an opportunity to raise questions at that meeting.

The full text of the Code is reproduced in Appendix 3.

4 Matters reserved for the board

A board cannot run a business at the day-to-day operational level, and must delegate extensive responsibilities to executive directors and management. However, the board remains responsible for the company and its business, and must therefore retain sufficient control. There are certain matters that ought to be reserved for decisions by the board of directors, which should not be delegated.

Code Provision A.1.1 states that there should be a formal schedule of matters specifically reserved for board decision-making. The annual report should include a statement of how the board operates, including a 'high-level statement' of which types of decision are taken by the board and which are delegated to executive management.

The ICSA's Guidance Note *Matters Reserved for the Board* offers guidance in this area. It provides a list of suggested matters to be reserved for the board. It recognises that some matters should be referred or delegated by the board to one of its committees (nomination, remuneration or audit committee), although recommendations by these committees should be subject to full board approval. The list should identify which transactions require multiple board signatures on the relevant documents.

4.1 Urgent matters

The Guidance Note also suggests that in drawing up the schedule of matters reserved for the board, procedures should be established for dealing with urgent matters that arise between regular board meetings. It recommends that to deal with such matters, a meeting should be held by telephone or video conferencing, including as many directors as possible. Directors unable to participate should be sent the relevant documents and have an opportunity to give their views to the chairman, another director or the company secretary before the meeting.

In dealing with urgent matters, there is a need to balance the need for urgency with the overriding principle that each director should be given as much information as possible, time to consider the matter properly and an opportunity to discuss the matter before the company commits itself to a decision.

4.2 The recommended schedule

The Guidance Note is set out in full in Appendix 4. Its recommended list contains 54 items, usefully grouped into 12 categories and indicating which decisions should not be delegated to a committee of the board. These are summarised below (not all of the 54 items are listed).

Strategy and management

The board has overall responsibility for strategy and management:

1 Responsibility for the overall management of the group
2 Approval of the group's long-term objectives and commercial strategy
3 Approval of the annual operating and capital expenditure budgets
4 Oversight of the group's operations
5 Reviewing the group's performance in the light of its objectives, strategy, business plans and budgets, and taking corrective action as necessary
6 Extending the group's activities into new business or geographical areas
7 Shutting down all or a material part of the group's business operations.

Structure and capital

The board also has responsibility for any changes to the capital structure, management structure and status of the company:

1 Changes to the group's capital structure
2 Changes to the corporate structure and management control structure
3 Changes to the company's status as a listed company or plc.

Financial reporting and controls

Most of the responsibilities for financial reporting and controls should not be delegated to a committee of the board. The matters for decision include:

1 Approval of preliminary announcements (interim and final results)
2 Approving the annual report and accounts
3 Approving the dividend policy, declaring the interim dividend and recommending the final dividend
4 Approving any significant change in accounting policies
5 Approval of treasury policies (including currency exposures and the use of financial derivatives).

Other categories of decision

The other categories of decision in the recommended schedule are as follows:

- *Internal controls*. Matters relating to the maintenance of a sound system of internal controls and risk management.
- *Contracts*. Matters relating to major capital projects and other contracts that are material either strategically or because of their size, including major acquisitions or disposals.
- *Communication*. Approval of resolutions to put to shareholders at a general meeting, circulars and listing particulars, and press releases.

- *Board membership and other appointments* (including succession planning for the board, and the appointment or removal of the external auditors and company secretary).
- *Remuneration.* Decisions include those relating to the remuneration policy for directors senior executives and non-executive directors, and share incentive plans for submission to the shareholders for approval.
- *Delegation of authority.* Decisions relating to approving the terms of reference for board committees and receiving reports from these committees.
- *Corporate governance matters.*
- *Policies.* The approval of policies on matters such as health and safety policy, environmental policy, corporate social responsibility, charitable donations and a share dealing code.
- *Other matters.* The schedule ends with a list of assorted other matters.

Given the responsibilities of the directors, Code Provision A.1.5 states that the company should arrange appropriate insurance cover in respect of legal action against its directors. Directors' and officers' liability insurance is covered in more detail in Chapter 2.

5 Frequency of board meetings

Combined Code Provision A.1.1 states that the board should meet 'sufficiently regularly to discharge its duties effectively'. Although there is no specific guidance on how frequent meetings should therefore be, Code Provision A.1.2 goes on to require disclosure in the annual report of the number of meetings of the board and board committees during the year and individual attendance at those meetings by the directors.

6 The executive committee (Excom)

Some of the more detailed tasks of the board should be delegated to board committees. The Combined Code promotes the roles of the nomination committee, remuneration committee and audit committee. These committees and their roles are described in later chapters.

The Combined Code does not give any consideration, however, to other committees that might be established, such as committees for risk management, health and safety, and corporate social responsibility.

An ICSA Guidance Note *Terms of Reference: Executive Committees* states that one of the key committees is the executive committee or Excom. This is the forum used by the Chief Executive Officer for major operational decisions. It is not formally constituted by the board of directors, but includes executive directors as well as other senior managers.

- However, in view of the importance of decisions taken by Excom, it should report back to the board, either by circulating minutes of its meetings to the board, or by means of a report to the board (oral or written) by the CEO.

- It is useful to appoint the company secretary as secretary to Excom, since this will help to avoid problems arising with governance issues.

Although the Combined Code requires companies to make available on their web-sites the terms of reference of the nomination, remuneration and audit committees, there is no such requirement for Excom. The Guidance Note suggests that companies might wish to consider making these available, in the interests of transparency and good corporate governance.

The Guidance Note provides an example of the terms of reference for such a committee, which include:

- the purpose of the committee (to develop and implement strategy and operational plans, policies, procedures and budgets, to monitor operational and financial performance, to assess and control risk, to prioritise and allocate resources, and to monitor the competition in each area of operations)
- the committee's membership
- the chairman and the secretary of the committee
- a quorum
- frequency of meetings
- notice of meetings
- conduct of meetings
- minutes of meetings
- the duties of the committee
- reporting responsibilities (the CEO, as Chair of the Committee, should report to the board of directors).

The duties of Excom should be specified in detail, and a suggested list is provided in the ICSA Guidance Note. They include:

- recommending objectives and strategy for the group in developing its business
- agreeing policy guidelines for business divisions based on agreed group strategy
- successful execution of strategy
- developing and reviewing business division objectives and budgets
- ensuring that appropriate levels of authority are delegated to senior management throughout the group
- reviewing the organisational structure of the group and recommending changes where appropriate
- ensuring the effective management of risk and application of internal controls within the group
- safeguarding the integrity of management information and financial reporting
- identifying new business opportunities outside the current core activities
- examining all major investments and divestments, with a view to making recommendations to the board of directors

- optimising the allocation and adequacy of the group's resources
- developing and implementing group policies on matters such as ethics, share dealing, risk management, Treasury policies, health and safety policy, and corporate social responsibility.

This list is not comprehensive. For further details, you are recommended to refer to the ICSA Guidance Note itself.

7 General purposes committee

The same ICSA Guidance Note provides a list of the duties and powers that are often delegated by the board of directors to a General Purposes Committee or Finance Committee, rather than to Excom. These include:

- approving the opening of new bank account facilities, the authorised signatories and their authority limits
- approving arrangements with financial institutions for dealing in financial instruments (money market instruments, currency instruments, interest rate instruments, futures and options, and sale and repurchase agreements)
- approving guarantees and indemnities up to a specified limit
- the allotment of shares under executive and employee share plans
- regular (monthly) reviews of treasury activities.

8 The company secretary and corporate governance

The corporate governance framework involves a range of laws, rules, principles and guidelines for practical application, and it is inevitable that the company secretary should be closely involved in the administration of corporate governance, through the support that he or she gives to the board and individual board members.

The 2003 Combined Code makes particular reference to the responsibilities of the company secretary for corporate governance. Supporting Principle A5 states that the company secretary is responsible for:

- ensuring good information flows within the board and its committees, and between senior management and non-executive directors;
- advising the board (through the chairman) on all governance matters;
- being available to give advice and support to individual directors, particularly in relation to the induction of new directors and assistance with professional development.

A brief list of some of the tasks and responsibilities of the company secretary reinforces this principle:

- The company secretary assists the chairman of the board with preparing for, conducting and reporting the outcome of board meetings and general meetings of the company. He or she attends those meetings, and takes the minutes.
- The company secretary will have some involvement in the counting of proxy votes from shareholders for a general meeting. Although the detailed counting is likely to be done by the company's registrars, the results should be sent to the company secretary. The company secretary is therefore well informed about shareholder voting intentions.
- Major shareholders are required by law to notify the company of changes in their shareholdings above 3 per cent, when the change takes the shareholding up or down by a percentage point or more. These notifications come to the company secretary, who (in the case of listed companies) must then notify a regulatory information service.
- Directors are required to notify the company of their transactions in shares of the company, by themselves or by related parties. This information should be notified to the company secretary, who (in the case of listed companies) must then notify an official news channel. The company secretary needs to be aware whether the share dealings breach any code (in the UK, a quoted company's code for directors' share dealings, which might be the same as the Model Code in the UK Listing Rules).
- The company secretary is likely to have the responsibility for assisting the chairmen of the committees of the board, i.e. the audit committee, remuneration committee and nominations committee. For example, the company secretary's office is likely to assist a chairman by checking the availability of the other committee members for a meeting and arranging the venue. He or she may also attend the meetings and take minutes.
- The company secretary will be responsible for the induction of new board directors, and possibly also for the training of directors.
- If he or she attends the meetings of the audit committee, the company secretary will have some involvement with the external auditors and internal auditors of the company and should be able to offer advice on matters of risk management.
- In some companies, the company secretary has the responsibility for arranging insurance cover for the group. In such cases, the company secretary is directly involved in an aspect of risk management.

The company secretary is close to the board of directors, without necessarily being a director. He or she is in a position to advise and assist the board chairman and NEDs. To provide this advice, he or she should have a proper understanding of corporate governance rules and practice. For example, the FSA has suggested that the company secretary should be involved in handling allegations by whistleblowers (see Chapter 12). He or she might also be asked to investigate cases of illicit share dealings by directors, potential conflicts of interest of individual directors or the independence of a particular non-executive director.

8.1 ICSA guidance on the corporate governance role of the company secretary

The ICSA Guidance Note, *Specimen Job Description for the Corporate Governance Role of the Company Secretary* provides a specimen job description, which includes the following key elements:

- ensuring the smooth running of the activities of the board of directors and the board committees, for example, by helping with planning the agendas for meetings and preparing papers for and presenting papers to the meetings;
- keeping under review all legal and regulatory developments affecting the company's operations, and making sure that the directors are properly briefed about them;
- ensuring that the interests of stakeholders are borne in mind when important business decisions are made, particularly those affecting employees. Keeping in touch with the debate on corporate social responsibility (CSR) and advising the board about its policies and practice with regard to CSR;
- acting as a 'confidential sounding board' to the chairman, NEDs and executive directors on matters that concern them, and taking a lead in dealing with difficult interpersonal issues, such as when a director is removed from the board;
- acting as a primary point of contact and source of advice and guidance for non-executive directors, with regard to the company and its activities, in order to help non-executive directors in their decsion-making process;
- acting as the 'conscience of the company', by providing an additional enquiring voice in relation to board decisions;
- ensuring compliance with the continuuing obligations of the UK Listing Rules. The Listing Rules require listed companies in the UK to comply with the provisions of the Combined Code or to explain their non-compliance. The company secretary should therefore be involved in ensuring either compliance with the Combined Code or that the board of directors provide satisfactory reasons for non-compliance;
- ensuring that the disclosures required by the Combined Code are observed;
- ensuring the dissemination of regulatory news announcements to the stock market, such as trading statements and information about share dealings by directors;
- managing relations with investors, particularly institutional investors, with regard to corporate governance matters;
- responsibility for the induction of new directors;
- making sure that the company avoids committing offences under the Financial Services and Markets Act 2000 and does not put out misleading information about its financial performance or trading condition (see Section 395 of the Act);
- ensuring compliance with the statutory requirements to file returns, such as the annual return and notification of changes in directors;

- arranging and managing the process of calling and holding the Annual General Meeting, and advising on matters to be raised at the meeting and put to the shareholders for a vote.
- The company secretary will often have additional responsibilities, relating perhaps to risk management, compliance with trading standards, or other executive issues. These will vary from one company to another.

8.2 Independence of the company secretary

The role of the company secretary in corporate governance is such that it is essential to ensure his or her independence from undue influence and pressure from a senior board member. The ICSA Guidance Note, *Reporting Lines for the Company Secretary*, comments:

> *Boards of directors have a right to expect the company secretary to give impartial advice and to act in the best interests of the company. However, it is incumbent on boards of directors to ensure that company secretaries are in a position to do so, for example by ensuring that they are not subject to undue influence of one or more of the board of directors. If the board fails to protect the integrity of the company secretary's position, one of the most effective in-built internal controls available to the company is likely to be seriously undermined. The establishment of appropriate reporting lines for the company secretary will normally be a crucial factor in establishing that protection.*

The Guidelines recommend that:

- in matters relating to his or her duties as an officer of the company, the company secretary should, through the chairman, be accountable to the board as a whole;
- if the company secretary has additional executive responsibilities on top of his or here 'core role', he or she should report to the chief executive officer or appropriate executive director on such matters;
- the company secretary's remuneration should be settled (or at least noted) by the board as a whole, or by the remuneration committee of the board on the recommendation of the chairman or chief executive.

9 Board committees

Article 72 of Table A also states that the board of directors may delegate any of its powers to a committee consisting of one or more directors, subject to any conditions the board may impose. The Combined Code includes provisions for an audit committee, remuneration committee and nomination committee, whose responsibilities are described in Chapters 9, 6 and 5.

CHAPTER

4 Board Structures and Balance

1 The composition of the board

A board consists of a chairman, the chief executive, a senior independent director and other executive and non-executive directors. The non-executives may or may not be independent (see below). There may also be a deputy chairman, and a nominated senior independent director.

The Articles of Association give extensive powers to the board of directors as a unit, and although the board can delegate powers to committees or individuals, the ability of the board to function effectively as a unit is a necessary requirement of good corporate governance.

1.1 Corporate governance and board composition

A board of directors should have the necessary skills, experience and integrity, both individually and collectively, to govern the company effectively:

- A lack of collective experience among the board members will affect the quality of decision-making by the board.
- The 'tone at the top' sets the pattern for the way in which a company conducts itself, and board members should give ethical leadership.
- Directors should not put their personal interests ahead of those of the company and its shareholders.

Domination of the board by one individual or by a small powerful group will increase the risk of unethical behaviour, decision-making in self-interest and also ill-judged decisions.

Size of the board

A Supporting Principle in the Combined Code (Principle A.3) states that:

- the board should not be so large as to be unwieldy, but

- it should be of sufficient size that the balance of skills and experience is appropriate for that company and its business, and that changes to the composition of the board can occur without undue disruption.

Objective decision-making and the contribution of board members

The Combined Code states that in order to have an effective board, 'all directors must take decisions objectively in the interests of the company'.

It is important that the directors should contribute constructively to board decisions, and in doing so should give their well-considered views. Where necessary, individuals should be prepared to disagree with the majority of the board, and let their views be known. Provision A.1.4 states that if directors have concerns about a matter that cannot be resolved, they should ensure that those concerns are recorded in the minutes of the board meetings at which the matter is discussed. If a non-executive director resigns as a result of any concern, he or she should provide a written statement to the chairman, for circulation to the board.

Balance of the board

To achieve balance and objectivity at board level:

- no one individual should have excessive powers, and
- there should be a significant number of independent directors on the board: independence is provided by non-executive directors.

Main Principle A.3 of the Combined Code states:

> *The board should include a balance of executive and non-executive directors (and in particular independent non-executive directors) such that no individual or small group of individuals can dominate the board's decision-making.*

This principle is concerned more generally with achieving a suitable balance on the board. It also introduces the idea that independent board members (independent NEDs) are important to prevent the domination of a board by one individual or a small group.

However, the Code also argues that executive directors bring an important element of balance to the board, and a Supporting Principle is that:

> *to ensure that power and information are not concentrated in one or two individuals, there should be a strong presence on the board of both executive and non-executive directors.*

2 Board roles

Within the framework of collective leadership by the board of directors, each board member also has a particular role to play. The most prominent roles are those of the board chairman, the CEO, the senior independent director and the chairmen of the main board committees. Combined Code Provision A.1.2 states that the annual report should identify the chairman, the deputy chairman (if there is one), the chief executive, the senior independent director and the chairmen and members of the nomination, audit and remuneration committees.

2.1 Role of the chairman

Supporting Principle A.2 of the Combined Code states that:

> *The chairman is responsible for leadership of the board, ensuring its effectiveness on all aspects of its role and setting its agenda. The chairman is also responsible for ensuring that the directors receive accurate, timely and clear information. The chairman should ensure effective communication with shareholders. The chairman should also facilitate the effective contribution of non-executive directors in particular and ensure constructive relations between executive and non-executive directors.*

In an appendix to the Combined Code, the *Higgs Suggestions for Good Practice* give guidance about what the role of the chairman should be, stating that the role of the chairman is 'pivotal' in creating the conditions for the effectiveness of the board as a whole and the individual directors (see Appendix 5). The responsibility of the chairman is to do the following:

- run the board and set its agenda, which should be forward-looking and concentrate on strategic matters
- ensure that members of the board receive accurate, timely and clear information to help them reach well-informed and well-considered decisions
- ensure effective communication with the shareholders, and ensure that all board members develop an understanding of the views of the major shareholders
- manage the board, and make sure that enough time is allowed for discussion of complex or contentious issues
- take the lead, using the company secretary as facilitator, in providing suitable induction for new directors
- take the lead, using the company secretary as facilitator, in identifying and meeting the development needs of individual directors
- ensure that the performance of the board as a whole and of individual directors is evaluated at least once a year
- encourage active engagement by all members of the board.

The effective chairman is therefore a team-builder. He or she should develop a board whose members communicate effectively between themselves and enjoy good relationships with each other. He or she should develop a close relationship of trust with the chief executive officer, giving support and advice whilst still respecting the CEO's responsibilities for executive matters. He or she should also ensure the effective implementation of board decisions, provide coherent leadership for the company and understand the views of the shareholders.

The chairman of the company is responsible for the functioning of the board of directors. He or she calls board meetings, sets the agenda and leads the meeting. The chairman also leads general meetings of the company and is the most prominent 'face' of the company in its dealings with shareholders and investment institutions (see Chapter 8).

The ICSA Guidance Note, *The Roles of the Chairman, Chief Executive and Senior Independent Director under the Combined Code*, (see Directory) comments:

> *The Chairman, under the Code, is responsible for ensuring the efficient use of the board's time and that the agenda is forward-looking, concentrating on strategy, rather than approving issues which should have been delegated to management. They must allow sufficient time to discuss complex or contentious issues and if necessary arrange for pre-board preparation. This should avoid non-executive directors being faced with unrealistic deadlines for decision-making.*

2.2 The role of the chief executive officer (CEO)

The CEO is the person responsible for the executive management of the company's operations. As the title suggests, he or she is the senior executive in charge of the management team and to whom all other executive managers report. Where there is an executive management committee, the CEO will be its chairman. Other executive managers might also be directors of the company, but the CEO is answerable to the board for the way the business is run and its performance.

The Combined Code does not specify the role of the CEO. However, there should be a clear division of responsibilities between the chairman of the board and the CEO. The exact division of esponsibilities may vary between different companies.

The ICSA Guidance Note, *The Roles of the Chairman, Chief Executive and Senior Independent Director under the Combined Code*, suggests that there should be a formal statement of their responsibilities and gives two approaches to presenting such a statement.

One of these approaches sets the reporting lines, key responsibilities and other responsibilities of the chairman and CEO side by side in the statement. The reporting lines and key responsibilities are contrasted as shown in the table on p. 54.

The Guidance Note also offers a sample Board Responsibilities Statement, as follows:

> *To achieve the maximum effectiveness of the board, the board accepts that the roles of Chairman and Chief Executive need to be split and clearly defined. The policy statement adopted by the board on [date] defines the role of the Chairman and Chief Executive. The Chairman is responsible for leadership of the board and creating the*

1 Reporting lines **Chairman**	**Chief Executive**
1.1 The Chairman reports to the board	1.1 The Chief Executive reports to the Chairman (acting on behalf of the board) and to the board directly
1.2 The Chairman is not responsible for executive matters regarding the Group's business. Other than the Chief Executive and the company secretary, no executive reports to the Chairman, other than through the board.	1.2 The Chief Executive is responsible for all executive management matters affecting the Group. All members of executive management report, either directly or indirectly, to him/her.
2 Key responsibilities **Chairman**	**Chief Executive**
2.1 The Chairman's principal responsibility is the effective running of the board.	2.1 The Chief Executive's principal responsibility is running the Group's business.
2.2 The Chairman is responsible for ensuring that the board as a whole plays a full and constructive part in the development and determination of the Group's strategy and overall commercial objectives.	2.2 The Chief Executive is responsible for proposing and developing the Group's strategy and overall commercial objectives, which he does in close consultation with the Chairman and the board.
2.3 The Chairman is the guardian of the board's decision-making processes.	2.3 The Chief Executive is responsible, with the executive team, for implementing the decisions of the board and its Committees.

conditions for overall board and individual director effectiveness, both inside and outside the boardroom. The Chief Executive is responsible for running the group's business. It should be noted that this document does not supersede the authorities delegated in the matters reserved for the board document approved by the board on [date].

2.3 The Combined Code on the positions of chairman and CEO

As leader of the management team and leader of the board of directors, the CEO and chairman are the most powerful positions on the board of directors.

- It is important for the proper functioning of the company that the chairman and CEO should be able to work well together.
- Acting in alliance, the chairman and CEO can dominate the board and its decision-making, particularly if the chairman also has executive responsibilities in the company's management.

When the same person holds the position of both chairman of the board and CEO, there is a possibility that he or she could become a domineering influence in decision-making in the company. There is also a potential risk that the individual will run the company for his or her own personal benefit, rather than in the interests of the shareholders and other stakeholders. The only ways to prevent a chairman-cum-CEO from dominating a company's board are to do the following:

- prohibit any individual from holding both positions, and/or
- have an influential group of directors capable of making their opinions heard and listened to.

It is unlikely that the Articles of Association will prevent the same individual from holding the office of both chairman and CEO, but in the interests of good corporate governance, the roles should be divided between two people. The chairman and the CEO would then each act as a check on the other, providing a better balance of power on the board.

It is now a generally accepted element of good corporate governance that in public companies, the roles of chairman and CEO should be held by two people, each independent of the other. Principle A.2 of the Combined Code states that:

> *There should be a clear division of responsibilities at the head of the company between the running of the board and the executive responsibility for running the company's business. No one individual should have unfettered powers of decision.*

This principle is supported by Code provisions:

- The roles of chairman and chief executive should not be exercised by the same individual. The division of responsibilities between these two roles should be set out in writing and agreed by the board (Provision A.2.1).
- On appointment, the chairman should meet the criteria for independence (see below) (Provision A.2.2).
- A chief executive should not go on to be the chairman of the same company (Provision A.2.2). If a CEO on leaving office becomes the company chairman, there is a strong risk that he or she will seek to interfere in the matters reserved for the CEO and so try to exert improper influence over the incoming CEO. The Code provision also states that if in exceptional circumstances the board decides that its CEO should move on to become the chairman, it should consult major shareholders in advance and set out its reasons to the shareholders both at the time of the appointment and in the next annual report.

There might be situations where it is appropriate for the same person to be both chairman and CEO. When a company gets into business or financial difficulties, for example, there is an argument in favour of appointing a single, all-powerful individual to run the company until its fortunes have been reversed. However, although combining the two roles might be expedient in the short term, it is much more difficult to justify over the longer term.

3 Non-executive directors (NEDs)

One function of non-executive directors is to improve the quality of decision-making by the board by:

- bringing a range of skills and experience to the deliberations of the board
- acting as a counterbalance, where necessary, to the influence of the chairman or CEO over board decision-making.

To be effective, a NED has to understand the company's business, but there appears to be a general consensus that the experience and qualities required of a non-executive director can be obtained from working in other industries or in other aspects of commercial and public life. Non-executives might therefore include individuals who:

- are an executive director in another public company
- hold non-executive director positions and chairmanship positions in other public companies
- have professional qualifications (for example partners in firms of solicitors)
- have experience in government, as politicians or former senior civil servants.

However, research has been carried out into identifying and recruiting suitable individuals as NEDs from a wider variety of sources and backgrounds. Recruiting NEDs is considered in more detail in Chapter 5.

Non-executive directors are expected not only to bring a wide range of skills and experience to the deliberations of the board, particularly in the area of strategy and business development, but also to ensure that there is a suitable balance of power on the board. A powerful chairman or chief executive officer might be able to dominate fellow-executive directors, but independent NEDs should be able to bring different views and independent thinking to the deliberations of the board. Decisions taken by the board should therefore be better and more in keeping with the aims of good corporate governance.

3.1 Higgs Guidance on the role of the non-executive director

The *Higgs Suggestions for Good Practice*, which are appended to the Combined Code, include guidance on the role of the non-executive director (see Appendix 6). This states that the role of a non-executive director has several key elements, which non-executives are perhaps in a better position to provide than executives. These are:

- *Strategy*. NEDs should constructively challenge and help to develop proposals on strategy.
- *Performance*. NEDs should scrutinise the performance of executive management in achieving agreed goals and objectives, and monitor the reporting of performance.
- *Risk*. NEDs should satisfy themselves about the integrity of financial information and that the systems of internal controls and risk management are robust.
- *People*. NEDs are responsible for deciding the level of remuneration for executive directors, and should have a prime role in appointing directors (and removing them where necessary) and in succession planning.

These particular roles explain the requirements for the audit and remuneration to consist entirely of independent NEDs and for the nomination committee to include a majority of independent NEDs.

In its response to the Higgs inquiry into the role of NEDs (leading to the Higgs Report in January 2003), the ICSA commented that the key role of NEDs was to bring an external 'real-world' focus to the board's discussions, particularly with regard to strategy and business development. Although the board should aim for unity and agreement in its decisions, NEDs should also play the role of 'devil's advocate' in challenging the views of the executive directors. Other aspects of the role of NEDs might be:

- opening up business opportunities through new contacts and experience;
- giving advice to executive directors;
- serving on board committees;
- safeguarding the interests of the shareholders and other stakeholders by making sure that these are considered when the board makes decisions;
- helping to maintain an ethical climate and encouraging probity in the conduct of the company's affairs;
- monitoring and reviewing excesses of executive directors.

3.2 Number of NEDs on the board

A key principle of good corporate governance is that there should be a sufficient number of independent NEDs on the board of directors to create a suitable balance of power and prevent the dominance of the board by one individual or by a small number of individuals.

The 1998 Combined Code required that:

- non-executive directors should comprise not less than one-third of the board; and
- a majority of the non-executives should be independent.

The 2003 Combined Code increases this requirement and offers a specific definition of independence (see below). However, recognising that the new requirement may prove difficult for smaller listed companies to implement, it also sets out differing requirements for large listed and smaller companies, defined as those outside the FTSE350 for the whole of the year immediately prior to the reporting year. Code Provision A.3.2 requires that:

- except for smaller companies, at least one half of the board, excluding the chairman, should be independent NEDs
- smaller companies should have at least two independent NEDs.

3.3 The role of non-executive directors on board committees

Independent non-executive directors are appointed to provide a counterbalance to powerful executive directors and to give the benefit of their experience and know-how to decision-making by the board. A further aspect of corporate governance is the extent to which executive directors should be kept away from some decision-making or monitoring responsibilities, through the delegation of certain responsibilities to committees of the board. A board committee might consist entirely or mostly of non-executive directors, and might be given:

- the power to make certain decisions on behalf of the board
- responsibility for investigating particular issues and making recommendations to the full board.

There are no statutory requirements to establish board committees, but three committees are recommended by the Combined Code:

1. a nomination committee
2. an audit committee
3. a remuneration committee.

The functions of the nomination, remuneration and audit committees are described in later chapters.

Boards might establish other committees, such as a risk management committee and an environment committee, but these are not dealt with by the Combined Code (except that the role and responsibilities of the audit committee are affected by the existence or non-existence of a risk committee of the board).

The Combined Code includes the specific recommendations about membership of board committees, shown in the table on p. 59.

4 Independence

Non-executive directors are either independent or non-independent, and the provisions of the Combined Code refer specifically to *independent* NEDs. A NED is not inde-

Committee	Membership
Nomination committee	A majority of the members should be independent NEDs. The chairman of the committee should be the chairman of the board or an independent NED.
Remuneration committee	All members should be independent NEDs. Large companies should have at least three members. Smaller companies should have at least two members.
Audit committee	All members should be independent NEDs. Large companies should have at least three members. Smaller companies should have at least two members. At least one member of the committee should have recent and relevant financial experience.

pendent if his or her opinions are likely to be influenced by someone else, in particular by the senior executive management of the company or by a major shareholder.

A person cannot be independent of a company if he or she personally stands to gain or otherwise benefit substantially from:

- income from the company, in addition to his or her fee as a non-executive (for example, fee income as a consultant);
- the company's reported profitability and movements in the company's share price.

An individual cannot be independent if he or she has been awarded a large number of share options by the company. Holding share options gives the individual a direct interest in the share price of the company around the time the options can be exercised. He or she might therefore favour decisions that improve the reported profitability of the company at this time, because good financial results are likely to be good for the share price.

4.1 Criteria for judging independence

Provision A.3.1 of the Combined Code requires the board to identify in the annual report each non-executive director it considers to be independent. Although this is a matter for the board's judgement, the Code provision sets out the circumstances in which independence would usually be questionable:

- where the director has been an employee of the company within the past five years
- where the director has a material business relationship with the company (or has had such a relationship within the past three years). This relationship might be as partner, shareholder, director or employee in another organisation that has a material business relationship with the company
- where the director receives (or has received) additional remneration from the company other than a director's fee, or is a member of the company's pension scheme, or participates in the company's share option scheme or a performance-related pay scheme
- where the director has close family ties with the company's advisers, directors or senior employees
- where the director has cross-directorships or has significant links with other directors through involvement in other companies or organisations
- where the director represents a significant shareholder
- where the director has served on the board for more than nine years since the date of his or her first election.

These criteria of independence should be applied to a chairman as well as other non-executive directors.

Where a board believes that a director is independent in spite of any of the above circumstances applying, it should state its reasons in the annual report.

4.2 Protecting the independence/effectiveness of board committees

As a way of protecting the independence and improving the effectiveness of board committees, the Combined Code includes the following Supporting Principles (Principle A.3):

- When deciding the chairmanship and membership of board committees, consideration should be given to the benefits of ensuring that committee membership is refreshed (i.e. membership rotation) and that undue reliance is not placed on particular individuals.
- The only individuals who are entitled to attend meetings of the nomination, remuneration and audit committees are the chairman and members of the committee, although other individuals may attend at the invitation of the committee.

5 Senior independent director

The Combined Code states that the board should appoint one of the independent NEDs to be the senior independent director (Code Provision A.3.3). Such an individual

> *should be available to shareholders if they have concerns which contact through the normal channels of chairman, chief executive or finance director has failed to resolve, or for which such contact is inappropriate.*

The senior independent director (SID) is therefore, in effect, a channel of communication between the company and its shareholders when normal channels do not work – perhaps when the principles of good corporate governance are not being applied.

To fulfil this role effectively, '*the senior independent director should attend sufficient meetings with a range of major shareholders to listen to their views in order to help develop a balanced understanding of the issues and concerns of major shareholders*' (Combined Code Provision D.1.1). The ICSA Guidance Note, *The Roles of the Chairman, Chief Executive and Senior Independent Director under the Combined Code*, comments additionally that: 'It must be emphasised that these are meetings that management would have as part of their normal investor relations programme, they are not special events or one-to-one meetings with the institution and SID, unless the shareholder has raised a concern with the SID that has not been dealt with in the normal manner.'

Critics of the concept of senior independent director argue that difficulties between a company and its shareholders should be resolved by the chairman, and the position of the SID should be superfluous. Opening up the possibility of an additional channel of communication for shareholders is perhaps more likely to confuse company–shareholder relationships rather than improve them.

The Combined Code includes the following provision with respect to the chairman, SID and other non-executive directors (Provision A.1.3):

- The chairman should hold meetings with the NEDs, without the executive directors present. (It is the chairman's responsibility to make sure that the NEDs contribute effectively to the board, and meetings without the executive directors present might help as a counter-balance to the tendency for the opinion of executive directors to dominate the deliberations of the board.)
- Led by the SID, the non-executive directors should meet at least annually, without the chairman being present, to discuss the chairman's performance and 'on other occasions as are deemed appropriate'.

The ICSA Guidance Note also suggests that the SID should chair the nomination committee when it is considering the succession to the position of chairman of the board of directors.

The senior independent director is seen as the main channel of communication between a company and it shareholders in the event that the normal channels of communications with the chairman or executive directors are ineffective. However, it can also be argued that all non-executive directors should meet with shareholders occasionally, in order to learn and understand their views. To some extent, this view is recognised in the Combined Code. Communications between shareholders and NEDs are described more fully in Chapter 7.

6 Criticisms of non-executive directors

There are differing views about the effectiveness of non-executive directors. The 'accepted' view is that NEDs bring experience and judgement to the deliberations of the board that the executive directors on their own would lack. An alternative view is that the effectiveness of NEDs can be undermined by several factors:

- A lack of knowledge about the business operations of the company. The quality of decision-making depends largely on the quality of information available to the decision-maker. However, the senior executives in a company control the information systems, and thus control the flow of information to the board. Lacking the 'insider knowledge' of executive managers about the business operations, and having to rely on the integrity of the information supplied to them by management and executive directors restricts the scope for NEDs to make a meaningful contribution to board decisions.
- NEDs often have executive positions in other companies and organisations, where most of their working time is spent. As a general rule, NEDs do not have an office at the company headquarters and may spend at most one or two days a month on the company's business. A further criticism of non-executive directors is that some individuals hold too many NED positions, so that they cannot possibly give sufficient time to any of the companies concerned. It would be argued, for example, that an individual cannot be an effective NED of a company if he is also the chief executive officer of another public company and holds four or five other NED positions in other companies.

The problems of access to information and time to perform board duties are addressed by the Combined Code and discussed in more detail in Chapter 5.

6.1 Threats to the objectivity of non-executives

Independent non-executive directors are supposed to bring an independent view to the deliberations of the board. However, they are in a difficult position:

- They are legally liable in the same way as executive directors. For example, they have the same fiduciary duties to the company, and the duty of skill and care.
- As fellow directors, they might also be reluctant to blow the whistle on their executive director colleagues.
- If they have been selected and appointed by the chairman or the chief executive officer, they will be less likely to ask tough questions about the way the company is being run. This is sometimes known as the 'St Thomas à Becket' problem, after the twelfth-century Archbishop of Canterbury. Becket was appointed as archbishop by Henry II, but then took a stand against him on issues concerning the roles of the king and the church in the governance of the country.

6.2 The Myners Report and criticisms of NEDs

The Myners Report in February 2002, a government-backed report into pension fund investment, criticised the boards of directors of public companies for being a 'self-perpetuating oligarchy', which failed to stand up for shareholders' rights against over-powerful executives. The report condemned non-executives as the 'missing link' in the chain of good corporate governance. In particular, it criticised the way in which NED appointments were made and the number of NED positions that some individuals held. The report suggested that:

- Some individuals held too many non-executive director positions in large public companies, more than they could possibly serve effectively.
- Non-executive directorships were frequently given to the executive directors of other listed companies, giving rise to the concerns about a 'you scratch my back and I'll scratch yours' mentality. A non-executive might tacitly undertake not to ask difficult questions or take a stand against executives on the board, provided that the non-executives of his or her own company act in the same way.
- Non-executives should help to make the board more accountable to the shareholders. However, shareholders only had opportunities to discuss the company's affairs with the non-executives in a formal setting, at general meetings of the company. Any other discussions between shareholders and non-executives were informal, if they took place at all.
- The law makes no distinction between executive and non-executive directors. In principle, the non-executives could be equally liable with the executive directors for negligence and failure of duty. Arguably, this threat of criminal or civil liability could make non-executives more inclined to support their executive colleagues.

CHAPTER

5 Board Appointments, Professional Development and Performance Evaluation

---

1 Board appointments

There are no regulations or Corporate Governance guidelines on the overall size of the board. So, unless a provision about the composition of the board is included in the company's Articles:

- there are no restrictions on making new appointments; and
- with the exceptions of the positions of chairman and chief executive officer, there is no requirement to replace individuals stepping down from the board.

It is an accepted principle of good corporate governance that the power over board appointments should rest with the whole board. In addition, recommendations about new appointments should not belong exclusively to the chairman and/or the CEO. In addition, appointments should be made on merit and against objective criteria.

Main Principle A.4 of the Combined Code recommends that

> *There should be a formal, rigorous and transparent procedure for the appointment of new directors to the board.*

2 The nomination committee

The Combined Code (Provision A.4.1) states that the nomination committee of the board should:

- lead the process for board appointments, and
- make recommendations to the board.

A majority of the committee's members should be independent non-executive directors, and the committee chairman should be either the board chairman or an independent NED. If the board chairman is the chairman of the nomination committee, he/she should not chair the committee when it is dealing with the succession to the chairmanship.

The existence of a majority of NEDs should ensure that the appointments process is not dominated by the chairman and CEO of the company.

The committee should consider new appointments to the board and make recommendations to the full board. The full board should then reach a decision about offering a position to the individual concerned, so that final responsibility for board appointments remains with the board as a whole.

2.1 The main duties of the nomination committee

The principal duties of the nomination committee are summarised in the *Higgs Suggestions for Good Practice*, attached to the Combined Code (see Appendix 7). These are that the nomination committee should:

- be responsible for identifying candidates to fill vacancies on the board, as and when they arise, and nominate them for approval by the board;
- before making an appointment, evaluate the balance of skills, knowledge and experience on the board, and on the basis of this evaluation, prepare a description of the role and capabilities required for the particular appointment;
- each year, review the time required from a non-executive director (performance evaluation should include an assessment of whether the NED is spending enough time on his or her duties);
- consider candidates for appointment from a wide range of backgrounds, and look beyond the 'usual suspects';
- give full consideration to succession planning;
- review regularly the structure, size and composition of the board, and make recommendations for any changes to the board;
- keep under review the leadership needs of the company, both executive and non-executive, with a view to ensuring that the company remains competitive;
- prepare an annual statement of the nomination committee for inclusion in the annual report. This should include a description of its activities, the process used for appointments (giving reasons if external advice or open advertising have not been used for the appointment of a chairman or non-executive director), the membership of the committee, the number of meetings and attendance over the course of the year;
- make available its terms of reference, explaining clearly its role and the authority delegated to it by the board;

- ensure that on appointment to the board, NEDs receive a formal letter of appointment, setting out what is expected of them, including time commitment and membership of board committees.

Recommendations by the nomination to the board should include:

- plans for the succession of NEDs and executive directors
- recommendations about the re-appointment of NEDs at the end of their term of office
- recommendations about the submission of any director for re-election by the shareholders under the retirement by rotation rules in the Articles of Association
- matters concerning the continuation in office of any director at any time.

2.2 Combined Code provisions on board nominations

The Combined Code includes several provisions about appointments to the board, some of which are duplicated in the Higgs Suggestions:

- The nomination committee should make available for inspection its terms of reference, explaining its role and the authority delegated to it by the board. A footnote to the Combined Code states that it is sufficient to make this information available by request and by including it as information on the company's web-site (Provision A.4.1).
- The committee should evaluate the skills, knowledge and experience of the board, and in the light of this evaluation prepare a description of the roles and responsibilities required for any new appointment (Provision A.4.2).
- For the appointment of a chairman, the nomination committee should prepare a job specification, including an assessment of the time required and recognising the need for the chairman's availability in times of crisis (Provision A.4.3).
- A chairman's other significant commitments should be disclosed to the board before an appointment is made, and included in the annual report. (Subsequent changes should also be disclosed and reported.) No individual should be appointed to a second chairmanship of a FTSE 100 company (Provision A.4.3).
- The terms and conditions of appointment of NEDs should be made available for inspection by any person at the company's registered office during normal business hours and at the AGM. The letter of appointment should set out the expected time commitment. NEDs should undertake to ensure that they will have sufficient time to meet this expected requirement. (Before their appointment, the other significant time commitments of NEDs should be disclosed to the board, and subsequent changes should also be reported.) (Provision A.4.4).
- A separate section of the annual report should describe the work of the nomination committee. This should include a description of the process used for appointments, and giving reasons if external advice or open advertising have not been used (Provision A.4.6).

It should be apparent that an important aspect of suitability for appointment is being able to make enough time available to perform the role of director properly. Code provision A.4.5 looks at the same issue from a different viewpoint, and states that the board should not allow one of its own executive directors to take on:

- more than one NED post in an FTSE 100 company, or
- the chairmanship of an FTSE 100 company.

2.3 ICSA Guidance Note on the terms of reference of the nomination committee

The Combined Code states that the majority of the members of the nomination committee should be non-executive directors, but gives no guidance as to what the overall size of the committee should be. An ICSA Guidance Note, *Terms of Reference: Nomination Committee*, recommends a committee of three for most companies, and possibly four or five in companies with a larger board of directors. Companies with a very small board might consider the responsibility for nominations to be a matter for the entire board. If so, the ICSA recommends that the board should sit as a nomination committee with an agenda specifically dedicated to nomination issues, rather than dealing with such issues as part of the agenda for a main board meeting.

It is also recommended that the company secretary should act as the secretary for the committee, because it is a responsibility of the company secretary to make sure that the board and its committees are properly constituted and advised. The company secretary can also play a valuable coordinating role, acting as a valued intermediary between the committee and the main board.

The Guidance Note suggests that the nomination committee should meet at least once a year, close to the financial year-end. A meeting at this time is necessary, if only to consider whether the directors retiring either by rotation or because they are reaching a predetermined age limit should be put forward for reappointment at the next annual general meeting. (The committee should then make recommendations to the main board on this matter.)

The Guidance Note also includes a list of the recommended duties of a nomination committee, most of which are included in the Higgs Suggestions. These are:

- regularly reviewing the structure, size and composition of the board, and making recommendations for changes when appropriate;
- identifying candidates to fill board vacancies when they arise, and nominating them for approval by the main board;
- keeping under review the leadership needs of the company;
- making recommendations to the board about plans for the succession of senior management, in particular for the board chairman and the CEO;
- making recommendations to the board for the re-appointment of NEDs at the end of their specified term of office.

Recommendations to the board about the appointment of a new company chairman should be considered by a meeting of all the directors, whereas recommendations about the appointment of a new CEO should be considered by a meeting of just the NEDs.

2.4 Practical aspects of board appointments

In practice, a nomination committee is likely to carry out its responsibilities by:

- using a firm of 'head-hunters' to find individuals outside the firm who might be suitable for appointment (as NED, CEO, finance director, and so on);
- vetting the candidates put forward by the head hunters; and
- making a selection and recommendation to the full board.

When an individual is appointed to the board, the appointment may be for a fixed term (which is usually the case with NEDs) or for an indeterminate length of time, subject to a minimum notice period.

The system of board nominations in UK public companies, particularly the appointment of NEDs, has been criticised for lack of rigour:

- In practice, the nominations system is often not independent enough, with the board chairman and chief executive having too much influence over nominations.
- Boards tend to prefer someone they know, someone they feel comfortable with.

This problem was addressed by the Higgs Report (2003) and by a subsequent report produced by the Tyson Committee, a committee set up by the DTI to look into the issue of recruiting and training NEDs (see below).

3 The appointment of NEDs

A decision to appoint a new NED might be triggered by the resignation of an existing NED, or to comply with corporate governance guidelines, or simply because the board has decided to alter its structure and increase the number of NEDs.

The responsibility for identifying an individual for recommendation to the board might be delegated to the nomination committee. In principle, the individual:

- will have suitable skills and experience that will add to the collective abilities of the board as a whole, and
- will be able and willing to give sufficient time to the company in order to fulfil his or her role properly.

The methods used to identify individuals for nomination as an NED vary, but in the past, the most common methods appear to have been:

- nominations by existing board members
- informal networks
- a personal approach to a particular individual
- nominations from investors
- nominations from professional advisers.

The criticism of these methods of nomination has been that they tend to restrict NED appointments to a relatively small circle of individuals. The Higgs Report on non-executive directors found that only 7 per cent of NEDs on UK public limited company boards were non-British nationals, only 6 per cent were women and only 1 per cent were from ethnic minorities. The majority of NEDs were white, middle-aged males, many with previous experience as a plc board director.

Consequently, alternative methods of identifying NEDs have emerged, in particular:

- recruitment agencies specialising in NED appointments
- registers of potential non-executive directors held by professional institutes (e.g. the ICAEW register).

3.1 The Tyson Report on recruiting and training NEDs

Following publication of the Higgs Report, the Department of Trade and Industry set up a task force under the chairmanship of Laura Tyson, Dean of the London Business School, to look into the recruitment and development of NEDs. The *Tyson Report on the Recruitment and Development of Non-Executive Directors* was published in June 2003 (see Directory and Appendix 10).

The main focus of the report was on the recruitment of NEDs. The report:

- argued that a range of different experiences and backgrounds amongst board members can enhance the effectiveness of the board, and
- suggested how a broader range of NEDs can be identified and recruited.

The need for a range of experiences and backgrounds

The report argued that NEDs have four broad responsibilities:

1. To provide advice and direction to the company's management on the development and evaluation of strategy.
2. To monitor the implementation of strategy by management and monitor performance against the strategic objectives.
3. To monitor the legal and ethical performance of the company.
4. To monitor the truthfulness and adequacy of the financial information provided by the company to investors and other stakeholders.

These responsibilities include appointing and appraising senior management, and where necessary removing them from office, and succession planning. The Tyson

Report suggested that to fulfil these responsibilities, a board with a range of backgrounds and experience is likely to be more effective than a board consisting of individuals with similar backgrounds and experience.

The report also referred to the identification in the Higgs Report of four personal qualities required of NEDs, and argues that in deciding whether an individual possesses these qualities, background and experience are not relevant. The four personal qualities are:

- integrity and high ethical standards
- sound judgement
- the ability and willingness to challenge and probe
- strong inter-personal skills.

The report therefore recommended that NEDs should be recruited by a formal process, advertising vacancies and preferably with formal interviews. The aim should be to ensure that the board as a whole possesses the necessary balance and range of skills and experience:

> *A company should begin a NED search by articulating its specific board needs taking into account the composition of existing board members. Only by analysing what its board lacks in skills and expertise can a company move forward to identify the best talent.*

Recruiting NEDs

The Report criticised the predominant current practice of appointing individuals to the position of NED through an informal process and without formal interviews. This 'traditional' method of recruitment has tended to overlook a number of potentially rich sources of NEDs, such as:

- The 'marzipan layer' of corporate management, just below board level. The CEO of a company might be willing to allow managers to act as NEDs of companies that are not competitors, although might be less willing if the demands on the individual's time become great. Another advantage of this source of NEDs is that the 'marzipan layer' includes a large number of women.
- Individuals in private sector companies
- Individuals in the public sector/non-commercial sector
- Individuals working for business consultancies or professional firms (lawyers, accountants) and retired professional accountants.

4 Information and induction

To be effective, all directors must be provided with suitable information. Principle A.5 of the Combined Code states:

The board should be supplied in a timely manner with information in a form and of a quality appropriate to enable it to discharge its duties.

- *The chairman is responsible for ensuring that the directors receive accurate, timely and clear information.*
- *Management has an obligation to provide this information, but the directors should seek clarification where necessary.*

Combined Code Provision A.5.2 states that all directors, and NEDs in particular, should have access to independent professional advice, at the company's expense, when they judge this necessary to perform their duties as directors properly.

4.1 Information, professional development and the company secretary

The Code also states that under the direction of the chairman, it is the responsibility of the company secretary to do the following:

- ensure good information flows within the board and its committees, and between management and NEDs
- facilitate induction for new board members and professional development for directors as required (see below)
- advise the board through the chairman on all governance matters.

Code Provision A.5.3 states that all directors should have access to the advice and services of the company secretary, who is responsible to the board for ensuring that board procedures are complied with.

4.2 Induction of new directors

Principle A.5 of the Combined Code states that all directors should receive induction on joining the board, and Code Provision A.5.1 states that this induction should be 'full, formal and tailored'. As part of this induction process, the company should offer to its major shareholders the opportunity to meet a new NED. However, both executive and non-executive directors should receive induction, even though the information provided might differ for each type of director.

The purpose of an induction programme should be to help the individual director to make an effective contribution to the board as quickly as possible. The Company Secretary should be involved arranging induction programmes (Code Principle A.5). The Higgs Suggestions state that the induction process for a new director should:

- build an understanding of the nature of the company, its business and the markets in which it operates
- build a link with the company's people
- build an understanding of the company's main relationships.

For a new NED, the company secretary should agree a programme of familiarisation with the company and its products or services. This might include:

- visits to key company sites
- product presentations
- meetings with senior management and staff
- meetings with major shareholders (should any such shareholders want one)
- meetings with external advisers of the company.

There should be an assessment of any specific training requirements for the new director, and provision of suitable training programmes.

As a part of the induction process, a new director should also be provided with certain information.

4.3 ICSA Guidance Note, *Induction of Directors*

At one time, it was considered 'best practice' to provide a new director with an 'induction pack' on his or her appointment, containing all the information that the director might find useful. However, the consequence of this practice was that new directors were often overwhelmed with a large volume of papers that they found difficult to read and assimilate. The ICSA therefore issued a Guidance Note, *Induction of Directors*, commenting:

> *The objective of induction is to inform the director such that he or she can become as effective as possible in their new role as soon as possible. The provision of reams of paper in one go is, obviously, not conducive to this process.*

The ICSA's current guidance is therefore that information should be provided to new directors in stages:

- essential information to be provided immediately on appointment, together with a comprehensive list of all the information that will eventually be provided;
- material to be provided over the first few weeks following the appointment, at the most appropriate time or when the director asks to receive it, if sooner.

The company secretary might also have a list of items that the new director might be made aware of at some stage, such as protocol, procedures and dress code at meetings, the reimbursement of expenses and procedures for matters such as signing off the accounts and announcing results.

Essential information to be provided immediately

Directors' duties

- An outline of the role of the director and a summary of his/her responsibilities and ongoing obligations (perhaps with more details where the individual has become a director for the first time).

- For listed companies, a copy of the UKLA Model Code; also details of the company's procedures regarding directors' share dealings and the disclosure of price-sensitive information.
- The company's guidelines on matters reserved for the board, the policy for directors obtaining independent professional advice and any other important policies and procedures.
- 'Fire drill' procedures (the procedures in place for dealing with matters such as hostile takeover bids).

The company's business

- Current strategic plan/business plan, market analysis, budget for the year with revised forecasts, three/five-year plan
- A copy of the latest annual report and accounts, and interim results as appropriate
- Explanation of key performance indicators
- A list of the major subsidiaries and associated companies of the group (and parent companies in the case of appointments to the board of a subsidiary)
- Summary details of the group's major insurance policies, including Directors' and Officers' liability insurance
- Details of any current or potential major litigation involving the company
- Treasury issues: the company's funding position and programme, and dividend policy
- A summary of the main events over the past three years; the corporate brochure; the company's mission statement; and other reports issued by the company over the past three years, such as an environmental report.

Board issues

- A copy of the company's Memorandum and Articles of Association, drawing attention to the most important provisions
- Minutes of the board meetings for the last three to six meetings
- Dates of future board meetings and of meetings of any board committees (if appropriate)
- A document explaining the procedures for board meetings, such as when the board papers are sent out before the meeting, and the normal location and duration of meetings
- A list of the current directors and company secretary, and the dates of their appointment. Biographical details and contact details of the other directors (and any key employees), including details of the executive responsibilities and board committees on which they sit
- Details of the committees of the board (audit, nomination, remuneration, etc.), their terms of reference and responsibilities, and membership. Where the director will be joining a committee, a copy of the minutes of its meetings in the previous 12 months.

Additional material to be provided in the first few months

- Copies of the company's main products/services brochures
- Copies of recent media reports on the company
- Details of the company's advisers (lawyers, bankers, auditors, registrars, etc.) and the name of the partner dealing with the company
- The company's risk management procedures and disaster recovery plans
- A copy of the Combined Code and the company's own corporate governance guidelines
- Brief history of the company
- Notices of any general meetings in the past three years, and the accompanying circulars
- Company organisation chart and management succession plans
- A copy of all management accounting reports since the last audited accounts
- Details of major shareholders; the company's investor relations policy
- The five largest customers of the company and the level of business done with them
- The five largest suppliers to the company
- Policies on health and safety, the environment, ethics and whistleblowing, and charitable and political donations
- Internal company telephone directory.

The full text of the ICSA Guidance Note is reproduced in Appendix 11.

4.4 New NEDs: meetings with institutional shareholders

The Combined Code states that companies should offer major shareholders the opportunity to meet with newly-appointed NEDs (Code Provision A.5.1) and that there should be opportunities for subsequent meetings if shareholders want them (Provision D.1.1). Many institutions will perhaps decline the opportunity to meet with new NEDs, but some may be keen on such meetings.

The *Hermes Guide for Shareholders and Independent Outside Directors*, published by Hermes Investment Management (see Directory), explains the nature of the conversations it would expect to have with NEDs. It suggests that induction meetings (i.e. meetings with a NED as part of the director's induction process) are likely to be brief. The number of meetings that a NED should expect to have will vary between companies, but there ought to be sufficient to give the NED an insight into the views held by its shareholders about the company.

The *Hermes Guide* also suggests the key issues that are likely to be discussed at induction meetings:

- *The appointment process*. Who made first contact with the individual? Did the appointment process work well, or could it have been better? Does the company have a formal list of the roles and responsibilities of its NEDs?

- *Skills and attitude*. What attracted you to the company? What do you think attracted the company to you? What unique skills and outlook do you bring to the board? How much time do you expect to spend on board duties? Do you expect to take on a specific role?
- *Perspectives on the company*. Do you see any problems at the company? What does the company do well? What is the company's competitive advantage, and is it being properly exploited? Are there further investment opportunities for the company to pursue? Where do you see the company in ten years' time?
- *Investment*. How many shares do you hold in the company? Do you expect to add to this shareholding in time? Explain the nature of the shareholder's investment (passive or active, long-term or short-term) and the reasons for investing in the company.

Hermes suggests in its guide that regular meetings between major shareholders and NEDs after the induction meeting should not be necessary, although if a shareholder has a genuine concern, it should expect NEDs to make themselves available to meet and discuss the problem.

5 Training and professional development

Main Principle A.5 of the Combined Code states that all directors should '*regularly update and refresh their skills and knowledge*'. Supporting Principle A.5 states that the company secretary should assist with the professional development of directors as required.

Training individual NEDs should be linked to the processes required by the Combined Code for the evaluation of board performance. Although training requirements will vary from one individual to another, and between executive and non-executive directors, subject areas for training might be:

- business strategy
- board dynamics
- corporate governance issues and legal requirements
- the company's products and services
- financial reporting

In the case of a non-executive director, the training process will include learning about the company's business, and getting to know its key executives. In the case of all directors, training could also involve learning about the statutory and regulatory duties, responsibilities and potential liabilities of directors.

The board chairman should be responsible for ensuring that new directors are suitably trained, but the chairman might ask the company secretary to arrange for a training programme to be devised and provided.

This proposal was put forward in the Higgs Report. The report comments:

> *On appointment, non-executive directors will already have relevant skills, knowledge, experience and abilities. Nevertheless, a non-executive director's credibility and*

> *effectiveness in the boardroom will depend not just on their existing capability but on their ability to extend and refresh their knowledge and skills ... The word 'training' in this context is not altogether helpful as it carries rather limited connotations of formal instruction in a classroom setting ... By contrast, what I envisage is continued professional development tailored to the individual.*

The need for continuing professional development can probably be readily accepted. The Tyson Report comments that NEDs require continual training and development, with specialist training necessary for individuals appointed to the remuneration committee or audit committee of the board.

It is not clear, however, what forms continuing professional development should take, nor how easily it can be provided. However, the Tyson Report commented that training courses are becoming more widely available, for example, in business schools: this might suggest a different view to that of Sir Derek Higgs, that formal classroom training might be suitable.

6 Directors' and officers' liability insurance

Directors and other officers of a company may become individually liable for certain 'wrongful acts' they commit (or are alleged to have committed), which could expose them to risks of civil litigation. A director who is sued individually could be obliged to incur defence costs and then be required to make a penalty payment or compensation payment on settlement of the case.

A company is legally permitted to indemnify a director or officer for costs incurred by the individual arising from personal liability for activities performed on behalf of the company. However, indemnification may still not apply in every situation. In some situations, the liability could be the sole personal responsibility of the director or officer. The main purpose of directors' and officers' liability insurance (D&O insurance) is to fill in these gaps, by protecting the personal assets of the individual director or officer.

6.1 Features of D&O insurance

The risks covered by D&O insurance are personal costs or losses as a consequence of 'wrongful acts' by the individual. Wrongful acts might be defined as 'actual or alleged breach of duty, breach of trust, misstatement, misrepresentation, omission or breach of warranty of authority, libel or slander'. The losses covered will include damages against an insured director or officer, out-of-court settlements, and costs incurred (professional fees, etc.).

It is worth noting that 'wrongful acts' include the personal liability of a director for statements made in the company's financial documents regarding the company's affairs. Directors are also personally liable to the external purchasers of a subsidiary company of the group for representations made prior to the sale (for example, over-stating profitability or making negligent misstatements about the subsidiary and its performance).

There are three broad types of D&O policy:

- a policy taken out by a company, covering its directors, company secretary and other named officers, providing cover for both indemnifiable risks and non-indemnifiable risks
- a policy taken out by a company, covering its directors, company secretary and other named officers, providing cover for non-indemnifiable risks only
- a policy taken out by an individual director, covering liability in his role as director or officer of several different companies.

An individual might therefore be covered by more than one insurance policy, and the liability of the different insurance companies in the event of a claim needs to be established.

D&O insurance policies have certain exclusions that are not covered by the policy. These are typically:

- fines, penalties and punitive damages imposed by a regulator or a criminal court
- criminal defence costs
- loss of earnings
- personal injury
- liabilities incurred in certain jurisdictions
- liabilities arising from an action brought by another individual who has D&O liability cover under the same insurance policy
- liability for fraudulent acts.

The insurance policy might provide for 'progress payments' of legal costs as a case progresses, but the policy might also provide for the insurance company to seek to recover the payments already made if the director is eventually found guilty of a fraudulent act.

Period of cover and limits of cover

An individual covered by D&O insurance should remain covered throughout the period during which he or she was a director or officer. However, a situation might occur when an individual incurs a loss for a liability after 'retirement', relating to events that occurred before retirement. A D&O policy might provide 'run-off cover' for individuals after their retirement, to cover this eventuality.

A policy provides cover up to a maximum amount:

- per claim, and/or
- per period (year).

D&O liability insurance and corporate governance

D&O liability insurance is relevant to corporate governance because directors are increasingly at risk from civil actions for 'wrongful acts', given the developments in best practice for corporate governance. Insurance protects individuals against the risk of inadvertently incurring a liability – a risk that might be so high that without insurance, individuals might be discouraged from agreeing to serve as director or company secretary.

The Higgs review into the effectiveness of NEDs noted the inadequacies and high costs of D&O cover. Insurance policies are not standard, and different policies cover differing liabilities and provide differing amounts of cover. Consequently, individuals are strongly advised to evaluate the D&O cover provided by a company before accepting a position as director.

An ICSA Guidance Note, *Directors' and Officers' Insurance* (2003) (see Appendix 12), considers this subject in detail, and includes the recommendations that before his or her appointment as director, an individual should:

- confirm that he or she will be covered by the policy
- confirm that the company will notify the insurance company of his/her appointment
- check the liabilities that are covered by the policy
- check the adequacy of the amount of cover
- check that the cover will continue for a suitable length of time after his or her 'retirement ('run-off cover').

The Companies (Audit, Investigations and Community Enterprise) Act 2004

The Companies (Audit, Investigations and Community Enterprise) Act 2004 relaxed the restrictions on companies indemnifying directors against liability and allows companies to pay directors' defence costs as they are incurred. This could affect the types of D&O policy taken out by companies.

The Act requires disclosure in the directors' report by companies that indemnify directors. Companies that do not indemnify directors will not have to make any disclosure.

7 Re-election of directors

Most company Articles of Association dictate that newly-appointed directors should retire at the next annual general meeting and submit themselves for re-election by the shareholders (Article 73, Table A), although the managing director and other directors with executive office are not required to submit themselves for re-election by rotation (Article 84, Table A).

The re-election of directors by the shareholders at annual general meetings is primarily a matter for the company's Articles of Association. However, the Combined Code includes the principle (Principle A.7) that:

> *All directors should be submitted for re-election at regular intervals, subject to continued satisfactory performance. The board should ensure planned and progressive refreshing of the board.*

The specific Code provisions are as follows:

- All directors should be subject to election by shareholders at the first annual general meeting after their appointment, and to re-election thereafter at intervals of no more than three years (Code Provision A.7.1). This Code provision applies to all board members, including the CEO.
- NEDs should be appointed for specified terms subject to re-election (and to Companies Acts provisions relating to the removal of directors). When a NED is proposed for election, the board should inform shareholders why it thinks the individual should be appointed (Code Provision A.7.2).
- When proposing re-election of a NED, the chairman should confirm to the shareholders that, following a formal performance evaluation, the individual's performance continues to be effective and shows a commitment to the role.
- Any term beyond six years (two three-year terms) for a NED should be subject to particularly rigorous review and take into account the need for progressive refreshing of the board.
- NEDs may serve longer than nine years (i.e. more than three three-year terms), but doing so could be relevant to the determination of whether the individual is independent (Code Provision A.7.2).

These provisions allow the shareholders some powers over board appointments, but in practice they are difficult to apply. In a large public company, it is difficult for 'activist' shareholders to gather a majority of votes against the re-election of particular directors.

Even so, the threat by some major shareholders to vote against the re-election of an individual, and the associated bad publicity this often creates in the media, could influence board thinking on certain contentious issues where the shareholders disagree with the board. Some activist investors have argued in favour of the annual re-election of all directors, giving the shareholders an opportunity each year to remove any individual from the board.

The requirement for the board to ensure planned and progressive refreshing means that re-election of current directors should not be 'automatic'.

8 Succession planning

The key positions on the board of directors are the chairman of the board and the chief executive officer. The individuals holding these positions will retire or resign at some time, for example, because the individual has reached retirement age or has come to the end of a fixed-term contract.

The board of directors should try to ensure a smooth succession, with a replacement lined up to take the place of the departing individual. In the case of a departing CEO, the successor might be an existing executive manager who has been 'groomed' for the succession. In the case of a departing non-executive chairman, the successor might be an external appointment. A smooth succession is desirable to avoid unexpected disruptions to the company's decision-making processes or unexpected changes in policy or direction. The succession can also be planned well in advance, so that the newly appointed individuals will have an opportunity to learn about their new role before the actual succession occurs.

A Supporting Principle in the Combined Code (Principle A.4) states that:

> *The board should satisfy itself that plans are in place for orderly succession for appointment to the board and to senior management, so as to maintain an appropriate balance of skills and experience within the company and its board.*

Principle A.7 also requires the board to ensure that there is a planned and progressive refreshing of the board membership, which should have implications for succession planning. Succession planning could be a matter delegated to the nomination committee.

9 Board performance evaluation

Following the Higgs Report, the revised Combined Code introduced new requirements for the performance evaluation of the board and individual directors. The Code requirements are quite short, and are set out below in full.

Main Principle (A.6) states that:

> *The board should undertake a formal and rigorous annual evaluation of its own performance and that of its committees and individual directors.*

Supporting Principle A.6 and Code Provision A.6.1 elaborate as follows:

> *Individual evaluation should aim to show whether each director continues to contribute effectively and demonstrate commitment to the role (including commitment of time for board and committee meetings and other duties). The chairman should act on the results of the performance evaluation by recognising the strengths and weaknesses of the board and, where appropriate, proposing new members be appointed to the board or seeking the resignation of directors.*

The board should state in the annual report how performance evaluation of the board, its committees and its individual directors has been conducted. The non-executive directors, led by the senior independent director, should be responsible for performance evaluation of the chairman, taking into account the views of executive directors.

The investor organisation Hermes has suggested that this section of the annual report should state that the performance evaluation has been carried out, giving a brief explanation of the process followed and a high-level review of observations from the process. In addition, it suggests that the board should be willing to discuss matters privately in more detail with shareholders if board performance has been an issue of some concern.

9.1 Performance evaluation guidelines

The requirement for performance evaluation was not in the previous Combined Code, and was only introduced in 2003. It still remains to be seen how it will operate in practice.

The *Higgs Suggestions for Good Practice* include some guidance on performance evaluation (see Appendix 13). The guidance does not go into detail about how the evaluation process should be conducted, nor what target measures of performance might be used in the evaluation. It simply suggests that:

- The board should state in the annual report how the evaluation has been conducted.
- The chairman is responsible for selecting an effective process of evaluation, and acting on its outcome.
- Using an external third party to carry out the evaluation will bring objectivity to the process. (This might suggest that unless the assistance of an external third party, such as a firm of consultants, is used, there is a risk that the process will not be objective.)

The Higgs Suggestions are limited mainly to providing a list of questions that should be considered, but the list is not exhaustive or definitive, and companies might take a different approach to suit their own particular circumstances. The answers to the questions should make an assessment of performance possible, and indicate in which areas performance might be improved.

Evaluation of the performance of the board as a whole and the board committees

- How well has the board performed against any objectives that were set?
- What has been the contribution of the board to the development and testing of strategy?
- What has been the contribution of the board to ensuring robust and effective risk management?
- Is the composition of the board and its committees appropriate? Do these have the right balance of knowledge and skills to maximise performance? Are relationships inside and outside the board working effectively?
- How has the board responded to any problems or crises that arose? Could (or should) these have been foreseen?
- Are the matters specifically reserved for the board the right ones?
- How well does the board communicate with the management team, employees and others? How effective is its use of the AGM and the annual report?
- Is the board as a whole up to date with the latest developments in the regulatory environment and the market?
- How effective are the board's committees (for example, in their role, their composition and their interaction with the board)?

Board processes

- Does the board receive the right amount and quality of timely information? How well does management respond to requests from the board for clarification or additional information?
- Do the board and the board committees hold enough meetings of suitable length to get through their business properly? Is time used effectively?
- Are board procedures flexible, and are they conducive to effective performance?

Performance evaluation of the chairman

The NEDs, led by the senior independent director, should be responsible for the performance evaluation of the chairman, taking into account the views of the executive directors. The Higgs Suggestions do not provide a full list of questions relating to performance evaluation of the chairman, but it does list five questions about matters relating to the chairman that would be relevant to assessing the performance of the board as a whole:

- Is the chairman demonstrating effective leadership of the board?
- Are relationships and communications with shareholders well managed?
- Are relationships and communications within the board constructive?
- Do the processes for setting the agenda for board meetings work well? Are board members able to raise issues and concerns?
- Is the company secretary being used effectively and to maximum value?

Performance evaluation of non-executive directors

The Combined Code requires that performance evaluation of the NEDs should include an assessment of the individual's continuing commitment to the role, in terms of commitment of time for board and committee meetings and other duties. (The Code does not specify NEDs in this context, but the commitment of time should not be an issue for executive directors.)

The Higgs Suggestions provide a list of questions for the assessment of each NED:

- How well prepared and well informed are they for board meetings? Is their attendance at meetings satisfactory?
- Do they show a willingness to spend time and effort learning about the company and its business? Are they willing to participate in events outside board meetings, such as site visits?
- What has been the quality and value of their contributions at board meetings?
- What has been their contribution to the development of (i) strategy; and (ii) risk management?
- How successfully have the brought their knowledge and experience to bear in the consideration of strategy?
- How effectively have they probed to test assumptions? Where necessary, how resolute are they in holding to their views and resisting pressure from others?

- How effectively have they followed up matters about which they have expressed concern?
- How good are their relationships with other board members, the company secretary and senior management?
- How actively and successfully do they refresh their knowledge and skills? Are they up-to-date with the latest developments in areas such as the corporate governance framework and financial reporting, and in the industry and market conditions?
- How well do they communicate with other board members, senior management and others (e.g. shareholders)? Can they present their views convincingly, yet diplomatically? Do they listen to the views of others?

The list excludes any specific questions about the performance of each NED on board committees, although some of the questions in this list could be applied to their committee work.

The Higgs Suggestions do not include a list of questions for the evaluation of the performance of executive directors.

9.2 Board evaluation programmes

A board evaluation programme might be formulated and implemented in a variety of ways. Some companies have developed an in-house programme, whereas others use external advisers and consultants. A variety of different board evaluation programmes are offered by different organisations. For example, the ICSA carries out Board Performance Evaluations as a service to companies, with services for:

- whole board evaluation
- remuneration, nomination and audit committee evaluation, and
- individual director evaluation.

The programme needs to involve both the board chairman, who has most of the responsibility for the programme, and the senior independent director, since the NEDs are responsible for evaluating the chairman's performance.

For the purpose of evaluation, key performance issues need to be identified, and these might relate to:

- the processes by which a board or board committee functions, such as
  - the frequency of meetings
  - the length of meetings
  - the administration of meetings
  - topics on the agenda for meetings
  - the number of committees and their roles
  - the flow of information to board members and between board members
  - the quality and quantity of the information
  - the selection and retirement of directors

- the performance of individuals
  - personal relationships
  - the collective performance of the board or committee as a team
  - individual performance and contribution

A programme might involve the use of:

- facilitators, providing guidance to the chairman, SID and others
- questionnaires, and
- possibly input from major shareholders.

At the end of an evaluation, the chairman and SID should report to the board on the results of the evaluation process. The board should then report to the shareholders in the annual report.

CHAPTER

Directors' Remuneration 6

1 Directors' remuneration as a corporate governance issue

Until the 1990s in the UK and even more recently in the US, directors' remuneration was not seen as a major problem of corporate governance. A sense of concern began with:

- media criticism of 'fat cat' top executives for being paid far more than they appeared to be worth, particularly top executives of newly-privatised utility companies who were receiving much larger remuneration packages for doing the same jobs as before privatisation; and
- criticisms by investment institutions of directors for receiving ever-increasing rewards even when their company performed badly and about large severance payments to outgoing senior executives who had been ousted from their job following poor company performance. High severance payments to unsuccessful directors were seen as 'rewards for failure'.

Directors' remuneration has tended to rise – often rapidly – regardless of company performance, whereas a principle of good corporate governance is that remuneration should be linked to some extent to company performance, so that directors will earn more if the company does well, but less if it does badly.

In the UK, the structure of directors' remuneration packages and reporting the remuneration of individual directors are seen as a significant aspect of good corporate governance, and a section of the Combined Code deals with the subject. The current requirements of the Combined Code originate largely from the work of the Greenbury Committee and the Greenbury Report (1995).

The main corporate governance issues concerning the level and make-up of directors' remuneration are as follows:

- Decisions on setting the remuneration packages of senior executives should not be taken by the executives themselves. Independent judgement should be brought to bear on negotiating remuneration levels. The Combined Code recommends that this responsibility should be delegated by the board to a remuneration committee.
- A significant part of the remuneration of senior executives should be incentive-related, so that individual executives receive higher rewards when the company's performance is such that shareholders should benefit.

1.1 The level and make-up of directors' remuneration

It is argued that within a system of good corporate governance, there should be a system of remuneration for directors that is:

- sufficient to attract individuals of suitable calibre, but also
- structured so as to motivate the individuals towards the achievement of performance levels that are in the best interests of the company and its shareholders, as well as their own personal interests.

Main Principle B.1 of the Combined Code states:

> *Levels of remuneration should be sufficient to attract, retain and motivate directors of the quality required to run the company successfully, but a company should avoid paying more than is necessary for this purpose. A significant proportion of executive directors' remuneration should be structured so as to link rewards to corporate and individual performance.*

A conceptual distinction should be made between:

- the unethical greed of individuals and a reasonable desire to be remunerated well and properly
- high rewards that are justified by performance and high rewards that are not justified.

In the US following the stock market collapse in 2002, Alan Greenspan, chairman of the US Federal Reserve, accused senior executives of 'infectious greed' during the period of the stock market boom in the late 1990s, when the size of reported corporate profits and rapidly increasing value of shares provided an 'outsized increase in opportunities for avarice'. In September 2002, the President of the Federal Reserve in the US, Bill McDonough, attacked the high levels of remuneration for chief executives as 'morally dubious'.

1.2 The remuneration package

It is important to remember that the corporate governance issues on remuneration extend to the entire remuneration package of individual directors, as well as to the remuneration policy generally. A remuneration package will consist of a number of elements, typically:

- Annual compensation (basic salary, pension contributions by the company for the individual, payments by the company into a personal pension scheme arrangement for the individual, a bonus (often a cash bonus) tied perhaps to the annual financial performance of the company and various perks, such as membership of the company's health insurance scheme, private use of company aircraft or boats, and so on).
- Long-term compensation, consisting of share option schemes or company shares ('restricted stock awards'), or the award of additional options depending on long-term performance indicators.
- An executive might also have a severance payment arrangement, whereby the company is committed to giving the individual a minimum severance payment if he or she is forced to leave the company.

It is often useful to think of a remuneration package as a combination of fixed and variable elements:

- The fixed elements are the remuneration received by the director regardless of performance, such as fixed salary and salary-related pension.
- The variable elements are the performance-related elements (cash bonuses, awards of share options or shares depending on performance, etc.).

A problem in negotiating a remuneration package with an executive is to decide on the balance between the fixed and the variable elements, and to agree on measures of performance as the basis for deciding on how much the performance-related payments should be. Linking remuneration to performance is not an easy task, however, for several reasons:

- Unsuitable measures of performance might be selected as a basis for deciding the reward. An individual might be rewarded for achieving performance that is of no significant benefit to the company.
- Many performance measures are linked to short-term results, such as the annual financial performance of the company. Achieving short-term targets might be detrimental to the company's longer-term interests, for example, by discouraging expenditure on longer-term investment to develop the company's businesses.
- Remuneration systems are based on historical performance, so that rewards are based on what has already happened, not what is happening now. This can result in a situation where directors are given performance rewards for the previous year's achievements when the company is currently suffering a downturn in its business and prospects.

- Severance payments to executives who are dismissed can be high, due to the contractual rights of the individual but are seen as 'rewards for failure'. The possibility of dismissing an individual is perhaps not discussed sufficiently when his or her remuneration package is originally negotiated.

2 The remuneration committee

The 1995 Greenbury Report reached the following conclusions:

- The formulation of remuneration packages for senior executive directors was a fundamental issue for good corporate governance.
- However, the system was open to abuse if executives could decide their own remuneration levels.
- Shareholders are not in a position to decide directors' remuneration, although they had a right to extensive information about it.
- Remuneration for executive directors should therefore be decided by a remuneration committee of the board, consisting entirely of independent non-executive directors.

2.1 Combined Code requirements for a remuneration committee

Combined Code (Main Principle B.2) states that:

> *There should be a formal and transparent procedure for developing policy on executive remuneration and for fixing the remuneration of individual directors. No director should be involved in deciding his or her own remuneration.*

It goes on to state (Provision B.2.1) that '*the board should establish a remuneration committee ... [which] should make available its terms of reference, explaining its role and the authority delegated to it by the board.*'

Note that the remuneration committee is responsible for both developing remuneration policy and for negotiating the remuneration of individual directors. Although these two matters are related, they are different.

- The remuneration committee should consist entirely of independent non-executive directors. In larger companies, the committee should consist of at least three members, and in smaller companies (i.e. companies below the FTSE 350) at least two members (Code Provision B.2.1).
- The remuneration committee should have delegated responsibility for setting the remuneration for all executive directors and the chairman (including pension rights and any compensation/severance payments). The remuneration committee should also recommend and monitor the level and structure of remuneration for senior management (Code Provision B.2.2).

- The board itself (or the shareholders, where required by the Articles of Association) should determine the remuneration of the non-executive directors. However, if permitted by the Articles, the board may delegate this responsibility to a committee, which might include the CEO (Code Provision B.2.3).
- The shareholders themselves, however, should normally be invited specifically to approve all new long-term incentive schemes and significant changes to existing schemes (Code Provision B.2.4).

The company should make available to the public (by supplying a copy on request and putting the information on the company's web-site) the terms of reference of the remuneration committee, explaining its role and the authority delegated to it by the board.

It is common in practice for a remuneration committee to use the services of external remuneration consultants. Where remuneration consultants are appointed, the company should also make publicly available a statement of whether they have any other connection with the company (Code Provision B.2.1).

The chairman of the board should arrange for the chairman of the remuneration committee to attend the AGM, to respond to any questions from shareholders on the committee's area of responsibility (Code Provision D.2.3).

Although not included in the Combined Code, the Higgs Review (2003) recommended that as a matter of good practice, the company secretary, or an individual designated by the company secretary, should act as secretary to the committee.

2.2 The principal duties of the remuneration committee

The Higgs Suggestions for Good Practice provide a summary of the principal duties of the remuneration committee (see Appendix 14). These are similar in many respects to a list of duties of the committee provided in the ICSA Guidance Note, *Terms of Reference: Remuneration Committee*.

Higgs suggested the following main duties for the committee:

- The committee should determine and agree with the main board the remuneration policy for the CEO, the board chairman, and any other designated executive managers. This policy should provide for executive managers to be given appropriate incentives for enhanced performance. (Deciding the remuneration of the NEDs should be the responsibility of the chairman and the executive directors. As a basic principle, no one should be involved in any decisions as to their own remuneration.)
- To maintain and assure his or her independence, the committee should also decide the remuneration of the company secretary.
- The committee should decide the targets for performance for any performance-related pay schemes operated by the company.
- It should decide the policy for and scope of pension arrangements for each executive director.

- It should ensure that the contractual terms for severance payments on termination of office are fair to both the individual and the company, that failure is not rewarded and that the director's duty to mitigate losses is fully recognised.
- Within the framework of the agreed remuneration policy, it should determine the remuneration package of each individual executive director, including bonuses, incentive payments and share options.
- It should be aware of and advise on any major changes in employee benefit structures throughout the company and group.
- It should agree the policy for authorising expense claims from the chairman and chief executive.
- It should ensure compliance by the company with the requirements for disclosure of directors' remuneration as required by the Directors' Remuneration Report Regulations 2002 (incorporated into the Companies Act 1985: see paragraph 7.2 on p. 98).
- It should be responsible for appointing any remuneration consultants to advise the committee.
- In the company's annual report, it should report the frequency of committee meetings and the attendance by members.
- It should make available to the public its terms of reference, setting out the committee's delegated responsibilities. Where necessary, these should be reviewed and updated each year.

The ICSA Guidance Note: *Terms of Reference: Remuneration Committee*, makes the following additional points:

- The committee should determine and agree with the board the framework or broad policy for the remuneration of the CEO, board chairman, executive directors, company secretary and any other senior executive managers that the committee has been designated to consider. (The remuneration of the NEDs should be a matter for the board chairman and the executive directors.) This broad policy should have the objective of ensuring that 'members of the executive management of the company are provided with appropriate incentives to encourage enhanced performance and are, in a fair and responsible manner, rewarded for their individual contributions to the success of the company'. The committee should also review the ongoing appropriateness and relevance of this policy.
- The committee should review the design of all share incentive plans for approval by the board and the shareholders.
- The committee chairman should report formally to the board on its proceedings after each meeting of the committee.
- It should also make recommendations to the board on any matter it deems appropriate within its remit, where action or improvement is needed.
- The committee should produce an annual report of the company's remuneration policy and practices, which should form part of the company's annual report, and

it should ensure that this report is put to the shareholders for approval at the AGM.

- At least once a year, the committee should review its own performance, constitution and terms of reference, to ensure that it is operating at maximum effectiveness. It should recommend to the board any changes it considers necessary.

The ICSA Guidance Note also suggests that the frequency of remuneration committee meetings will vary between companies and over time, but it recommends that there should be at least two committee meetings each year, one of these around the end of the year to enable the committee to review the company's remuneration report.

3 Remuneration package size and structure

The remuneration package offered to a senior executive has to be sufficient to attract him or her to accept the position. There is a perception that there are not enough individuals available to meet the demand with sufficient skills and talent to fill a senior executive post successfully. If this perception is correct, it is a sellers' market and talented executives can command ever-increasing remuneration packages, that companies are forced to pay to get the person they want.

3.1 The size of the remuneration package

The Combined Code (Principle B.1) states that:

> *Levels of remuneration should be sufficient to attract, retain and motivate directors of the quality required to run the company successfully, but a company should avoid paying more than is necessary for this purpose.*

Companies often use remuneration consultants, who give advice on remuneration packages, including basic salary levels for senior executives. Consultants might use competitive pay data to recommend a basic package for senior executives. Competitive pay data are simply information about the rewards that are being paid to senior executives in other top companies. At first sight, it would seem that this is a sensible way of setting a total value for a remuneration package.

Unfortunately, over-reliance on competitive pay data is likely to result in a sharp upward spiral in executive remuneration, since companies may be advised to offer above-average remuneration in order to attract above-average individuals. If every top company believes it must do the same, remuneration packages will inevitably rise at a very fast rate.

A Supporting Principle in the Combined Code (Principle B.1) is that the remuneration committee should judge where to position the company relative to other companies, but they should use caution in making this judgement

> *in view of the risk of an upward ratchet of remuneration levels with no corresponding improvement in performance*.

The committee should also consider pay and employment conditions elsewhere within the group, especially when deciding the annual salary increases for the executive directors.

One of the arguments in favour of high remuneration for top executives of international companies has been that high pay is necessary to stop executives being poached by other global companies. However, a report in 2002 by the International Corporate Governance Network (ICGN) argued that there is no international market for top executives, and so there is no point in structuring remuneration packages to prevent top executives from being lured to companies in other countries, the US in particular. The ICGN report admitted that some multinational companies face global competition for top executives, so have to offer packages that match those paid to top US executives. However, the number of multinationals in this position was much smaller than the number of companies using the international competition argument to boost top executives' pay.

3.2 The Combined Code on the structure of the remuneration package

The remuneration package for an executive director should be a mixture of fixed payments and a performance-related element. Principle B.1 of the Combined Code states that:

> *A significant proportion of executive directors' remuneration should be structured so as to link rewards to corporate and individual performance*.

Code Provision B.1.1 goes on to state that the performance-related elements should be designed so as to align the interests of the executive director with those of the company's shareholders, and should give the director '*keen incentives to perform at the highest levels*'.

However, Code Provision B.2.4 states that the shareholders should be invited specifically to approve all new long-term incentive schemes and significant changes to existing schemes.

3.3 Performance-based incentives

Performance-based incentives reward executives, often with one or more cash bonus payments, if actual performance during a review period reaches or exceeds certain predetermined targets. A performance target might be for an annual period, with the executive rewarded according to the financial performance of the company as measured by annual profit after taxation (earnings or earnings growth), annual profit before interest and taxation (PBIT), or annual earnings before interest, taxation, depreciation and amortisation (EBITDA).

There are several problems with using profit measures as a basis for a reward system:

- Annual profitability can often be manipulated within the accounting rules, so that executives seeking a high current annual bonus might be able to make the profit more than the profit that would be reported if more conservative accounting policies and judgements were applied.

- Achieving profit targets does not necessarily mean that the shareholders benefit. Higher annual profits do not automatically guarantee higher dividends and higher share prices. However, an ideal bonus system is one that links rewards to executives with the benefits accruing to shareholders, so that the interests of directors and shareholders are in alignment.

Alternatively, performance could be measured in terms of the benefits obtained by shareholders. Total shareholder return (TSR) is the total return on investment achieved for shareholders during the review period. This is the sum of the dividends paid to shareholders plus the change in the market value of the shares. The drawback to shareholder-return-based performance incentives is that share prices are volatile, so that the returns made by shareholders over the previous twelve-month period could fluctuate sharply with even daily stock market share price movements. Such volatility will undermine confidence in any bonus scheme.

Other types of remuneration scheme are to reward executives on the basis of achieving:

- a number of different performance targets, some of them non-financial; or
- longer-term strategic objectives.

A chief executive might have two or even more bonus schemes, with one bonus payment linked to short-term financial results and another linked to longer-term strategic achievements. A problem with rewarding executives for long-term performance, however, is that an incoming chief executive inherits the long-term results of the efforts of his or her predecessor. The chief executive might also move on to another position before the full impact of his or her own efforts is fully appreciated.

3.4 Combined Code provisions on the design of performance-related remuneration

Schedule A to the Combined Code contains provisions for the design of performance-related remuneration schemes that remuneration committees are expected to apply:

- The committee should consider whether the directors should be eligible for annual bonuses. If so, performance criteria should be 'relevant, stretching and designed to enhance shareholder value'. There should be upper limits to annual bonuses, and these limits should be disclosed. There may be a case for an annual bonus to be part-paid in shares which the director is required to hold for a 'significant period'.
- The committee should consider whether the directors should be eligible for benefits under long-term incentive schemes. Traditional share option schemes should be weighed against other types of long-term incentive scheme. In normal circumstances the benefits under such schemes should not be receivable in less than three

years (for example, share options should not be exercisable within three years, and the granting of fully-paid shares should not be within three years). Directors should be encouraged to hold their shares for a further period after they have been granted or share options have been exercised (subject to the need to finance any costs of purchase or any associated tax liabilities).

- Any proposed new long-term incentive scheme should be approved by the shareholders. A new scheme should preferably replace an existing scheme, or should at least form part of a well-considered overall plan that incorporates the new scheme with existing schemes. The total rewards that are potentially available under such schemes should not be excessive.
- Payouts or grants under all incentive schemes (including new grants under share option schemes) should be subject to challenging performance criteria that reflect the company's objectives. Consideration should be given to criteria that reflect the company's performance relative to a group of other companies in some key measure, such as total shareholder return.
- Grants of share options and under other long-term incentive schemes should normally be phased in rather than awarded in one large block.
- As a general rule, only the basic salary should be pensionable (i.e. there should be no pension rights attached to bonuses and other rewards and payments).
- The remuneration committee should consider the consequences for pension costs to the company of any increases in basic salary or other pensionable remuneration, especially for directors close to retirement.

4 Share options and restricted stock awards

Share options granted under company share option schemes can align the interests of senior executives (as option holders) with their shareholders, since while the executives have their options, they have a personal interest in seeing the share price go up. However, there are a number of governance problems with share option awards as part of a remuneration package:

- Options for executive directors are a particular bone of contention, especially when options are granted in large blocks. The temptation for the directors is to focus on ensuring that the company's share price is as high as possible when the time comes for exercising the options. There might even be a temptation to manipulate the profits to improve the look of the company's financial performance when the options become eligible for exercise, as a way of giving upward impetus to the share price. An alternative to the issue of share options in large blocks is a phased grant of options to an individual in smaller quantities over several years. If options are granted more regularly to an individual, but in smaller amounts, the individual will have an interest in the long-term growth in the share price.

- It has been argued by some commentators that there should be controls over the sale of shares by executives after they have exercised options, in the form of a *minimum retention ratio*. Option holders would be required to hold on to a minimum proportion of the shares they acquire by exercising options for a minimum length of time after exercising the options. The only shares they might be permitted to sell would be enough to cover the cost of buying the shares.
- *The exercise price*. Provision B.1.2 of the Combined Code states that executive share options should not be offered at a discount, except as permitted by the provisions of the Listing Rules. This means that if the market price of a share is £5.00 when share options are granted to an executive under an executive option scheme, the exercise price should be no lower than £5.00.
- *The size of option awards*. A share option scheme will set a limit on the number of shares for which options may be issued. In the UK, this might be up to about 5 per cent of the existing issued share capital of the company. In a well-governed company, the award of options to individuals is likely to be made by the remuneration committee.

An alternative to stock options is restricted stock. Restricted stock is shares in the company given free to the executive concerned, but on condition that they are held for a minimum period of time after they have been granted. This arrangement has the advantage for the shareholders of giving the executive a long-term interest in dividends and share price performance. A possible attraction for executives is that unlike share options, which can go 'under water' when the share price falls, restricted stock will always have some value unless the company goes bankrupt.

4.1 Financial reporting and share-based payments

The international accounting standard IFRS2 *Share-based payments* (and the equivalent UK accounting standard FRS20) require that from 1 January 2005 (1 January 2006 in the case of unlisted companies), the awarding of shares and share options to employees should be recognised as an expense in the income statement. (The debit in the income statement is matched by a credit in a capital account.) The fair value of the share options should be assessed at the time of their grant, and charged as an expense accordingly.

Accounting issues might therefore have a strong influence on remuneration decisions. Since companies are now required to include a charge in the income statement whenever they award shares or share options, it seems probable that they will be more cautious than in the past about the number of options they grant, in order to avoid excessive charges against profit.

5 Compensation for loss of office: severance payments

A company might come under pressure from its institutional shareholders to limit severance payments to senior executives who are unsuccessful and so are forced to leave the company, having lost the support of both shareholders and fellow directors.

When an executive director or other senior executive is dismissed from office, there is usually a compensation payment for loss of office:

- The service contract of a director might provide for the payment of compensation for loss of office.
- Alternatively, a company might be required to give the individual a minimum period of notice, typically one year or six months in the UK. If an individual is asked to leave, he or she might be paid for the notice period, without having to work out the notice.

Shareholder concerns regarding compensation for loss of office arise in cases where an individual is dismissed for having performed badly. A large compensation payment can seem annoying, because it seems that the individual is being rewarded for failure. The actual amount of compensation that is paid for loss of office could be a matter of long and difficult negotiations, involving solicitors on both sides.

The Combined Code contains two provisions on service contracts and compensation for termination of office:

- When negotiating the terms of appointment of a new director, the remuneration committee should consider what compensation commitments the company would have in the event of early termination of office. More specifically, the aim should be to avoid rewarding poor performance. The committee should 'take a robust line' on reducing the amount of compensation to reflect a departing director's obligation to mitigate losses.
- Notice periods in a contract should be set at one year or less. If it is necessary to offer a longer notice period to a director coming into the company from outside, the notice period should subsequently be reduced to one year or less 'after the initial period'.

The reference to taking a robust line on a director's duty to mitigate losses is a suggestion that a director's contract should provide for a payment of compensation in stages, which would be halted in the event of the director finding employment elsewhere.

From a good corporate governance perspective, it is generally undesirable that a confidentiality agreement should apply to the details of any compensation agreement. In the UK, the Listing Rules require listed companies to give details, in their annual report and accounts, of any compensation for loss of office paid to any director.

A joint statement by the Association of British Insurers and the National Association of Pension Funds, which goes into some detail on severance payment arrangements, is described in paragraph 9.4 on p. 105.

6 The remuneration of non-executive directors

A provision in the Combined Code (B.2.3) is that the board (or, if required by the Articles of Association, the shareholders) should decide the remuneration of non-executive directors. It is usual for a non-executive director to receive a fixed annual fee for his or her services, for attending board meetings, some committee meetings and general meetings of the company. A conscientious non-executive should also spend some time visiting parts of the company, to meet its executives and see how it operates. Combined Code Provision B.1.3 states that the level of remuneration for NEDs should reflect the time commitment and responsibilities of the role.

Non-executive directors may receive other forms of remuneration or reward from the company, in addition to a basic fee, but these will put the independence of the non-executive in doubt.

Provision B.1.3 of the Combined Code states that the remuneration for NEDs should not include share options. However, if, exceptionally, share options are granted:

- shareholder approval should be sought in advance
- shares acquired by exercising the options should be held for at least one year after the NED leaves the board, and
- the granting of options could affect the NED's status as 'independent'.

7 Remuneration details and policy: disclosure

There is no suggestion in the Combined Code that shareholders should get involved in making remuneration decisions themselves. Shareholder involvement, however, is desirable, and there are two ways in which this might happen:

1 Disclosure of remuneration details for each director.
2 Shareholder voting on remuneration policy.

Until 2002, the main rules for listed companies about the disclosure of details of their directors' remuneration were provided by the UK Listing Rules. The Listing Rules requirements have been superseded by amendments to the Companies Act 1985, introduced by the Directors' Remuneration Report Regulations 2002. These regulations deal with both the disclosure of the remuneration details of individual directors and shareholder approval for the company's remuneration policy.

The regulations apply to 'quoted' companies, which are UK companies whose shares are listed on the Official List of the London Stock Exchange or on an official exchange of any other EEA state, the New York Stock Exchange or NASDAQ. The regulations do not apply to AIM-companies, nor to private companies.

7.1 Shareholder approval of remuneration policy

A distinction should be made between two different types of shareholder vote on executive remuneration:

- Shareholders might be invited to vote on the company's remuneration policy for the directors. This vote could be binding on the company, so that if the shareholders voted against a remuneration policy, the remuneration committee (or whoever is responsible for remuneration policy in the company) would have to devise a new policy.
- Alternatively, a shareholder vote might not have the power to bind the company, but simply be treated as a form of advice.

Shareholders do not vote on the remuneration package of individual directors. Once a remuneration package has been agreed between a company and a director, there is a binding contract, and shareholders could not be allowed the right to alter the contract details, since this would put the company in breach of contract.

The Companies Act gives shareholders the right to vote on the remuneration report, but the vote is advisory only, and not binding on the company. Effectively, this means that the vote allows shareholders to give their opinions about the company's remuneration policy, and, if there is a strong negative vote, expect the board of directors/remuneration committee to re-consider their position for the future. Shareholders are not permitted to vote on the remuneration package of individual directors, although in practice, shareholders can use a vote against the remuneration policy to express their disapproval of the package for a particular individual such as the chairman or CEO.

7.2 Directors' remuneration report

Quoted companies are required to prepare a directors' remuneration report, which must be approved by the board and signed on its behalf (s234B, s234C of the Companies Act 1985). A copy must be circulated to shareholders in the same way as the annual report and accounts, and it is normal for the report to be included in the same document.

Shareholders must vote at the annual general meeting on a resolution (ordinary resolution) to approve the report (s241A CA1985). This is an advisory vote only. 'No entitlement of a person to remuneration is made conditional on the resolution being passed.'

The report must contain extensive disclosures about directors' remuneration, which are set out in Schedule 7A to the Companies Act. A distinction is made between items that are not subject to audit and items that are. The auditors in their audit report must state whether in their opinion the auditable part of the report has been prepared properly in accordance with the Act. A signed copy of the report must also be filed with the

Registrar of Companies, in the same way as the annual accounts, the directors' report and the auditors' report.

Information not subject to audit

Items to be included in the directors' remuneration report that are not subject to audit are as follows:

- The names of the directors who were members of the remuneration committee, and details about any remuneration consultants that were used (name, nature of services provided).
- A statement of the company's policy on directors' remuneration for the next financial years and the years after that (i.e. a forward-looking policy statement).
- A line graph showing the total shareholder return (TSR) on the company's shares over a five-year period, and the TSR on a holding of a portfolio of shares over the same period representing a named broad equity market index. The graph can therefore be used to compare shareholder returns on the company's shares with those of a market index. The Act specifies how TSR should be calculated.
- Information about the service contract for each director: the date of the contract, its unexpired term and details of any notice periods; any compensation payable for early termination of the contract and any other provisions in the contract affecting the liability of the company in the event of early termination (i.e. severance terms).

The forward-looking statement on the company's policy on directors' remuneration must include the following details, for *each director*:

- details of the performance conditions that apply to decide the director's entitlement to share options or an award under a long-term incentive scheme, and an explanation of why these performance conditions were chosen;
- a summary of the methods used to decide whether these performance conditions have been met, and an explanation of why these methods were chosen;
- a description of any proposed significant amendment to the terms and conditions affecting the director's entitlement to share options or awards under a long-term incentive scheme (and an explanation of the reasons for the proposed change);
- where the director's entitlement to share options or award under a long-term incentive scheme are not subject to meeting certain performance conditions, an explanation of why this is the case;
- the relative importance of those elements of the director's remuneration that are related to performance and those which are not.

The policy statement should also summarise and explain the company's policy on the duration of contracts with directors and the notice periods and termination payments under these contracts.

Information subject to audit

The remuneration report must contain the following items which are subject to audit.

- A table showing, for each director, the total remuneration for the year, broken down into salary and fees, bonuses, expenses received, compensation for loss of office and other severance payments, and non-cash benefits.
- A table showing, for each director, details of interests in share options, both beneficial and non-beneficial. (Beneficial options are options held in the name of the director or a connected person, such as the director's spouse or child under 18.) The information disclosed should include details of options awarded or exercised during the year, options that expired unexercised during the year, and any variations to the terms and conditions relating to the award or exercise of options. For options exercised during the year, the disclosures should show the market price of the shares when the options were exercised. For options not yet expired, the disclosures should give details of the price paid for their award (if any), the exercise price, the date from which the options may be exercised and the date they expire. Also the market price of the shares at the end of the year, and the highest and lowest market prices reached during the year.
- For each director, details of any long-term incentive schemes (other than share options). These should show the director's interest in each scheme at the start of the year and the end of the year, any changes during the year, and details of when the awards/entitlements can be taken.
- For each director, details of pension contributions or entitlements. The nature of the disclosures will vary according to whether the pension scheme is a defined benefit scheme or a defined contribution scheme.
- For each director, details of any excess pension benefits received or receivable in the year. Excess retirement benefits are benefits in excess of the director's contractual entitlement.
- Significant payments made during the year to former directors of the company.
- The total amount of any payments made to third parties for the services of any director.
- An explanation and justification of any element of directors' remuneration, other than basic salary, which is pensionable.

7.3 Additional requirements recommended by the Combined Code

The Combined Code makes further recommendations about remuneration for directors and senior executives:

- Shareholders should be asked to approve all new long-term incentive schemes (Code Provision B.2.4).
- If grants under a share option scheme or long-term incentive scheme are made in one block, rather than phased over time, this should be explained and justified (Schedule A).

8 Directors' service contracts

The service contract of a director with his or her company should ideally be in written form, but might not be. A service contract sets out the terms and conditions of the director's appointment, including the duration of the appointment (with a fixed-term contract) or the required minimum period of notice of termination (with a 'rolling' contract).

Companies are required (by Section 318 of the Companies Act 1985) to keep a copy of all written service agreements with directors. Each written service contract should be available for inspection by shareholders free of charge, and a copy should be kept at the company's registered office, or its principal place of business, or in the same place as its register of shareholders.

Individuals who are not shareholders may also inspect a director's service contract on payment of a prescribed fee (Companies (Inspection and Copying of Registers, etc.) Regulations 1991). In addition, the Listing Rules require, for listed companies, that:

- Directors' service contracts should be available for inspection by shareholders during normal business hours.
- Copies of directors' service contracts must be available for inspection at the location of the AGM for at least 15 minutes before the meeting starts and until it ends.
- The notice convening the AGM must specify that copies of written service contracts will be available for inspection, or that no such written contracts exist.

In the directors' report in the annual report and accounts, there should be a statement of the unexpired term of the service contract of any director who is being proposed for re-election at the AGM.

The issues that raise the most concerns about directors' service contracts are:

- remuneration, including pension rights;
- the term of the contract or period of notice;
- payments to which the director would be entitled on termination of the contract.

The Combined Code states that notice periods or contract periods should be for one year or less (Code Provision B.1.6). Should it be necessary to offer a director joining from outside the company a notice period or contract period in excess of one year, the period should be reduced to one year or less after the initial period.

The views of the association of British Insurers (ABI) and the National Association of Pension Funds (NAPF) on two-year contracts are that as a general rule, they should not be offered to incoming senior executives as an inducement to join. The notice period for contracts should be one year or less. If all companies take this line, executives will stop asking for contracts with a notice period in excess of one year. Two-year deals should be acceptable only for struggling companies.

9 Institutional shareholder views on directors' remuneration

The associations of institutional investors have developed strong views on directors' remuneration. The views of the Association of British Insurers, including a joint statement with the National Association of Pension Funds, are set out below, and are reproduced in full in Appendix 18.

The Association of British Insurers regularly reviews its guidelines for members on executive remuneration. Its revised guidelines, published in December 2004, contains:

- basic principles on executive remuneration
- guidelines on remuneration structure
- guidelines on share incentive schemes
- a joint statement with the National Association of Pension Funds on severance pay for senior executives.

The ABI principles and guidelines are reproduced in full in Appendix 15.

9.1 ABI principles for executive remuneration

Although the board is accountable to shareholders for remuneration policy, the main responsibility for executive remuneration is seen to lie with the remuneration committee:

- Remuneration committees should maintain a timely and constructive dialogue with the company's major institutional shareholders and with the ABI, on matters relating to senior executive remuneration such as changes in remuneration policy and share incentive schemes. Any proposed departure from the stated remuneration policy should be subject to approval by the shareholders.
- Companies must ensure that their remuneration committee is properly established with appropriate powers and authority.
- Boards should be able to demonstrate that senior executive remuneration arrangements are linked to the company's business strategies and objectives, and are regularly reviewed. Overall arrangements should be prudent, well communicated and accord with current best practice.
- The remuneration committee should guard against the possibility of unjustified windfall gains when designing a share-based incentive plan.
- The committee should have regard to pay and conditions throughout the company. It should make comparisons with caution, in view of the risk of an upward ratchet in remuneration levels with no corresponding improvement in performance. It should not pay more than is necessary.
- The committee should pay particular attention to arrangements for key executives who are not directors.

- All new share-based incentive schemes should be submitted to the shareholders for approval.
- When there is any type of performance-linked enhancement with respect to share incentives or incentive bonus arrangements, there should be a separate shareholder vote.
- Shareholders consider it inappropriate for the chairman or NEDs to receive incentives geared to share price performance. The granting of incentives linked to share price performance is 'not appropriate' since this could affect the ability of the chairman or NEDs 'to provide impartial oversight and advice'.

9.2 ABI guidelines on remuneration structure

The ABI's guidelines on remuneration structure go into some detail on specific aspects of remuneration packages. They include the following:

- Remuneration packages should strike a suitable balance between *fixed pay* (e.g. basic salary) and *variable pay* (e.g. bonuses), and between *short-term and long-term objectives*.
- The remuneration committee should consider market rates of remuneration, but should not pay more than is necessary to attract a suitable individual to a senior management position.
- *Annual cash bonuses* can be a suitable method of providing short-term incentives.
- The performance targets for individuals should be disclosed in the annual remuneration report, subject to considerations of confidentiality. There should be disclosure of the basic parameters used for performance targets for the financial year being reported on.
- Shareholders should not normally support *transaction bonuses* (i.e. the payment of a bonus to executives for the successful completion of a specific transaction, such as a takeover). A payment of any transaction bonus should be subject to shareholder consent.
- There should be clear disclosures of *pension liabilities* to senior executives.
- Institutional shareholders should encourage companies to require that senior executives should build meaningful shareholdings in their company. It might be appropriate for share incentive schemes to include a rule that participants in the scheme should retain a proportion of the shares they obtain under the terms of the scheme.

9.3 ABI Guidelines for share incentive schemes

The ABI supports share incentive schemes that link remuneration to performance and align the interests of senior executives with those of the company's shareholders. However, these schemes involve either a commitment of shareholder funds or a dilution of equity, and it is therefore important that schemes should be:

- well designed, forming a coherent element in the overall remuneration package, and
- properly costed.

The guidelines on share incentive schemes are quite long, but the key elements are as follows:

- *General principles*. A share incentive scheme should link remuneration to performance and effectively align the long-term interests of management with those of shareholders. There should be limits on the dilution of shareholders' equity and on the participation of individuals in such schemes. Schemes should be clearly evaluated and its costs disclosed. Phased grants and the award of grants on a sliding scale according to performance should be encouraged.
- *Remuneration committees*. Remuneration committees should regularly review all share incentive schemes to ensure that they remain effective. Substantial or exceptional amendments to scheme rules should be submitted to shareholders for prior authorisation.
- *Disclosure*. There should be full disclosure of share incentive schemes (the basis and rationale for the scheme, its details and its cost) in the remuneration report. Disclosure should include details of scheme limits and limits to individual participation in these schemes.
- *Performance conditions and criteria*. The granting of awards should be conditional on meeting performance criteria. The greater the level of the potential award to an individual, the more stretching and demanding the performance criteria should be. Total shareholder return (TSR) relative to a suitable index or peer group is generally acceptable as a performance criterion, but whatever performance criterion (or criteria) it selects, the remuneration committee should explain their choice and demonstrate that it is both robust and demanding.
- *Granting of awards*. Performance conditions should be measured over a period of three years or more, and the use of even longer performance periods should be encouraged in order to motivate individuals to achieve sustained improvements in financial performance.
- *Accrual of dividends*. For long-term incentive schemes the statement recommends that, from the date of the grant of options to a scheme participant, companies should accrue the equivalent of the dividends paid to shareholders and that this accrued dividend should be paid to the participant when the shares are eventually vested in him or her.
- *Change of control provisions*. Scheme rules should state that there will be no automatic waiving of performance conditions in the event of a change of control of the company, and any payment should be based on the underlying financial performance of the company that is subject to a change of control. (This measure, introduced as a result of shareholder dissatisfaction with the incentives paid to Carlton chairman Michael Green following the merger of Carlton and Granada in 2004, is intended to discourage windfall gains following a company takeover or merger.)

- *Cost.* The cost of a share incentive scheme should be disclosed at the time shareholder approval is sought for the scheme. The information disclosed should include the cost of all incentive arrangements, the potential value of the awards to individuals participating in the scheme, the expected value of the award at the outset and the maximum dilution that may arise through issuing shares to satisfy scheme entitlements.
- *Dilution limits.* Where an incentive scheme provides for the issue of new shares, the rules of the scheme must ensure that, aggregating all the company's schemes together, commitments to issue new shares must not exceed 10 per cent of the issued ordinary share capital in any ten-year rolling period. Commitments to issue new shares under executive (discretionary) schemes should normally not exceed 5 per cent of the issued ordinary share capital in any ten-year rolling period.
- *Participation.* Participation in share incentive schemes should be restricted to bona fide employees and executive directors, and should be subject to appropriate limits for individual participation.
- *Phasing of awards/grants and timing.* The phasing of awards and grants is encouraged, for several reasons. Phased awards reduce the risk of unexpected outcomes due to share price volatility, and eliminate the problem that any limit on individual participation will encourage early exercise. They also lessen the likelihood of problems due to underwater options. The rules of a scheme should also provide that awards of shares or options should be granted only within a 42-day period following the publication of the company's results.
- *Pricing of options on shares.* Prices at which shares or options are granted should usually be not less than the mid-market price immediately preceding the grant.
- *Life of a scheme.* The life of any such scheme should not exceed ten years.

9.4 Joint ABI/NAPF statement on severance pay

The ABI and NAPF have also produced a joint statement (reviewed December 2004) on severance pay. The statement was a result of the concern about severance payments to senior executives ousted from their companies as a result of poor corporate performance. High levels of compensation on leaving office were seen as unjustifiable 'rewards for failure'. The joint statement comments:

> *It is unacceptable that failure, which detracts from the value of an enterprise and which can threaten the livelihood of employees, can result in large payments to its departing leaders. Executives, whose remuneration is already at a level which allows for the risk inherent in their role, should show leadership in aligning their financial interests with those of their shareholders.*

On the other hand, the ABI/NAPF acknowledge that incoming executives should be offered some protection against downside risk in their contracts, and that having agreed a contract with the company, the individual is protected by contract rights.

Nevertheless, the joint statement argues that boards should have remuneration policies that avoid making payments that are not properly merited. From the outset, when agreeing a remuneration package with an individual senior executive, boards should both calculate the potential cost of a sudden termination of employment and also consider the potential reputational risk to the company of being obliged to make a high severance payment to an unsuccessful departing executive. Although shareholders should hold the board of directors accountable for excessive severance payment terms, the main responsibility for arranging suitable severance terms in an individual's contract lies with the remuneration committee.

Principles for negotiating severance terms

- The terms of an individual's contract should not commit companies to making payments for failure. Boards should resist pressure from incoming individuals for generous severance terms in their contract.
- In agreeing the remuneration package with an individual, the link between remuneration and performance must be absolutely clear in the wording of the contract. A suitable way forward might be to favour lower fixed pay in a remuneration package and a larger element of performance-related variable pay, with the contract specifying that the payment of the variable element depends on performance. Investors do not expect executives to be automatically entitled to cash payments other than basic pay. Bonuses should be cut or eliminated when individual performance is poor.
- Although the maximum notice period should be one year, a shorter notice period might be appropriate where severance pay would otherwise be too high.
- When a matter is taken to litigation, the courts take account of some elements of variable pay, such as bonuses, when deciding on the awards for a departing executive. However, the size of this payment can be limited by attaching clear performance conditions (rather than unclear or ambiguous conditions) to variable pay.

Contract details

- The ABI/NAPF would approve of a contract that provided for phased payments to an individual after termination of employment, with the payments ceasing if the individual finds fresh employment.
- A liquidated damages approach is not normally desirable. This is an approach involving an agreement at the outset on the amount that will be paid in the event of the individual's dismissal. The statement recommends that if a liquidated damages approach is taken, the approach should be modified so that there is an agreement in advance that in the event of the individual's dismissal, the parties will go to arbitration to decide how much should be paid.
- The employment contract might possibly include a provision that it is the duty of the individual, in the event of severance of employment, to mitigate his or her losses.

The ABI/NAPF statement goes on to discuss the problem that in UK law, it is not normally possible for under-performance to be established as grounds for summary dismissal of an individual without compensation. It refers to the Employment Act 2002, under which a statutory disciplinary procedure is implicit in every employment contract, including those of executive directors, and suggests that boards should be prepared to make use of these statutory procedures against under-performing executives where appropriate.

An executive's contract might therefore include a provision that following dismissal as a result of disciplinary procedures against the individual, a shorter notice period will apply than the normal notice period in the contract (typically 12 months). The ABI/NAPF statement suggests one week's notice for every year of service up to a maximum of 12 weeks. However, without a specific provision in the contract for shorter notice periods, the individual will be entitled to the full contractual notice period, even if dismissed following disciplinary procedures.

The statement also makes certain comments about pension settlements for an outgoing executive. Boards should make a clear distinction between the individual's contractual entitlement to pension arrangements and discretionary enhancements agreed as part of the severance settlement. Contracts for executives should state that the individual's pension will not be enhanced in the event of early termination unless the board is satisfied that the enhancement is merited. Ominously perhaps, the statement adds that shareholders are likely to question enhancement decisions that do not seem merited, and might vote against the remuneration policy if they are not satisfied.

CHAPTER

7 Shareholders and Shareholder Relations

1 The relationship between the board and the shareholders

In listed public companies, the management is separate from the ownership. The shareholders need to rely on management to run the company in the interests of the shareholders. Management in return should be able to rely on the support of the shareholders, particularly where new initiatives, such as a proposed takeover, have to be put to a vote at a company general meeting.

Relations between the company's board and its shareholders are an important aspect of corporate governance, although there are two inter-related issues:

- From the company's perspective, the directors should recognise that although their legal duties are to the company, the shareholders of the company are its owners. The board should therefore keep the shareholders well informed about what the company is doing.
- From the shareholders' perspective, only institutional shareholders have the time, as well as the understanding, to monitor the performance of companies and the activities of their boards.

Traditionally, institutional investors have possibly taken the view that if they disapprove of a particular company or its management, they can always sell their shares and invest somewhere else.

Another view is that many investments by institutional shareholders may be of a long-term nature. 'Activist' shareholders would argue that over the long term, companies that are better governed will create more value than those that are badly governed. It is therefore in the self-interest of institutional investors, and the clients or beneficiaries they represent, to encourage companies to adopt best practices in corporate governance. This argument is by no means universally accepted, but it remains an important rationale for shareholder activism.

The Combined Code seeks to provide shareholders with opportunities to be more involved in corporate governance. Under company law, the powers and rights of shareholders are fairly restricted, and in most circumstances a company's directors could, in strict legal terms at least, run their company without significant shareholder involvement. In order to appreciate the contribution of the Combined Code to corporate governance in this area, it is useful to look at the powers and rights of shareholders under company law.

2 Shareholders' powers and rights

2.1 Shareholders' powers

Shareholders powers are fairly restricted in law, although there is some debate as to how extensive these powers are. In the context of corporate governance, shareholders' powers relate to the actions that shareholders can take to make decisions for the company, or to affect decisions taken by the directors with which they disagree.

The most significant powers of the shareholders relate to their voting powers in general meeting, although the matters on which they can make decisions are fairly limited (electing or re-electing directors, appointing or re-appointing the external auditors, approving the directors' remuneration report, decisions on authorised share capital, approving or reducing the proposed final dividend, etc.).

Shareholder powers in company law include the following:

- Under Section 35(2) of the Companies Act 1985 a shareholder may bring proceedings to court to prevent the company from doing something *ultra vires* (outside the scope of the objects clause in its Memorandum of Association). However, given that objects clauses are now commonly given a general wording, this power is not usually significant.
- Under Section 459 of the Companies Act 1985, a shareholder can petition the court for an order the grounds that the company's affairs are being conducted in a way that is unfairly prejudicial to some or all of its members. The court may then issue an order, for example to regulate the company's affairs or to prevent the company from following a particular course of action.
- Under Section 368 of the Companies Act 1985, shareholders representing at least 10 per cent of the voting shares can call an extraordinary general meeting.
- Under Section 459 of the Companies Act 1985, shareholders representing at least 5 per cent of the voting shares can arrange for a resolution to be put to the annual

general meeting, and ask for the company to circulate to other shareholders a message of up to 1,000 words that they have written on the subject matter of the resolution.

2.2 Shareholders' rights

Use of voting rights

The rights of shareholders relate mainly to the issues on which they may vote in general meetings of the company. In the UK, most shareholder voting requires a simple majority (an ordinary resolution) or a 75 per cent majority vote (a special resolution).

- In the past, it has been common for shareholders to 'rubber stamp' proposals by the directors at general meetings and to support the directors with very few questions asked. Most general meetings of a company are attended by very few shareholders and most shareholders vote by proxy.
- Some investors believe that shareholders should use their voting rights more actively, voting against proposed resolutions where appropriate. 'Activist' shareholder groups might try to encourage shareholders to vote against specific resolutions in a general meeting, to show their disapproval of certain policies of the board. There appears to be a growing interest in shareholders' voting rights among some institutional investment organisations, and there have been some calls for company meetings to be brought into the technology age, with electronic voting.

New share issues and shareholders' rights

An important aspect of the balance of power between directors and shareholders is the authority of directors to issue new shares and the rights of shareholders in any new share issue. In the UK, the major elements in the legislation are as follows:

- The amount of the authorised share capital is specified in the company's Memorandum of Association and to issue shares in excess of the current authorised limit requires prior shareholder approval for increasing the authorised share capital.
- The directors cannot increase the issued share capital without prior approval from the shareholders (Section 80 of the Companies Act 1985). In theory, this could mean that the directors must always go to the shareholders for approval when they want to issue new shares, such as when employees wish to exercise share options. A compromise arrangement is usually reached by listed public companies, whereby the shareholders grant authority to the directors to issue new shares up to a certain maximum amount. This authority is usually given to the directors by a resolution at the annual general meeting, and the authority typically lasts for one year, until the next annual general meeting (when another resolution is put forward to renew the authority for a further twelve months).
- Under UK company law, shareholders have pre-emption rights when new shares are issued for cash (Section 89 of the Companies Act 1985), giving them the right to

subscribe for the new shares in proportion to their existing shareholding. This rule protects shareholders against an erosion of their stake in the company. However, the shareholders can vote to disapply their pre-emption rights. Within certain limits, this might be a reasonable requirement of the directors, for example, to allow the company to issue new shares under share option schemes. It is therefore usual to pass a resolution at the annual general meeting of a listed company that the shareholders should disapply their pre-emption rights and allow the directors to issue new shares to other investors, but only up to a specified limit in the number of new shares.

The investor protection committees or IPCs of the Association of British Insurers (ABI) and the National Association of Pension Funds (NAPF) have issued guidelines on pre-emption rights, recommending to their members that resolutions to disapply pre-emption rights at an annual general meeting should be approved, provided that:

- the total number of 'non-pre-emptive' shares issued in any year does not exceed 5 per cent of the company's issued share capital; and
- the total number of 'non-pre-emptive' shares issued in any rolling three-year period should not exceed 7.5 per cent of the company's issued share capital.

Proposals by a board of directors to disapply pre-emption rights for more shares should not be approved by the shareholders, the guidelines recommend, unless the board of directors has explained its reasons to the shareholders, and the shareholders have accepted them. In addition, the guidelines recommend that the price of any such shares issued by the directors should normally not be at a discount of more than 5 per cent to the current share price at the time of the issue.

Rights to remove a director from office

The shareholders of a company should have rights under the constitution of the company to remove a director from office. In UK law, if the shareholders are dissatisfied with a director, they have the right under the Companies Act 1985 (Section 303) to remove a director from office by an ordinary resolution in general meeting.

A group of shareholders proposing to remove a director from office have the right to call for a resolution on the matter at a general meeting of the company, under either Section 368 or Section 376, provided they represent the required minimum of the total voting rights., When a group of shareholders puts forward a proposal to remove a director, the board cannot refuse to put the issue to a general meeting for a vote. In practice, however, shareholder initiatives of this sort are most unlikely to happen.

Election and re-election of directors

Shareholders could hold individual directors to account for their actions by voting against their initial election (after appointment) or their re-election. (The Table A Articles of Association provide for one-third of the directors to retire by rotation.)

The retirement of directors by rotation and standing for re-election offers the shareholders an opportunity to vote a director out of office. However, most shareholders tend to vote in support of the directors, and it is currently still difficult for active shareholders to vote successfully against the re-election of any director.

Case example

In September 2002, the finance director of Anite plc, a UK IT software and services company, resigned in the face of strong criticism from investors who were angry at the company's remuneration policy and acquisition strategy.

- The individual concerned was one of the highest-paid finance directors among UK technology companies, and his remuneration for the year to 30 April 2002 had risen 10 per cent despite a collapse in the company's performance compared with the previous year.
- Bonuses for the chief executive and the finance director were based on the profits before tax, exceptional items and goodwill, rather than earnings (profits after tax).
- The company had a policy of growth through acquisitions, and had made seventeen acquisitions since April 2000. These resulted in large amounts of purchased goodwill, and the amortisation of this goodwill reduced earnings, but not profits before goodwill.
- The acquisitions were made with an open-ended purchase price. The final purchase price depended on the performance of the purchased assets, with an 'earn-out' for the sellers of the acquired companies. All the purchases were paid for with new Anite shares.
- The Anite share price fell by about 80 per cent in the year to 30 April 2002, which meant that more shares had to be issued to pay for new acquisitions. The result was a big dilution in earnings per share.
- The dilution in earnings per share had no effect, however, on the bonuses of the CEO and finance director. On the contrary, the new acquisitions added to profits before tax, exceptional items and goodwill, even though profits after exceptional items and goodwill fell.
- The finance director, who was closely associated with the funding of the acquisitions, was therefore put under pressure to resign by shareholders. However, questions remained about the responsibility of the whole board for both the directors' remuneration policy and the acquisition funding policy.

Although the finance director was not removed from office by a vote of the shareholders at an annual general meeting, the threat of shareholders would exercising this right was apparently sufficient in this case to achieve the desired result.

Other voting rights of shareholders

Shareholders also have some other rights under company law or (in the case of listed companies) the UK Listing Rules.

- Shareholders in larger companies vote each year to re-elect the external auditors. In practice, however, it is very unusual for a group of shareholders to try to prevent the re-election of auditors, against the wishes of the board of directors. Shareholders vote each year at the annual general meeting to approve the proposed final dividend for the previous year. However, the shareholders can vote only to reduce the final dividend proposed by the directors, and cannot vote to increase it above the proposed amount. Votes against the final proposed dividend are uncommon.
- The shareholders in a company have a right to certain information about the financial performance and financial situation of the company. This is provided by the annual report and accounts and, in the case of listed companies, by interim accounts for the first half of each financial year. Shareholders use this financial information to make judgements about how well or badly the company has been run.
- Shareholders are required to vote each year at the annual general meeting on the directors' remuneration report (Section 234C of the Companies Act 1985), although this vote is advisory only, and is not binding on the board of directors.

The Listing Rules require that for significant 'transactions' (typically, a large acquisition or the sale of a business of the company), the company must notify the stock market, send a circular to the shareholders giving information about the transaction, and obtain the prior approval of the shareholders before the transaction can go ahead.

This rule applies only to significant transactions. A major public company is able to enter into a number of smaller transactions that are not significant. Provided the acquisitions are for cash, or the authority of the shareholders has already been obtained to allot any extra shares that might be needed to finance the transactions, the board of directors can buy up a number of smaller companies, without the shareholders having any say in the matter.

3 The Combined Code and shareholder relations

A view taken in the original Combined Code in 1998, and developed in the revised Code in 2003, is that good relations between a company and its shareholders are desirable. The responsibility for good relations ought to be shared by the boards of companies and institutional shareholders.

The Code therefore has separate sections on:

- the company's relations with all its shareholders. This section of the Code includes not just principles, but also provisions. As with the other provisions in the Code, listed companies should comply with them or explain their non-compliance.

- the responsibilities of institutional investors. This section of the Code consists of Main Principles and Supporting Principles, but there are no Code provisions. However, the Code is consistent with statements and guidelines issued by the main UK institutional shareholder representative groups.

4 Relations with shareholders: the company's responsibilities

The Combined Code identifies two areas of responsibility for companies:

- maintaining a dialogue with their institutional shareholders, and
- making constructive use of the AGM.

4.1 Maintaining a dialogue with institutional shareholders

A Main Principle of the Code (D.1) is that:

> *There should be a dialogue with shareholders based on the mutual understanding of objectives. The board as a whole has responsibility for ensuring that a satisfactory dialogue with shareholders takes place.*

The Code recognises that for shareholders, most contact with a company is contact with the chief executive or finance director. However, the chairman (and senior independent director and other directors as appropriate) should maintain enough contact with shareholders to understand their isues and concerns. The board should keep in touch with shareholder opinion in whatever ways are most suitable.

The Code states a number of practical requirements for maintaining dialogue (Code Provision D.1.1):

- The chairman should ensure that the views of the shareholders are communicated to the board as a whole.
- The chairman should discuss strategy and governance with the major shareholders.
- Non-executive directors should be given the opportunity to attend meetings with major shareholders.
- If requested to attend meetings with major shareholders, NEDs should expect to attend them. (Note: The Combined Code states that companies should offer major shareholders the opportunity to meet newly-appointed non-executive directors (Provision A.5.1), although it is uncertain whether major shareholders will wish to take advantage of the opportunity.)
- The senior independent director should attend enough meetings with a range of major shareholders to listen to their views, in order to develop a 'balanced understanding' of their concerns and views.

In the annual report, the board should report on the steps that have been taken to ensure that members of the board, especially the NEDs, develop an understanding of the views of the shareholders, for example, through face-to-face meetings, analysts' or brokers' briefings or surveys of shareholder opinion (Code Provision D.1.2).

4.2 Constructive use of the Annual General Meeting

The Code states that:

> *The board should use the AGM to communicate with investors and to encourage their participation* (Main Principle D.2).

The 1998 version of the Combined Code required the board to communicate with and encourage the participation of private investors, but the word 'private' was deleted from the 2003 revised Code.

The Combined Code suggests that relations with smaller private shareholders should be maintained through constructive use of the annual general meeting. The provisions of the Code are concerned mainly with:

- encouraging attendance at the AGM;
- giving shareholders an opportunity to ask questions and to hear about the company during the meeting;
- giving shareholders the opportunity to use their vote and greater openness in voting procedures at the annual general meeting.

The Combined Code provisions are as follows.

Encouraging attendance

The company should arrange for the notice of the AGM and the related papers to be sent to the shareholders at least 20 working days before the meeting (Code Provision D.2.4). The minimum notice of an AGM required by the Companies Act (Section 369) is just 21 calendar days.

Giving shareholders an opportunity to ask questions

The board chairman should arrange for:

- the chairmen of the audit, nomination and remuneration committees to be available to answer questions, and
- all directors to attend (Code Provision D.2.3).

Voting procedures

- At the AGM, there should be a separate resolution for each substantially separate issue (Code Provision D.2.2). This requirement is intended to prevent the practice of combining two or more issues, one 'popular' and the other more controversial, into a single resolution. Each issue will then be voted on separately.
- The company should count all proxy votes. After the resolution has been dealt with on a show of hands, the company should indicate the level of proxy votes lodged for

and against the resolution, *and the number of abstentions*. The company should also make sure that votes cast are properly received and recorded (Code Provision D.2.1).

The reference to counting the number of abstentions was introduced into the revised Combined Code in 2003, and had not been included in the original 1998 Code. However, the Code goes into no further detail. The issue of abstentions in proxy voting was subsequently taken up by the Myners Report to the Shareholder Voting Working Party and an ICSA Guidance Note. These are described below.

4.3 Investor relations programmes

The Combined Code does not make any recommendations about the development and application of investor relations progammes. However, its emphasis on good communications between a company and its shareholders is consistent with a formal programme for investor relations, which might consist of:

- a planned schedule of presentations to both existing and potential investors
- presentations to stock market analysts
- where appropriate, arranging site visits for major shareholders
- providing a facility for shareholders to vote by proxy by e-mail

A key feature of an investor relations policy should be to make information available to investors on the company's web-site. A web-site can be used to:

- present information about the company
- update investors regularly about developments in the company's business, and with the most recently published financial information
- present a calendar of important events, such as dividend payments dates.

The Investor Relations Society has published Best Practice Guidelines for using the company's web-site (see Directory).

5 The Combined Code and institutional shareholders

The Combined Code sets out a number of principles relating to the responsibilities of institutional shareholders for ensuring good corporate governance. For institutional investors, however, more significant guidance has been provided by their own professional and voluntary organisations, such as the ABI and NAPF. However, the Combined Code is consistent with the views of the main institutional investor organisations. The principles in the Code are set out below, as an introduction to the institutional shareholder perspective on corporate governance.

The section of the Combined Code on institutional investors has three sets of principles, relating to:

- dialogue with companies
- evaluating the corporate governance disclosures by companies
- shareholder voting.

5.1 Dialogue with companies

Just as companies should maintain a dialogue with shareholders, so too should institutional shareholders enter into a dialogue with companies 'based on the mutual understanding of objectives (Main Principle E.1). The Code also states that institutional shareholders should apply the principles set out in the ISC's Guidance Note, *The Responsibilities of Institutional Shareholders and Agents: Statement of Principles* (see below and Appendix 16).

5.2 The evaluation of corporate governance disclosures

The Code encourages institutional investors to take a reasoned and flexible approach to judging the compliance of companies with corporate governance requirements:

- When evaluating company disclosures on corporate governance, particularly those relating to board structure and composition, institutional shareholders 'should give due weight to all relevant factors drawn to their attention' (Main Principle E.2).
- Institutional shareholders should consider carefully the explanations by companies for any departure from the Combined Code provisions 'and make reasoned judgements in each case'.
- If they do not accept the company's position, they should explain their views in writing to the company, and be prepared to enter a dialogue if necessary.
- They should avoid a 'box-ticking' approach to checking compliance with the Code and assessing a company's corporate governance.

In making their evaluation of a company's corporate governance arrangements, institutional investors should bear in mind in particular the size and complexity of the company and the size and nature of the risks that it faces.

5.3 Shareholder voting

The Combined Code encourages attendance at AGMs by institutional investors and reasoned use of their votes. The Code states that: '*Institutional investors have a responsibility to make considered use of their votes*' (Main Principle E.3).

- They should take steps to ensure that their voting intentions are being translated into practice. (Although the Code does not go into further detail, this Supporting Principle addresses issues such as the way in which discretionary proxy votes are given and used.)

- On request, institutional shareholders should make available to their clients information on the proportion of resolutions on which votes were cast and non-discretionary proxy votes cast. (The accountability of institutional investors to their clients for the way they have voted is an issue that has been recognised by the institutions' shareholder representative bodies.)
- Major shareholders should attend AGMs 'where appropriate and practicable'. Companies and registrars should facilitate this.

6 Shareholder activism

'Shareholder activism', in its popular definition, is a term used to describe actions by shareholders to use their powers and influence when they disagree with the corporate governance arrangements or the policies of companies in which they invest. The main guidance on corporate governance and shareholder activism is provided to institutional investors by their various representative bodies, notably the ABI, the NAPF and the Institutional Shareholders' Committee (ISC).

Although it is tempting to think of 'activism' as confrontational, it is more appropriate to explain it in terms of encouraging shareholders, and institutional shareholders in particular, to have a more active involvement with the companies in which they invest. Active involvement will normally mean supporting the board, constructive dialogues with the board and a considered use of votes at general meetings.

6.1 The Myners Committee and relations between companies and institutional investors

The Myners Committee, set up by the Department of Trade and Industry to look into the relationship between listed companies and their investors, and to consider how companies and institutional investors could work more closely together, produced an influential report in 2001. The report suggested that in an ideal world, the board of a company would have:

- clear objectives for the company;
- a well-formulated strategy for achieving these objectives;
- a financing policy to pay for implementation of the strategy; and
- capital expenditure and revenue plans.

All of these it communicates annually to institutional investors and brokers.

The board should also arrange regular meetings with the shareholders to discuss long-term issues facing the company. In addition, it should have a clearly defined and articulated policy for the remuneration of executive directors that it also discusses openly with shareholders.

In a 2001 report to the Chancellor of the Exchequer on institutional investment in the UK, Paul Myners criticised the lack of activism amongst institutional investors, favouring government regulation to force institutions to take involvement with their companies more seriously. He wrote:

> *In the world we now face, an ever-higher premium is likely to be placed on efficiency and flexibility. This review's conclusion is that our present structures fall short on both counts. In short, it finds that savers' money is too often being invested in ways that do not maximise their interests. It is likely to follow too that capital is being inefficiently allocated in the economy. This report therefore sets out a blueprint for change. At the heart of it is a belief that clear incentives and tougher customer pressures need to be driven throughout the savings and investment industry.*

7 Institutional shareholder guidelines on corporate governance

7.1 ISC Statement of Principles

In 2002, the ISC published a statement of principles on the responsibilities of institutional shareholders and their agents, the fund managers, as they should be applied to UK listed companies. It can be seen as a statement on shareholder activism. The introduction to the statement comments:

> *The policies of activism set out below do not constitute an obligation to micro-manage the affairs of investee companies, but rather relate to procedures designed to ensure that shareholders derive value from their investments by dealing effectively with concerns over under-performance. Nor do they preclude a decision to sell a holding, where this is the most effective response to such concerns.*

Setting out policy on the discharge of responsibilities

Institutional investors and their agents should have a clear statement of their policy on activism and how they will discharge their responsibilities to their beneficiaries. The responsibilities should address each of the following matters:

- how investee companies will be monitored. For monitoring to be effective, there should be an active dialogue with the company's board and senior management
- the policy for requiring investee companies to comply with the core requirements of the Combined Code
- the policy for meeting an investee company's board and senior management.
- the strategy on intervention
- an indication of the circumstances when further action might be taken and what the nature of that action might be
- the policy on voting.

Institutional shareholders and their agents (fund managers) should agree which of them should discharge these responsibilities and arrangements for agents to report back.

Monitoring performance

Institutional shareholders and/or their agents will review annual reports and accounts, circulars issued by companies and general meeting resolutions. They may attend general meetings where they may raise questions. Investee companies will also be monitored to decide when and if it is necessary to enter into an active dialogue with its board and senior management. The monitoring process should include measures to obtain satisfaction that the company's board of directors and sub-committees are effective, and that the non-executive directors have 'adequate oversight'.

Institutional investors must remain aware that if they become too involved in the affairs of a company and too knowledgeable (i.e. in receipt of information that has not been publicly disclosed), they could become insiders. As insiders they would be restricted from dealing in the company's shares under the insider dealing legislation (Criminal Justice Act 1993) or market abuse legislation (Financial Services and Markets Act 2000).

> *In summary, institutional shareholders … will endeavour to identify problems at an early stage to minimise any loss in shareholder value. If they have concerns and do not propose to sell their holdings, they will seek to ensure that the appropriate members of the investee company's board are made aware of them. It may not be sufficient just to inform the Chairman and/or Chief Executive. However, institutional shareholders … may not wish to be made insiders. Institutional shareholders … will expect investee companies to ensure that information that could affect their ability to deal in the shares of the company is not conveyed to them without their agreement.*

Intervention

Effective monitoring of investee companies will enable institutional investors to exercise their votes, and if necessary intervene, in an informed way. Institutional investors should set out the circumstances in which they will actively intervene, which might be in connection with concerns about:

- strategy
- company performance
- the company's acquisitions or disposals strategy
- a failure by the NEDs to hold executive management properly to account
- a failure of internal controls
- an unjustifiable failure to comply with the Combined Code
- inadequate remuneration policy/packages
- inadequate succession planning or
- the company's approach to corporate social responsibility.

Institutional shareholders should vote all their shares at general meetings. They should not automatically support the board, and if they have been unable to obtain a resolution of their concern, they should either abstain or vote against the appropriate resolution. It is good practice to notify the company about this voting intention in advance, giving the reasons why.

Evaluating and reporting
Institutional shareholders should monitor and evaluate the effects of their activism. Their agents (fund managers) should report regularly to their clients (institutional investors) giving details on how they have discharged their responsibilities.

However, the Code does not make it mandatory for institutions to vote at general meetings, although voting is recommended 'where practicable' and institutions must be prepared to intervene 'where necessary'.

This initiative by the ISC was seen at the time as an attempt by institutional investors to avoid legislation by the government compelling them to become more active in exercising their shareholders' rights. The head of investment affairs at the ABI was reported to have commented, with respect to voting against the board of directors if they did not respond to shareholder concerns: 'We will have a red card in the pocket and we will not be afraid to use it. Clearly, we hope this will focus minds on improving shareholder value.'

7.2 NAPF corporate governance policy

The National Association of Pension Funds published a document in December 2003 setting out its policy on corporate governance, following a comprehensive review. This policy will be the basis for research and recommendations on how to vote at company meetings by Research Recommendations and Electronic Voting (RREV), a corporate governance organisation (and voting advisory service) established jointly by NAPF and Institutional Shareholder Services (ISS) in January 2004. This policy was reviewed but not amended substantially, at the end of 2004.

The NAPF policy document consists of a number of underlying principles and additional issues of general guidance, and a lengthy list of voting guidelines.

Its *underlying principles*, not surprisingly, are based on the view that the NAPF wants the companies in which its members invest to succeed:

- The interests of management should be aligned with the long-term interests of shareholders; therefore managers should hold shares in the business for which they are responsible.
- The board of directors is the agent of the owners of the company, its shareholders.
- Shareholders should normally be supportive of management, but should vote against the management if necessary. Confrontation between the shareholders and the board is a sign of failure.

- The NAPF gives robust support to the Combined Code, but has some 'minimal' additional requirements.

Additional issues listed in the NAPF document include:

- Informed use of votes is an obligation on shareholders, even though it is not a legal duty. Active voting by shareholders is therefore recommended.
- Engagement by shareholders with their companies is a necessary part of good ownership.
- Shareholders should expect companies to comply with the Combined Code wherever appropriate, and to explain clearly the reasons for any non-compliance. 'Boiler plate' excuses for non-compliance will not be sufficient.
- The NAPF gives full support to the role of independent NEDs. 'The status of Independent Non-Executive Directors is a bastion of security for shareholders.'

To this end, the NAPF *voting guidelines* are largely supportive of the Combined Code, but some of the specific guidelines are worth noting:

- Companies should implement the proposals of Higgs on the size, balance and structure of boards (as set out in the revised Combined Code) by 31 October 2004 at the latest.
- *Appraisal of performance of board members*. Annual reports should confirm that any directors proposed for re-election at the AGM has recently had a performance evaluation.
- *Remuneration of directors*. The NAPF calls on companies to publish data on the ratio between the pay of directors and the pay of other workers in the company, and to provide an explanation of remuneration policy.
- *Directors' contracts*. Executive directors should not be employed without a contract.

The NAPF has indicated that it will follow a policy of recommending active voting to its members. If explanations by companies for non-compliance with its governance policies are unsatisfactory, it could recommend voting against the re-election of the chairman, senior independent director or chairman of the board's nomination committee.

The Statement of Underlying Principles and Additional Issues from the NAPF Corporate Governance Policy are reproduced in full in Appendix 17.

7.3 ABI Guidelines

The following principles are included in the ABI's Guidelines to its members:

- Shareholders should be concerned about the composition and structure of the board of directors and should support the role played by non-executive directors and the creation of remuneration, audit and nominations committees.
- Shareholders should practise responsible voting. Responsible voting is defined as the application of informed decisions about how to vote, within the framework of a

'considered' corporate governance policy. This policy should be based on the principles and provisions in the Combined Code. As a guiding rule, the board of directors should be given positive support by shareholders, unless there are reasons for voting against any particular resolution. The ABI argued that positive support from institutional shareholders over a period of time should alert the board to the importance of retaining and maintaining this support and should make the board concerned whenever this support is not given on any particular issue. The guidelines also recommend that whenever an institutional investor judges it appropriate to vote against a resolution at a general meeting, it is important if possible to let the company know in advance. This will give time for the problem to be considered by the board and for consultations to take place before the vote.

- Although shareholders are recommended to support the board of directors, the ABI guidelines also suggest that they should also be ready to defend their rights and interests. Shareholders should support incentive schemes for executives, but within prudent limits that avoid excessive dilution of the earnings of existing shareholders. Performance-related incentive schemes that align the interests of the executives and the shareholders are favoured. The guidelines also express concern about arrangements that provide for excessive amounts of new shares to be issued by a company to persons other than existing shareholders, for example, under share option schemes. Members are recommended to oppose any resolution by a company that would give the directors authority to issue new shares except by way of a rights issue, where the number of new 'non-rights issue' shares would exceed a certain limit. The limit is set at 5 per cent of the issued share capital in any one year and 7.5 per cent of the issued share capital over any rolling three-year period.

7.4 ICGN Guidelines for members

In 2003, the International Corporate Governance Network (www.icgn.org), a group of major international institutional investors, published a similar statement on the responsibilities of institutional investors.

The ICGN statement is compatible with the more detailed corporate governance practices in different countries. It comments:

> *Institutional investors have a general responsibility to ensure that investments are managed exclusively in the financial interests of their beneficiaries … As a matter of best practice, in discharging this responsibility, institutional shareholders should contribute to improving and upholding the corporate governance of companies and markets in which they invest.*

However, the scale of their involvement with any individual company will depend on considerations of cost-effectiveness.

The aim of their involvement should be the preservation and growth of the long-term value of the companies in which they invest. Appropriate actions for discharging their responsibilities might be:

- voting
- supporting the company in respect of good corporate governance
- maintaining constructive communications with the board on governance policies and practices in general
- expressing specific concerns to the board, either directly or in shareholders' meetings
- making a public statement
- submitting proposals for inclusion on the agenda of a general meeting
- submitting a nominee for appointment to the board
- convening a shareholders' meeting
- forming an alliance with other investment organisations, either in general or in specific cases
- taking legal action
- lobbying the government
- including corporate governance issues in the investment decision process.

As a general rule, however, institutional shareholders should not interfere in the day-to-day management of companies.

The ICGN considers that showing concern about good corporate governance is a key issue. 'It is clear that institutions risk failing to meet their responsibilities as fiduciaries if they disregard serious corporate governance concerns that may affect the long-term value of their investment.'

8 Electronic communications with shareholders

It has been argued that communications between companies and shareholders (both ways) could be improved with greater use of electronic methods, particularly web-sites and e-mail.

- Companies should be able to communicate more effectively with their shareholders, and provide a greater range and depth of information more quickly than they could using written communications by post.
- Shareholders might be more willing to participate in voting at general meetings if they are able to submit proxy votes conveniently by e-mail or via the company's web-site, rather than by voting form and post.

8.1 UK law on electronic communications

The Electronic Communications Act 2000 legalised 'e-signatures' and the Companies Act 1985 (Electronic Communication) Order 2000 gives companies and shareholders the option of communicating electronically in some instances where communication in writing was previously compulsory.

- A company can *seek the agreement of its shareholders* to the distribution of certain documents either through electronic communications (e.g. e-mail) or by web-site, rather than in writing. These documents include the annual accounts and notices of meetings.
- Shareholders may also be permitted to appoint proxies electronically, by e-mail or fax, to vote on their behalf at general meetings. However, the law does not (yet) permit shareholders or their proxies to vote electronically.

Changes to permit electronic communications need the agreement of the shareholders, but are voluntary. There is no requirement for a change to the Articles of Association for the Order to take effect.

8.2 ICSA guidelines on electronic communications with shareholders

The ICSA has issued a Best Practice Guide, *Electronic Communications with Shareholders*, relating to the Order (see Appendix 18). The points of Recommended Best Practice include the following:

- A company should amend its Articles specifically to provide for the use of electronic communications with shareholders (even though this is not a legal requirement).
- The facility should be offered to all shareholders on equal terms. Provision of the facility should not discriminate between shareholders (i.e. those using the facility and those not doing so).
- Shareholders should be given the option to continue to receive communications through the post, in hard copy form. The invitation to use electronic communications should be repeated at least once a year to those shareholders who continue to receive hard copy material.
- When the information available electronically on a web-site includes notice of a general meeting, the 'notice of availability' sent to the shareholders should draw attention to this fact, together with the date, time and location of the meeting, the deadline for submitting proxy votes and details of any special business to be raised at the meeting. (Note: a 'notice of availability' is the message to the shareholder giving notification that new information is available on the company's web-site. The notice should include a hyperlink to the web-site, to make it easier for the recipient of the message to access the information.)
- When information or notifications of availability (of information on the web-site) are sent out to shareholders, the company should use a system for producing a list of recipients or a total number of messages sent, as 'proof of sending'.
- When shareholders are able to appoint proxies electronically, each shareholder should be allocated a discrete identifier which must be entered on the electronic proxy form.
- Where a poll is not demanded for a resolution, electronic proxy forms should be retained for one month after the meeting. Where a poll is demanded, the forms should be retained for one year.

- Shareholders opting to communicate electronically should be warned that if they file an electronic proxy voting form containing a virus, the company will not accept it.
- The company should alert shareholders to the fact that the company's obligation to communicate electronically ends with the transmission of the message, and the company cannot be responsible for failed transmissions that are outside their control. However, in the case of failed transmissions, the company should send a written communication to the shareholder within 48 hours of the failure.
- Shareholders not wishing to communicate electronically should continue to have the option of receiving communications in writing by post. However, the company should re-issue its invitation to them to communicate electronically at least once a year, normally with the notice of the next annual general meeting.

9 Voting and proxy votes

9.1 Responsible voting

The meaning of 'responsible voting' is well defined in a joint statement (1999) by the Association of British Insurers and the National Association of Pension Funds: 'Responsible voting involves the application of informed decisions reached within the framework of considered corporate governance policy.'

Institutional shareholders should support the board of directors unless they have good reason not to. When a shareholder thinks that it should vote against the board, it should first make representations to the board in time for the problem to be considered, with a view to reaching a satisfactory solution.

The ABI and NAPF guidelines to their members support of the principle of responsible voting, and these organisations also liaise closely with members through their respective voting (advisory) services.

9.2 The Myners Report to the Shareholder Voting Working Party

In January 2004 Paul Myners, chairman of the Shareholder Voting Working Party, published a report: *Review of the Impediments to Voting UK Shares*. The review was prompted by continuing concerns about 'lost' proxy votes. There are known to be instances where the votes of shares have not been received at the company general meeting, even though the beneficial owners had wanted to vote.

The Report identified four key issues:

1. It would appear that the beneficial owners of shares do not give sufficient attention to voting. The voting chain can be complex, but the same system is used for corporate actions and works much better for these.
2. The existing voting system is largely paper-based and prone to error. The Newbold Report in 1999 (sponsored by the NAPF) and a report by the Shareholder Voting

Working Group in 2001 recommended the use of electronic voting. In January 2003, CRESTCo introduced a system for recording proxy votes electronically, but the initial take-up by the date of the Myners report had been disappointing.

3 Custodians often hold shares for investment managers or beneficial owners in an omnibus nominee account. The nominee account is the legal owner of the shares and so has the voting entitlement. When shares are held in an omnibus nominee account, there is no clear audit trail as to who is the beneficial owner of the shares. It is therefore difficult for the beneficial owner to arrange for its voting instructions to be carried out. This problem does not exist when the custodian holds the shares for a client in a designated nominee account.
4 Section 372(5) of the Companies Act 1985 requires companies to fix the latest time for receiving proxy votes as no more than 48 hours before the general meeting. The Uncertificated Securities Regulations state:

> *for the purposes of determining which persons are entitled to attend or vote at a meeting, and how many votes such persons may cast, the … issuer may specify in the notice of the meeting a time, not more than 48 hours before the time fixed for the meeting, by which a person must be entered on the relevant register of securities in order to have the right to attend and vote at the meeting.*

Arguably, 48 hours is an insufficient time to avoid administrative difficulties and the 'record date' – i.e. the date on which voting entitlements are set – should be longer than 48 hours before the meeting.

9.3 Recommendations in the Myners Report

The Myners Report made several recommendations, to the members of the Shareholder Voting Working Group and its sponsoring organisations.

Beneficial owners

Beneficial owners of shares should ensure that their agreements with parties that are accountable to them (e.g. investment managers and custodians):

1 include specific service standards for voting
2 establish a chain of responsibility for voting and an information flow that enables all the parties to meet their responsibilities, and
3 require those that are responsible to report back on how they have discharged their obligations.

They should also decide a voting policy and ensure that it is implemented. In this respect, an institution should speak with one voice:

> *There are concerns that, on occasion, those responsible for voting issues are presented … as the institution's voice on the issue, when they might not necessarily represent the*

> *views of the portfolio manager ... with whom the issuer's management have been encouraged to communicate ... Within the investing institution, the left hand appears to be disconnected from the right hand.*

The Report also supports the ISC Principle that institutional investors should have a 'stated and regularly reviewed policy on voting UK shares which is public'.

Beneficial owners should make enquiries within the next three months as to whether their agents and others will have introduced electronic voting facilities before the end of 2004.

They should consider requiring their shares to be registered by its custodian in a designated nominee account.

They should hold the investment manager to account for the manner in which the votes have been cast.

Electronic voting

The Report recommended the adoption of electronic voting:

> *I firmly believe electronic voting will enhance the efficiency of the process for voting UK shares and reduce the extent to which votes are 'lost'. The slow take-up of electronic voting in 2003 was unsatisfactory ... Issuers in at least the FTSE 350, investment managers, custodians and proxy voting agencies should all have introduced, or introduce, the necessary system changes so that electronic voting capabilities are universally available as soon as practicable. Furthermore beneficial owners should over the next three months make direct and specific enquiries of their agents ... to establish the extent to which they have, or will have, introduced electronic voting capabilities to be used this year.*

Stock lending

The beneficial owners of shares should be fully aware of the implications of stock lending. If the shares they own beneficially are lent, the legal ownership passes for the duration of the 'loan' to the other party, and the right to vote is temporarily lost. This is because the legal nature of a stock lending agreement is an absolute transfer of title against an irrevocable undertaking to return equivalent securities at a future date. The Report also comments: 'I am aware that on occasion shares can be borrowed for the express purpose of acquiring votes.'

The Report recommends that:

> *Borrowing of shares for the purpose of voting is not appropriate, as it gives a proportion of the vote to an agent which has no relation to the agent's economic stake in the company.... It is important that beneficial owners are fully aware of the implications for voting if they agree to their shares being lent. In particular, when a resolution is contentious I start from the position that the lender should automatically recall the related stock, unless there are good economic reasons for not doing so.*

Investment managers

Investment managers should report to their clients on how they have executed their voting responsibilities. However, the Report did not recommend that investment managers should be required to make public how they have voted. Mr Myners commented: 'I am not yet persuaded that public disclosure should be made mandatory but believe that the market will increasingly expect such disclosure.'

The Report also recommended that investment managers should introduce electronic voting capabilities in 2004 if they had not done so already.

On the issue of stock lending, they should:

- automatically recall lent stock when a resolution at a forthcoming general meeting is contentious, and
- not vote stock held as collateral.

Procedures at company meetings

The Report made several recommendations with the intention of giving proxies more voice at company meetings.

The Table A Articles of Association (Regulation 46) provide that unless a poll is called, a resolution voted at a company meeting should be decided on a show of hands, with one vote per member present but excluding proxies in attendance (unless the Articles provide otherwise).

Table A also states that a poll may be called by:

- the chairman
- two members either present in person or represented by a proxy
- a member or members representing not less than 10 per cent of the total voting rights.

Most proxy forms name the 'chairman of the meeting' as the default proxy, and most shareholders appoint the chairman as their proxy at the meeting. There is no statutory definition of the chairman's role as proxy or his obligations to call for a poll. A chairman has a duty to 'ascertain the true sense of the meeting' (*Second Consolidated Trust Ltd v Ceylon Amalgamated Tea and Rubber Estates Ltd* (1942)). Where a chairman as proxy is aware that if a poll were to be called, the outcome would be different from that reached on a show of hands, he has a duty to call a poll if permitted to do so under the articles of association.

The Report found the current situation unsatisfactory and made the following recommendations:

- On the basis that attendance at company meetings can be unrepresentative, and in the interests of transparency and equity, a poll should be called on *all resolutions* at company meetings.
- Companies should disclose, on their web-sites and in summary in annual reports, the results of polls at general meetings.

- The Listing Rules (Rule 13.28) require companies to issue proxy forms that provide for two-way voting ('for' or 'against') on all issues, but the Report stated that 'the existence of a significant number of *votes consciously withheld* evidences the existence of concerns'. It therefore recommended that proxy forms should provide a 'vote withheld' box and when declaring the results of a poll a company should publish the number of votes received, the numbers 'for' and 'against' the resolution and the number of votes consciously withheld. However, in accordance with the current legal position, only the votes 'for' and 'against' should be taken into account when deciding whether or not the resolution has been carried.
- Section 372 of the Companies Act 1985 provides that members are entitled to appoint a proxy to attend a company meeting and vote on their behalf, but a proxy has the right to speak at a meeting only in the case of a private company. Unless the articles of association provide otherwise, a proxy can only vote on a poll, not a show of hands. The Report recommended that company law should be changed to give more rights to proxies, so that they can speak and vote on a show of hands as well as a poll. Until the law is changed, companies should be encouraged to allow proxies to speak and vote on a show of hands, and if necessary amend their articles to allow this to happen.

9.4 ICSA Guidance Notes on shareholder voting

Some of the recommendations in the Myners have since been developed by the ICSA in two guidance notes.

ICSA *Guidance Note:* Proxy Voting: Abstentions

An ICSA Guidance Note on proxy voting and abstentions was published in August 2004. It noted that institutional shareholders, following the Myners Report, are under increasing pressure to vote by proxy and to reveal their voting record to their beneficial investors. Since some institutional investors might actually want to abstain from voting on a particular resolution, the ICSA has recommended that proxy voting forms should allow shareholders four choices, for each resolution:

- instructing the proxy to vote for the resolution
- instructing the proxy to vote against the resolution
- giving a 'vote withheld' instruction, as a positive abstention from voting
- giving the proxy discretion in the way that he or she votes.

ICSA *Guidance Note:* Disclosing proxy votes

The ICSA published another guidance note, also in August 2004, on best practice for companies on disclosing proxy voting details. It supports the view stated in the Hampel Report that disclosure of proxy votes, after the resolution has been decided on a show of hands, will provide information about the total number of votes for which proxy voting instructions had been received and the weight of shareholder opinion revealed by those votes. 'Publication is thus likely to encourage an increase in shareholder voting' (Hampel Report).

The Guidance Note suggests that best practice is for companies to publish details of proxy votes for each resolution:

- on paper, for handing out to shareholders at the end of a general meeting, and
- on the company's web-site, for a reasonable period of time after the general meeting.

The guidance note also considers the point in the Combined Code that the company should count all proxy votes (except where a poll is called for), indicate the proxy votes for and against and the number of abstentions. Although it would be possible to disclose the actual number of abstentions, the Guidance Note suggests that the information disclosed should leave it to the user to calculate the number of abstentions. The recommended disclosures are:

- the total number of issued shares with voting entitlements and the number of shares for which proxy voting instructions were received, and
- for each resolution, of the proxy votes cast for or against the resolution, the number and percentage (1) voting for, (2) voting against and (3) cast by the chairman with discretionary voting power.

The sum of (1), (2) and (3) is always 100 per cent, and the number of abstentions is calculated as the difference between the total number of votes cast for the resolution and the number of shares for which proxy voting instructions were received.

CHAPTER

8 Reporting and Disclosure

1 Governance, reporting and disclosure

An essential feature of good corporate governance is communication between a company and its shareholders (and other stakeholders). A large element of communication is reporting to shareholders and the disclosure of information that might be relevant to shareholders in making decisions about their investment in the company.

Reporting by companies to the shareholders, and the nature of the disclosures in reports, have been based in the past almost exclusively on financial reporting. With the development of good practice in corporate governance, measures have been introduced to:

- improve the reliability of financial reporting (for example, with the clarification of the role of the audit committee)
- inform shareholders about risk as well as returns, and to satisfy shareholders that the company has adequate risk management systems in place (for example, with the disclosure requirements for the Operating and Financial Review and the Combined Code requirement for an annual review of internal control and risk management systems by the board)
- provide more financial information, or financial information in a more understandable form (for example, with the disclosure requirements for the Operating and Financial Review and the Directors' Remuneration Report Regulations)
- provide more information of a non-financial nature.

This chapter provides a review of disclosure requirements that are associated with measures to enhance corporate governance. The disclosure requirements for companies have developed over time. They are a mixture of statutory and other regulatory requirements together with voluntary disclosures.

2 The annual report and accounts

The requirement for companies (with some exceptions) to prepare an annual report and accounts remains a key element of the reporting by companies to their shareholders.

Section 226 of the Companies Act 1985 states that individual companies have a duty to prepare a balance sheet and a profit and loss account, and Section 227 imposes the requirement on parent companies to prepare consolidated accounts for the group as a whole. Section 234 contains the requirement for companies to prepare a directors' report, containing:

- a fair review of the development of the company and its subsidiaries during the year, and the company's or group's financial position as at the end of the year, and
- the amount that the directors recommend should be paid as a final dividend for the year.

All shareholders and debenture holders are entitled to receive a copy of the annual report and accounts (s238) and the directors must lay the accounts before the company at the annual general meeting (s241).

The Companies Act includes some specifications about the format and content of financial reports. The statutory requirements are extended substantially by financial reporting standards, such as the requirements for companies to include a cash flow statement and a statement of changes in equity in the annual financial statements, and to report the earnings per share for the financial year.

Financial reporting and external audit are covered in detail in Chapter 9.

3 The UK Listing Rules

The UK Listing Rules extend the reporting and disclosure requirements for listed companies, and are a significant element in the corporate governance framework in the UK.

3.1 UK Listing Rules and financial reporting

Chapter 12 of the Listing Rules extend the financial reporting requirements:

- Companies are required to prepare a half-yearly financial report on their activities and profit for the first six months of their financial year (Rule 12.46). This is the interim statement. The minimum contents of the interim statement are also set out in the Listing Rules.
- Companies are required to make a preliminary statement of their annual results and dividends through a Regulatory Information Service within 120 days of the end of the period to which the results relate (Rule 12.40).

- Certain information which must be included in the annual report and accounts, in addition to the requirements of the Companies Act and financial reporting standards, is set out in Rule 12.42. This includes a requirement that if the results in the period under review differ by 10 per cent or more from any published forecast or estimate previously made by the company, the company should provide an explanation of the difference.

Listed companies are required to make announcements to the stock market, through a Regulatory Information Service, of any major new development which is not public knowledge and which, by virtue of its effect:

- may lead to a substantial movement in the value in the market price of the company's listed securities, or
- in the case of debt securities, may affect the ability of the company to meet its financial commitments.

Companies are also required to announce to the stock market:

- changes in their financial condition
- changes in their performance or
- changes in the company's expectations of its future performance,

which, if the information were to become public knowledge, might lead to a substantial movement in the value in the market price of the company's listed securities.

Other disclosure requirements in the Listing Rules, which companies must announce to the market through a Regulatory Information Service, include:

- changes relating to their capital (such as alterations in capital structure): (Rule 9.10)
- changes in major interests in shares of the companies (in connection with Sections 198–208 of the Companies Act): (Rule 9.11)
- changes in the shareholdings of directors and connected persons, such as the sale or purchase of shares and the granting of share options): (Rule 16.13).

A consequence of the UK Listing Requirements for disclosures through a Regulatory Information Service, and for an interim statement, is that listed companies are required to make more reports and disclosures to their shareholders and the market throughout the year, and not just provide an annual historical statement of financial results.

3.2 The going concern statement

Listed companies incorporated in the UK must include a statement by the directors in its annual report that the business is a going concern. This statement must be reviewed by the auditors before publication (Rule 12.42).

The requirement for directors to report that the business is a going concern, with supporting assumptions and qualifications as necessary, is also a provision of the Combined Code (Provision C.1.2). Although the Combined Code duplicates the UK Listing Rules in this respect, the Code may be applied by non-listed companies. A sample going concern statement is given in Chapter 9.

3.3 The UK Listing Rules and the Model Code

The UK Listing Rules require listed companies to apply rules for dealing in the companies shares by directors that are no less stringent than the Model Code.

The Code states that directors should not deal in shares of the company during certain close periods, except in exceptional circumstances. The Listing Rules impose the disclosure requirement that if a director is permitted to deal in the company's shares during a close period, the company should provide the stock market through a Regulatory Information Service with a statement of what those exceptional circumstances were (Rule 16.16). (See coverage of insider dealing in Chapter 2.)

3.4 The UK Listing Rules: comply or explain

The UK Listing Rules add further support to the corporate governance regime in the UK by requiring disclosure by listed companies of the extent of their compliance or non-compliance with the Combined Code.

The Combined Code consists of Main Principles, Supporting Principles and practical provisions:

- A UK listed company must include in its annual report and accounts a narrative statement of how it has applied the *principles* of the Combined Code, providing an explanation that enables the shareholders to evaluate how the principles have been applied (Rule 12.43(a)).
- A UK listed company must include in its annual report and accounts a statement as to whether or not it has complied throughout the accounting period with the *provisions* of the Combined Code. If a company has not complied with the Code provisions, or has complied with only some of them or has complied for only a part of the accounting period, it must specify:
  - which provisions it has not complied with
  - where relevant, for what part of the accounting period the non-compliance continued.

It must also give reasons for the non-compliance (Rule 12.43(b)). Rule 12.43(b) is the so-called 'comply or explain' rule.

Examples of compliance statements

Statements about compliance with the Combined Code, in accordance with the 'comply or explain' requirement of the Listing Rules, vary in their wording. Examples of compliance statements, relating to the 1998 Combined Code, are shown below:

> *Diageo's board and executive committee are committed to achieving the highest standards of corporate governance, corporate responsibility and risk management in directing and controlling the business. They are pleased to report that the company has complied throughout the year with the provisions of Section 1 of the Combined Code on Corporate Governance issued in 1998.... The Combined Code was substantially revised during the year.... The board reviewed its corporate governance practices during the year in the light of the new code and US regulatory changes, and implemented a number of changes, which are disclosed below. The new Code applies to Diageo's financial year beginning on 1 July 2004 and accordingly the board will report on compliance with the new Code next year.*
>
> *(Diageo plc, 2004 annual report)*

> *The directors consider that for the year ended 3 April 2004 the company complied with all the provisions of the existing Code and has put in place procedures to enable it to report future compliance with the new Code, which takes effect for Marks & Spencer from 4 April 2004.*
>
> *(Marks & Spencer plc, 2004 annual report)*

> *As a Company listed on the official list of the London Stock Exchange, Barclays is required to state how it has applied the principles in the United Kingdom Listing Authority's Combined Code on Corporate Governance or, where these have not been applied, to provide an explanation accordingly.*
>
> *For the year ended 31st December 2003, Barclays complied with the existing Combined Code save for the formal appointment of a Senior Executive Director. As set out in our letter to shareholders on 6th November 2003, making such an appointment is a priority for the Board during 2004. However, the Group has in Sir Brian Jenkins a Deputy Chairman and independent non-executive director who is available as a point of contact for shareholders if required.*
>
> *(Barclays Bank plc, 2003 annual report)*

4 Directors' remuneration report

Prior to the Directors' Remuneration Report Regulations 2002, disclosure requirements relating to directors' remuneration were provided by the UK Listing Rules and the Combined Code.

The effect of the Regulations has been to replace the former disclosure requirements with statutory requirements in the Companies Act. These can be summarised as follows:

- The directors of a quoted company should prepare a directors' remuneration report each year, containing information specified in Schedule 7A of the Companies Act. The information not subject to audit is listed in Part 2 of Schedule 7A and the information subject to audit is listed in Part 3 of the Schedule (s234B Companies Act 1985).
- Information required to be shown in the report in respect of a particular individual should link the information to that individual by name (Schedule 7A, Part 1 Companies Act).
- The information to be disclosed in the remuneration report includes details of the remuneration committee. If the company has a remuneration committee, the directors' remuneration report should include:
  - the name of each committee member
  - the name of any person who provided advice or services to the committee that was of material assistance, and in the case of these persons who are not directors, the nature of the services provided and whether that person was appointed by the committee (Schedule 7A, Part 2 Companies Act).
- The directors' remuneration report should be approved by the board, and signed by a director and the company secretary (s234C). A signed copy should be delivered to the registrar (s242).
- At the annual general meeting, shareholders should vote on an ordinary resolution approving the directors' remuneration report for the year. However, no entitlement of a person to remuneration should be conditional on the resolution being passed (s241A).

Directors' remuneration is covered in more detail in Chapter 6.

5 The Operating and Financial Review (OFR)

Financial statements are historical in outlook and contain no non-financial information. Although they help users to understand the prospects for the company, it is argued that more information should be provided to give users a much better understanding. This information can be provided in an annual Operating and Financial Review (OFR) by the company.

It has been best practice for some years for listed companies to publish an OFR with their annual report and accounts, and a statement of best practice has been issued by the Accounting Standards Board (revised 2003).

Draft Regulations have now been issued, containing proposals to amend the Companies Act and require all quoted companies to include an OFR in their annual report and accounts, for reporting years starting on or after 1 April 2005. (For quoted companies with a financial year ending 31 December, the first mandatory OFR would therefore be for the year ending 31 December 2006.)

Where shareholders have agreed to receive summary financial statements, companies are not required to send them the full OFR. Instead, these shareholders should be notified of the availability of the OFR on the company's web-site.

The government proposals are based on the White Paper, *Modernising Company Law* (2002). This stated the following fundamental principles for an OFR:

- There should be a statutory requirement to publish an OFR each year. Publishing an OFR should not simply be a matter of 'best practice'.
- It should be mandatory for the largest companies.
- It should contain certain information to meet a 'high level objective of greater transparency'.
- In addition, it should also reflect those matters on which, in the opinion of the board of directors, are relevant to an understanding of the company.

It is also intended that the OFR Regulations should implement certain requirements of the EU's Accounts Modernisation Directive 2003, which calls for the publication of certain information by companies of medium size or larger. 'Medium-sized' is defined by reference to company law. In the UK, a company is either small or medium-sized if it meets at least two of the three requirements set out below:

	Small	***Medium-sized***
Annual turnover	Not more than £5.6 million	Not more than £22.8 million
Balance sheet net assets	Not more than £2.8 million	Not more than £11.4 million
Number of employees	Not more than 50	Not more than 250

The Directive requires medium-sized and large companies:

- to report on the principal risks and uncertainties facing their businesses, and
- to include key performance indicators relevant to their particular business.

The Directive allows for governments to allow an exemption to medium-sized companies from giving some of the non-financial reporting information.

5.1 Contents of an OFR

The Regulations for quoted companies to produce an OFR each year will be introduced by statutory instrument, amending the Companies Act 1985. There will be a new Schedule 7ZA to the Act, specifying the contents of the Review. Some minimum requirements must be included, but the directors should use their judgement deciding what additional information would be appropriate for disclosure.

The Regulations state that the OFR should provide a balanced and comprehensive analysis, for the company and its subsidiaries, of:

- the development and performance of the business during the financial year
- the position as at the end of the year
- the main trends and factors underlying the development, performance and position of the business during the financial year
- the main trends and factors likely to affect the development, performance and position of the business in the future.

As a minimum requirement, an OFR should include, for the company and its subsidiaries:

- a statement of the business, its objectives and strategy
- a description of the resources available to them
- a description of the main risks and uncertainties facing them
- a description of the capital structure, treasury policies and liquidity of the company and its subsidiaries.

However, the information in an OFR must be sufficient to enable shareholders to assess the strategies of the company and their potential to succeed. Beyond these minimum requirements, the Regulations state that the OFR should include additional information 'to the extent necessary to comply with these general requirements'.

The further information that should therefore be included will vary between companies, but might relate, for example, to the following:

- employees
- environmental matters
- social and community issues
- business relationships
- receipts from and returns to shareholders
- key performance indicators (both financial and non-financial in nature, for example, relating to employee and environmental matters).

The directors must use their judgement in deciding what to include and exclude. The information included in the Review is likely to be a mix of quantitative and qualitative information and financial and non-financial information.

At the time of writing, the OFR Regulations have not yet been introduced, and some changes are expected to the draft Regulations. In a written statement to the House of Commons, the Secretary of State confirmed that directors will be expected to be open and candid with the information that they include in the OFR, and they will be able to make a distinction between:

- statements made in good faith, and
- statements made on the basis of objectively verifiable data.

Guidance notes to the OFR can then alert users to treat with caution those statements made on the basis of good faith.

5.2 Other proposals for the OFR

The draft OFR Regulations also included the following provisions:

- Responsibility for *enforcing* the new regulations should be given to the Financial Reporting Review Panel (FRRP).
- The Accounting Standards Board (a part of the Financial Reporting Council) should be responsible for issuing Standards for the preparation of the OFR. These Standards should have the same authority as accounting standards.
- The directors should be required to state whether the OFR has been prepared in accordance with the OFR Standards, and to explain any departures from them.
- There should be a criminal offence, punishable by a fine, of 'recklessly approving an OFR'.

The original draft Regulations also included a requirement that the external auditors should be required to express an opinion 'after due and careful enquiry' on the process that has been followed by the directors in producing the OFR, and the propriety of the process used. The original proposals also stated that the auditors should review the 'process' involved in preparing the OFR. However, it was recognised that this might deter directors from reporting openly.

The Regulations were therefore changed to the less stringent requirement that directors should act with 'due care, skill and diligence' in preparing the OFR, and that the external auditors should state whether the information in the OFR is consistent with the financial statements and any other matters that might have come to their attention during their audit.

5.3 *The Operating and Financial Review: Practical Guidance for Directors*

In December 2002, the DTI set up a working group under the leadership of Rosemary Radcliffe, which published *The Operating and Financial Review: Practical Guidance for Directors* during 2004, after the publication of the draft Regulations.

The Guidance report addresses some of the key issues about deciding what to include in the report. Some of the Guidance is set out below:

- The OFR should cover long-term as well as short-term issues. A mandatory OFR, 'by emphasising the need for directors to think and manage in this broader context and to report accordingly, has the capacity to enhance corporate performance and bring, as a consequence, substantial benefits to shareholders and all other stakeholders'.
- Although the OFR Regulations themselves state that the aim of the OFR is to enable the shareholders to assess the company's strategies, the Guidance suggests that the directors should take a broader view and consider all stakeholders. It gives as an example producers and retailers of foodstuffs, who might need to address in the OFR customers' concerns about the health implications of pesticides in foods, or more general concerns about obesity and genetically modified foods. Failure to address these concerns could damage perceptions by customers of the producer's or retailer's brands.
- The board should act collectively: 'Whatever arrangements may be made for doing the detailed work of preparation, the whole board will want to be involved in the process of deciding what should and should not be included in the OFR.'
- 'A balance between historic [*sic*] review and a focus on the future is key to the OFR.... Directors will have to strike a balance between analysis of past and present performance and discussions of trends and likely future performance.' The directors will also have to decide the appropriate time period for looking at future performance. This is likely to vary according to the length of the life cycle of the company's business operations.
- The OFR will include quantitative and qualitative data, and financial and non-financial data. There should also be appropriate performance indicators, measured quantitatively wherever possible. However, the Guidance gives a company's plans to embark on a new business venture as an example of when qualitative data could be very important. A qualitative assessment of the depth, breadth and relevance of top management's experience in relation to the venture, and its plans to fill key gaps in this experience, would be vital to an assessment of the venture's chances of success.
- The OFR Regulations require a description of the main risks and uncertainties facing the business to be included in the Review. The Guidance suggests that 'a particularly important issue related to risk is reputational risk. This is inextricably linked to the licence to operate and is a critical value driver. Reputation, and thus competitive advantage, may be won or lost through the ability to deliver

consistently against explicit or implicit promises made to investors and ... customers, suppliers and employees.'

- The nature and size of items to be included in the OFR are a matter of judgement and may depend on particular circumstances. The Guidance gives as an example the resignation of directors from a subsidiary company. If just one director resigns, this would probably not merit any mention in the OFR; however, if a number of directors resign within a short space of time from the same subsidiary, this might well merit disclosure. The key test for deciding whether to include an item should be the potential future significance of the issue.
- There should be consistency in disclosure from one year to the next. This does not mean that if an issue is included once, it should be mentioned in the OFR in every succeeding year. However, if an issue is dropped from the OFR, it will be appropriate to mention the fact and explain the reason.

The Guidance also gives six criteria for assessing the process used for making judgements about what to include in the OFR:

a) The process should be planned, and there should be an emphasis on transparency, with the process being recorded and communicated to everyone involved in preparing the OFR.
b) The process should provide for appropriate consultation within the business (management and other employees) and with shareholders and other key groups.
c) The process should ensure that all relevant existing information and comparators are taken into account, from both internal and external information sources.
d) The process should be comprehensive.
e) The process should be consistent.
f) The process should be subject to review.

The draft Regulations included a requirement for periodic review by the external auditors, who should give an opinion on whether the directors had used 'due and careful enquiry' in preparing the OFR. However, this proposal met with strong resistance, and was dropped.

5.4 The ASB's first exposure draft of a Reporting Standard

The OFR Regulations give the UK Accounting Standards Board the responsibility for issuing Reporting Standards for the OFR, building on its existing statement, *Operating and Financial Review*. The ASB issued an exposure draft for a first Reporting Standard ('RED1') in November 2004. This is intended to provide a basic framework that directors should apply in order to comply with the Regulations; the draft is reproduced in Appendix 19.

In an introductory summary, the draft Reporting Standard states that directors should address the OFR to *investors*, setting out their analysis of the business, with a *forward-looking orientation*, to assist investors to asses the company's strategies and the potential for those strategies to succeed. However, the information provided in the OFR 'will also be of relevance to other stakeholders'.

The draft Reporting Standard sets out several principles essential to the preparation of an OFR:

- The OFR should set out an analysis of the business as seen through the eyes of the board of directors.
- It should focus on matters that are of relevance to investors.
- It should have a forward-looking orientation.
- It should complement and supplement the financial statements 'in order to enhance the overall corporate disclosure'. Where relevant, for example, the OFR should provide additional explanation of amounts recorded in the financial statements.
- It should be comprehensive and understandable. However, this does not mean that the OFR should cover everything. 'The objective is quality, not quantity.'
- The OFR should be balanced and neutral, dealing in an even-handed way with both good and bad aspects.
- It should be comparable over time.

The draft Reporting Standard also sets out a framework for the disclosures to be made in the OFR. This framework is based on the requirements in the draft OFR Regulations, but goes into more detail about the nature of the disclosures.

6 Combined Code disclosure requirements

The provisions of the Combined Code include a variety of disclosure requirements, which are set out as a checklist in Schedule C of the Code.

6.1 Disclosures in the annual report about the board

The annual report should contain:

- a statement of how the board operates, including a high-level statement of which types of decisions are taken by the board and which are delegated to management (Provision A.1.1)
- the name of the chairman, the deputy chairman (where there is one), the chief executive, the senior independent director and the chairmen and members of the nomination, audit and remuneration committees (A.1.2)
- the number of meetings of the board and of these committees, and individual attendance by directors (A.1.2)
- the name of each non-executive director that the board considers to be independent, with reasons where necessary (A.3.1). Although the chairman should meet the

independence criteria on appointment, this test of independence is not relevant to the chairman
- when a new chairman is appointed, his or her other significant commitments and any changes to such commitments during the year (A.4.3)
- details of how the performance evaluation of the board, its committees and its individual directors has been conducted (A.6.1)
- information about the steps the board has taken to ensure that members of the board, and in particular the NEDs, develop an understanding of the views of the major shareholders about their company (D.1.2).

If exceptionally a board decides that a chief executive should become chairman, the board (having consulted major shareholders in advance) should set out its reasons to shareholders in the next annual report (A.2.2).

6.2 Disclosures in the annual report about board committees

The annual report should contain:

- a separate section describing the work of the nomination committee, including the process it has used for board appointments. An explanation should be given if neither an external search consultancy nor open advertising has been used in the appointment of a chairman or a NED (A.4.6).
- a description of the work of the remuneration committee, as required by the Directors' Remuneration Report Regulations (Schedule 7, Companies Act). In addition, when a company releases an executive director to serve as a NED elsewhere, the remuneration report should include a statement as to whether or not the director will retain such earnings and, if so, what the remuneration is (B.1.4).
- a separate section describing the work of the audit committee in discharging its responsibilities (C.3.3).

6.3 Other disclosures in the annual report

The Combined Code also requires other disclosures in the annual report. Some of these may be contained within the report of the audit committee:

- The directors should explain their responsibility for preparing the accounts. There should also be a statement by the auditors about their reporting responsibilities (C.1.1).
- The directors should report that the business is a going concern, with supporting assumptions or qualifications as necessary. (See also the UK Listing Rules, Rule 12.42.)
- At least annually, the board should conduct a review of the group's system of internal controls and should report to shareholders that they have done so (C.2.1). This report to shareholders is likely to be included within the annual report (see Chapter 10).

- Where there is no internal audit function, the audit committee should consider annually whether there is a need for such a function. Where it decides there is no such need, the reasons for the absence of an internal audit function should be included in the relevant section of the annual report (i.e. within the report of the audit committee) (C.3.5).
- If the board does not accept the recommendation of the audit committee on the appointment, re-appointment or removal of the external auditors, there should be a statement from the audit committee explaining their recommendation and setting out the reasons why the board has taken a different position (C.3.6).
- If the external auditor provides non-audit services, there should be a statement about how auditor objectivity and independence are safeguarded (C.3.7).

6.4 Disclosures in papers to shareholders accompanying a recommendation to elect or re-elect a director

In papers to shareholders accompanying a recommendation to elect or re-elect a director, the board should:

- provide sufficient biographical details and any other relevant information, to enable shareholders to make an informed decision on their election (A.7.1)
- in the papers accompanying a resolution to elect a NED, why they believe the individual should be elected (A.7.2).

When proposing re-election of a NED, the chairman should confirm to shareholders that, following formal performance evaluation, the individual's performance continues to be effective and to demonstrate commitment to the role (A.7.2).

6.5 Disclosures in papers to shareholders accompanying a recommendation to appoint or re-appoint the external auditors

In papers to shareholders accompanying a recommendation to appoint or re-appoint the external auditors, if the board has not accepted the recommendation of the audit committee, there should be a statement from the audit committee explaining their recommendation and setting out the reasons why the board has taken a different position (C.3.6).

6.6 Information to be made publicly available

The following information should be made available to the public. This requirement can be met by making the information available on the company's web-site and by making it available on request. The information to be made available is:

- the terms of reference of the nomination committee and the authority delegated to it by the board (A.4.1)

- the terms of reference of the remuneration committee and the authority delegated to it by the board (B.2.1)
- the terms of reference of the audit committee and the authority delegated to it by the board (C.3.3)
- where remuneration consultants are used, a statement of whether they have any other connection with the company (B.2.1).

The terms and conditions of appointment of non-executive directors should be made available for inspection by any person, at the company's registered office during normal business hours and at the AGM, for 15 minutes prior to the meeting and during the meeting (A.4.4).

7 Sustainability reporting

Companies may decide voluntarily to publish a sustainability report (or social and environmental report) each year. These reports are often included within the published annual report and accounts document. These reports, and their content, are described in more detail in Chapter 11.

CHAPTER

9

Financial Reporting and External Audit

1 Financial reporting and corporate governance

Communications with shareholders are a key element in good corporate governance. The main instruments of communication for a listed company are:

- the annual and interim financial statements (and publication of the preliminary announcement of the annual financial results)
- the directors' report
- the Operating and Financial Review (for periods starting on or after 1 April 2005; see Chapter 8)
- voluntary statements and reports, such as a Chairman's statement with the annual report and accounts or a sustainability report
- information placed on the company's web-site.

Non-financial elements of reporting and disclosures are considered in Chapter 8. This chapter focuses on the financial statements of companies, and the corporate governance issues relating to them.

Financial reporting and the external audit of companies lie at the heart of corporate governance. The Cadbury Committee was set up as a direct consequence of concerns about the quality of financial reporting in the UK and the ability of the auditing profession to provide sufficient assurances to the investment community about the reliability of company financial statements.

There are three ways in which published financial statements could be misleading:

1 There could be a fraudulent misrepresentation of the affairs of the company, where the company's management deliberately presents a false picture of the financial position and performance.
2 The company might use accounting policies whereby it presents its reported position and profits more favourably than would be the case if more conservative accounting policies were used.
3 They are historical in outlook, and are not forward-looking in any way. Financial statements contain only financial information, and do not give users any information of a non-financial nature. The financial statements could be complex and difficult for investors to understand. It would be possible, particularly in companies whose business is itself quite complex, to present financial statements in a way that readers will find difficult to comprehend properly.

2 Financial reporting: directors' duties and responsibilities

The directors of a company have certain legal duties with regard to financial reporting:

- They have a duty to prepare annual company accounts and, in the case of a parent company, consolidated accounts for the group (Sections 226–227 of the Companies Act 1985). The annual accounts must be approved by the board and signed by a director on behalf of the board. (Note: The Companies Act states that the period allowed for laying the annual accounts before the company in the AGM and delivering a copy of the accounts to the Registrar is ten months after the end of the relevant financial period for private companies, and seven months for public companies (s244 CA1985). The UK Listing Rules add a further requirement that the preliminary statement of the company's annual financial results must be notified to a Regulatory Information Service within 120 days of the end of the accounting period to which the statement relates (Rule 12.40)).
- They have a duty to prepare a directors' report, which must be approved by the board and signed on its behalf by a director or the company secretary (Sections 234 and 234A).
- The directors of a quoted company have a duty to prepare a directors' remuneration report, which must be approved by the board and signed on its behalf by a director or the company secretary (Sections 234B and 234C).
- These accounts and reports must be laid before the shareholders in general meeting (Section 241) and the shareholders must be invited to approve the directors' remuneration report (Section 241A).
- In respect of each financial year the directors must file with the Registrar of Companies a copy of the annual accounts, the directors' report, the auditors' report and, in the case of quoted companies, the directors' remuneration report (Section 242).

2.1 Combined Code requirements

The Combined Code places additional requirements and responsibilities on the directors with regard to financial reporting, and states that the financial reports should be balanced and understandable:

- Principle C.1 states: 'The board should present a balanced and understandable assessment of the company's position and prospects.' This requirement applies not only to the statutory financial reports, but also to interim reports, other price-sensitive reports and reports to the regulators.
- The directors should explain in the annual report their responsibility for preparing the accounts (Provision C.1.1) (see below).
- The auditors must provide a statement about their reporting responsibilities (Provision C.1.1).
- The directors should also report that the business is a going concern (Provision C.1.2, see below). This requirement is also included in the UK Listing Rules (12.42), which requires listed companies incorporated in the UK to include in the annual report and accounts a statement by the directors that the business is a going concern, 'with supporting assumptions or qualifications as necessary'. This statement should be reviewed by the auditors before publication.

Statement of directors' responsibilities

A typical statement of directors' responsibilities for a UK listed company might be as follows:

> *The directors are required by company law to prepare financial statements for each accounting period that give a true and fair view of the company and group as at the end of the period and the profit or loss of the group for that period.*
>
> *The directors confirm that appropriate accounting policies have been used and applied consistently, and reasonable and prudent judgements and estimates have been made in the preparation of the accounts for the year ended [date]. The directors also confirm that applicable accounting standards have been followed, any material departures being disclosed and explained in the notes to the financial statements, and that the financial statements have been prepared on the going concern basis.*
>
> *The directors are responsible for ensuring proper accounting records are kept which disclose with reasonable accuracy at any time the financial position of the company and the group and to enable them to comply with the Companies Act 1985. They are also responsible for taking steps to safeguard the assets of the company and the group and to prevent and detect fraud and other irregularities.*

Having made such a statement of responsibilities, the directors must also accept liabilities arising out of a failure to carry them out.

Going concern statement

In the context of corporate governance, an important part of the corporate governance report of UK listed companies is the going concern statement. This is a statement by the directors that the company is a going concern, and will be for the next 12 months. If, for any reason, the company subsequently suffers financial collapse, each director could be liable to anyone suffering a loss (e.g. shareholders, bondholders, lending banks) having relied on that statement.

A typical going concern statement within a corporate report might be as follows:

> *The directors, on the basis of current financial projections and facilities available, have a reasonable expectation that the company and group have adequate resources to continue in operational existence for the foreseeable future. The directors accordingly continue to adopt the going concern basis in the preparation of the group's financial statement.*

3 UK Listing Rules: disclosure requirements

Rule 12.42 of the UK Listing Rules specifies a variety of items that should be disclosed in the annual report and accounts. These include:

- a commentary on published forecasts or estimated, where these differ from actual results by more than 10 per cent
- a statement showing the beneficial and non-beneficial interests of directors in shares of the company as at the end of the year, and changes in those interests since that time
- major shareholding interests in the company.

3.1 Summary Financial Statements

A listed public company may take advantage of the Companies (Summary Financial Statement) Regulations 1995 (SI 1995/2092) to send its annual report and accounts to shareholders in a summary form rather than sending the full report and accounts. The principle underlying the Regulations is that many shareholders are not interested in the full details of a company's report and accounts and will be satisfied with a summary.

The Regulations have been incorporated in the Companies Act 1985 (Section 251). However, a copy of the full report and accounts should be sent to any shareholder who wishes to receive it.

Section 251 also specifies that 'a summary financial statement is also to be treated as sent to an entitled person where the company and that person have agreed to his having access to summary financial statements on a web site (instead of their being sent to him).'

> *These summary financial statements are a summary of information contained in the Reed Elsevier Annual Reports and Financial Statements 2003. They do not contain sufficient information to allow as full an understanding of the results and state of affairs of the Reed Elsevier businesses and the parent companies as would be provided by the full Annual Reports.*
>
> *Shareholders who wish to receive, free of charge, a copy of the Annual Reports and Financial Statements for the year ended 31 December 2003, or in the future, should write to the registered offices.*
>
> *(Reed Elsevier)*

> *This Annual Review and the* summary financial statement *do not contain sufficient information to allow as full an understanding of the results of the group and state of affairs of the company or of the group as is provided by the full financial statements, directors' report, directors' remuneration report and report of the auditor contained in the annual report.*
>
> *Any shareholder or debenture holder requiring more detailed information has the right to obtain, free of charge, a copy of the company's annual report by contacting the company at [address] and may elect to continue to do so for future financial years.*
>
> *(Diageo plc)*

The Regulations (together with relevant accounting standards) specify what the Summary Financial Statements should contain. The Regulations require that there should be a prominent statement to the effect that the Summary Financial Statements will not provide sufficient information to allow as full an understanding of the company's financial affairs as the full report and accounts. Examples of such statements are given above.

3.2 Interim accounts

The UK Listing Rules require listed companies to prepare a half-yearly report ('interim accounts') on its activities and profit and loss for the first six months of the financial year (Rule 12.46). This must be published within 90 days of the end of the period to which it relates (Rule 12.48) and contain certain specified information.

The Listing Rules are supported by a Statement of the Accounting Standards Board on *Interim Reports*, which has 'persuasive rather than mandatory force'. The ASB recommends, for example, that interim reports should be available within 60 days of the end of the period, and goes into greater detail about what the statements should contain. Companies that comply with international accounting standards are subject to IAS34 *Interim Financial Reporting*, which applies to all companies that are required to publish interim accounts by their government, securities regulator, stock exchange or accountancy body.

3.3 Preliminary statement of annual results

The UK Listing Rules require listed companies to provide a preliminary statement of its annual results to a Regulatory Information Service, for disclosure to the market. The preliminary statement should be issued 'without delay after board approval' and in any case no later than 120 days after the end of the financial year (Rule 12.40).

The financial information in the preliminary statement should include at least the items required by the Listing Rules for inclusion in the half-year report, and in addition it should indicate the final proposed dividend.

4 External audit

The purpose of an independent audit is to make sure, as far as reasonably possible, that the financial statements are objective and can be relied on. The audit report has two main purposes:

1. to give an expert and independent opinion about whether the financial statements give a true and fair view of the financial position of the company as at the end of the financial year covered by the report, and of its financial performance during the year;
2. to give an expert and independent opinion on whether the financial statements comply with the relevant laws.

Auditors of listed companies are also required to review the company's compliance with aspects of the Combined Code of corporate governance, and to obtain evidence to support the company's statement (in the annual report and accounts) of its compliance with the Code.

There is a popular misconception that the auditor is responsible for detecting fraud or error in a company's financial statements. This is not the case.

- The management of the company has the responsibility for preventing and detecting fraud and error. This is achieved by implementing an adequate system of accounting and 'internal controls'.
- The auditor has no responsibility for detecting fraud or error. However, the auditor will assess the risk or possibility that fraud or error might have caused the financial statements to be materially misleading. The auditor should therefore design audit procedures that will provide reasonable reassurance that material fraud or error has not occurred, and that the financial statements give a true and fair view of the company's financial position and performance.

Auditors are potentially liable to shareholders and others who suffer loss as a result of negligence in carrying out an audit. Negligence would arise from failure to comply properly with professional audit guidelines, and from a failure to carry out the audit with due skill, care, diligence and expedition.

4.1 The audit report

Section 235 of the Companies Act 1985 requires that the audit report on the annual report and accounts must state whether in the auditors' opinion the annual accounts have been properly prepared in accordance with the Companies Act and in particular whether they give a true and fair view:

- in the case of an individual balance sheet, of the state of affairs of the company as at the end of the financial year
- in the case of an individual profit and loss account, of the profit or loss for the period, and
- in the case of group accounts, of the state of affairs as at the year end and the profit or loss for the year for the group as a whole.

The auditors should also consider whether the information in the directors' report is consistent with the information in the financial statements, and they should make a statement in their report if they believe them not to be consistent (s235(3)).

When the annual report and accounts include a drectors' remuneration repor, the auditors must also report on the auditable part of the report and state whether in their opinion that part of the remuneration report has been prepared in accordance with the requirements of the Companies Act (s235(4)).

Rule 12.43A of the UK Listing Rules also requires the auditors to review the company's statement the 'comply or explain' requirement with regard to compliance with the Combined Code, but only insofar as it relates to the following Combined Code provisions:

- Provision C.1.1: reporting responsibilities. The requirement for an explanation by the directors in the annual report of their reponsibility for preparing the annual accounts and a statement by the auditors about their reporting responsibilities.
- Provision C.2.1: internal control review. The requirement of the board to conduct a review at least annually of the effectiveness of the group's system of internal control and to report to the shareholders that they have done so. (Note: There is no requirement for the directors to *give their evaluation* of the effectiveness of the internal controls.)
- Provisions C.3.1–C.3.7: provisions relating to the audit committee and the auditors.

4.2 Auditors' liability to third parties

The auditors have a legal duty of care to the company and its shareholders.

Case example

The Caparo case

In the *Caparo* case (*Caparo Industries plc* v *Dickman and others* [1990]), it was held by the House of Lords that auditors did not owe a duty of care in audit reports to third parties that they did not know at the time. The auditors of a company had negligently audited its accounts, and as a result the company reported a profit of £1.2 million instead of a loss of £400,000. Relying on these accounts, the respondents in the case made a successful takeover bid for the company. They subsequently brought an action against the auditors for breach of duty of care and skill. In ruling in the auditors' favour, the House of Lords held that there was no liability, since the auditors did not owe a duty of care to a member of the public. Their duty was simply to the company and its shareholders.

Case example

The Bannerman case

As a result of the Caparo case, it was considered that the auditors of a company did not hold a duty of care to any third party, until the subject came up for consideration again in the *Bannerman* case (*Royal Bank of Scotland* v *Bannerman Johnstone Maclay* [2002]). This was a case in the Scottish courts, and so was not binding on English courts, but it drew from leading English court cases and so is considered to have significant legal implications for England and Wales as well as Scotland. (At the time of writing, this case is going through an appeals procedure.)

In this case, Bannerman were the auditors of a company that arranged an overdraft facility with the bank. The overdraft facility letter between the bank and the company contained a requirement for the company to send the bank a copy of its audited annual accounts at the end of each year. In 1998, the company went into receivership owing over £13 million to the bank, which claimed that due to fraud, the accounts for the previous year were materially incorrect and the auditors were negligent. The bank also claimed that it had relied on the auditors' unqualified opinion to continue providing the overdraft facility to the company. In its defence, the audit firm claimed that it had no duty of care to the bank.

The judge ruled that although there had been no direct contact between the audit firm and the bank, the auditors would have known about the facility letter. The knowledge they would have gained during the course of their audit work was therefore sufficient, *in the absence of any disclaimer*, to create a duty of care to the *continued*

bank. In the judge's view, the absence of a disclaimer was a crucial feature of the case.

In response to the outcome of the *Bannerman* case, PricewaterhouseCoopers decided to include a disclaimer of liability to third parties using its audit reports. In January 2003, the Institute of Chartered Accountants in England and Wales recommended that its members place an additional paragraph in the audit report stating explicitly that audit work is undertaken solely for the shareholders of the company, and disclaiming responsibility to any third parties. The US Securities and Exchange Commission (SEC) subsequently stated that these paragraphs would need to be removed from any reports issued by SEC registrants.

A disclaimer within the audit report might be worded as follows:

> *Our responsibility is to audit the financial statements and the auditable part of the report on directors' remuneration in accordance with relevant legal and regulatory requirements and United Kingdom Auditing Standards issued by the Auditing Practices Board. This report, including the opinion, have been prepared for, and only for, the company's members as a body in accordance with section 235 of the Companies Act 1985 and for no other purpose. We do not, in giving this opinion, accept or assume responsibility for any other purpose or to any other person to whom this report is shown or into whose hands it may come, save where expressly agreed by our prior consent in writing.*

Audit practice on this issue appears to differ between audit firms, and not all audit firms folow the ICAEW recommendation and include a disclaimer.

5 Auditor independence

The external auditor should be independent of the client company, so that the audit opinion will not be influenced by the relationship between the auditor and the company. The auditors are expected to give an unbiased and honest professional opinion to the shareholders about the financial statements. An unqualified audit report is often seen by investors as a 'clean bill of health' for the company. However, doubts have been expressed about the independence of the external auditors. It might be argued that unless suitable corporate governance measures are in place, a firm of auditors might reach opinions and judgements that are heavily influenced by their wish to maintain good relations with the management of a client company.

Auditors are expected to act with integrity and honesty, and to follow a code of ethics in the work they do. The corporate governance problem is that there can be pressures on auditors to ignore ethical considerations and to allow their judgement to be affected by other considerations.

5.1 Threats to auditor independence and ethical standards for auditors

Perhaps the most significant threat to auditor independence is that the audit firm relies on the company's management to secure its appointment and reappointment as the company's auditor. Although listed companies now give the responsibility to the audit committee for recommending the appointment or non-reappointment of the auditors (see below)), the opinions of senior management may nevertheless be influential in the matter of auditor selection. The auditors may therefore, to some extent, be reliant for future audit work from the company on the views of the management whose financial statements it is their job to audit. In addition, the audit firm has to rely extensively on management for the information and explanations needed to enable them to carry out their audit work.

Professional guidelines are given to auditors by both national and international bodies. International guidelines have been issued by the International Federation of Accountants (IFAC). The IFAC Code of Ethics for Professional Accountants (2001) identifies certain ways in which the integrity, objectivity and independence of the auditors might be put at risk:

- An audit firm should not have to rely on a single company for a large proportion of its total fee income, because undue dependence on a single audit client could impair objectivity. IFAC does not specify what amounts to 'undue dependence' on a single client.
- A risk to objectivity and independence arises when the audit firm or anyone closely associated with it (such as an audit partner) has a mutual business interest with the company or any of its officers. Similarly, objectivity could be threatened when there is a close personal relationship between a member of the audit firm and an employee of the company.
- The audit firm should not have a client company in which a partner holds a significant number of shares.
- The IFAC Code does not have any objection in principle to an audit firm providing non-audit services (such as consultancy services) to a client, although the auditor should not perform any management functions in a company nor take any management decisions.

In the UK, oversight of auditing standards and ethics in auditing has been given to the Auditing Practices Board, which is a part of the Financial Reporting Council. The APB issued its first five Ethical Standards for auditors, effective for audits of financial statements beginning on or after 15 December 2004. These first five ethical standards, ES1–ES5, cover:

- integrity, objectivity and independence
- financial, business, employment and personal relationships
- long association with the audit engagement

- fees, remuneration and evaluation policies, litigation, gifts and hospitality
- non-audit services provided to audit clients.

The Ethical Standards (ES) establish principles and essential procedures for auditors in their audit work, and on the whole do not make specific regulations. The APB states that the company's audit committee has the main responsibility for ensuring that the ethical standards are met. However, the APB has banned three practices on ethical grounds:

- Contingent fees must not be charged for audit work. These are fees where the amount payable is dependent on the outcome of the audit.
- The auditor firm must not provide tax services to an audit client where the tax charges payable may be dependent on the outcome of the audit.
- The auditors must not accept non-audit work in circumstances where the objectives of the non-audit work are not consistent with the objectives of an audit.

In a consultation document issued at the same time as ES1–ES5, the APB stated that: 'The management threat will be unacceptably high where audit firms provide internal audit services that involve the auditors making decisions or taking judgements that should properly be made by management.'

Some of the governance issues relating to external audits are discussed in further detail below.

5.2 Non-audit work for a client by an audit firm

Suggestions for regulatory measures to ensure auditor independence have included proposals to restrict the amount of non-audit work, or the type of non-audit work, that the firm of auditors is permitted to carry out for a client company. Non-audit work might include:

- consultancy on taxation issues, for example, helping a group of companies to minimise tax liabilities by setting up subsidiaries in countries with a low-tax regime
- investigating targets for a potential takeover bid
- helping a company to construct a bid for a major government contract;
- providing advice and expert assistance on IT systems.

The main problem with auditors doing non-audit work is that when the firm audits transactions recommended by its consultancy arm, it is unlikely to take an independent view.

Audit firms have denied that fees from non-audit work will affect their independence, arguing that the individuals who work as consultants for a client company, for example, on IT projects, are not the same individuals who work on the company audit. Even so, activist shareholder groups continue to challenge this assertion.

There are three broad approaches to the regulation of non-audit work by audit firms.

1 There could be no restrictions at all on non-audit work by the audit firm. Some audit firms have argued that they have already separated their audit partnerships from their consultancy partnerships, and the risk to auditor independence from non-audit work is therefore not significant.
2 There should be a total prohibition on non-audit work for a corporate client by the audit firm. The large audit firms have argued that this would be an unreasonable and unnecessary restriction.
3 There should be a partial prohibition on non-audit work for a corporate client by the audit firm. This could take either of two forms. There could be a prohibition on audit firms from taking on certain types of consultancy work where their independence as auditors could be put at risk, for example, tax planning advice work. However, audit firms would be free to carry out other types of non-audit work. The second approach to restricting non-audit work would be to set a limit on the amount of fees an audit firm could earn from non-audit work, expressed perhaps as a proportion of the fees it earns from the audit. For example, a limit might be imposed restricting non-audit fees to, say, 50 per cent of the fees from the audit work.

The difficulty with a partial restriction on non-audit work is that rules would have to be devised and agreed as to what permissible and non-permissible non-audit work should be, or what the maximum amount of non-audit fee income should be.

5.3 Rotation of audit firm or audit partner

Whilst recognising the importance of auditor independence, there has been disagreement about the extent to which regulatory measures should be imposed.

Audit firm rotation

One suggestion is that there should be a regular rotation of auditors, whereby the auditors of a company should be replaced by another firm after a given number of years. Rotation would enhance auditor independence because a firm of auditors would have little to gain by going along with the wishes of the client company, and carrying out a less than rigorous audit, if it knows that it will soon lose the audit work anyway. The work of outgoing auditors would also be subject to review – and criticism – by the firm of auditors taking their place.

A disadvantage of auditor rotation is that the incoming firm of auditors might need one or two years to get to know the business of the client company, and might be unable to conduct an audit to the same standard as their predecessor.

If the argument in favour of auditor rotation is accepted, however, there is still scope for disagreement about how frequently auditor rotation should occur. Regular rotation might involve changing auditors every five years or so. An alternative argument is that auditor rotation should be much more occasional, say, every ten or fifteen years.

Audit partner rotation

An alternative argument put forward by the major accountancy firms is that the requirement for rotation should apply, not to the firm of auditors, but to the individual partner of a firm in charge of the audit. In the case of large companies, there is also an argument for a regular rotation of other senior audit managers, as well as the lead partner. The Auditing Practices Board (APB) has specified a mandatory rotation every five years, for the audit engagement partner and the independent partner for a listed company audit (APB Ethical Standard 3).

5.4 Directorships and senior management positions for former auditors

Yet another potential threat to auditor independence is the practice whereby public companies appoint a former auditor to their board, as chief financial officer/finance director. It could be reasoned that if an auditor sees the possibility of a lucrative promotion to the board of a major public company, he or she will do nothing to threaten the relationship he or she has with the management of the company. A suggestion for countering this risk is that public companies should not be allowed to appoint a former auditor of the company to the board for at least a minimum time (say, two years) after the individual concerned has left the audit firm.

5.5 Companies (Audit, Investigations and Community Enterprise) Act 2004

One of the aims of the Companies (Audit, Investigations and Community Enterprise) Act 2004 (which amends the Companies Act) is to enhance the independence of the audit process.

It gives additional rights to auditors to require information and explanations:

- Auditors previously had the right to require officers of the company (directors, managers and the company secretary) to provide information. The Act extends this right to all employees of the company.
- Whereas previously it was a criminal offence for an officer of the company to provide misleading, false or deceptive information and explanations to the auditors, the Act makes it a criminal offence to *fail to provide* information or explanations when these are required of them.
- The directors of the company are required to include a statement in their annual report to the effect that, in the case of each person who was a director at the time the report was approved: '(a) so far as the director is aware, there is no relevant audit information of which the company's auditors are unaware and (b) he has taken all the steps that he ought to make himself aware of any relevant audit information and to establish that the company's auditors are aware of that information.'

It gives the Secretary of State powers to issue regulations requiring companies to publish more information about non-audit work performed by the auditors for the company.

6 The audit committee

The Combined Code requires a board of directors to present a balanced and understandable assessment of the company's position and prospects. The Code also requires the board to maintain a sound system of internal control (see Chapter 10). A further principle (C.3) is that the board should establish formal and transparent arrangements for:

- considering how they should apply the financial reporting and internal control principles, and
- maintaining an appropriate relationship with the company's auditors.

It should do this by setting up an audit committee. The Code's provisions relating to the audit committee are based on the Smith Report (see below and Appendix 20). The main roles of this committee should be (Code Provision C.3.2):

- to monitor the integrity of the company's financial statements and any formal announcements relating to the company's financial performance. In doing so, it should review 'significant financial judgements' that these statements and announcements contain
- to review the company's internal financial controls
- unless the role is assigned to a separate board risk committee, or taken on by the full board, to review the company's internal control and risk management systems
- to monitor and review the effectiveness of the company's internal audit function
- to make recommendations to the board in relation to the appointment, re-appointment or removal of the company's external auditors, for putting to the shareholders for approval in general meeting of the company
- to approve the remuneration and terms of engagement of the external auditors
- to review and monitor the independence and objectivity of the external auditors, and also the effectiveness of the audit process, taking into account relevant UK professional and regulatory requirements
- to develop and implement the company's policy on using the external auditors to provide non-audit services. This should take into account any relevant external ethical guidance on the subject. The committee should report to the board, identifying actions or improvements that are needed and recommending the steps to be taken.

The terms of reference of the audit committee, including the role and authority delegated to it by the board, should be made available to the public. (Providing copies on request, and making the information available on the company's web-site will be sufficient for this purpose.)

A separate section of the annual report should describe the work of the audit committee (Code Provision C.3.3). This 'puts the spotlight on the audit committee and gives it an authority that it might otherwise lack' (the Smith Guidance).

6.1 The Smith Guidance

Further guidance on audit committees is provided in *The Smith Guidance*, which is annexed to the Combined Code and based on the recommendations of the Smith Report (see Appendix 20). The Smith Report was originally published in January 2003 (at the same time as the Higgs Report) by a committee set up by the Financial Reporting Council (under the chairmanship of Sir Robert Smith) to consider the role of audit committees.

The Smith Guidance makes the following comments about the role and responsibilities of the audit committee:

- The audit committee arrangements within each company need to be proportionate to the task, and will differ according to the size, complexity and risk profile of the company.
- All the board directors have a duty to act in the best interests of the company, but the audit committee has a particular role, 'acting independently from the executive, to ensure that the interests of shareholders are properly protected in relation to financial reporting and internal control'.
- The principle of the unitary board is not affected by the creation of an audit committee. All directors are equally responsible in law for the company's affairs. The audit committee is a committee of the board, and any disagreement within the board, including disagreement between the audit committee members, should be resolved at board level.
- Where there are disagreements between the audit committee and the rest of the board that cannot be resolved, the audit committee should have the right to report the issue to the shareholders as part of the report to shareholders on its activities.
- The company's management is under an obligation to make sure that the audit committee is kept properly informed and should take the initiative in providing the committee with information, instead of waiting to be asked. The executive directors should also have regard to their common law duty to provide all directors, including the audit committee members, with all the information they need to discharge their duties as directors of the company. (This guidance is crucial. The audit committee can only do its work properly if it is kept properly informed by the executive management.)
- The core functions of the audit committee are concerned with 'oversight', 'assessment' and 'review' of other functions and systems in the company. It is not the

committee's duty to carry out those functions; for example, management remains responsible for preparing the financial statements and the auditors remain responsible for preparing the audit plan and carrying out the audit.

- However, the high-level oversight function can sometimes lead to more detailed work. The Smith Guidance gives as an example a situation where the audit committee are unhappy with the explanations of management and the auditors about a particular financial reporting decision, 'there may be no alternative but to grapple with the detail and perhaps seek independent advice.'
- For groups, the audit committee of the parent company will usually have to review activities relating to subsidiaries within the group. The board of the parent company must ensure that there is adequate co-operation within the group to allow the audit committee of the parent company to do its job properly.
- The board should decide just what the role of the audit committee should be, and the terms of reference should be tailored to the company's particular circumstances. However, the audit committee should review its terms of reference and effectiveness annually, and recommend any necessary changes to the board (Smith Guidance, Note 3.3). The board should also review the effectiveness of the audit committee annually.

6.2 Composition of the audit committee

The audit committee should consist of at least three members (or at least two members in the case of smaller companies, outside the FTSE 350). All its members should be independent non-executive directors. The Smith Guidance adds that:

- the chairman of the company should not be a member of the committee, and
- appointments to the committee should be made to the board on the recommendation of the nomination committee (if there is one), in consultation with the audit committee chairman
- appointments should be for a period of up to three years, extendable by no more than two additional three-year periods, and provided that the committee member remain independent during that time.

The board should satisfy itself that at least one member of the committee has recent and relevant financial experience (Provision C.3.1). The Smith Guidance adds that it is desirable that this person should have a professional qualification from one of the professional accountancy bodies (Guidance Note 2.17). The degree of financial literacy required from the other committee members will vary according to the nature of the company.

Remuneration, induction and training of committee members

The Smith Guidance adds that the audit committees have wide-ranging and time-consuming work to do, and companies must make the necessary resources available.

This includes making suitable payments to the members of the audit committee, in view of the responsibilities they have and the time they must commit to the work. The amount of remuneration paid to the audit committee members should take account of the remuneration paid to other members of the board. The committee chairman's responsibilities and time commitments will normally be greater than those of the other committee members, and this should be reflected in his or her remuneration.

The committee should have the support of the company secretary and should have access to the services of the company's secretariat.

Audit committee members must also be given suitable induction and training. Ongoing training should include keeping the committee members up to date on developments in financial reporting and related company law. It may, for example, include understanding financial statements, the application of particular accounting standards, the regulatory framework for the company's business, the role of internal and external auditing, and risk management. Both induction and training can take various forms, including attendance at formal courses and conferences, internal company talks and seminars and briefings by external advisers.

6.3 Audit committee meetings

The audit committee chairman should decide the timing and frequency of committee meetings, in consultation with the company secretary, and there should be as many meetings as the role and responsibilities of the committee require. The Smith Guidance (Notes 2.7–2.10) suggests that:

- There should be no fewer than three committee meetings each year, timed to coincide with key dates in the financial reporting and audit calendar. For example, meetings might be held when the audit plans are available for review and when interim statements, preliminary announcements and the full annual report are near completion. Most audit committee chairmen will probably want to call meetings more frequently.
- Sufficient time should be allowed between audit committee meetings and meetings of the main board to allow any work arising out of the committee meeting to be carried out and reported to the board as appropriate.
- Only the audit committee chairman and members are entitled to attend meetings of the committee. It is for the committee to decide whether other individuals should be invited to attend for a particular meeting or a particular agenda item. It is expected that the audit lead partner and the company's finance director will be invited regularly to attend meetings.
- At least once a year, the audit committee should meet, without management being present, the external and internal auditors, to discuss matters relating to its responsibilities and issues arising from the audit.

7 Audit committee responsibilities

7.1 Financial reporting

It is the responsibility of management, not the audit committee, to prepare complete and accurate financial statements. It is the responsibility of the audit committee to review the significant financial reporting issues and judgements that are made in connection with these statements.

- The audit committee should consider significant accounting policies used to prepare the statements, and any changes to them, and any significant estimates or judgements on which the statements have been based.
- Management should inform the committee about the methods they have used to account for significant or unusual transactions, where the accounting treatment is open to different approaches.
- Taking the external auditors' views into consideration, the committee should consider whether the company has adopted appropriate accounting policies and made appropriate estimates and judgements.
- The committee should also consider the clarity and completeness of the disclosures in the financial statements.

If the committee is not satisfied with any aspect of the proposed financial reporting by the company, it should report its views to the board (Smith Guidance, Note 4.3).

The committee should also review related information presented with the financial statements, including the Operating and Financial Review (OFR) and the corporate governance statements relating to audit and risk management.

7.2 Internal audit

The audit committee is required to monitor the effectiveness of the company's internal audit activities (Code Provision C.3.5). If the company does not have an internal audit function:

- the committee should consider annually whether there is a need for an internal audit function and make a recommendation to the board, and
- the absence of an internal audit function should be explained in the relevant section of the annual report.

The role and responsibilities of the audit committee with regard to internal audit and risk management are described in more detail in Chapter 10.

7.3 Appointment, re-appointment or removal of the external auditors

The audit committee is the body responsible for oversight of the company's relations with its external auditors (Smith Guidance, Note 4.13).

The Combined Code states that the audit committee has the *primary responsibility for making a recommendation* to the board on the appointment, re-appointment or removal of the external auditors. If the board does not accept this recommendation, it should:

- include in the annual report, and in any papers recommending the appointment or re-appointment of the auditors, a statement from the audit committee explaining its recommendation, and
- giving the reasons why the board has taken a different position (Code Provision C.3.6).

If the audit committee recommends to the board that new external auditors should be selected, the committee should 'oversee' the selection process (Smith Guidance, Note 4.15). The committee's recommendation should be based on the following assessments:

- the qualification and expertise of the auditors
- the resources of the auditors
- the independence of the auditors
- the effectiveness of the audit process.

The assessment should cover all aspects of the audit service provided by the audit firm, and in carrying out the assessment the committee should obtain from the audit firm a report on its own internal quality control procedures (Smith Guidance, Note 4.16).

If the external auditors resign, the audit committee should investigate the issues that gave rise to the resignation, and consider whether any action is needed.

Terms and remuneration of the auditors

The audit committee should *approve* the terms of engagement of the external auditors and the remuneration to be paid to the auditors for their audit services. (Note: the committee should approve the terms and remuneration, but is not required to negotiate them itself.) It should satisfy itself that the amount of the fee payable for the audit services is appropriate, and that an effective audit can be carried out for such a fee. (Note: The fee should not be too large, nor should it be too low. A low audit fee creates a risk that the audit might be of an inadequate scope or quality.)

The committee should review and agree the engagement letter issued by the external auditors at the start of each audit, to make sure that it has been updated to reflect any changes in circumstances since the previous year.

The committee should also review the scope of the audit with the auditor. If it is not satisfied that the proposed scope is adequate, the committee should arrange for additional audit work to be undertaken (Smith Guidance, Note 4.19).

7.4 Auditor independence

If the external auditors provide non-audit services to the company, the annual report should explain how auditor independence and objectivity are safeguarded (Code Provision C.3.7).

The audit committee should have procedures for ensuring the independence and objectivity of the external auditors annually (Smith Guidance, Note 4.21). The Smith Guidance suggests various measures for the committee to take:

- The committee should seek reassurance that the auditors and their staff have no family, financial, employment, investment or business relationship with the company (other than in the normal course of business).
- The committee should seek from the audit firm, annually, information about the firm's policies and processes for maintaining independence and monitoring compliance with relevant requirements, such as those regarding the rotation of audit partners and staff.
- The committee should agree with the board the company's policy on employing former employees of the external auditor. Particular attention should be given to the company's policy on former employees of the auditor who were members of the audit team and then moved directly to the company. This policy should be drafted, and the audit committee should monitor its application. The committee should monitor the number of former employees of the external auditor who now hold senior positions within the company, and consider in the light of their findings whether there may be some impairment (or *appearance* of impairment) in the auditors' judgement and independence with regard to the audit.
- The committee should monitor the audit firm's compliance with ethical guidance in the UK about the rotation of audit partners, and the level of fees the company pays as a proportion of the overall fee income of (i) the firm; (ii) the office of the firm responsible for the audit; and (iii) the audit partner.
- The audit committee should develop and recommend to the board the company's policy in relation to the provision of non-audit services by the external auditors. The committee's objective should be to ensure that the provision of such services does not impair the independence or objectivity of the auditors.

7.5 Provision of non-audit services

In developing the company's policy on the provision of non-audit services by the external auditor, the audit committee should consider:

- whether the skills and experience of the audit firm make it a suitable supplier of the non-audit services
- whether there are safeguards in place for ensuring that there would be no threat to the objectivity and independence of the auditors arising from the provision of these services
- the nature of the non-audit services and the fees for these services
- the level of fees for individual non-audit services and the fees in aggregate for these services, relative to the size of the audit fee
- the criteria governing the compensation of the individuals who perform the audit.

The audit committee should set and apply a formal policy specifying the types of non-audit work:

- from which the external auditors are excluded
- for which the external auditors can be engaged without referral to the audit committee
- for which a case-by-case decision is necessary. In these cases, it may be appropriate to give a general pre-approval for certain classes of work, subject to a fee limit decided by the audit committee and ratified by the board. If the external auditor subsequently provides any of these services, the engagement of the auditors should then be ratified at the next audit committee meeting.

The policy may also set fee limits generally or for particular classes of non-audit work.

In deciding its policy on the provision of non-audit work by the external auditors, the committee should take into account relevant ethical guidance, but a guiding set of principles should be that the external auditor should not be engaged for non-audit work if the result is that:

- the external auditor audits work done by itself
- the external auditor makes management decisions for the company
- a mutuality of interest is created, or
- the external auditor is put in the role of advocate for the company (Smith Guidance, Note 4.28).

These issues are addressed in further detail in guidance to audit committees issued by the Institute of Chartered Accountants in England and Wales, see below.

If the external auditors do provide non-financial services, the annual report should explain to shareholders how auditor independence and objectivity are safeguarded (Combined Code, Provision C.3.7).

7.6 Whistleblowing

The audit committee should *review the arrangements* by which employees of the company may, in confidence raise concerns about possible improprieties in financial reporting or other matters (Code Provision C.3.4). The objective of the audit committee should be to make sure that arrangements are in place for:

- the 'proportionate and independent' investigation of such matters and
- appropriate follow-up action.

The committee is not required to be part of the whistleblowing procedures itself; it is simply required to review the system and procedures that are in place.

The law in the UK on whistleblowing is described in Chapter 12.

7.7 The audit committee and communication with shareholders

The Smith Guidance includes some matters relating to the communication by the audit committee to the company's shareholders.

The terms of reference of the audit committee should be made available.

The separate section in the annual report about the work of the audit committee should include:

- a summary of the role of the audit committee
- the names and qualifications of the audit committee members during the period
- the number of audit committee meetings
- a report on the way the audit committee has discharged its responsibilities
- if the external auditors provide non-audit services, an explanation of how auditor objectivity and independence are safeguarded.

The chairman of the audit committee should be present at the AGM to answer questions on the audit committee report and matters within the scope of the audit committee's responsibilities.

7.8 Disclosures about audit independence

During 2002, the Association of British Insurers held up several company reports as providing good examples. An extract from one of these, the corporate governance report of Unilever for the year to 31st December 2001, is reproduced below:

> ***Auditors***
> *Subject to the annual appointment of auditors by the shareholders and in addition to our ongoing process of monitoring the auditors' performance, we undertake a formal review every three years. The next review is currently in progress. The directors' recommendation resulting from this review will be put to the AGM for approval in 2003. Both the Executive Committee and the auditors have for many years had safeguards to avoid the possibility that the auditors' objectivity and independence could be compromised, in particular, our procedures in respect of other services provided by PricewaterhouseCoopers.*
>
> ***Audit-related services***
> *This is work that, in their position as the auditors, they must or are best placed to undertake. It includes formalities relating to borrowings, shareholder and other circulars, various other regulatory reports, and work in respect of acquisitions and disposals.*
>
> ***Tax consulting***
> *In cases where they are best suited, we use the auditors. All other significant tax consulting work is put to tender.*

General consulting
All significant general consulting projects are put out to tender. Prior to 2002, PricewaterhouseCoopers were only permitted to tender when we and they were satisfied that the nature of the work presented no potential threat to the independence of the audit team. Additionally such projects were not awarded to PricewaterhouseCoopers without the prior approval of the Executive Committee. From the beginning of 2002, in recognition of increasing public concern over the effect of consulting services on auditors' independence, our policy is that the external auditors will not be invited to tender for any further general consulting work.

8 The audit committee and the annual audit cycle

The Smith Guidance goes into some detail on the annual audit cycle, and the relationship between the audit committee and the external auditors during this process (Guidance Notes 4.30–4.35):

- At the start of each annual audit, the audit committee should make sure that appropriate plans are in place for the audit.
- The committee should consider whether the auditors' overall work plan (including the planned levels of materiality and the proposed resources to carry out the audit) seems consistent with the scope of the audit engagement. This assessment should have regard to the seniority, expertise and experience of the audit team.
- The audit committee should review, with the external auditors, the findings of their work. As a part of this review, the committee should: (i) discuss with the auditors any major issues that arose during the audit (and whether these have been resolved); (ii) review key accounting or audit judgements; and (iii) review levels of errors identified during the audit and obtain explanations as to why certain errors might remain unadjusted.

The Smith Guidance states that the audit committee should review:

- the audit representation letters from management, before they are signed, and consider whether the information provided is complete and appropriate, based on the knowledge the committee has
- the management letter from the auditors, and the responsiveness of the company's management to the auditors' findings and recommendations.

8.1 Management representations

Representation letters from the company's management are a part of the audit evidence collected and considered by the auditors. These deal with matters for which other audit evidence does not exist; therefore the auditors are relying on what management tell them. Representations are required:

- from the directors, acknowledging their collective responsibility for the financial statements and confirming that they have approved them, and
- with regard to matters where knowledge of the facts is confined to management (for example, management's intention to sell off a division of the business) or where there is a matter of judgement and opinion (for example, with regard to the trading position of a major customer and debtor, or the likely outcome of litigation in progress).

8.2 Management letter

As a by-product of the audit process, the auditors will normally make recommendations to management about improvements in internal controls. These recommendations are known as management letters.

8.3 Audit review by the committee

At the end of the audit cycle, the audit committee should assess the effectiveness of the audit process (Smith Guidance, Note 4.35). As a part of this assessment, the committee should:

- review whether the auditors have met the agreed audit plan and consider the reasons for any changes
- consider the 'robustness and perceptiveness' of the auditors, in their handling of key accounting and audit judgements, and in their commentary on the appropriateness of the company's internal controls
- obtain feedback about the conduct of the auditors from key people within the company, such as the finance director and the head of internal audit
- review the auditor's management letter, to assess whether it is based on a good understanding of the business and to establish whether the auditors' recommendations have been acted on (and if not, why not).

9 Guidance for audit committees

9.1 ICSA Guidance Note on the terms of reference for the audit committee

The ICSA Guidance Note: *Terms of Reference: Audit Committee.* presents model terms of reference for an audit committee, which are applicable to organisations in the public and not-for-profit sectors as well as to companies.

The Guidance Note stresses the need for formal written terms of reference as follows:

> *Not only should companies go through a formal process of considering their internal audit and control procedures and evaluating their relationship with their external auditor, but they must be seen to be doing so in a fair and thorough manner. It is, therefore, essential that the Audit Committee is properly constituted with a clear remit and identified authority.*

In addition to providing model terms of reference, the Guidance Note makes the following points:

- The Higgs Review stated that as good practice the company secretary (or an individual designated by the company secretary) should act as secretary to the audit committee, with responsibility for ensuring that both the board and the committee are properly advised. He or she should be able to play the role of intermediary between them.
- The Smith Report recommended that the company secretary should attend meetings of the audit committee.
- The company secretary is responsible for ensuring that the board of directors and its committees, incuding the audit committee, are properly constituted and advised.

The Guidance Note also comments that:

> *Although the responsibility for internal controls clearly remains with the board as a whole, the company secretary would normally have the day-to-day task of reviewing the internal control procedures of the company and responsibility for drafting the governance report.*

The frequency of audit committee meetings should be specified in the terms of reference. As a general rule, the committee should meet quarterly, although the Combined Code provides that the Committee should meet at least three times a year.

The Guidance Note also suggests that the annual report of the Audit Committee to shareholders will need to disclose:

- the role and main responsibilities of the Committee
- the membership of the committee and the relevant qualifications of the members; the appointment proccess and fees paid in respect of membership
- the number of meetings and attendance levels
- a description of the main activities during the year to:
  - monitor the integrity of the financial statements
  - review the integrity of the internal financial control and risk management systems
  - review of the independence of the external auditors and the provision of non-audit services
  - the oversight of the external audit process and how its effectiveness was assessed

- an explanation of the recommendation of the board to the shareholders on the appointment of the auditors.

9.2 ICAEW Guidance for Audit Committees

The Institute of Chartered Accountants in England and Wales has also issued a series of booklets, *Guidance for Audit Committees*. They include titles on *Company Reporting and Audit Requirements*, *Working with Your Auditors*, *Reviewing Auditor Independence* and *Evaluating Your Auditors*. These booklets, which are written for the benefit of members of audit committees, can be viewed on the ICAEW web-site (www.icaew.co.uk).

Evaluating the auditors

The Smith Report on audit committees for the Financial Reporting Council recommended that audit committees:

- should have the primary responsibility for recommending the appointment, reappointment and removal of the company's auditors, and
- should assess, on an annual basis, the qualifications, expertise and resources, effectiveness and independence of the external auditors.

If the company decides to recommend a change of auditors to its shareholders, the audit committee should oversee the process of selecting the new auditors.

Guidance to audit committees on carrying out these tasks has been published by the Institute of Chartered Accountants in England and Wales in *Evaluating Your Auditors*, a booklet in a series on *Guidance for Audit Committees*.

Recommending the appointment or re-appointment of the auditors

The appointment or re-appointment of the auditors must be made each year by the company's shareholders (Sections 384 and 385 of the Companies Act 1985). The audit committee's responsibility is to make a recommendation each year to the board about the appointment of new auditors or the re-appointment of the existing auditors. The board either accepts or rejects the recommendation, and in turn puts a resolution to the shareholders at the annual general meeting.

The board of directors is not required to accept the audit committee's recommendation, but if it does not, the directors' report should include a statement from the audit committee and an explanation of why the board does not accept its views.

The ICAEW guidance suggests that frequent changes of the company's auditors is undesirable, because the process of putting an audit out to tender is both time-consuming and costly. The annual review of the auditors is therefore normally likely to be concerned mainly with improving the quality and effectiveness of the audit and the relationship between the company and the auditors rather than with deciding on a recommendation to the board.

When the audit committee is not considering a change of auditors, its assessment is likely to be made in the short time window between the completion of the annual audit and its recommendation to the board. The board must make its own recommendation to the shareholders by the time the notice of the annual general meeting is sent out to the shareholders.

When the audit committee decides to recommend a change of auditors, the selection process will probably have to begin much earlier, before the end of the accounting year; otherwise time will run out because of the pressures on the company's accounting staff around the year-end to produce the audited financial statements.

The annual assessment of the auditors

The audit committee will not have time to conduct the annual assessment of the auditors, and most of the work will be done by the company's management (e.g. senior accounting staff). However, the audit committee must retain overall control of the process, to ensure that it is fair and free from management bias.

The ICAEW recommends that the assessment process should be carried out with openness, and should involve the audit firm itself. The audit firm should provide a report to the audit committee about its internal quality control procedures. Openness can be achieved by ensuring that the company documents its needs and expectations from the audit each year, perhaps in the letter of engagement or in the review of the audit plan. This document can then be used at the end of the audit to review the extent to which the company's stated needs and expectations have been met. The ICAEW guideline adds that if the company sets specific performance criteria for the auditors, these too should be documented.

The Smith Report sets out four criteria against which the auditors should be assessed:

- *Qualifications*. This should usually not be a problem. The auditors should be registered auditors and the audit engagement partner should be a 'responsible individual' under the Audit Regulations. The audit committee might want to satisfy themselves that all the key members of the audit team are suitably qualified individuals.
- *Expertise and resources*. The audit committee can check the expertise of individual members of the audit team, the audit team as a whole and the audit firm itself. Information about the qualifications and experience of the audit team members should be obtained from the audit firm. The audit committee might want to look for sufficient continuity in the team membership from one year to the next. The expertise of the audit firm itself should be apparent from its documented audit manuals and procedures. The audit firm should also have sufficient resources to be able to handle the audit for the company.
- *Effectiveness*. Effectiveness is a composite of competence, procedural arrangements, quality control and quality assurance. The ICAEW guideline suggests two ways of checking on the effectiveness of the audit and the audit firm. First, the audit firm is

required by the professional accountancy bodies to monitor its compliance with the Audit Regulations, auditing standards, technical standards and legal requirements. Audit firms now publish annual reports on their activities, which consider amongst other things audit quality and auditor independence. Second, the audit committee can also review the audit. For example, did the auditors seem to understand the company's business properly? Did any issues come up during the audit, and how were they dealt with? Did the auditors make any useful suggestions for improvements in the company's internal controls?

- *Independence*. The audit committee should review the independence of the auditors (see below).

The audit committee should also evaluate the quality of the auditors by considering:

- the quality of leadership provided by the audit engagement partner, and
- the quality of succession planning within the audit firm, i.e. for the rotation of key audit partners.

Reviewing auditor independence

The ICAEW's guidance to audit committees on reviewing auditor independence stresses that the prime responsibility for ensuring its independence and objectivity rests with the audit firm itself. However, the audit committee should each year ask the audit firm for information about its policies and procedures for remaining independent.

The responsibilities of the audit committee should be to:

- seek reassurance that the audit firm and its staff have no family, financial, employment investment or business relationship with the company
- develop and implement a policy on using the audit firm to provide non-audit services without putting its independence and objectivity into question
- hold discussions with the auditors on matters such as the provision of non-audit services, audit partner rotation, the dependence of the audit firm on fee income from the company and employment by the company of audit firm partners and staff.

The ICAEW emphasises in its guidance that the key issue is ensuring the independence of the auditors. The audit opinion must be free from bias, and the auditors must therefore be objective in reaching their opinion.

The guidance lists the threats to auditor independence, and states that the onus for considering these threats and putting suitable safeguards in place rests with the audit firm.

- *Self-interest*. The audit firm or an individual auditor might benefit from a financial interest in the company, or might have a conflict of interest in some matter affecting the company. For example, the audit firm might rely heavily on its fee income from the company, or an auditor might be hoping to obtain a job with the company.

- *Self-review threat.* This arises from the possibility that the auditors might, as part of their audit, have to review work previously done by the company by the audit firm. The audit team could be under pressure not to criticise work done or advice given by their colleagues.
- *Advocacy threat.* This arises when the audit firm finds itself in a position where it is promoting the client company's position or opinion, such that its objectivity is compromised. This could occur, for example, if the audit firm speaks on behalf of the company in litigation or assists with the resolution of disputes between the company and a third party.
- *Familiarity threat.* Auditors are at risk of becoming too sympathetic to the company. This can occur simply through a long-term association of a senior auditor with the annual audits of the company. The threat is even greater if a close family member of one of the auditors is a director or senior manager in the company, or if a former audit partner is now a senior manager in the company, for example, the finance director. Independence can also be threatened by gifts from the company, or hospitality.
- *Intimidation threat.* Members of the audit team might be influenced by intimidation from individuals in the company. Intimidation could take the form of a threat to replace the auditors, or pressure to complete some aspects of the audit work in an unreasonably short time, or even pressure from a dominant personality in the client company.

Non-audit services and auditor independence

Questions can be raised about auditor independence when the audit firm does non-audit work for the company, in addition to the audit. Non-audit services could consist of preparing accounts and financial statements for the client, tax services (consultancy, etc.), valuations, internal audit services, the provision and installation of IT systems, corporate finance services, and so on.

The main problems are likely to be:

- a reluctance of the audit team to criticise work done by or advice given by their colleagues
- fee income. Fee income from non-audit services could become large in relation to audit fee income, such that the independence of the audit firm must be brought into question.

The ICAEW guidelines suggest that the threat to auditor independence from providing non-audit services will vary according to the nature of the services and the circumstances of each case. It is unlikely, for example, that auditors can remain independent if the firm prepares the company's accounts and financial statements.

The audit committee should develop a policy for making recommendations to the board about the appointment of the audit firm to do non-audit work. The ICAEW suggests that this policy should take into consideration:

- whether the audit firm has the skills and experience to do the work
- whether there are safeguards in place to protect the audit firm's independence and objectivity
- the nature of the non-audit work
- the levels of fees for non-audit work compared with the size of the audit fee.

The audit committee might wish to balance the advantages of using audit firm staff for non-audit work, which will give them a better understanding of the company and its business, against the threat to their independence.

9.3 Hiring former audit firm staff: effect on audit firm independence

The Smith Report recommended that the audit committee should review the company's policy for employing former staff of the audit firm in senior management positions. The ICAEW's guidance on this matter is that a threat to auditor independence will arise if a key audit team member takes a key management job in the company *unless* at least two years have elapsed since completion of the relevant audit work.

Audit partner rotation

The ICAEW places requirements on audit firms to rotate audit partners for the audits of listed companies, as a necessary measure for protecting auditor independence. From 1st January 2003:

- the lead audit engagement partner should be changed at least every five years, and the individual should not return to the audit for at least five years
- other senior audit partners should not work on the audit for more than seven years, with no return for at least two years.

10 Ethical Standards for auditors

In October, the Auditing Practices Board (a part of the Financial Reporting Council) issued its first five Ethical Standards for auditors, containing basic principles and essential practices for ethical conduct. The Standards, which are all effective for financial statements for periods commencing on or after 15 December 2004, are:

- ES1: Integrity, objectivity and independence
- ES2: Financial, business, employment and personal relationships
- ES3: Long association with the audit engagement
- ES4: Fees, remuneration and evaluation policies, litigations, gifts and hospitality
- ES5: Non-audit services provided to audit clients.

A brief summary of each Ethical Standard is set out below.

ES1: Integrity, objectivity and independence

An audit firm should establish policies and procedures, appropriately documented and communicated, which are designed to ensure that for each audit that it undertakes, the firm (including the audit engagement team and anyone else in a position to influence the conduct of the audit) should act with integrity, objectivity and independence.

The firm should be alert to the threats to objectivity and perceptions of independence. These threats are categorised as follows:

- *Self-interest threat.* This is the risk arising from self-interest of the auditor or audit firm.
- *Self-review threat.* This could arise whenever the audit team has to review non-audit work carried out for the client by anyone in the audit firm.
- *Management threat.* This could arise whenever the audit firm takes on work for the client where it will have to make decisions and judgements that are a management task. The auditor should not be in a position of acting in a management capacity for the audit client.
- *Advocacy threat.* This could occur whenever the audit form takes on work for the client where it acts as an advocate for the client in an adversarial context.
- *Familiarity threat (or trust threat).* This is the risk from trusting someone working for the audit client because of familiarity and having got to know the person.

The audit firm should designate a partner as the ethics partner with responsibility for the adequacy of the firm's policies and procedures on ethical issues, and for providing guidance to individual partners.

ES2: Financial, business, employment and personal relationships

This Ethical Standard provides requirements and guidance on circumstances arising out of financial, business, employment and personal relationships with the audit client (and people working for it), which may create threats to the auditor's objectivity and perceived loss of independence. It also suggests safeguards that might in some circumstances either eliminate the risk or reduce it to an acceptable level.

ES3: Long association with the audit engagement

The audit form should establish policies and procedures for monitoring the length of time that audit engagement partners, key audit partners and senior staff of the firm serve as members of the audit engagement team for a particular audit client. Where any individual has a long association with an audit, the firm should assess the threats to his or her objectivity and independence, and should apply safeguards to reduce the risks to an acceptable level.

The risks can be reduced through a rotation of the audit partner and senior staff on the audit. As a guideline, the Ethical Standard suggests that for non-listed company audits, rotation for any individual should be made within ten years. For listed companies, the suggested rotation period is shorter:

- No one should act as the audit engagement partner for a continuous period of more than five years, after which he or she should not be re-appointed to a position of responsibility for to the same audit for at least a further five years.
- No one should act as a key audit partner for a continuous period of more than seven years.
- The position of senior staff on an audit should be reviewed after seven years.

ES4: Fees, remuneration and evaluation policies, litigations, gifts and hospitality

This Ethical Standard provides requirements and guidance on specific circumstances, arising out of fees, economic dependence, litigation, remuneration and evaluation of partners and staff, and receiving gifts and hospitality, that could threaten the objectivity of the auditor and create a perceived loss of independence.

The Standard states, for example, that:

- an audit firm should not undertake audit work on a contingency fee basis
- where it is expected that the fees from a particular client for audit and non-audit work will regularly exceed 10 per cent of its annual income, the audit firm should not act as auditor to the client and should either resign or not stand for reappointment.

ES5: Non-audit services provided to audit clients

For the auditing profession, this is the most controversial of the first five Ethical Standards. This Ethical Standard provides requirements and guidance on specific circumstances arising from the provision of non-audit services to an audit client, which could threaten the objectivity of the auditor and create a perceived loss of independence:

- Where the audit engagement partner considers it probable that a reasonable and informed third party would regard a proposed non-audit engagement as being such a threat, and safeguards to eliminate the threat or reduce it to an acceptable level are not available, the firm should not take on the non-audit engagement.
- The audit engagement partner should ensure that the reasons for deciding to take on any non-audit work for an audit client, and any safeguards adopted to reduce the risk of a threat to objectivity and independence, are appropriately documented.

The Ethical Standard goes on to specify whether an audit form should or should not take on particular types of non-audit work:

- Internal audit work can be taken on, subject to sufficient safeguards being in place to protect the objectivity and perceived independence of the external audit.
- However, an audit firm should not undertake an engagement to design, provide or implement an IT system for an audit client, where the system concerned would be a significant part of the accounting system or the audit firm would be required to undertake a part of the role of management for the audit client.
- An audit firm should not undertake valuation services for an audit client, when the valuation would both involve considerable subjective judgement by the valuer and the valuation could also have a material effect on the financial statements.
- The Standard specifies situations in which it is appropriate or inappropriate for the audit firm to provide tax services, corporate finance services and transaction-related services (such as due diligence investigations for a proposed takeover, or providing information to sponsors in relation to a prospectus or other investment circular) to an audit client.
- An audit firm should not provide litigation support services to an audit client, where this could involve an estimation of the likely outcome of a pending legal matter that could have a material effect on the disclosures in the financial statements, and a significant amount of subjective judgement is required.
- The audit firm should not undertake to provide recruitment services where this would involve the firm in making decisions about the employment of any employee or director of the audit client. For audit clients that are a listed company, the audit firm should not provide any recruitment services at all in relation to a key management position in the audit client itself or a significant affiliate.
- An audit firm should not provide accounting services to any audit client that is a listed company, except in an emergency.

11 The Sarbanes–Oxley Act (SOX) (s302) and financial reporting

UK companies with a US listing are subject to the requirements of s302 of the Sarbanes–Oxley Act 2002 with respect to financial reporting. Section 302 requires that in the annual or quarterly reports of the company, the CEO and chief financial officer (CFO) of the company must certify that they have reviewed the report and accounts and:

- the report does not contain any untrue statement and there is no misleading omission
- the accounts and other financial statements in the report give a fair view of the financial position and results of the company.

The CEO and CFO must certify their responsibility for establishing and maintaining the internal controls of the company (over disclosures and financial reporting), and that they have:

- designed internal controls to make sure that they receive reports on material information about the company (and its subsidiaries)
- evaluated the effectiveness of the internal controls within the previous 90 days
- presented in their report their conclusions about the effectiveness of those controls.

The CEO and CFO must also certify that they have disclosed to the external auditors and the audit committee:

- any material weaknesses in the internal controls
- any fraud involving management or other employees with a significant involvement in internal controls.

They must also disclose:

- any changes in internal controls, or
- other factors that might significantly affect the internal controls.

The consequences for UK companies with a US listing would appear to be that these companies must establish procedures for ensuring compliance with s302 (and s404) of SOX. They might do this by:

- requiring individual managers to provide an opinion about the effectiveness of the internal controls for which they are responsible, and/or
- setting up formal procedures for the approval of external disclosures, for example by establishing disclosure committees.

The relationship between corporate governance requirements in the UK and the US in this, and other, areas is summarised in Appendix 25.

CHAPTER

10

Internal Control, Risk Management and Internal Audit

1 Risk and corporate governance

Risk management is relevant to corporate government in two ways:

- It is the responsibility of the board of directors to look after the assets of their company and to protect the value of their shareholders' investment. This includes a duty to take measures to prevent losses through error, omission, fraud and dishonesty. Control measures are provided through a system of internal control. A principle of the UK Combined Code is that: '*The board should maintain a sound system of internal control to safeguard shareholders' investment and the company's assets.*'
- It is also argued that the board of directors should be responsible for making sure that all risks are managed properly. A company should protect itself against serious downside risks, such as losses through fire damage, flood damage, theft, accident claims by employees, and so on, and the board should be satisfied that a management system is in place for monitoring and controlling these risks. Executive managers take many business decisions where returns are difficult to predict, and there is upside risk as well as downside risk. The board should be satisfied that in their decision-making, managers take risk into account as well as expected returns. Similarly, when the board takes major investment decisions itself or decides on corporate strategy, risks as well as expected returns should be properly assessed.

The Cadbury Committee described risk management as 'the process by which executive management, under board supervision, identifies the risk arising from business ... and establishes the priorities for control and particular objectives'. The Committee took the view that risk management should be systematic and embedded in the company's procedures and that there should be a culture of risk awareness. The importance of risk management for a company is that a failure to monitor, control and contain risks could lead to financial collapse.

The Cadbury Committee argued the need not just for an effective system of internal control but also for broader risk management. This view was not generally accepted at the time, but the significance of risk management, and of the board's responsibility to shareholders for proper risk management, was eventually accepted 'officially' in the UK as an element of corporate governance with the publication of the Combined Code in 1998.

In relation to corporate governance, there are three main areas relating to controls and risk management:

1 the board's responsibility for the system of internal control, and reviewing internal financial controls
2 the responsibility of the audit committee for reviewing all the company's internal control systems and risk management systems (unless this responsibility is given to a separate committee or dealt with by the full board)
3 internal audit.

2 Defining an internal control system: the COSO Framework

An internal control system consists of a 'control environment' and control procedures. Although there are different ways in which an internal control system can be defined and analysed, a widely accepted 'standard' was published in the US in 1992 by the Committee of Sponsoring Organizations of the Treadway Commission (COSO) as a report entitled *Internal Control – Integrated Framework*. This is commonly known as the COSO Framework, and has influenced the approach to internal control of many organisations world-wide, including the AICPA in the US, the Basle Committee on Banking Supervision and the Turnbull Committee in the UK.

The COSO Framework defined internal control as 'a process, effected by an entity's board of directors, management and other personnel, designed to provide reasonable assurance regarding the achievement of objectives' in three particular areas:

- the effectiveness and efficiency of operations
- the reliability of financial reporting
- compliance with applicable laws and regulations.

This definition of internal control is much more extensive than internal controls applied just to financial reporting and accounting.

The COSO Framework states that an internal control system has five elements:

- A *control environment.* Without a suitable control environment, internal controls are unlikely to operate effectively. The responsibility for ensuring that a company has a sound system of internal control rests with the board of directors, which must establish the policies on risk and control. It must also ensure that the organisation operates with integrity and ethical values. Management has the responsibility for putting the board's policies into practice, but employees also have a responsibility for ensuring that the controls devised by management are implemented. There should be a culture of control embedded in the operations of the organisation, and the culture is created by the board of directors and senior management, who set the 'tone at the top'.
- *Risk identification and assessment.* There should be a system within the organisation for the regular review of risks, identifying new risks and identifying changes or developments in existing risks. Risks that have been identified should be assessed, to establish their materiality (in terms of probability of occurrence and the likely cost or loss in the event that they do happen). Internal controls may have to be devised to meet new risks or risks that have previously been undetected.
- *Control activities (internal controls).* In a report on internal control systems, based on the COSO Framework, the Basle Committee on Banking Supervision stated the principle that:

  > *Control activities should be an integral part of the daily activities of [an organisation]. An effective internal control system requires that an appropriate control structure is set up, with control activities defined at every business level. These should include: top level reviews; appropriate activity controls for different departments or divisions; physical controls; checking for compliance … and follow-up on non-compliance; a system of approvals and authorisations; and a system of verification and reconciliation.*

- *Information and communication.* An internal control system must have effective channels of communication to ensure that staff understand their roles and responsibilities, and adhere to them, and that other relevant information reaches the appropriate personnel.
- *Monitoring.* There must be regular monitoring and review of the efficiency and effectiveness of the internal control system. One method of carrying out independent reviews of the proper application of internal controls is internal audit.

When the Combined Code refers to internal control, it refers to all aspects of an internal control system, not just the internal controls (control activities).

3 Internal audit

Internal audit is defined as

> *an independent appraisal activity established within an organisation as a service to it. It is a control which functions by examining and evaluating the adequacy and effectiveness of other controls.*
>
> (CIMA, *Official Terminology*)

> *The objective of internal auditing is to assist members of the organisation in the effective discharge of their responsibilities. To this end internal auditing furnishes them with analyses, appraisals, recommendations, counsel and information concerning the activities reviewed.*
>
> (*Institute of Internal Auditors*)

An organisation might have an internal audit unit or section, which carries out investigative work. An internal audit function should act independently of executive managers, and would report either to the board itself, the audit committee, the chief executive officer or the finance director.

The work done by any internal audit unit is not prescribed by regulation, but is decided by management or by the board (or audit committee). The possible tasks of internal audit include the following.

- *Reviewing the internal control system.* Traditionally, an internal audit department has carried out checks on the financial controls in an organisation, possibly in collaboration with the external auditors. The checks would be to establish whether suitable financial controls exist, and, if so, whether they are applied properly and are effective. Reports by internal auditors can provide reassurance on internal controls as effective, or might recommend changes and improvements where weaknesses are uncovered.
- *Special investigations.* Internal auditors might conduct special investigations into particular aspects of the organisation's operations.
- *Examination of financial and operating information.* Internal auditors might be asked to investigate the timeliness of reporting and the accuracy of the information in reports.
- *Value for money audits.* A VFM audit is an investigation into an operation or activity, to establish whether it is economical, efficient and effective.
- *Reviewing compliance* by the organisation with particular laws or regulations.
- *Risk assessment.* Internal auditors might be asked to investigate aspects of risk management, and in particular the adequacy of the mechanisms for identifying, assessing and controlling significant risks to the organisation, from both internal and external sources.

4 Combined Code requirements: internal control and risk management systems, and internal audit

A Main Principle (C.2) of the Combined Code is that:

> *The board should maintain a sound system of internal control to safeguard shareholders' investment and the company's assets.*

The Code goes on to state that the board should establish formal and transparent arrangements for considering how they should apply the financial reporting and internal control principles (Main Principle C.3).

The *board* is required, at least annually, to conduct a review of the group's systems of internal controls, and should report to the shareholders that they have done so (Code Provision C.2.1):

> *The review should cover all controls, including financial, operational and compliance controls and risk management.*

In other words, the board's responsibility for reviewing internal controls and risk management extends beyond financial matters to the business operations and regulatory compliance.

The Code also states that the audit committee should have delegated responsibilities for some or all of these matters. Code Provision C.3.2 includes in the main responsibilities of the audit committee:

- to review the company's internal financial controls
- unless reviewed by a separate board risk committee consisting of independent directors or by the board as a whole, to review the company's internal control and risk management systems (i.e. extending beyond just internal financial controls)
- to monitor and review the effectiveness of the internal audit function.

Where there is no internal audit function, the audit committee should consider annually whether there is a need for one, and make a recommendation to the board. The reasons for the absence of an internal audit function should be explained in the relevant section of the annual report (Code Provision C.3.6).

5 The Turnbull Committee Report on internal control

In the UK, a working party was set up by the Institute of Chartered Accountants in England and Wales after the publication of the first Combined Code in 1998. This working party, known as the Turnbull Committee, published guidelines to listed companies on how to apply the principles of the Combined Code with respect to internal controls and risk management. The Report was entitled *Internal Control: Guidance for Directors on the Combined Code*.

The Guidance is intended to do the following:

- reflect sound business practice, in which internal control is embedded in the business processes by which a company pursues its business objectives
- remain relevant over time, in a continually changing business environment
- enable each company to apply the guidance in a way that reflects its particular circumstances.

The Turnbull Report, which is based on the COSO Framework, is now known as the Turnbull Guidance and included as an annexe to the 2003 revised Combined Code. The Guidance is considered in some detail below and is reproduced in Appendix 22.

6 Establishing and maintaining a sound system of internal control

The board of directors is responsible for maintaining a sound system of internal control. The Turnbull Guidance states that the board should:

- set appropriate policies on internal control
- seek regular assurance to satisfy itself that the system is operating effectively
- ensure that the system of internal control is effective in managing risks in the way that it has approved.

In deciding its policies for internal control and assessing what constitutes an effective system of internal control, the board should consider the following factors:

- the nature and extent of the risks facing the company
- the extent and categories of risk that it regards as acceptable for the company to bear
- the likelihood that the risks will materialise
- the company's ability to reduce the incidence and impact on the business of the risks that do materialise
- the costs of operating particular controls relative to the benefits to be obtained from managing the risks they control (Turnbull Guidance, Paragraph 17).

6.1 Elements of a sound system of internal control

The Turnbull Guidance describes a sound system of internal control quite broadly, stating that it should have three elements:

1 It should facilitate the effective and efficient operation of the company, by enabling it to respond to any significant risks to the achievement of the company's objectives. These might be 'business, operational, financial, compliance and other risks'. The

company's objectives include the safeguarding of assets from inappropriate use, loss or fraud, and ensuring that liabilities are identified and managed.
2 It should ensure the quality of both internal (management) and external reporting.
3 It should help to ensure compliance with laws and regulations and also with the company's internal policies concerning the conduct of business.

The internal control system therefore includes control activities, communication processes and processes for monitoring the continued effectiveness of the system. It should:

- 'be embedded in the operations of the company and form part of its culture';
- be capable of responding quickly to risks to the business as they emerge and develop;
- include procedures for reporting immediately to the management responsible and control failings that have been identified and any corrective action that has been undertaken.

The report emphasises that a sound system of internal control cannot provide certain protection against a company suffering losses or breaches of laws or regulations or failing to meet its business objectives. The possibility will always exist of 'poor judgement in decision-making, human error, control processes being deliberately circumvented by employees and others, management overriding controls and the occurrence of unforeseen circumstances'.

6.2 Reviewing the effectiveness of internal control

The Turnbull Guidance states that 'reviewing the effectiveness of internal control is an essential part of the board's responsibilities'. The Combined Code states that the authority to conduct the review should be delegated to the audit committee, but the board as a whole is responsible for the statements on internal control in the company's annual report and accounts. The review of internal control should therefore be carried out at least annually.

The system of internal control consists of a large number of control activities and communication and monitoring procedures, and it would be impossible for the board or a committee of the board to conduct detailed investigations:

- An essential feature of a sound system of internal control is a continuous monitoring of the system.
- The board should not rely solely on the monitoring processes that are built into the system as internal controls. It should also receive regular reports on internal control. 'Internal controls considered by the board should include all types of controls including those of an operational and compliance nature, as well as internal financial controls' (the Turnbull Report).

Management is accountable to the board for monitoring the internal control system, and should provide an assurance to the board that it has done so. 'The reports from management to the board should … provide a balanced assessment of the significant risks and the effectiveness of the system of internal control in managing those risks.' Any significant control failings or weaknesses that have been identified should be discussed in the management reports, including the impact they have had or could have, and the measures that have been taken to rectify them.

When reviewing management reports, the board (audit committee) should:

- consider what are the significant risks and assess how they have been identified, evaluated and managed
- assess the effectiveness of the related system of internal control in managing those significant risks (having particular regard to any significant failings or weaknesses in internal control that have been reported)
- consider whether the necessary actions are being taken to deal with identified failings or weaknesses
- consider whether the findings of the review indicate a need for more extensive monitoring of the internal control system (the Turnbull Guidance, paragraph 31).

The board (audit committee) should undertake an *annual assessment* for the purpose of making its public statement on internal control. This should consider, in particular:

- the changes, since the previous annual assessment, in the nature and extent of significant risks and the company's ability to respond to changes in its business and external environment
- the scope and quality of management's risk monitoring, the system of internal control and the work of the internal audit function (and other providers of assurance)
- the extent and frequency of reports to the board (audit committee) on risk monitoring and internal control
- the incidence of significant failings or weaknesses in control that have been identified in the period, and their actual or potential impact on the company's financial performance or condition
- the effectiveness of the company's public reporting processes.

Whenever the board (audit committee) becomes aware at any time of a significant failing or weakness in internal control, it should:

- find out how the failing or weakness arose
- re-assess the effectiveness of management's processes for designing, operating and monitoring the system of internal control (the Turnbull Guidance, Paragraph 34).

6.3 The board's statement on internal control

The board should present an annual report to shareholders on its review of the effectiveness of the company's internal control. The Turnbull Guidance adds:

- The board may wish to provide additional information in the annual report to assist understanding of the company's risk management processes and system of internal control.
- The report should explain that the system of internal control is designed to manage rather than eliminate risk, and can only provide reasonable assurance, not absolute assurance, against material misstatement or financial loss.
- The report should summarise the process the board (or audit committee) has applied in reviewing the effectiveness of the system of internal control.
- The board should ensure that its disclosures provide meaningful high-level information and do not give a misleading impression.

7 The annual review of internal audit

The Combined Code requires the audit committee to monitor and review the effectiveness of the internal audit function. Where there is no internal audit function, the audit committee should consider annually whether there is a need for one, and make a recommendation to the board (Code Provision C.3.6).

The Turnbull Guidance suggests that the need for an internal audit function will depend on the nature of the company and its activities, and on factors such as company size, diversity and complexity of activities, number of employees, and so on. Some particular aspects of risk and internal control might be monitored by specialist units, such as health and safety experts, lawyers and environmental experts.

The Guidance adds:

> *In the absence of an internal audit function, management needs to apply other monitoring processes in order to assure itself and the board that the system of internal control is functioning as intended. In these circumstances, the board will need to assess whether such processes provide sufficient and objective assurance.*

When undertaking its assessment of the need for an internal audit function, the audit committee should:

- look at trends or other factors relevant to the company's activities, markets or external environment that have changed and that have increased (or are expected to increase) the risks facing the company
- consider internal factors, such as organisational restructuring or changes in reporting processes or information systems, that might have led to an increased risk
- consider other matters such as adverse trends that are evident from the monitoring of internal control systems, or an increase in the incidence of unexpected occurrences.

8 The role of the board (audit committee) in risk management

The Combined Code states that unless either there is a separate board risk committee consisting of independent directors or the full board considers the matter itself, the audit committee should be responsible for reviewing the company's internal control and risk management systems, not just financial controls.

Some guidance is given by the Turnbull Guidance to the board of directors on how to carry out an assessment of risks. An appendix to the report provides a list of questions to which there ought to be satisfactory answers.

On risk assessment

- Does the company have clear objectives? Have these been communicated in a way that provides effective direction to employees on risk management and control issues?
- Are significant risks assessed on an ongoing basis? Significant risks could relate to market risk (adverse movements in market prices, including the company's own share price), and credit risk, liquidity risk, technological risk, legal risk, health and safety risk, environmental and reputational risk, and business probity issues.
- Do management and others have a clear understanding of what risks are acceptable to the board? In other words, is the board satisfied that management know the extent of the risks they can expose the company to without taking appropriate risk reduction or risk hedging measures?

On the control environment and control activities

- Does the board have a clear strategy for dealing with significant risks, and is there a policy on how to manage them?
- Do the company's culture and performance reward systems support the business objectives and risk management and internal control system? In other words, does the incentive system for senior management recognise the need for risk management as well as profit growth?
- Does senior management demonstrate through their actions as well as their policies a commitment to both competence and integrity?
- Are authority, responsibility and accountability clearly defined clearly, so that decisions are made and actions are taken by the appropriate people?
- Does the company communicate to its employees what is expected of them, and the scope of their freedom to act? The guidelines indicate the scope of this question by stating that it applies to areas such as customer relations, service levels, health and safety and environmental protection, security of assets, business continuity issues, expenditure and accounting and financial reporting.
- How are processes and controls adjusted to adapt to new risks or operational deficiencies?

On information and communication

- Do management and the board receive regular and relevant reports on actual performance compared with business objectives and the related risks, suitable for decision-making and management review purposes?
- Are periodic reporting procedures effective in communicating a proper account of the company's performance and prospects?

On monitoring

- Are processes embedded within the company's operations for monitoring the effective application of internal control and risk management?
- Is there appropriate communication to the board (or board committees) on the monitoring of risk and control matters?
- Are there specific arrangements for management monitoring and reporting to the board on risk and control matters of particular importance? These matters would include fraud and other illegal acts that could adversely affect the company's reputation or financial position.

8.1 Review of the Turnbull Guidance

The Financial Reporting Council established a working group in 2004, led by Douglas Flint, to review the Turnbull Guidelines, which by that time were five years old. The group issued a consultation document in December 2004, and the consultation period was due to run out on 2 March 2005. It is intended that any changes proposed by the working group should be implemented by listed companies for their financial year beginning on or after 1 January 2006.

The main questions raised by the consultation paper are:

- Should the Guidance continue to retain a high-level risk-based approach to the review of internal control, or should it move to a more detailed prescriptive approach?
- Should the Guidance continue to cover all controls, or should it be restricted to a review of just financial controls?
- Are the current disclosure requirements adequate?
- Should the board's private assessment of the effectiveness of the internal control system be turned into a public statement in the annual report and accounts of their assessment of its effectiveness?
- Should the role of the external auditors in the review be extended?

9 The Sarbanes–Oxley Act (Section 404) and the assessment of internal controls

UK companies with a US listing that have to register with the SEC are subject to the regulatory requirements of the Sarbanes–Oxley Act 2002 (SOX) with regard to the assessment of internal controls, and must comply with these requirements for reporting years ending on or after 15 July 2005. The SOX requirements are currently more rigid and prescriptive than those in the UK.

Section 404(a) directs the SEC to set rules requiring companies ('SEC registrants') to include an internal control in their annual report:

> *The Commission shall prescribe rules requiring each annual report … to contain an internal control report, which shall –*
>
> *(1) state the responsibility of management for establishing and maintaining an adequate internal control structure and procedures for financial reporting; and*
>
> *(2) contain an assessment, as of the end of the most recent fiscal year of the issuer, of the effectiveness of the internal control structure and procedures of the issuer for financial reporting.*

The SEC applied the requirements of s404(a) in its own Rule 33-8238. This Rule includes the requirements that:

(a) 'The management of each … issuer … must evaluate, with the participation of the issuer's principal executive and principal finance officers, … the effectiveness, as of the end of each fiscal year, of the issuer's internal control over financial reporting. The framework on which management's evaluation of the issuer's internal control over financial reporting is based must be a suitable, recognized control framework that is established by a body or group that has followed due-process procedures, including the broad distribution of the framework for public comment.'

(b) 'The management of each … issuer … must evaluate, with the participation of the issuer's principal executive and principal finance officers, … any change in the issuer's internal control over financial reporting that has occurred during each of the issuer's fiscal quarters, or fiscal year in the case of a foreign private issuer, that has materially affected, or is likely to materially affect, the issuer's internal control over financial reporting.'

(c) 'The term internal control over financial reporting is defined as a process designed by, or under the supervision of, the issuer's principal executive and principal finance officers … and effected by the issuer's board of directors, management and other personnel, to provide reasonable assurance regarding the reliability of financial reporting and the preparation of financial statements for external purposes in accordance with generally-accepted accounting principles and includes those policies and procedures that:

(1) pertain to the maintenance of records that in reasonable detail accurately and fairly reflect the transactions and dispositions of the assets of the issuer

(2) provide reasonable assurance that the transactions are recorded as necessary … and that receipts and expenditures … are being made only in accordance with authorizations of management and directors …

(3) provide reasonable assurance regarding prevention or timely detection of unauthorized acquisition, use or disposition of the issuer's assets that could have a material effect on the financial statements.'

(d) Companies should maintain evidence, including documentation, to provide reasonable support for management's assessment of the effectiveness of internal control over financial reporting.

Control deficiencies should be classified in accordance with PCAOB Auditing Standard No. 2, which identifies the following types of control deficiency:

- A *control deficiency*. This exists when the design or operation of a control does not allow management or employees to prevent or detect errors and misstatements in a timely manner. A control deficiency can be caused by either a deficiency in the design of the control or in its operation.
- A *significant deficiency*. This is a control deficiency that adversely affects the company's ability to 'initiate, authorize, record, process or report external financial data reliably', such that there is 'more than a remote likelihood' that a misstatement that is 'more than inconsequential' could occur in the financial statements.
- A *material weakness*. This is a significant deficiency that results in 'more than a remote likelihood' that a material misstatement in the financial statements will not be prevented or detected.

Management are required to disclose any material weaknesses in the company's internal control system for financial reporting, and are not permitted to conclude that the internal control is effective if one or more material weaknesses exist.

Section 404 of SOX requires companies to include in their annual report a report on 'internal control over financial reporting'. This report should set out:

- a statement of management's responsibility for establishing and maintaining adequate internal controls over the company's financial reporting
- a statement identifying the framework used by management for evaluating the efficiency and effectiveness of the internal control over financial reporting
- an assessment by management of the effectiveness of the internal control over financial reporting, as at the end of the most recent fiscal year (and any 'material weakness' in internal control)
- disclosure of any material weakness in the company's internal control over financial reporting that management has identified
- a statement that the external auditors have issued an 'attestation report' on management's assessment of the company's internal control over financial reporting. This attestation report by the auditors should be filed as part of the company's annual report.

In order to prepare this report on internal control, management must:

- undertake a review of the effectiveness of internal controls over financial reporting (the 'review' requirements'), and
- maintain evidence to provide reasonable support for management's assessment of the effectiveness of internal controls (the 'documentation requirements').

9.1 Rule 404 and the Turnbull Guidance

Under SEC Rule 33-8238, the Turnbull Guidance is recognised as an acceptable framework for the conduct of the assessment of the internal controls over financial reporting. In December 2004, the FRC issued guidance to UK companies registered with the SEC on the use of the Turnbull Guidelines for the purpose of s404(a).

In its guidance, the FRC made the following general comments about the use of Turnbull in a US context:

- Although the Turnbull Guidance is an acceptable framework for s404 purposes, all SEC Rules and US security laws must be complied with. In particular, companies must meet the requirements regarding appropriate documentation of processes and testing (in order to demonstrate compliance).
- Responsibility for compliance with s404(a) rests with the management of the company, whereas the Turnbull Guidance was written in a UK corporate governance context, in which the responsibility lies with the board of directors.
- The Turnbull Guidance was also written within the context of the 'comply or explain' requirement of UK Listing Rule 12.43A. In a US context, companies using the Turnbull Guidance as a framework for meeting s404 requirements *must* comply with all the Turnbull guidelines.
- Compliance with s404 calls for careful preparation, particularly with regard to documentation and testing. SEC Rule 33-8238 states that companies should maintain evidence, including documentation,

9.2 Comparing s404 of Sarbanes–Oxley with the Combined Code and Turnbull Guidance

There are significant differences between the requirements of SOX and the Combined Code/Turnbull Guidance. For UK companies without a US listing:

- there is no requirement for management to report on the effectiveness of internal control, only to state each year that they have reviewed the system of control
- there is no requirement for the auditors to report to shareholders on the directors' statement on internal control
- however, Section 404 applies to internal control over financial reporting only, whereas the review of internal control in the UK covers operational controls, compliance with laws and regulations and risk management.

CHAPTER

11

Corporate Social Responsibility (CSR)

1 Definitions of CSR

Many investors expect companies to operate in a socially responsible manner, and also to provide information about the nature of their policies and activities in this area.

Since CSR is concerned with the way in which companies are run, and with communications with stakeholders (particularly shareholders and the investment community), it is appropriate to regard CSR as an issue in corporate governance.

There are many different definitions of CSR:

> *While there is no single, commonly accepted definition of corporate social responsibility, or CSR, it generally refers to business decision-making linked to ethical values, compliance with legal requirements, and respect for people, communities and the environment.*
>
> *(Business for Social Responsibility: www.bsr.org)*

> *The government sees CSR as the business contribution to our sustainable development goals. Essentially, it is about how business takes account of its economic, social and environmental impacts in the way it operates – maximising the benefits and minimising the downsides. Specifically, we see CSR as the voluntary actions that business can take, over and above compliance with minimum legal requirements, to address both its own competitive interests and the interests of wider society.*
>
> *(The Department of Trade and Industry's CSR web-site: www.csr.gov.uk)*

> *CSR is used synonymously with 'corporate citizenship' and encompasses environmental, social and economic aspects of business impacts and performance.*
>
> *(International Institute for Environment and Development)*

> *The continuing commitment by business to behave ethically and contribute to economic development while improving the quality of life of the workforce ... the local community and society at large.*
>
> (*The World Business Council for Sustainable Development*, 1998)

2 The issues in CSR

One problem with CSR is that the issues facing companies, and their potential significance, vary from one company to another and from one industry to another according to its particular circumstances. The general principles of CSR might be relatively easy to establish, but the application of principles to particular circumstances is more complex.

Business in the Community, a voluntary group of UK companies working for the application of responsible business practices, has set out five principles that companies should apply:

- to treat employees fairly and with respect
- to operate in an ethical way and with integrity
- to respect basic human rights
- to sustain the environment for future generations
- to be a responsible neighbour in their communities.

More specifically, CSR issues include the following.

2.1 Ethical behaviour

Companies should behave in an ethical manner, with the lead given by its top managers. Behaving ethically covers all aspects of CSR, but includes avoiding corrupt practices and not using bribery to influence decisions by customers and governments.

More controversially, ethical behaviour might be extended to taxation matters, such as choosing not to use tax avoidance schemes and contributing a fair share in taxation to government spending on the community.

Inevitably, there are differences of opinion about what is meant by 'ethical', since views can differ sharply. For example, there are fiercely opposing views about how companies should exploit scientific change, such as stem cell research and genetic modification, and whether experimentation on animals should be permitted for research and the development of new products.

2.2 Sustainable development

Sustainable development has been defined as; 'development which meets the needs of the present without compromising the ability of future generations to meet their own needs (the UN Conference on the Environment and Development or 'Earth Summit' 1992). Issues relating to sustainable development include:

- reduction in pollution, and the view that the polluters should pay for the pollution they cause
- climate change and action to reduce the adverse impact of change; reductions in harmful emissions
- the preservation of natural resources or their replacement (e.g. timber, fish stocks)
- conserving the biodiversity of life and the preservation of species
- waste minimisation (waste reduction, re-cycling, re-use of materials) and the safe disposal of waste
- energy efficiency.

2.3 Human rights issues

Human rights issues relate to the community generally, as well as to employees and the employees of suppliers and customer organisations. Issues include:

- the prohibition of slavery
- the prohibition of child labour
- the right to personal safety and security (health and safety at work issues; issues relating to the effect of products on the health of consumers)
- the right to freedom from discrimination, on grounds of race, religion, sex, age, etc.
- the prohibition of torture and the degrading treatment of individuals
- the right to form trade unions
- the right to rest and leisure (working hours issues)
- the right to an adequate living standard (pay issues)
- the right to education.

Human rights issues relate not only to the company itself, but to suppliers and the countries where suppler firms are located. All companies in the supply chain, including retailers and providers of high-quality branded goods, might be adversely affected by publicity about the use of child labour or 'sweat shop labour' by suppliers.

3 Why does CSR matter?

CSR can be significant for companies, particularly listed companies, for several reasons. These reasons are linked to initiatives taken by investor and lending institutions, which themselves are influenced by the attitudes of governments and the public in general.

- Some shareholders and investment institutions regard corporate social responsibility as an indication of good corporate governance, and their support for the board of directors might be influenced by the CSR policies of the company.

- Ethical investment institutions are constrained in the investments they make by ethical considerations, and need to obtain as much information as they can from companies about their CSR policies and practices, in order to make their investment decisions.
- Governments are giving support to the voluntary disclosure of information by companies about CSR issues, and are encouraging companies to give more attention to CSR issues and the disclosure of information about these issues. The OECD has issued guidelines for multinational enterprises on CSR issues and disclosure (see paragraph 4).
- Ethical issues might be a factor in lending decisions by both public sector lending institutions and private sector banks. The World Bank and other development banks require borrowers to respect environment and human rights as a precondition of lending. (In 2004, a number of banks adopted the Equator Principles to the provision of project finance. These provide a framework for banks to manage environmental and social issues when they consider requests for project financing. The principles are applied to direct project loans with a total capital cost of $50 million or more, globally and across all industry sectors. They provide a standardised method of assessing projects, whereby lenders ensure that the projects they finance are developed in a manner that is socially responsible and environmentally sound. The banks that have adopted the Principles account for about 75 per cent of all project loans (globally) by commercial banks.)
- Public awareness of CSR issues continues to develop, and information about companies and CSR is widely reported and publicised.
- CSR has become a recognised issue in corporate governance by drawing attention to the relationships between a company and its stakeholders, other than its shareholders: 'Governance systems are increasingly expected to extend beyond their traditional focus on investors to address diverse stakeholders' (GRI Framework 2002).

CSR issues can affect the value of companies:

- Adverse publicity and adverse shareholder reaction can damage a company's perceived 'reputation' in the market place. Reputation risk is now recognised by many companies as a significant risk that needs to be monitored and managed.
- Social and environmental issues might also provide opportunities for companies to develop their businesses. CSR can provide opportunities as well as risks.

The potential significance risks to companies from CSR issues from a financial rather than an ethical perspective are:

- brand reputation (reputation risk), and
- stakeholder preferences. Employees might prefer working for ethical organisations, customers might prefer buying from them and suppliers might prefer dealing with them. Perhaps even more significantly, investors might prefer holding the securities of ethical companies (and companies with good governance practices).

However, as yet, there is no clear link between CSR and short-term shareholder value.

4 Deciding a CSR policy

Companies need to decide whether they should have a policy on CSR. For many companies, particularly large public companies, the need for a policy on CSR may be driven by investor expectations. Multinational companies could base their CSR policy on diversity in CSR practice between different countries, or a consistent policy worldwide in all countries in which the mulitnaitonal (and its suppliers) operate.

The CSR policy objective of a multinational might therefore be:

- compliance with national and local laws
- applying the same high standards worldwide, regardless of national and local laws, or
- aiming for standards that are higher than those actually required in any country or jurisdiction.

The OECD has issued *Guidelines for Multinational Enterprises* (first published in 2000, revised 2004). This includes the requirements that multinationals should:

- contribute to economic, social and environmental progress
- aim to achieve sustainable development
- respect human rights
- avoid exemptions in local laws
- disclose its CSR policies and CSR information.

5 CSR and shareholders

Much of the pressure for enhanced sustainability reporting has come from investment institutions and associations, or is aimed at providing investors with the CSR-related information they require.

5.1 ABI Disclosure Guidelines

In October 2001, the Association of British Insurers issued *Disclosure Guidelines on Socially Responsible Investment* (see Appendix 23). These are aimed at both companies and investment institutions, and set out the issues about social, environmental and ethical (SEE) performance that be included in a company's annual report. The Guidelines take the form of disclosures that investment institutions should expect to see in the annual reports of listed companies.

They state that the annual report should describe the company's policies and procedures for managing the risks to short-term and long-term value arising out of SEE matters:

- The annual report 'should include information about the extent to which the company has complied with its policies and procedures for managing risks arising from SEE matters'.
- 'If the annual report and accounts state that the company has no such policies and procedures, the board should provide reasons for their absence.'

Although SEE disclosures are voluntary, the Guidelines suggest that shareholders might be encouraged to vote against boards that persistently ignore their concerns.

5.2 CSR indices: FTSE and Dow Jones indices

Both the FTSE and Dow Jones have developed a series of share price indices for companies that meet certain criteria for 'good' CSR values. Dow Jones publish a Dow Jones Sustainability Index series, and FTSE have a FTSE4Good Index series (with a FTSE4Good UK, FTSE4Good Europe and FTSE4Good US index).

Companies are admitted to a relevant index if they meet suitable CSR criteria, which have been tightened up over time, and they are removed if they fail to meet them.

Investors wishing to invest ethically can use the indices to monitor the performance of their investments. FTSE have argued that the introduction of the series has resulted in a much greater attention by listed companies to CSR issues.

5.3 Corporate Responsibility Exchange (CRE)

The London Stock Exchange has established a Corporate Responsibility Exchange. This is an on-line service based on a central data bank of corporate governance and CSR information, and companies subscribing to the service submit information to the Exchange. The CRE also has links to FTSE4Good and Business in the Community.

The aim of the CRE is to improve the efficiency of communications of corporate responsibility data, and to reduce the administrative burdens on companies that might otherwise be required to respond to large numbers of CSR questionnaires from proxy voting agencies and other investor services.

- Companies only need to complete one corporate responsibility questionnaire each year.
- Investors or their agents wanting to obtain corporate reponsibility information about companies can obtain it conveniently from the CRE site instead of having to approach each company individually.

6 CSR, the UK Government and the EU

6.1 UK government initiatives

Government initiatives for companies to act in a socially responsibly way vary from country to country and industry to industry, and are written into legislation such as employment law and laws on environmental protection and waste disposal.

The UK government has taken the view that most CSR initiatives should be undertaken voluntarily by business, but that the government should actively encourage the adoption of best practice.

- The government published a sustainable development policy for the UK in 1999 (*A Better Quality of Life*), which set out indicators on progress towards achieving a sustainable society. At the 2002 World Summit on Sustainable Development, the government made a commitment to actively promote corporate responsibility and accountability.
- The Sustainable Development Commission, an independent advisory body to the government, produced a report in 2004 on progress towards achieving a sustainable society which called for some policy changes. This led to a major review and consultation on sustainable development strategy, begun in April 2004.
- Since 2001, the government has maintained a web-site on CSR issues: www.societyandbusiness.gov.uk or www.csr.gov.uk.
- The government has issued guidelines on environmental reporting (greenhouse gas emissions, waste and water).
- In 2004, the DTI gave its support to the CSR Academy, which has been established as a collaboration between five partner organisations to promote CSR learning, and develop a programme of training activities.

6.2 European Commission intiatives

Like the UK, the European Commission also currently takes the view that CSR and CSR reporting should be essentially voluntary.

- The EC is developing a CSR strategy that covers consumer concerns and environmental, social and economic issues. This strategy will be focussed in those areas where EC involvement can add value.
- The strategy will support international legal obligations such as human rights and environmental treaties.

The EC strategy has the following aims:

- to improve awareness of the benefits of CSR for business and society as a whole
- to develop methods of exchanging information about good CSR practice between businesses and member states

- to develop codes of conduct for environmental, human rights and labour issues, and with regard to corrupt practices
- to develop management skills in CSR and promote the development of CSR standards
- to encourage companies to provide 'triple bottom line' reporting (economic, social and environmental reporting).

7 CSR reporting and disclosure

7.1 Government initiatives for CSR reporting

To date, most government initiatives on CSR disclosures by companies have been based on the view that disclosures should be voluntary, but that companies should be encouraged to provide CSR information, primarily by:

- providing a CSR report (possibly called a Social and Environmental Report or a Sustainability Report) as a part of or as a supplement to the annual report and accounts (and to make similar information available on the company's web-site), and
- providing information on CSR issues on request to institutional investors or their agents (e.g. proxy voting agencies).

7.2 CSR reporting guidelines

A major element of best practice in CSR is that companies should publish an annual CSR report (Sustainability Report, or Social and Environmental report). However, at the moment there is no accepted standard or format for these reports. Although many companies produce them, their content, format and style vary considerably.

GRI Guidelines

Perhaps the best-established set of guidelines for CSR reporting are the *GRI Guidelines*. The Global Reporting Initiative, now an institution of the United Nations, was set up in 1997 with the objective of raising sustainability reporting to the same level as financial reporting. It first published *Sustainability Reporting Guidelines* in 2000. (These were amended in 2002 and the next version is due in 2006.) The Guidelines present principles for companies to apply in preparing Sustainability Reports and also specific content guidelines.

The GRI has issued (and continues to issue) a range of documents, including:

- *Guidelines*. This is the foundation document, providing an outline of the core content of sustainability reports that is broadly relevant to all organisations, regardless of size, industry sector or location.

- *Technical protocols*. These are intended to help companies to apply the Guidelines. Each technical protocol addresses a specific 'indicator' (e.g. energy use, child labour) and how these may be measured (in quantitative or qualitative terms) for reporting purposes, by providing detailed definitions, procedures and formulae.
- *Sector supplements*. These address issues that are relevant to a specific industry sector. They supplement but do not replace the Guidelines.

The GRI Guidelines state that a Sustainability Report should include sections on:

- *Vision and strategy*. The organisation's strategy with regard to sustainability, including a statement from the CEO.
- *Profile*. An overview of the company's structure and operations, and the scope of the report.
- *Governance structure and management systems*. A description of the organisation structure, policies and management systems, including the company's efforts at stakeholder engagement.

There should be a GRI content index. This is a table identifying where specific items of relevant information can be found in the report.

The Guidelines also provide a detailed list of quantitative and qualitative indicators for the following issues:

- Economic indicators, relating to economic issues
- Environmental indicators
- Social indicators, divided into several sub-categories:
  - labour practices and decent work
  - human rights
  - society
  - product responsibility.

For details of the Guidelines, visit www.globalreporting.org.

Other CSR reporting initiatives

In spite of the GRI Guidelines, CSR reporting by companies lacks consistency in content and format. However, there have been several initiatives to provide companies and investors with information about the CSR reports that companies do produce.

- Copies of CSR reports by companies are available on the web-site: www.iosreporting.org.
- Business in the Community has issued an Impact on Society reporting framework. This gives practical guidelines for measuring and reporting CSR performance.

7.3 CSR and the Operating and Financial Review

The annual Operating and Financial Review, which will be a statutory requirement for larger companies, should cover any significant risks arising from social or environmental issues. The OFR will not replace CSR reports, and will not require the inclusion of references to CSR issues. However, the OFR should include certain topics 'whenever the directors in good faith judge them *material*'. These will include corporate governance; values and structures; an account of key relationships with employees, customers, suppliers and others; and policies and performance on environmental, community, social, ethical and reputational issues.

8 Other CSR initiatives and organisations

Social Accountability System SA8000

Social Accountability International is a US-based not-for-profit organisation that promotes standards for maintaining just and decent working conditions throughout the supply chain. It establishes standards relating to child labour, forced labour, health and safety, the right to collective bargaining, discrimination at work, working hours and pay.

SA8000 provides a third-party verification system, and companies meeting the required standards throughout their supply chain can apply for and obtain a SA8000 certificate.

AccountAbility

The Institute of Social and Ethical Accountability (www.accountability.org.uk) is an organisation with international membership committed to enhancing the CSR performance of organisations and competence of individuals.

In 1999 it launched an AA1000 Framework. This is an accountability standard focusing on accounting, auditing and reporting of ethical and social issues, built around the engagement of companies with their stakeholders. This complements the GRI sustainability reporting guidelines, by dealing with how sustainability reports should be prepared, checked and used rather than what they should contain. A major element of the AA1000 Framework is the guidance it provides on stakeholder engagement.

In March 2003, AccountAbility issued an AA1000 Assurance Standard.

SIGMA

SIGMA is an acronym for Sustainability – Integrated Guidelines for Management. The Project SIGMA initiative was launched in the UK in 1999 as a partnership between the British Standards Institution, Forum for the Future and AccountAbility, with support from the Department of Trade and Industry. It has developed Guidelines (2003) giving practical advice to the management of companies on how to develop and implement policies for sustainability. These are available on www.projectsigma.com.

Business in the Community Corporate Responsibility Index

Business in the Community (BitC) is an association of UK companies whose aim is to promote CSR, largely by benchmarking and exchanging information on CSR practices. In 2002 it launched an initiative to produce a voluntary Corporate Responsibility Index. This index is calculated by giving 'scores' to participating companies in relation to business practices in the areas of:

- the community
- the environment
- the market place, and
- the work place.

The answers in the survey are converted into an index score (up to 100) and the scores of each company are then used to provide a ranking. The 2002 survey results were published in *The Sunday Times*. The results of a 2004 survey are due to be reported in *The Sunday Times* during 2005.

The BitC CRI scores can be used by participating companies:

- to assess their progress over time on CSR issues, and
- to compare their own progress with the progress of other companies in the survey, and particularly those in the same business sector.

9 Codes of ethics

Companies that develop a policy on CSR might do so within the framework of a code of ethics. In the UK, the adoption of a code of ethics by companies is voluntary. Several institutions have been established to promote business ethics, such as the International Business Ethics Institute in the US, the Institute of Business Ethics in the UK and the European Business Ethics Network in the Netherlands.

In the US, Section 406 of the Sarbanes–Oxley Act (SOX) requires companies to make an annual disclosure of whether it has adopted a code of ethics for its CEO and senior financial officers, and if not, why not. The code must be made available to the public, and changes to or waiver of the code must be reported.

In January 2003, the SEC announced that in accordance with s406 SOX, companies under its jurisdiction would be required to disclose in their annual reports for financial years ending on or after 15 July 203 whether they have adopted a code of ethics applicable to:

- its CEO
- its chief financial officer, and
- other senior managers with accounting and financial functions.

A code of ethics and business conduct is a written code that should deal with:

- honest and ethical conduct
- avoiding conflicts of interest

- handling situations in which an individual has an opportunity for personal gain through the use of company property or because of his or her position in the company
- confidentiality
- fair dealing with customers, suppliers, employees and competitors
- protection and proper use of the company' assets
- compliance with laws and regulations
- encouraging the reporting of illegal and unethical behaviour by others
- full, fair, accurate, timely and understandable disclosures in company reports and other public communications
- compliance with laws and regulations
- prompt internal reporting of violations of the code
- accountability for compliance with the code.

In practice, although the SOX requirement for a code of ethics is restricted to the CEO and senior financial managers, companies might choose to extend it to all their employees.

9.1 How serious are companies about CSR?

The growth in CSR reporting has been criticised as a public relations exercise by companies rather than a recognition of social and ethical issues in corporate governance.

In October 2002, there was a reported disagreement between the Institute of Directors (IoD) and a think tank, the Institute for Public Policy Research (IPPR). The IoD had commissioned a survey of 500 businesses, which was used by the IPPR to prepare a report that questioned the commitment of UK companies to corporate social responsibility. The IPPR report, with which the IoD disagreed, was said to include the findings that there was a considerable amount of hypocrisy shown by companies and a large gulf between the 'supportive rhetoric' on CSR and the reality. For example, in only 40 per cent of the companies surveyed were social and environmental issues discussed at board meetings; only a third of companies had a board member with responsibility for environmental issues; and just over one-fifth had a board member with responsibility for social issues.

The 2003 annual report by the Environment Agency, *Spotlight on Business*, commented that the Agency supported the requirement in the planned legislation for listed companies to disclose information about environmental risk matters in the Operating and Financial Review. However, it added: 'While almost 90 per cent of FTSE listed companies mention the environment in their existing annual reports, they are generally not disclosing sufficient information to meet the new OFR requirements.'

It seems highly probable that pressures for CSR reporting and greater disclosures will continue to grow.

CHAPTER

Whistleblowing 12

1 The nature of whistleblowing

A whistleblower is an employee who provides information about his or her company which he or she reasonably believes provides evidence of:

- a violation of a law or regulation by the company;
- a miscarriage of justice;
- financial malpractice; or
- a danger to public health or safety.

In the government sector, a whistleblower might also provide evidence of a gross waste of public funds or gross mismanagement.

A feature of whistleblowing is that the individual concerned has been unable to get a response from the company's management through normal lines of reporting, which has forced the individual to go to someone else with the information. The whistleblower presumably hopes that the recipient of the information will take action to deal with the misdemeanour.

There is a strong connection between corporate governance and whistleblowing. An employee may honestly believe that there is, has been or could soon be serious malpractice by someone within the company, but feel unable to report his or her concerns in the normal way.

The board of directors and senior management have a responsibility for monitoring potential risks within their company. This responsibility includes a need to recognise that whistleblowing by an employee would help to uncover significant risks, and procedures should therefore exist to encourage 'honest' whistleblowing, whilst at the same time discouraging malicious and unjustifiable accusations and allegations from employees against their bosses.

Concerns about whistleblowing have grown in recent years, for three main reasons:

1. A huge amount of information about a company is held on computer files, which are accessible to many employees. Individual employees prepared to spend the time to look closely into a matter are likely to discover a large amount of information that they might not 'officially' be supposed to know, or information that no one else has yet become aware of. Companies are now aware, for example, that they could become liable for information held as e-mail messages in the files of employees.
2. In many companies, there is a strong culture of loyalty to the company. Employees who question or criticise the actions of management might be considered to be 'traitors'. Despite laws designed to protect them, whistleblowers run the risk of retaliatory action from their company. When they report their suspicions, they may be sacked on the grounds of making false and malicious allegations. It would certainly appear to be the case that whistleblowers are more likely to be dismissed than rewarded. This is particularly the case when the whistleblower passes the information to someone outside the company, such as a newspaper.
3. Individual whistleblowers played an important role in uncovering information about financial and accounting mismanagement at Enron (2001) and WorldCom (2002), and in criticising the handling of security information by the FBI before the September 11 terrorist attacks in New York. The public became aware not only that organisations were being mismanaged, but that honest attempts to reveal the problems were being disregarded by senior management.

Whistleblowers can put their job at risk. An employer taking retaliatory action may claim that sacking the employee had nothing to do with the revelations the employee had made, or claim that the employee was sacked because his or her statements were vindictive and untrue.

2 Whistleblowing: best practice

Companies rightly should not want to encourage malicious whistleblowing. On the other hand, it would be inappropriate to treat whistleblowers as 'enemies' and 'traitors'. The problems facing whistleblowers relate to weaknesses in corporate governance. If an employee has a genuine, honest concern about something happening within the company, which he or she believes to be dishonest or improper, there should be a way for the employee's concerns to be brought to the attention of management and dealt with in a constructive way. Having a system for listening to employees' concerns should be a part of an effective risk management system within the organisation, because diligent employees can act as an early warning system of problems.

In practice, employees may feel obliged to take their concerns to someone *outside the organisation* (such as the press or a government regulator), risking the anger of the employer for breach of proper procedures.

2.1 Internal procedures for dealing with whistleblowers' allegations

A company should have a fair system for dealing internally with accusations from whistleblowers, so that an honest individual does not feel under threat when making an allegation. Employees ought to know what those procedures are.

Since whistleblowing is not a regular event, a company may simply try to deal with each case on its merits when it arises, without any formal procedures or channels of complaint being established. The employee will therefore not know whom to complain to, and will probably go to the most senior manager available – possibly the chief executive.

A problem with dealing with whistleblowing incidents on an *ad hoc* basis is that the accusations may relate to the senior executive directors themselves. An employee who believes the chief executive officer or finance director to be guilty of wrongdoing will have no option other than to resign or take the complaint to an external authority, such as the press or the police.

It may therefore be more appropriate to establish a formal internal channel for dealing with whistleblowers:

- If the company has a culture of ethical conduct, it should be prepared to encourage whistleblowing, and should provide a channel for reporting complaints and allegations by employees about their bosses. At the same time, it should make clear its policy about disciplining employees found to have been malicious in making allegations.
- Although it will often be necessary to involve senior executives in the investigation of allegations, the channel for complaints should not be to senior executive management or the board. One possible arrangement would be for allegations to be made to the company secretary, who would then arrange for the senior non-executive director to be notified. This NED, or a committee of NEDs, could then decide how the allegation should be investigated.
- An allegation might be investigated on behalf of a company by a firm of solicitors, because of the possibility of criminal activity or a misdemeanour that could expose the company to a large civil liability. If so, the solicitors asked to do the work should not have a close relationship with the company, so that the investigation can be independent. For example, the company should not be a large client of the solicitors for other legal work.

3 The Combined Code on whistleblowing

The Combined Code includes the Provision (C.3.4) that the audit committee should review arrangements by which staff may, in confidence, raise concerns about possible concerns 'in matters of financial reporting or other matters'. The committee's objective should be to ensure that arrangements are in place for the proportionate and independent investigation of such matters and for appropriate follow-up action.

The system within a company to receive and deal with allegations from whistleblowers is an element of the system of internal control. The Turnbull Guidelines (Appendix to the Guidelines) suggest that when the board carries out its annual review of the effectivness of risk and control procedures, one of the questions it might ask is: 'Are there established channels of communication for individuals to report suspected breaches of laws or regulations or other improprieties?'

4 Combining internal and external procedures

In the UK, the Financial Services Authority is responsible for the supervision of firms in the financial services industry. It has recognised the potential importance of whistleblowers in revealing corruption and malpractice in an industry where non-professional investors are known to be vulnerable. It would like to see a combination of internal procedures for dealing with whistleblowers, backed by an external system for cases where internal procedures do not exist or are inadequate.

The FSA has suggested that firms should have internal procedures for dealing constructively with information provided by whistleblowers, in their own 'enlightened self-interest'. These procedures could include the following arrangements:

- The employer should make a formal statement to all employees that it takes seriously any genuine whistleblowing (and the allegations of whistleblowers).
- The employer should also indicate to employees what it would regard as a 'failure' in the system, sufficient to justify whistleblowing.
- There should be respect for individuals who 'blow the whistle'.
- The firm should give an assurance to its employees that it will take every measure to ensure that there is no victimisation of a whistleblower.
- The system should provide employees with an opportunity to voice their concerns outside the line management structure, but still within the organisation.
- The FSA suggests that whistleblowers should be able to take their concerns to the internal auditor or the company secretary, who should then investigate the problem. Another suggestion is that the focal point for receiving allegations from whistleblowers should be the audit committee.
- However, employees making false claims or allegations should be subject to disciplinary measures by the employer.

The firm should also indicate how the employee may, if necessary, take the complaint to an outside body for investigation. In the UK financial services industry, the FSA has set up a Whistleblowing Line, so that employees of financial services firms can voice their concerns if they do not feel they will be dealt with properly by the firm.

5 Legal protection for whistleblowers: Public Interest Disclosure Act 1998

In the UK, a 'Whistleblower's Charter' was turned into the Public Interest Disclosure Act 1998, which came into force in 1999. Under the terms of this Act, workers are given protection when they disclose information they reasonably believe will expose financial malpractice, dangers to health and safety, or miscarriages of justice in their employer's organisation. Employees making a 'qualifying disclosure' have the right not to suffer any detriment at the hands of the employer, under the pretence of redundancy, demotion or failure to receive promotion. If a whistleblower is penalised by the employer, he or she can take a claim for retaliatory action to an industrial tribunal. (Industrial tribunals also hear cases of unfair dismissal.) There is no limit to the size of award a tribunal can make against an employer and in favour of a dismissed employee.

The Act also states that any 'gagging' clause in an employee's service contract is void. A gagging clause forbids the employee from voicing concerns about illegal activity, etc. in the organisation to the authorities, and gives the employer the right to sack the individual for whistleblowing.

A 'qualifying disclosure' protected by the Act must normally satisfy three criteria:

1 It should be made in good faith.
2 It should be made in the reasonable belief that the information tends to reveal (although might not provide conclusive proof of) a criminal offence, a failure to comply with a legal obligation, a danger to the health or safety of one or more individuals, or damage (or the threat of damage) to the environment.
3 It is made to the employer under an internal whistleblowing procedure (or, in certain circumstances, to another person).

The Act also recognises that it is not always sufficient to have internal whistleblowing procedures and, in exceptional circumstances, individuals making an external disclosure are also protected. These circumstances might arise if four criteria are met:

1 The disclosure must be made in good faith.
2 It should not be made for personal gain.
3 It is reasonable for the disclosure to be made outside the employer organisation.
4 The employee reasonably believes that he or she will be victimised by making the disclosure to the employer, or the employee has already made the disclosure to the employer (with no effect), or the employee believes that by making the disclosure to the employer, evidence of the malpractice will be concealed or destroyed.

5.1 Whistleblowing cases

A review of recent whistleblowing cases can be found on the web site of Public Concern at Work (www.pcaw.co.uk). This has summarised the application of the Act by Employment Tribunals and the higher courts as follows:

- Cases have confirmed that whistleblowers do not lose their right to statutory protection because they are mistaken in their allegations.
- There is a test of good faith. Allegations should be made in good faith, and in some cases, claims have been dismissed which on the facts have clearly been without merit.
- The causation of the detriment to a worker is determined by the facts of the case, not by law.

There have been cases where information given to the media has been a protected disclosure under the Act.

6 ICSA Best Practice Guide on whistleblowing

The ICSA issued a Best Practice Guide on whistleblowing in 1999, in response to the Public Interest Disclosure Act. The Guide states that an internal whistleblowing procedure will be effective only if it has the confidence of the employees, who are its intended users. Confidence in the system will be obtained only if the employer is genuinely committed to the procedure. The Guide recommends that employees' representatives should be involved in establishing the procedure and monitoring its implementation.

- The internal whistleblowing procedures should be documented and a copy should be given to every employee.
- It should set out the key aspects of the procedure, such as the person to whom employees should report their suspicions or concerns. This might be the company secretary.
- It should contain a statement that the employer takes malpractice or misconduct seriously, and is committed to a culture of openness in which employees can report legitimate concerns without fear of penalty or punishment.
- It should give examples of the type of misconduct for which employees should use the procedure and set out the level of proof that there should be in an allegation. (Although positive proof might not be required, a whistleblower should be able to provide good reasons for his or her concern.)
- It should make clear that false or malicious allegations will result in disciplinary action against the individual making them.

- An external whistleblowing route should be offered, as well as an internal reporting procedure.
- The document should set out the procedures by which an allegation will be investigated.

The ICSA Guide also includes a model whistleblowing procedure, which is reproduced in Appendix 24.

7 The Sarbanes–Oxley Act on whistleblowing procedures

In 2003, the SEC introduced a rule in accordance with SEC Section 301 of the Sarbanes–Oxley Act 2002. This requires the audit committees of companies to establish procedures for the receipt, retention and treatment of complaints regarding:

- accounting
- internal accounting controls and
- auditing matters.

Section 806 of the Act also states that a company cannot dismiss, demote, suspend, threaten, harass or otherwise discriminate against an employee because the employee has been involved in a securities-related or fraud-related investigation against the company.

This part of the legislation was prompted to a large extent by the highly publicised cases of whistleblowers at Enron and WorldCom, whose allegations were ignored.

The SOX regulation is restricted to whistleblowing on accounting and audit issues, and the UK legislation and governance guidelines are broader in the subject matter of whistleblowing allegations they cover. However, UK companies with a US listing need to consider the implications of the US regulation for the role and responsibilities of their audit committee. SOX is not inconsistent with the Combined Code in this area, but it imposes additional tasks on the committee, notably the requirement to retain a record of whistleblowing allegations and how they were treated.

Appendices

Contents

Appendix 1

The Combined Code on Corporate Governance

SECTION 1 COMPANIES

A.1 DIRECTORS

A.1 The Board

Main Principle

Every company should be headed by an effective board, which is collectively responsible for the success of the company.

Supporting Principles

The board's role is to provide entrepreneurial leadership of the company within a framework of prudent and effective controls which enables risk to be assessed and managed. The board should set the company's strategic aims, ensure that the necessary financial and human resources are in place for the company to meet its objectives and review management performance. The board should set the company's values and standards and ensure that its obligations to its shareholders and others are understood and met.

All directors must take decisions objectively in the interests of the company.

As part of their role as members of a unitary board, non-executive directors should constructively challenge and help develop proposals on strategy. Non-executive directors should scrutinise the performance of management in meeting agreed goals and objectives and monitor the reporting of performance. They should satisfy themselves on the integrity of financial information and that financial controls and systems of risk management are robust and defensible. They are responsible for determining appropriate levels of remuneration of executive directors and have a prime role in appointing, and where necessary removing, executive directors, and in succession planning.

Code Provisions

A.1.1 The board should meet sufficiently regularly to discharge its duties effectively. There should be a formal schedule of matters specifically reserved for its decision. The annual report should include a statement of how the board operates, including a high level statement of which types of decisions are to be taken by the board and which are to be delegated to management.

A.1.2 The annual report should identify the chairman, the deputy chairman (where there is one), the chief executive, the senior independent director and the chairmen and members of the nomination, audit and remuneration committees. It should also set out the number of meetings of the board and those committees and individual attendance by directors.

A.1.3 The chairman should hold meetings with the non-executive directors without the executives present. Led by the senior independent director, the non-executive directors should meet without the chairman present at least annually to appraise the chairman's performance (as described in A.6.1) and on such other occasions as are deemed appropriate.

A.1.4 Where directors have concerns which cannot be resolved about the running of the company or a proposed action, they should ensure that their concerns are recorded in the board minutes. On resignation, a non-executive director should provide a written statement to the chairman, for circulation to the board, if they have any such concerns.

A.1.5 The company should arrange appropriate insurance cover in respect of legal action against its directors.

A.2 Chairman and chief executive

Main Principle

There should be a clear division of responsibilities at the head of the company between the running of the board and the executive responsibility for the running of the company's business. No one individual should have unfettered powers of decision.

Supporting Principle

The chairman is responsible for leadership of the board, ensuring its effectiveness on all aspects of its role and setting its agenda. The chairman is also responsible for ensuring that the directors receive accurate, timely and clear information. The chairman should ensure effective communication with shareholders. The chairman should also facilitate the effective contribution of non-executive directors in particular and ensure constructive relations between executive and non-executive directors.

Code Provisions

A.2.1 The roles of chairman and chief executive should not be exercised by the same individual. The division of responsibilities between the chairman and chief executive should be clearly established, set out in writing and agreed by the board.

A.2.2 The chairman should on appointment meet the independence criteria set out in A.3.1 below. A chief executive should not go on to be chairman of the same company. If exceptionally a board decides that a chief executive should become chairman, the board should consult major shareholders in advance and should set out its reasons to shareholders at the time of the appointment and in the next annual report.

A.3 Board balance and independence

Main Principle

The board should include a balance of executive and non-executive directors (and in particular independent non-executive directors) such that no individual or small group of individuals can dominate the board's decision taking.

Supporting Principles

The board should not be so large as to be unwieldy. The board should be of sufficient size that the balance of skills and experience is appropriate for the requirements of the business and that changes to the board's composition can be managed without undue disruption.

To ensure that power and information are not concentrated in one or two individuals, there should be a strong presence on the board of both executive and non-executive directors.

The value of ensuring that committee membership is refreshed and that undue reliance is not placed on particular individuals should be taken into account in deciding chairmanship and membership of committees.

No one other than the committee chairman and members is entitled to be present at a meeting of the nomination, audit or remuneration committee, but others may attend at the invitation of the committee.

Code Provisions

A.3.1 The board should identify in the annual report each non-executive director it considers to be independent. The board should determine whether the director is independent in character and judgement and whether there are relationships or circumstances which are likely to affect, or could appear to affect, the director's judgement. The board should state its reasons if it determines that a director is independent notwithstanding the existence of relationships or circumstances which may appear relevant to its determination, including if the director:

- has been an employee of the company or group within the last five years;
- has, or has had within the last three years, a material business relationship with the company either directly, or as a partner, shareholder, director or senior employee of a body that has such a relationship with the company;
- has received or receives additional remuneration from the company apart from a director's fee, participates in the company's share option or a performance-related pay scheme, or is a member of the company's pension scheme;
- has close family ties with any of the company's advisers, directors or senior employees;
- holds cross-directorships or has significant links with other directors through involvement in other companies or bodies;
- represents a significant shareholder; or
- has served on the board for more than nine years from the date of their first election.

A.3.2 Except for smaller companies, at least half the board, excluding the chairman, should comprise non-executive directors determined by the board to be independent. A smaller company should have at least two independent non-executive directors.

A.3.3 The board should appoint one of the independent non-executive directors to be the senior independent director. The senior independent director should be available to shareholders if they have concerns which contact through the normal channels of chairman, chief executive or finance director has failed to resolve or for which such contact is inappropriate.

A.4 Appointments to the Board

Main Principle

There should be a formal, rigorous and transparent procedure for the appointment of new directors to the board.

Supporting Principles

Appointments to the board should be made on merit and against objective criteria. Care should be taken to ensure that appointees have enough time available to devote to the job. This is particularly important in the case of chairmanships.

The board should satisfy itself that plans are in place for orderly succession for appointments to the board and to senior management, so as to maintain an appropriate balance of skills and experience within the company and on the board.

Code Provisions

A.4.1 There should be a nomination committee which should lead the process for board appointments and make recommendations to the board. A majority of members of the nomination committee should be independent non-executive directors. The chairman or an independent non-executive director should chair the committee, but the chairman should not chair the nomination committee when it is dealing with the appointment of a successor to the chairmanship. The nomination committee should make available (8) its terms of reference, explaining its role and the authority delegated to it by the board.

A.4.2 The nomination committee should evaluate the balance of skills, knowledge and experience on the board and, in the light of this evaluation, prepare a description of the role and capabilities required for a particular appointment.

A.4.3 For the appointment of a chairman, the nomination committee should prepare a job specification, including an assessment of the time commitment expected, recognising the need for availability in the event of crises. A chairman's other significant commitments should be disclosed to the board before appointment and included in the annual report. Changes to such commitments should be reported to the board as they arise, and included in the next annual report. No individual should be appointed to a second chairmanship of a FTSE 100 company (9).

A.4.4 The terms and conditions of appointment of non-executive directors should be made available for inspection (10). The letter of appointment should set out the expected time commitment. Non-executive directors should undertake that they will have sufficient time to meet what is expected of them. Their other significant commitments should be disclosed to the board before appointment, with a broad indication of the time involved and the board should be informed of subsequent changes.

A.4.5 The board should not agree to a full time executive director taking on more than one non-executive directorship in a FTSE 100 company nor the chairmanship of such a company.

A.4.6 A separate section of the annual report should describe the work of the nomination committee, including the process it has used in relation to board appointments. An explanation should be given if neither an external search consultancy nor open advertising has been used in the appointment of a chairman or a non-executive director.

A.5 Information and professional development

Main Principle

The board should be supplied in a timely manner with information in a form and of a quality appropriate to enable it to discharge its duties. All directors should receive induction on joining the board and should regularly update and refresh their skills and knowledge.

Supporting Principles

The chairman is responsible for ensuring that the directors receive accurate, timely and clear information. Management has an obligation to provide such information but directors should seek clarification or amplification where necessary.

The chairman should ensure that the directors continually update their skills and the knowledge and familiarity with the company required to fulfil their role both on the board and on board committees. The company should provide the necessary resources for developing and updating its directors' knowledge and capabilities.

Under the direction of the chairman, the company secretary's responsibilities include ensuring good information flows within the board and its committees and between senior management and non-executive directors, as well as facilitating induction and assisting with professional development as required.

The company secretary should be responsible for advising the board through the chairman on all governance matters.

Code Provisions

A.5.1 The chairman should ensure that new directors receive a full, formal and tailored induction on joining the board. As part of this, the company should offer to major shareholders the opportunity to meet a new non-executive director.

A.5.2 The board should ensure that directors, especially non-executive directors, have access to independent professional advice at the company's expense where they judge it necessary to discharge their responsibilities as directors. Committees should be provided with sufficient resources to undertake their duties.

A.5.3 All directors should have access to the advice and services of the company secretary, who is responsible to the board for ensuring that board procedures are complied with. Both the appointment and removal of the company secretary should be a matter for the board as a whole.

A.6 Performance evaluation

Main Principle

The board should undertake a formal and rigorous annual evaluation of its own performance and that of its committees and individual directors.

Supporting Principle

Individual evaluation should aim to show whether each director continues to contribute effectively and to demonstrate commitment to the role (including commitment of time for board and committee meetings and any other duties). The chairman should act on the results of the performance evaluation by recognising the strengths and addressing the weaknesses of the board and, where appropriate, proposing new members be appointed to the board or seeking the resignation of directors.

Code Provision

A.6.1 The board should state in the annual report how performance evaluation of the board, its committees and its individual directors has been conducted. The non-executive directors, led by the senior independent director, should be responsible for performance evaluation of the chairman, taking into account the views of executive directors.

A.7 Re-election

Main Principle

All directors should be submitted for re-election at regular intervals, subject to continued satisfactory performance. The board should ensure planned and progressive refreshing of the board.

Code Provisions

A.7.1 All directors should be subject to election by shareholders at the first annual general meeting after their appointment, and to re-election thereafter at intervals of no more than three years. The names of directors submitted for election or re-election should be accompanied by sufficient biographical details and any other relevant information to enable shareholders to take an informed decision on their election.

A.7.2 Non-executive directors should be appointed for specified terms subject to re-election and to Companies Acts provisions relating to the removal of a director. The board should set out to shareholders in the papers accompanying a resolution to elect a non-executive director why they believe an individual should be elected. The chairman should confirm to shareholders when proposing re-election that, following formal performance evaluation, the individual's performance continues to be effective and to demonstrate commitment to the role. Any term beyond six years (e.g. two three-year terms) for a non-executive director should be subject to particularly rigorous review, and should take into account the need for progressive refreshing of the board. Non-executive directors may serve longer than nine years (e.g. three three-year terms), subject to annual re-election. Serving more than nine years could be relevant to the determination of a non-executive director's independence (as set out in provision A.3.1).

B. REMUNERATION

B.1 The Level and Make-up of Remuneration

Main Principles

Levels of remuneration should be sufficient to attract, retain and motivate directors of the quality required to run the company successfully, but a company should avoid paying more than is necessary for this purpose. A significant proportion of executive directors' remuneration should be structured so as to link rewards to corporate and individual performance.

Supporting Principle

The remuneration committee should judge where to position their company relative to other companies. But they should use such comparisons with caution, in view of the risk of an upward ratchet of remuneration levels with no corresponding improvement in performance. They should also be sensitive to pay and employment conditions elsewhere in the group, especially when determining annual salary increases.

Code Provisions

Remuneration policy

B.1.1 The performance-related elements of remuneration should form a significant proportion of the total remuneration package of executive directors and should be designed to align their interests with those of shareholders and to give these directors keen incentives to perform at the highest levels. In designing schemes of performance-related remuneration, the remuneration committee should follow the provisions in Schedule A to this Code.

B.1.2 Executive share options should not be offered at a discount save as permitted by the relevant provisions of the Listing Rules.

B.1.3 Levels of remuneration for non-executive directors should reflect the time commitment and responsibilities of the role. Remuneration for non-executive directors should not include share options. If, exceptionally, options are granted, shareholder approval should be sought in advance and any shares acquired by exercise of the options should be held until at least one year after the non-executive director leaves the board. Holding of share options could be relevant to the determination of a non-executive director's independence (as set out in provision A.3.1).

B.1.4 Where a company releases an executive director to serve as a non-executive director elsewhere, the remuneration report (12) should include a statement as to whether or not the director will retain such earnings and, if so, what the remuneration is.

Service Contracts and Compensation

B.1.5 The remuneration committee should carefully consider what compensation commitments (including pension contributions and all other elements) their directors' terms of appointment would entail in the event of early termination. The aim should be to avoid rewarding poor performance. They should take a robust line on reducing compensation to reflect departing directors' obligations to mitigate loss.

B.1.6 Notice or contract periods should be set at one year or less. If it is necessary to offer longer notice or contract periods to new directors recruited from outside, such periods should reduce to one year or less after the initial period.

B.2 Procedure

Main Principle

There should be a formal and transparent procedure for developing policy on executive remuneration and for fixing the remuneration packages of individual directors. No director should be involved in deciding his or her own remuneration.

Supporting Principles

The remuneration committee should consult the chairman and/or chief executive about their proposals relating to the remuneration of other executive directors. The remuneration committee should also be responsible for appointing any consultants in respect of executive director remuneration. Where executive directors or senior management are involved in advising or supporting the remuneration committee, care should be taken to recognise and avoid conflicts of interest.

The chairman of the board should ensure that the company maintains contact as required with its principal shareholders about remuneration in the same way as for other matters. .

Code Provisions

B.2.1 The board should establish a remuneration committee of at least three, or in the case of smaller companies two, members, who should all be independent non-executive directors. The remuneration committee should make available its terms of reference, explaining its role and the authority delegated to it by the board. Where remuneration consultants are appointed, a statement should be made available of whether they have any other connection with the company.

B.2.2 The remuneration committee should have delegated responsibility for setting remuneration for all executive directors and the chairman, including pension rights and any compensation payments. The committee should also recommend and monitor the level and structure of remuneration for senior management. The definition of 'senior management' for this purpose should be determined by the board but should normally include the first layer of management below board level.

B.2.3 The board itself or, where required by the Articles of Association, the shareholders should determine the remuneration of the non-executive directors within the limits set in the Articles of Association. Where permitted by the Articles, the board may however delegate this responsibility to a committee, which might include the chief executive.

B.2.4 Shareholders should be invited specifically to approve all new long-term incentive schemes (as defined in the Listing Rules) and significant changes to existing schemes, save in the circumstances permitted by the Listing Rules.

C. ACCOUNTABILITY AND AUDIT

C.1 Financial Reporting

Main Principle

The board should present a balanced and understandable assessment of the company's position and prospects.

Supporting Principle

The board's responsibility to present a balanced and understandable assessment extends to interim and other price-sensitive public reports and reports to regulators as well as to information required to be presented by statutory requirements.

Code Provisions

C.1.1 The directors should explain in the annual report their responsibility for preparing the accounts and there should be a statement by the auditors about their reporting responsibilities.

C.1.2 The directors should report that the business is a going concern, with supporting assumptions or qualifications as necessary.

C.2 Internal Control

Main Principle

The board should maintain a sound system of internal control to safeguard shareholders' investment and the company's assets.

Code Provision

C.2.1 The board should, at least annually, conduct a review of the effectiveness of the group's system of internal controls and should report to shareholders that they have done so. The review should cover all material controls, including financial, operational and compliance controls and risk management systems.

C.3 Audit Committee and Auditors

Main Principle

The board should establish formal and transparent arrangements for considering how they should apply the financial reporting and internal control principles and for maintaining an appropriate relationship with the company's auditors.

Code Provisions

C.3.1 The board should establish an audit committee of at least three, or in the case of smaller companies two, members, who should all be independent non-executive directors. The board should satisfy itself that at least one member of the audit committee has recent and relevant financial experience.

C.3.2 The main role and responsibilities of the audit committee should be set out in written terms of reference and should include:

- to monitor the integrity of the financial statements of the company, and any formal announcements relating to the company's financial performance, reviewing significant financial reporting judgements contained in them;
- to review the company's internal financial controls and, unless expressly addressed by a separate board risk committee composed of independent directors, or by the board itself, to review the company's internal control and risk management systems;
- to monitor and review the effectiveness of the company's internal audit function;
- to make recommendations to the board, for it to put to the shareholders for their approval in general meeting, in relation to the appointment, re-appointment and removal of the external auditor and to approve the remuneration and terms of engagement of the external auditor;
- to review and monitor the external auditor's independence and objectivity and the effectiveness of the audit process, taking into consideration relevant UK professional and regulatory requirements;
- to develop and implement policy on the engagement of the external auditor to supply non-audit services, taking into account relevant ethical guidance regarding the provision of non-audit services by the external audit firm; and to report to the board, identifying any matters in respect of which it considers that action or improvement is needed and making recommendations as to the steps to be taken.

C.3.3 The terms of reference of the audit committee, including its role and the authority delegated to it by the board, should be made available. A separate section of the annual report should describe the work of the committee in discharging those responsibilities.

C.3.4 The audit committee should review arrangements by which staff of the company may, in confidence, raise concerns about possible improprieties in matters of financial reporting or other matters. The audit committee's objective should be to ensure that arrangements are in place for the proportionate and independent investigation of such matters and for appropriate follow-up action.

C.3.5 The audit committee should monitor and review the effectiveness of the internal audit activities. Where there is no internal audit function, the audit committee should consider annually whether there is a need for an internal audit function and make a recommendation to the board, and the reasons for the absence of such a function should be explained in the relevant section of the annual report.

C.3.6 The audit committee should have primary responsibility for making a recommendation on the appointment, reappointment and removal of the external auditors. If the board does not accept the audit committee's recommendation, it should include in the annual report, and in any papers recommending appointment or re-appointment, a statement from the audit committee explaining the recommendation and should set out reasons why the board has taken a different position.

C.3.7 The annual report should explain to shareholders how, if the auditor provides non-audit services, auditor objectivity and independence is safeguarded.

D. RELATIONS WITH SHAREHOLDERS

D.1 Dialogue with Institutional Shareholders

Main Principle

There should be a dialogue with shareholders based on the mutual understanding of objectives. The board as a whole has responsibility for ensuring that a satisfactory dialogue with shareholders takes place.

Supporting Principles

Whilst recognising that most shareholder contact is with the chief executive and finance director, the chairman (and the senior independent director and other directors as appropriate) should maintain sufficient contact with major shareholders to understand their issues and concerns.

The board should keep in touch with shareholder opinion in whatever ways are most practical and efficient.

Code Provisions

D.1.1 The chairman should ensure that the views of shareholders are communicated to the board as a whole. The chairman should discuss governance and strategy with major shareholders. Non-executive directors should be offered the opportunity to attend meetings with major shareholders and should expect to attend them if requested by major shareholders. The senior independent director should attend sufficient meetings with a range of major shareholders to listen to their views in order to help develop a balanced understanding of the issues and concerns of major shareholders.

D.1.2 The board should state in the annual report the steps they have taken to ensure that the members of the board, and in particular the non-executive directors, develop an understanding of the views of major shareholders about their company, for example through direct face-to-face contact, analysts' or brokers' briefings and surveys of shareholder opinion.

D.2 Constructive Use of the AGM

Main Principle

The board should use the AGM to communicate with investors and to encourage their participation.

Code Provisions

D.2.1 The company should count all proxy votes and, except where a poll is called, should indicate the level of proxies lodged on each resolution, and the balance for and against the resolution and the number of abstentions, after it has been dealt with on a show of hands. The company should ensure that votes cast are properly received and recorded.

D.2.2 The company should propose a separate resolution at the AGM on each substantially separate issue and should in particular propose a resolution at the AGM relating to the report and accounts.

D.2.3 The chairman should arrange for the chairmen of the audit, remuneration and nomination committees to be available to answer questions at the AGM and for all directors to attend.

D.2.4 The company should arrange for the Notice of the AGM and related papers to be sent to shareholders at least 20 working days before the meeting.

SECTION 2 INSTITUTIONAL SHAREHOLDERS

INSTITUTIONAL SHAREHOLDERS

E.1 Dialogue with companies

Main Principle

Institutional shareholders should enter into a dialogue with companies based on the mutual understanding of objectives.

Supporting Principles

Institutional shareholders should apply the principles set out in the Institutional Shareholders' Committee's "The Responsibilities of Institutional Shareholders and Agents — Statement of Principles", which should be reflected in fund manager contracts.

E.2 Evaluation of Governance Disclosures

Main Principle

When evaluating companies' governance arrangements, particularly those relating to board structure and composition, institutional shareholders should give due weight to all relevant factors drawn to their attention.

Supporting Principle

Institutional shareholders should consider carefully explanations given for departure from this Code and make reasoned judgements in each case. They should give an explanation to the company, in writing where appropriate, and be prepared to enter a dialogue if they do not accept the company's position. They should avoid a box-ticking approach to assessing a company's corporate governance. They should bear in mind in particular the size and complexity of the company and the nature of the risks and challenges it faces.

E.3 Shareholder Voting

Main Principle

Institutional shareholders have a responsibility to make considered use of their votes.

Supporting Principles

Institutional shareholders should take steps to ensure their voting intentions are being translated into practice.

Institutional shareholders should, on request, make available to their clients information on the proportion of resolutions on which votes were cast and non-discretionary proxies lodged.

Major shareholders should attend AGMs where appropriate and practicable. Companies and registrars should facilitate this.

Schedule A: Provisions on the design of performance related remuneration

1 The remuneration committee should consider whether the directors should be eligible for annual bonuses. If so, performance conditions should be relevant, stretching and designed to enhance shareholder value. Upper limits should be set and disclosed. There may be a case for part payment in shares to be held for a significant period.

2 The remuneration committee should consider whether the directors should be eligible for benefits under long-term incentive schemes. Traditional share option schemes should be weighed against other kinds of long-term incentive scheme. In normal circumstances, shares granted or other forms of deferred remuneration should not vest, and options should not be exercisable, in less than three years. Directors should be encouraged to hold their shares for a further period after vesting or exercise, subject to the need to finance any costs of acquisition and associated tax liabilities.

3 Any new long-term incentive schemes which are proposed should be approved by shareholders and should preferably replace any existing schemes or at least form part of a well considered overall plan, incorporating existing schemes. The total rewards potentially available should not be excessive.

4 Payouts or grants under all incentive schemes, including new grants under existing share option schemes, should be subject to challenging performance criteria reflecting the company's objectives. Consideration should be given to criteria which reflect the company's performance relative to a group of comparator companies in some key variables such as total shareholder return.

5 Grants under executive share option and other long-term incentive schemes should normally be phased rather than awarded in one large block.

6 In general, only basic salary should be pensionable.

7 The remuneration committee should consider the pension consequences and associated costs to the company of basic salary increases and any other changes in pensionable remuneration, especially for directors close to retirement.

Schedule B: Guidance on liability of non-executive directors: care, skill and diligence

1 Although non-executive directors and executive directors have as board members the same legal duties and objectives, the time devoted to the company's affairs is likely to be significantly less for a non-executive director than for an executive director and the detailed knowledge and experience of a company's affairs that could reasonably be expected of a non-executive director will generally be less than for an executive director. These matters may be

relevant in assessing the knowledge, skill and experience which may reasonably be expected of a non-executive director and therefore the care, skill and diligence that a non-executive director may be expected to exercise.

2 In this context, the following elements of the Code may also be particularly relevant. (i) In order to enable directors to fulfil their duties, the Code states that:
   - The letter of appointment of the director should set out the expected time commitment (Code provision A.4.4); and
   - The board should be supplied in a timely manner with information in a form and of a quality appropriate to enable it to discharge its duties. The chairman is responsible for ensuring that the directors are provided by management with accurate, timely and clear information. (Code principles A.5).

   (ii) Non-executive directors should themselves:
   - Undertake appropriate induction and regularly update and refresh their skills, knowledge and familiarity with the company (Code principle A.5 and provision A.5.1) – Seek appropriate clarification or amplification of information and, where necessary, take and follow appropriate professional advice. (Code principle A.5 and provision A.5.2)
   - Where they have concerns about the running of the company or a proposed action, ensure that these are addressed by the board and, to the extent that they are not resolved, ensure that they are recorded in the board minutes (Code provision A.1.4). – Give a statement to the board if they have such unresolved concerns on resignation (Code provision A.1.4)

3 It is up to each non-executive director to reach a view as to what is necessary in particular circumstances to comply with the duty of care, skill and diligence they owe as a director to the company. In considering whether or not a person is in breach of that duty, a court would take into account all relevant circumstances. These may include having regard to the above where relevant to the issue of liability of a non-executive director.

Schedule C: Disclosure of corporate governance arrangements

The Listing Rules require a statement to be included in the annual report relating to compliance with the Code, as described in the preamble. For ease of reference, the specific requirements in the Code for disclosure are set out below:

The annual report should record:

- a statement of how the board operates, including a high level statement of which types of decisions are to be taken by the board and which are to be delegated to management (A.1.1);
- the names of the chairman, the deputy chairman (where there is one), the chief executive, the senior independent director and the chairmen and members of the nomination, audit and remuneration committees (A.1.2);
- the number of meetings of the board and those committees and individual attendance by directors (A.1.2);

- the names of the non-executive directors whom the board determines to be independent, with reasons where necessary (A.3.1);
- the other significant commitments of the chairman and any changes to them during the year (A.4.3);
- how performance evaluation of the board, its committees and its directors has been conducted (A.6.1);
- the steps the board has taken to ensure that members of the board, and in particular the non-executive directors, develop an understanding of the views of major shareholders about their company (D.1.2).

The report should also include:

- a separate section describing the work of the nomination committee, including the process it has used in relation to board appointments and an explanation if neither external search consultancy nor open advertising has been used in the appointment of a chairman or a non-executive director (A.4.6);
- a description of the work of the remuneration committee as required under the Directors' Remuneration Reporting Regulations 2002, and including, where an executive director serves as a non-executive director elsewhere, whether or not the director will retain such earnings and, if so, what the remuneration is (B.1.4);
- an explanation from the directors of their responsibility for preparing the accounts and a statement by the auditors about their reporting responsibilities (C.1.1);
- a statement from the directors that the business is a going concern, with supporting assumptions or qualifications as necessary (C.1.2);
- a report that the board has conducted a review of the effectiveness of the group's system of internal controls (C.2.1);
- a separate section describing the work of the audit committee in discharging its responsibilities (C.3.3);
- where there is no internal audit function, the reasons for the absence of such a function (C.3.5);
- where the board does not accept the audit committee's recommendation on the appointment, reappointment or removal of an external auditor, a statement from the audit committee explaining the recommendation and the reasons why the board has taken a different position (C.3.6); and
- an explanation of how, if the auditor provides non-audit services, auditor objectivity and independence is safeguarded (C.3.7).

The following information should be made available (which may be met by making it available on request and placing the information available on the company's website):

- the terms of reference of the nomination, remuneration and audit committees, explaining their role and the authority delegated to them by the board (A.4.1, B.2.1 and C.3.3);
- the terms and conditions of appointment of non-executive directors (A.4.4);

- the tems of reference of any remuneration consultants, together with a statement of whether they have any other connection with the company (B.2.1).

The board should set out to shareholders in the papers accompanying a resolution to elect or re-elect:

- sufficient biographical details to enable shareholders to take an informed decision on their election or re-election (A.7.1).
- why they believe an individual should be elected to a nonexecutive role (A.7.2).
- on re-election of a non-executive director, confirmation from the chairman that, following formal performance evaluation, the individual's performance continues to be effective and to demonstrate commitment to the role, including commitment of time for board and committee meetings and any other duties (A.7.2).

The board should set out to shareholders in the papers recommending appointment or reappointment of an external auditor:

- if the board does not accept the audit committee's recommendation, a statement from the audit committee explaining the recommendation and from the board setting out reasons why they have taken a different position (C.3.6).

Appendix 2

Directors' Duties: Extract from the White Paper on Company Law Reform, March 2005

PART B

DIRECTORS

CHAPTER 1

GENERAL DUTIES

Introductory provisions

B1 Scope and application of general duties

(1) The general duties specified in sections B2 to B8 are owed by a director of a company to the company.

(2) The duties apply to shadow directors as they apply to directors, subject to any necessary adaptations.

(3) A person who ceases to be a director continues to be subject:

   (a) to the duty in section B6 (duty to avoid conflicts of interest) as regards the exploitation of any property, information or opportunity of which he became aware at a time when he was a director, and

   (b) to the duty in section B7 (duty not to accept benefits from third parties) as regards things done or omitted by him before he ceased to be a director.

To that extent those duties apply to a former director as to a director, subject to any necessary adaptations.

The general duties

B2 Duty to act within powers

As a director of a company you must:

(a) act in accordance with the company's constitution, and

(b) only exercise powers for the purposes for which they are conferred.

B3 Duty to promote the success of the company for the benefit of its members

(1) As a director of a company you must act in the way you consider, in good faith, would be most likely to promote the success of the company for the benefit of its members as a whole.

(2) Where or to the extent that the company is established for purposes other than the benefit of its members, your duty is to act in the way you consider, in good faith, would be most likely to achieve those purposes.

(3) In fulfilling the duty imposed by this section you must take account (where relevant and so far as reasonably practicable) of:

(a) the likely consequences of any decision in both the long and the short term,

(b) any need of the company:

(i) to have regard to the interests of its employees,

(ii) to foster its business relationships with suppliers, customers and others,

(iii) to consider the impact of its operations on the community and the environment, and

(iv) to maintain a reputation for high standards of business conduct,

and

(c) the need to act fairly as between members of the company who have different interests.

(4) The duty imposed by this section has effect subject to any enactment or rule of law requiring directors, in certain circumstances, to consider or act in the interests of creditors of the company.

B4 Duty to exercise independent judgment

(1) As a director of a company you must exercise independent judgment.

(2) This duty is not infringed by your acting:

(a) in accordance with an agreement duly entered into by the company that restricts the future exercise of discretion by its directors, or

(b) in a way authorised by the company's constitution.

B5 Duty to exercise reasonable care, skill and diligence

(1) As a director of a company you must exercise reasonable care, skill and diligence.

(2) This means the care, skill and diligence that would be exercised by a reasonably diligent person with:

(a) the knowledge, skill and experience that may reasonably be expected of a director in your position, and

(b) any additional knowledge, skill or experience that you in fact have.

B6 Duty to avoid conflicts of interest

(1) As a director of a company you must avoid a situation in which you have, or can have, a direct or indirect interest that conflicts, or possibly may conflict, with the interests of the company.

(2) This applies in particular to the exploitation of any property, information or opportunity (and it is immaterial whether the company could take advantage of the property, information or opportunity).

(3) This duty is not infringed:

(a) if there is no real possibility of a conflict of interest;

(b) if the conflict of interest arises in relation to a proposed transaction or arrangement with the company (but see section B8 (duty to declare interest in proposed transaction with company));

(c) if the conflict of interest arises in relation to a transaction or arrangement duly entered into by the company;

(d) if authorisation has been given by the company in accordance with subsection (4).

(4) Authorisation by the company may be given:

(a) by the matter being proposed to the members of the company and authorised by them; or

(b) where the company is a private company and nothing in the company's constitution invalidates such authorisation, by the matter being proposed to and authorised by the directors; or

(c) where the company is a public company and its constitution includes provision enabling the directors to authorise the matter, by the matter being proposed to and authorised by them in accordance with the constitution.

(5) If you or any other interested director participate in the proceedings required by subsection (4)(b) or (c), the authorisation is effective only if it would have been effectively agreed to without the participation of any interested director.

(6) Any reference in this section to a conflict of interest includes a conflict of interest and duty and a conflict of duties.

B7 Duty not to accept benefits from third parties

(1) As a director of a company you must not accept a benefit from a third party conferred by reason of:

(a) your being a director, or

(b) your doing (or not doing) anything as director.

(2) A 'third party' means a person other than the company, an associated company or a person acting on behalf of the company or an associated company.

(3) Benefits received by you from a person by whom your services (as a director or otherwise) are provided to the company are not regarded as conferred by a third party.

(4) This duty is not infringed:

(a) if there is no real possibility of a conflict of interest;

(b) if the matter has been proposed to the members of the company and authorised by them.

(5) Any reference in this section to a conflict of interest includes a conflict of interest and duty and a conflict of duties.

B8 Duty to declare interest in proposed transaction with the company

(1) As a director of a company you must declare the nature and extent of any interest, direct or indirect, you have in a proposed transaction or arrangement with the company.

(2) If an earlier declaration of interest proves to be, or becomes, inaccurate or incomplete (for instance, because of subsequent changes in the matters to which it relates, you must make a further declaration.

(3) Any declaration required by this section:

(a) may be made to the other directors or to the members of the company, and

(b) must be made before the company enters into the transaction or arrangement.

(4) You will be regarded as failing to comply with the duty imposed by this section if you fail to make a declaration, or fail to declare fully the nature and extent of your interest, because you are unaware of matters of which you ought reasonably to be aware.

(5) In Chapter 2 (declaration of interest: further provisions), sections B12 to B15 impose other requirements that you must comply with, but they are not part of the duty imposed by this section; and sections B16 to B19 contain supplementary provisions, including provisions about exceptions, notices and sole directors, that apply both in relation to those requirements and in relation to the duty imposed by this section.

Supplementary provisions

B9 Cases within more than one of the general duties

Except as otherwise provided, more than one of the general duties may apply in any given case and the operation of any of them is not affected by the application or otherwise of any of the others.

B10 Relationship between general duties and other rules

(1) The general duties are based on certain common law rules and equitable principles as they apply in relation to directors and have effect in place of those rules and principles as regards the duties owed to a company by a director.

(2) The general duties shall be interpreted and applied in the same way as common law rules or equitable principles, and regard shall be had to the corresponding common law rules and equitable principles in interpreting and applying the general duties.

(3) In a case where section B6 (duty to avoid conflicts of interest) or section B8 (duty to declare interest in proposed transaction or arrangement) is complied with by disclosure to or authorisation by the directors, the transaction or arrangement is not liable to be set aside by virtue of any common law rule or equitable principle requiring the consent or approval of the members of the company.

This is without prejudice to any enactment, or provision of the company's constitution, requiring such consent or approval.

(4) The application of section B8 (duty to declare interest in proposed transaction or arrangement) is not affected by the fact that the case also falls within Chapter 3 (transactions requiring shareholder approval).

(5) Where Chapter 3 applies (transactions requiring shareholder approval) and:

(a) approval is given under that Chapter, or

(b) the matter is one as to which it is provided that approval is not needed,

it is not necessary also to comply with section B6 (duty to avoid conflicts of interest) or section B7 (duty not to accept benefits from third parties).

(6) Except as otherwise provided, the general duties have effect notwithstanding any other enactment or rule of law or anything in the company's constitution.

B11 Civil consequences of breach of general duties

The consequences of breach (or threatened breach) of any of the general duties are the same as would apply if the corresponding common law rule or equitable principle applied.

Appendix 3
ICSA Code on Good Boardroom Practice

1 The board should establish written procedures for the conduct of its business which should include the matters covered in this Code. A copy of these written procedures should be given to each director. Compliance should be monitored, preferably by an audit committee of the board, and breaches of the procedures should be reported to the board.

2 The board should ensure that each director is given on appointment sufficient information to enable him to perform his duties. In particular, guidance for non-executive directors should cover the procedures:

(i) for obtaining information concerning the company; and

(ii) for requisitioning a meeting of the board.

3 In the conduct of board business, two fundamental concepts should be observed:

(i) each director should receive the same information at the same time; and

(ii) each director should be given sufficient time in which to consider any such information.

4 The board should identify matters which require the prior approval of the board and lay down procedures[1] to be followed when, exceptionally, a decision is required before its next meeting on any matter not required by law to be considered at board level.

5 As a basic principle, all material contracts, and especially those not in the ordinary course of business, should be referred to the board for decision prior to the commitment of the company.

6 The board should approve definitions of the terms 'material'[2] and 'not in the ordinary course of business' and these definitions should be brought to the attention of all relevant persons.

7 Where there is any uncertainty regarding the materiality or nature of a contract, it should normally be assumed that the contract should be brought before the board.

8 Decisions regarding the content of the agenda for individual meetings of the board and concerning the presentation of agenda items should be taken by the chairman in consultation with the company secretary.

9 The company secretary should be responsible to the chairman for the proper administration of the meetings of the company, the board and any committees thereof. To carry out this responsibility the company secretary should be entitled to be present at (or represented at) and prepare (or arrange for the preparation of) minutes of the proceedings of all such meetings.

10 The minutes of meetings should record the decisions taken and provide sufficient background to those decisions. All papers presented at the meeting should be clearly identified in the minutes and retained for reference. Procedures for the approval and circulation of minutes should be established.

11 Where the articles of association allow the board to delegate any of its powers to a committee, the board should give its prior approval to:

(i) the membership and quorum of any such committee;

(ii) its terms of reference; and

(iii) the extent of any powers delegated to it.

12 The minutes of all meetings of committees of the board (or a written summary thereof) should be circulated to the board prior to its next meeting and the opportunity should be given at that meeting for any member of the board to ask questions thereon.

13 Notwithstanding the absence of a formal agenda item, the chairman should permit any director or the company secretary to raise at any board meeting any matter concerning the company's compliance with this Code of Practice, with the company's memorandum and articles of association and with any other legal or regulatory requirement.

Notes

1 If it is practicable, the approval of all the directors should be obtained by means of a written resolution. In all cases, however, the procedures should balance the need for urgency with the overriding principle that each director should be given as much information as possible and have an opportunity to requisition an emergency meeting of the board to discuss the matter prior to the commitment of the company.

2 Different definitions of the term 'material' should be established for 'contracts not in the ordinary course of business' and 'contracts in the ordinary course of business'. Financial limits should be set where appropriate.

Appendix 4
ICSA Guidance Note: Matters Reserved for the Board

No matter how effective a Board of directors may be it is not possible for the directors to have hands on involvement in every area of the company's business. An effective Board controls the business but delegates day to day responsibility to the executive management. That said there are a number of matters which are required to be or, in the interests of the company, should only be decided by the Board of directors as a whole.

It is incumbent upon the Board to make it clear what these matters reserved for the board are. The Combined Code states that 'There should be a formal schedule of matters specifically reserved for [the Board's] decision'[1] and that the annual report should contain a 'high level statement of which types of decisions are to be taken by the Board and which are to be delegated to management'.[1]

The Combined Code also states that 'The Board's role is to provide entrepreneurial leadership of the company within a framework of prudent and effective controls which enables risk to be assessed and managed. The Board should set the company's strategic aims, ensure that the necessary financial and human resources are in place for the company to meet its objectives and review management performance. The Board should set the company's values and standards and ensure that its obligations to its shareholders and others are understood and met.'[2]

ICSA has produced this Guidance Note to aid directors and company secretaries in drawing up such a schedule of matters reserved for the board. The original version of this document was first published in the February 1993 edition of *The Company Secretary* and has been adopted as a precedent by a number of writers on corporate governance. It has been updated to incorporate more recent developments in best practice.

The relative importance of some matters included in this Guidance Note will vary according to the size and nature of the company's business. For example, all companies will have a different view on the establishment of the financial limits for transactions which should be referred to the Board. Equally, there may well be items not mentioned in the Guidance Note which some companies (for example those subject to additional forms of external regulation) would wish to include in their own schedule.

Multiple signatures

In drawing up a schedule of matters reserved for the board, companies should clarify which transactions require multiple Board signatures on the relevant documentation.

Delegation

Certain of the matters included in this Guidance Note should, under the provisions of the Combined Code, be the subject of recommendations by the audit, nomination or remuneration committee. However, full delegation is not normally permitted in these cases as the final decision on the matter is required to be taken by the whole Board.

Urgent matters

In drawing up a schedule of matters reserved for the board it is important to establish procedures for dealing with matters which often have to be dealt with urgently, often between regular Board meetings. It is recommended that a telephone or video conference meeting should be held in which as many directors as possible participate. This allows directors the opportunity to discuss the matter and ask questions. Any director who cannot attend should still be sent the relevant papers and have the opportunity to give their views to the Chairman, another director or the company secretary before the meeting. If the matter is routine and discussion is not necessary the approval of all the directors may be obtained by means of a written resolution. In all cases however the procedures should balance the need for urgency with the overriding principle that each director should be given as much information as possible, the time to consider it properly and an opportunity to discuss the matter prior to the commitment of the company.

The following schedule has been produced to assist Boards of directors and company secretaries in preparing a schedule of matters reserved for the board in accordance with good corporate governance.

Items marked * are not considered suitable for delegation to a committee of the Board, for example because of Companies Act requirements or because, under the recommendations of the Combined Code, they are the responsibility of an audit, nomination or remuneration committee, with the final decision required to be taken by the Board as a whole.

SCHEDULE OF MATTERS RESERVED FOR THE BOARD

CA refers to the Companies Act 1985

CC refers to the Combined Code

LR refers to the UKLA Listing Rules

References to Audit, Nomination or Remuneration refer to the Board committee which will consider the item and make recommendations to the board for its final decision.

1. Strategy and Management

1.1 Responsibility for the overall management of the group. (CC A.1)

1.2 Approval of the group's long term objectives and commercial strategy. (CC A.1)

1.3 Approval of the annual operating and capital expenditure budgets and any material changes to them.

1.4 Oversight of the group's operations ensuring:

- competent and prudent management
- sound planning
- an adequate system of internal control
- adequate accounting and other records
- compliance with statutory and regulatory obligations.

1.5 Review of performance in the light of the group's strategy, objectives, business plans and budgets and ensuring that any necessary corrective action is taken. (CC A.1)

1.6 Extension of the group's activities into new business or geographic areas.

1.7 Any decision to cease to operate all or any material part of the group's business.

2. Structure and capital

2.1 Changes relating to the group's capital structure including reduction of capital, share issues (except under employee share plans), share buy backs [including the use of treasury shares].

2.2 Major changes to the group's corporate structure.

2.3 Changes to the group's management and control structure.

2.4 Any changes to the company's listing or its status as a plc.

3. Financial reporting and controls

3.1 *Approval of preliminary announcements of interim and final results. (CC C.1 Audit)

3.2 *Approval of the annual report and accounts, [including the corporate governance statement and remuneration report].[3] (CA s. 233, s. 234C, LR 9.35, CC C.1 Audit)

3.3 *Approval of the dividend policy.

3.4 *Declaration of the interim dividend and recommendation of the final dividend.3 (LR 9.35)

3.5 *Approval of any significant changes in accounting policies or practices. (Audit)

3.6 Approval of treasury policies [including foreign currency exposure and the use of financial derivatives].

4. Internal controls

4.1. Ensuring maintenance of a sound system of internal control and risk management including:

- receiving reports on, and reviewing the effectiveness of, the group's risk
- and control processes to support its strategy and objectives
- undertaking an annual assessment of these processes
- approving an appropriate statement for inclusion in the annual report. (CC C.2, C.2.1 Audit)

5. Contracts

5.1 Major capital projects.

5.2 Contracts which are material strategically or by reason of size, entered into by the company [or any subsidiary] in the ordinary course of business, for example bank borrowings [above £xx million] and acquisitions or disposals of fixed assets [above £xx million].

5.3 Contracts of the company [or any subsidiary] not in the ordinary course of business, for example loans and repayments [above £xx million]; foreign currency transactions [above £xx million]; major acquisitions or disposals [above £xx million].

5.4 Major investments [including the acquisition or disposal of interests of more than 5 per cent in the voting shares of any company or the making of any takeover offer].

6. Communication

6.1 Approval of resolutions and corresponding documentation to be put forward to shareholders at a general meeting. (LR 14.1)

6.2 *Approval of all circulars and listing particulars [approval of routine documents such as periodic circulars about scrip dividend procedures or exercise of conversion rights could be delegated to a committee]. (LR 14.1, 16.1, 5.2)

6.3 *Approval of press releases concerning matters decided by the Board.

7. Board membership and other appointments

7.1 *Changes to the structure, size and composition of the Board, following recommendations from the nomination committee. (Nomination)

7.2 *Ensuring adequate succession planning for the Board and senior management. (CC A.4, A.7)

7.3 *Appointments to the Board, following recommendations by the nomination committee. (CA s. 282, Nomination)

7.4 *Selection of the Chairman of the Board and the Chief Executive. (Nomination)

7.5 *Appointment of the Senior Independent Director. (CC A.3.3, Nomination)

7.6 *Membership and Chairmanship of Board committees. (Nomination)

7.7 *Continuation in office of directors at the end of their term of office, when they are due to be re-elected by shareholders at the AGM and otherwise as appropriate. (Nomination)

7.8 *Continuation in office of any director at any time, including the suspension or termination of service of an executive director as an employee of the company, subject to the law and their service contract. (Nomination)

7.9 *Appointment or removal of the company secretary. (CA s283, s286, CC A.5.3)

7.10 *Appointment, reappointment or removal of the external auditor to be put to shareholders for approval, following the recommendation of the audit committee. (CA s384, CC C.3.2, Audit)

7.11 Appointments to boards of subsidiaries.

8. Remuneration

8.1 *Determining the remuneration policy for the directors, company secretary and other senior executives. (Remuneration)

8.2 Determining the remuneration of the non-executive directors, subject to the articles of association and shareholder approval as appropriate. (CC B.2.3)

8.3 *The introduction of new share incentive plans or major changes to existing plans, to be put to shareholders for approval. (Remuneration)

9. Delegation of Authority

9.1 *The division of responsibilities between the chairman, the chief executive [and other executive directors,] which should be in writing. (CC A.2.1)

9.2 *Approval of terms of reference of Board committees. (CC A.4.1, B.2.1, C.3.1)

9.3 *Receiving reports from Board committees on their activities.

10. Corporate governance matters

10.1 *Undertaking a formal and rigorous review [annually] of its own performance, that of its committees and individual directors. (CC A.6)

10.2 *Determining the independence of directors. (CC A.3.1)

10.3 *Considering the balance of interests between shareholders, employees, customers and the community.

10.4 Review of the group's overall corporate governance arrangements.

10.5 *Receiving reports on the views of the company's shareholders. (CC D.1.1)

11. Policies

11.1 Approval of policies, including:

- code of conduct
- share dealing code
- health and safety policy
- environmental policy
- communications policy [including procedures for the release of price sensitive information]
- corporate social responsibility policy
- charitable donations policy. (CC A.1)

12. Other

12.1 The making of political donations.

12.2 Approval of the appointment of the group's principal professional advisers.

12.3 Prosecution, defence or settlement of litigation [involving above £xx million or being otherwise material to the interests of the group].

12.4 Approval of the overall levels of insurance for the group including directors' and officers' liability insurance [and indemnification of directors].

12.5 Major changes to the rules of the group's pension scheme, or changes of trustees or [when this is subject to the approval of the company] changes in the fund management arrangements.

12.6 This schedule of matters reserved for Board decisions.

Matters which the Board considers suitable for delegation are contained in the terms of reference of its Committees.

In addition, the Board will receive reports and recommendations from time to time on any matter which it considers significant to the Group.

Notes

1 The Combined Code on Corporate Governance – July 2003, A1.1.

2 The Combined Code on Corporate Governance – July 2003 A.1, first Supporting Principle.

3 These items are often considered by the whole Board but with the final formal decision being delegated to a committee (set up solely for that purpose). This allows time for any changes requested at the Board meeting to be incorporated into the final document before publication.

Appendix 5
Guidance on the Role of the Chairman (Higgs Guidance)

The chairman is pivotal in creating the conditions for overall board and individual director effectiveness, both inside and outside the boardroom. Specifically, it is the responsibility of the chairman to:

- run the board and set its agenda. The agenda should take full account of the issues and the concerns of all board members. Agendas should be forward looking and concentrate on strategic matters rather than formulaic approvals of proposals which can be the subject of appropriate delegated powers to management;
- ensure that the members of the board receive accurate, timely and clear information, in particular about the company's performance, to enable the board to take sound decisions, monitor effectively and provide advice to promote the success of the company;
- ensure effective communication with shareholders and ensure that the members of the board develop an understanding of the views of the major investors;
- manage the board to ensure that sufficient time is allowed for discussion of complex or contentious issues, where appropriate arranging for informal meetings beforehand to enable thorough preparation for the board discussion. It is particularly important that non-executive directors have sufficient time to consider critical issues and are not faced with unrealistic deadlines for decision-making;
- take the lead in providing a properly constructed induction programme for new directors that is comprehensive, formal and tailored, facilitated by the company secretary;
- take the lead in identifying and meeting the development needs of individual directors, with the company secretary having a key role in facilitating provision. It is the responsibility of the chairman to address the development needs of the board as a whole with a view to enhancing its overall effectiveness as a team;
- ensure that the performance of individuals and of the board as a whole and its committees is evaluated at least once a year; and
- encourage active engagement by all the members of the board.

The effective chairman:

- upholds the highest standards of integrity and probity;
- sets the agenda, style and tone of board discussions to promote effective decision-making and constructive debate;
- promotes effective relationships and open communication, both inside and outside the boardroom, between non-executive directors and executive team;
- builds an effective and complementary board, initiating change and planning succession in board appointments, subject to board and shareholders' approval;

- promotes the highest standards of corporate governance and seeks compliance with the provisions of the Code wherever possible;
- ensures clear structure for and the effective running of board committees;
- ensures effective implementation of board decisions;
- establishes a close relationship of trust with the chief executive, providing support and advice while respecting executive responsibility; and
- provides coherent leadership of the company, including representing the company and understanding the views of shareholders.

Appendix 6

Guidance on the Role of the Non-Executive Director (Higgs Guidance)

As members of the unitary board, all directors are required to:

- Provide entrepreneurial leadership of the company within a framework of prudent and effective controls which enable risk to be assessed and managed;
- Set the company's strategic aims, ensure that the necessary financial and human resources are in place for the company to meet its objectives, and review management performance; and
- Set the company's values and standards and ensure that its obligations to its shareholders and others are understood and met.

In addition to these requirements for all directors, the role of the non-executive director has the following key elements:

- Strategy. Non-executive directors should constructively challenge and help develop proposals on strategy.
- Performance. Non-executive directors should scrutinise the performance of management in meeting agreed goals and objectives and monitor the reporting of performance.
- Risk. Non-executive directors should satisfy themselves on the integrity of financial information and that financial controls and systems of risk management are robust and defensible.
- People. Non-executive directors are responsible for determining appropriate levels of remuneration of executive directors, and have a prime role in appointing, and where necessary removing, executive directors and in succession planning.

Non-executive directors should constantly seek to establish and maintain confidence in the conduct of the company. They should be independent in judgement and have an enquiring mind. To be effective, non-executive directors need to build a recognition by executives of their contribution in order to promote openness and trust.

To be effective, non-executive directors need to be well-informed about the company and the external environment in which it operates, with a strong command of issues relevant to the business. A non-executive director should insist on a comprehensive, formal and tailored induction. An effective induction need not be restricted to the boardroom, so consideration should be given to visiting sites and meeting senior and middle management. Once in post, an effective non-executive director should seek continually to develop and refresh their knowledge and skills to ensure that their contribution to the board remains informed and relevant.

Best practice dictates that an effective non-executive director will ensure that information is provided sufficiently in advance of meetings to enable thorough consideration of the issues facing the board. The non-executive director should insist that information is sufficient, accurate, clear and timely.

An element of the role of the non-executive director is to understand the views of major investors both directly and through the chairman and the senior independent director.

The effective non-executive director:

- upholds the highest ethical standards of integrity and probity;
- supports executives in their leadership of the business while monitoring their conduct;
- questions intelligently, debates constructively, challenges rigorously and decides dispassionately;
- listens sensitively to the views of others, inside and outside the board;
- gains the trust and respect of other board members; and
- promotes the highest standards of corporate governance and seeks compliance with the provisions of the Code wherever possible.

Appendix 7

Summary of the Principal Duties of the Nomination Committee (Higgs Guidance)

There should be a nomination committee which should lead the process for board appointments and make recommendations to the board.

A majority of members of the committee should be independent non-executive directors. The chairman or an independent non-executive director should chair the committee, but the chairman should not chair the nomination committee when it is dealing with the appointment of a successor to the chairmanship.

Duties

The committee should:

- be responsible for identifying and nominating for the approval of the board, candidates to fill board vacancies as and when they arise;
- before making an appointment, evaluate the balance of skills, knowledge and experience on the board and, in the light of this evaluation, prepare a description of the role and capabilities required for a particular appointment;
- review annually the time required from a non-executive director. Performance evaluation should be used to assess whether the non-executive director is spending enough time to fulfil their duties;
- consider candidates from a wide range of backgrounds and look beyond the 'usual suspects';
- give full consideration to succession planning in the course of its work, taking into account the challenges and opportunities facing the company and what skills and expertise are therefore needed on the board in the future;
- regularly review the structure, size and composition (including the skills, knowledge and experience) of the board and make recommendations to the board with regard to any changes;
- keep under review the leadership needs of the organisation, both executive and non-executive, with a view to ensuring the continued ability of the organisation to compete effectively in the marketplace;
- make a statement in the annual report about its activities; the process used for appointments and explain if external advice or open advertising has not been used; the membership of the committee, number of committee meetings and attendance over the course of the year;
- make available its terms of reference explaining clearly its role and the authority delegated to it by the board; and
- ensure that on appointment to the board, non-executive directors receive a formal letter of appointment setting out clearly what is expected of them in terms of time commitment, committee service and involvement outside board meetings.

The committee should make recommendations to the board:

- as regards plans for succession for both executive and non-executive directors;
- as regards the re-appointment of any non-executive director at the conclusion of their specified term of office;
- concerning the re-election by shareholders of any director under the retirement by rotation provisions in the company's articles of association;
- concerning any matters relating to the continuation in office of any director at any time; and
- concerning the appointment of any director to executive or other office other than to the positions of chairman and chief executive, the recommendation for which would be considered at a meeting of the board.

This guidance has been compiled with the assistance of ICSA who have kindly agreed to produce updated guidance on their website www.icsa.org.uk in the future.

Appendix 8

Sample Letter of Non-Executive Director Appointment (Higgs Guidance)

On [date], upon the recommendation of the nomination committee, the board of [company] ('the Company') has appointed you as non-executive director. I am writing to set out the terms of your appointment. It is agreed that this is a contract for services and is not a contract of employment.

Appointment

Your appointment will be for an initial term of three years commencing on [date], unless otherwise terminated earlier by and at the discretion of either party upon [one month's] written notice. Continuation of your contract of appointment is contingent on satisfactory performance and re-election at forthcoming AGMs.

Non-executive directors are typically expected to serve two three-year terms, although the board may invite you to serve an additional period.

Time commitment

Overall we anticipate a time commitment of [number] days per month after the induction phase. This will include attendance at [monthly] board meetings, the AGM, [one] annual board away day, and [at least one] site visit per year. In addition, you will be expected to devote appropriate preparation time ahead of each meeting.

By accepting this appointment, you have confirmed that you are able to allocate sufficient time to meet the expectations of your role. The agreement of the chairman should be sought before accepting additional commitments that might impact on the time you are able to devote to your role as a non-executive director of the company.

Role

Non-executive directors have the same general legal responsibilities to the company as any other director. The board as a whole is collectively responsible for the success of the company. The board:

- provides entrepreneurial leadership of the company within a framework of prudent and effective controls which enable risk to be assessed and managed;
- sets the company's strategic aims, ensures that the necessary financial and human resources are in place for the company to meet its objectives, and reviews management performance; and
- sets the company's values and standards and ensures that its obligations to its shareholders and others are understood and met.

All directors must take decisions objectively in the interests of the company.

In addition to these requirements of all directors, the role of the non-executive director has the following key elements:

- Strategy. Non-executive directors should constructively challenge and help develop proposals on strategy;
- Performance. Non-executive directors should scrutinise the performance of management in meeting agreed goals and objectives and monitor the reporting of performance;
- Risk. Non-executive directors should satisfy themselves on the integrity of financial information and that financial controls and systems of risk management are robust and defensible; and
- People. Non-executive directors are responsible for determining appropriate levels of remuneration of executive directors and have a prime role in appointing, and where necessary removing, executive directors and in succession planning.

Fees

You will be paid a fee of £[amount] gross per annum which will be paid monthly in arrears, [plus [number] ordinary shares of the company per annum, both of] which will be subject to an annual review by the board. The company will reimburse you for all reasonable and properly documented expenses you incur in performing the duties of your office.

Outside interests

It is accepted and acknowledged that you have business interests other than those of the company and have declared any conflicts that are apparent at present. In the event that you become aware of any potential conflicts of interest, these should be disclosed to the chairman and company secretary as soon as apparent.

[The board of the Company have determined you to be independent according to provision A.3.1 of the Code.]

Confidentiality

All information acquired during your appointment is confidential to the Company and should not be released, either during your appointment or following termination (by whatever means), to third parties without prior clearance from the chairman.

Your attention is also drawn to the requirements under both legislation and regulation as to the disclosure of price sensitive information. Consequently you should avoid making any statements that might risk a breach of these requirements without prior clearance from the chairman or company secretary.

Induction

Immediately after appointment, the Company will provide a comprehensive, formal and tailored induction. This will include the information pack recommended by the Institute of Chartered Secretaries and Administrators (ICSA), available at www.icsa.org.uk. We will also arrange for site visits and meetings with senior and middle management and the Company's auditors.

We will also offer to major shareholders the opportunity to meet you.

Review process

The performance of individual directors and the whole board and its committees is evaluated annually. If, in the interim, there are any matters which cause you concern about your role you should discuss them with the chairman as soon as is appropriate.

Insurance

The Company has directors' and officers' liability insurance and it is intended to maintain such cover for the full term of your appointment. The current indemnity limit is £ [amount]; a copy of the policy document is attached.

Independent professional advice

Occasions may arise when you consider that you need professional advice in the furtherance of your duties as a director. Circumstances may occur when it will be appropriate for you to seek advice from independent advisors at the company's expense. A copy of the board's agreed procedure under which directors may obtain such independent advice is attached. The Company will reimburse the full cost of expenditure incurred in accordance with the attached policy.

Committees

This letter refers to your appointment as a non-executive director of the Company. In the event that you are also asked to serve on one or more of the board committees this will be covered in a separate communication setting out the committee(s)'s terms of reference, any specific responsibilities and any additional fees that may be involved.

This sample appointment letter has been compiled with the assistance of ICSA who have kindly agreed to produce updated guidance on their website www.icsa.org.uk in the future.

Appendix 9

Pre-Appointment Due Diligence Checklist for New Board Members (Higgs Guidance)

Why?

Before accepting an appointment a prospective non-executive director should undertake their own thorough examination of the company to satisfy themselves that it is an organisation in which they can have faith and in which they will be well suited to working.

The following questions are not intended to be exhaustive, but are intended to be a helpful basis of the pre-appointment due diligence process that all non-executive directors should undertake.

Questions to ask

- What is the company's current financial position and what has its financial track record been over the last three years?
- What are the key dependencies (e.g. regulatory approvals, key licences, etc.)?
- What record does the company have on corporate governance issues?
- If the company is not performing particularly well, is there potential to turn it round and do I have the time, desire and capability to make a positive impact?
- What are the exact nature and extent of the company's business activities?
- Who are the current executive and non-executive directors, what is their background and their record and how long have they served on the board?
- What is the size and structure of the board and board committees and what are the relationships between the chairman and the board, the chief executive and the management team?
- Who owns the company, i.e. who are the company's main shareholders and how has the profile changed over recent years? What is the company's attitude towards, and relationship with, its shareholders?
- Is any material litigation presently being undertaken or threatened, either by the company or against it?
- Is the company clear and specific about the qualities, knowledge, skills and experience that it needs to complement the existing board?
- What insurance cover is available to directors and what is the company's policy on indemnifying directors?
- Do I have the necessary knowledge, skills, experience and time to make a positive contribution to the board of this company?
- How closely do I match the job specification and how well will I fulfil the board's expectations?

- Is there anything about the nature and extent of the company's business activities that would cause me concern both in terms of risk and any personal ethical considerations?
- Am I satisfied that the internal regulation of the company is sound and that I can operate effectively within its stated corporate governance framework?
- Am I satisfied that the size, structure and make-up of the board will enable me to make an effective contribution?
- Would accepting the non-executive directorship put me in a position of having a conflict of interest?

Sources of information

- Company report and accounts, and/or any listing prospectus, for the recent years.
- Analyst reports.
- Press reports.
- Company web site.
- Any Corporate Social Responsibility or Environmental Report issued by the company.
- Rating agency reports.
- Voting services reports.

Published material is unlikely to reveal wrong-doing, however a lack of transparency may be a reason to proceed with caution.

This guidance has been compiled with the assistance of ICSA who have kindly agreed to produce updated guidance on their website www.icsa.org.uk in the future.

Appendix 10

The Tyson Report on the Recruitment and Development of Non-Executive Directors (June 2003): Executive Summary

The report by Derek Higgs on the Role and Effectiveness of Non-Executive Directors raised the agenda of boardroom effectiveness. This report provides another piece of the jigsaw by highlighting how a range of different backgrounds and experiences among board members can enhance board effectiveness and by exploring how a broader range of non-executive directors can be identified and recruited.

The selection of each non-executive director (NED) should rest on a careful assessment of the needs and challenges of a particular company and on a broad, transparent and rigorous search that reflects this assessment.

Factors such as a company's size and age, the makeup of its customer and employee base, the extent of its participation in global markets, its future strategies, and its current board membership are important determinants of its NED requirements.

Diversity in the backgrounds, skills, and experiences of NEDs enhances board effectiveness by bringing a wider range of perspectives and knowledge to bear on issues of company performance, strategy and risk. Board diversity can also send a positive and motivating signal to customers, shareholders and employees, and can contribute to a better understanding by the company's leadership of the diverse constituencies that affect its success.

Broader, more rigorous and more transparent search processes for NEDs would not only enhance board talent and effectiveness but would also foster greater diversity in the background, experience, age, gender, ethnicity and nationality of NEDs.

Many UK companies would benefit from extending their searches for NEDs to new pools of talent. Possible sources of talented candidates that traditional, largely informal, search processes have tended to overlook include: the so-called 'marzipan' layer of corporate management just below board level; unlisted companies and private equity firms; business services and consultancies; and organisations in the non-commercial sector.

In addition, despite the increasing globalisation of business, the NEDs of UK companies tend to be domestic citizens rather than foreign nationals. Such board membership represents a potential mismatch between the international issues a company faces and the knowledge that its domestic board members can bring. Such a mismatch is likely to compromise the global competitive strength of British-based companies over time.

To help individuals from non-traditional sources who want to be considered for NED positions, we describe the role of executive search firms in identifying potential NED candidates and we suggest what individuals can do to be considered for these positions. We also note that a growing number of non-commercial organisations such as the Association of Chief Executives of Voluntary Organisations (ACEVO) are developing databases of qualified individuals interested in NED positions. Individuals with successful leadership careers in the non-commercial and public sectors have the attributes, skills and experience relevant to commercial NED positions.

We provide information showing that large non-commercial organisations are comparable in scale and complexity to large commercial organisations.

We decided against developing our own list of qualified candidates of individuals from the non-commercial sector with the skills and experience relevant to NED positions in the commercial sector. Developing a list of candidates without a careful assessment of company needs and without a broad, rigorous and transparent search process would be inconsistent with our recommendations about how companies should select their NEDs.

As NED responsibilities continue to expand, companies will have to provide more training and evaluation for their board members. Companies should provide thorough induction programmes for all new NED appointees and should provide ongoing training opportunities for incumbent NEDs. Companies should also evaluate the performance of their boards on a regular basis, and NED training should be linked to the findings of such assessments. Training and evaluation processes are likely to be particularly important for companies committed to building diverse boards and to realising the benefits of diversity among their members.

Although board training is currently available in a variety of ways, there are possible gaps between what providers of training are offering and what companies need. We recommend an initiative to bring together companies and training providers to establish guidelines to ensure that training programmes for directors are providing what is needed, and that useful information about such programmes is easily accessible on a timely basis. London Business School has offered to play a full part in such discussions.

We recommend an initiative to monitor both progress on achieving rigorous and transparent processes for NED appointments and progress on building more diverse boardrooms. Such an initiative should provide reliable measures of board composition for individual companies, should disseminate best-practice examples of how individual companies build more diverse and meritocratic boards, and should foster research on the impact of board diversity on board and company performance.

Optimising board membership is vital for company performance and competitiveness. It can also play an important role in restoring shareholder and public trust in UK boardrooms.

Appendix 11
ICSA Guidance Note: Induction of Directors

Since the publication of the ICSA Best Practice Guide *The Appointment and Induction of Directors*, it has become apparent that some newly appointed directors have been completely overwhelmed with the sheer volume of documents and other papers provided by the well-meaning company secretary to such an extent that some have been completely put off by it.

The objective of induction is to inform the director such that he or she can become as effective as possible in their new role as soon as possible. The provision of reams of paper in one go is, obviously, not conducive to this process. It is therefore recommended that, on appointment, a new director be provided with certain key, essential information together with a comprehensive list of other information that will be made available subsequently.

More recently we have seen the publication of the Higgs Report on the role and effectiveness of non-executive directors. That report includes various recommendations including, as Annex I, an induction checklist. ICSA worked closely with the Higgs Review team on the creation of that checklist and, in order to enable it to be kept brief and to the point, undertook to produce this Guidance Note providing more comprehensive details of the material that should be considered for inclusion in an induction pack provided to new directors on, or during the weeks immediately following their appointment.

The following list is divided into three parts. The first includes the essential material that should be provided immediately and the second, material that should be provided over the first few weeks following the appointment, as and when deemed most appropriate. The director should, however, be provided immediately with a comprehensive list of the material being made available in total, together with an undertaking to provide it earlier if required. The third list covers items which the company secretary might consider making the director aware of.

Note that some information may have already been provided during the director's due diligence process prior to appointment, or along with the appointment letter. Whilst duplication should be avoided, care should be taken to provide any updates that may be necessary.

The topics contained within this note should be supplied to all newly appointed directors, both executive and non-executive, however the secretary will need to gauge the level of previous knowledge and adjust them accordingly, particularly in regard to the appointment of executive directors.

Essential information to be provided immediately

The following information is felt to be essential and needs to be given to the director prior to the first board meeting. Methods of delivery vary. Some of the information needs to be sent to the director with his appointment letter; but some could be deferred until a meeting after the board papers have been issued, so that the company secretary can review the board pack with the director before the first meeting highlighting any relevant issues.

Directors' Duties

- Brief outline of the role of a director and a summary of his/her responsibilities and ongoing obligations under legislation, regulation and best practice.
- Copy of UKLA Model Code, and details of the company's procedure regarding directors' share dealings and the disclosure of price sensitive information.
- The company's guidelines on:
  - Matters reserved for the board;
  - Delegated Authorities;
  - The policy for obtaining independent professional advice for directors;
  - Other standing orders, policies and procedures of which the director should be aware.
- 'Fire Drill' procedures (the procedures in place to deal with such as hostile takeover bids).

The Company's Business

- Current strategic/business plan, market analysis and budgets for the year with revised forecast, and three-/five-year plan.
- Latest annual report and accounts, and interims as appropriate.
- Explanation of key performance indicators.
- List of major domestic and overseas subsidiaries, associated companies and joint ventures, including any parent company(ies).
- Summary details of major group insurance policies including D&O liability insurance.
- Details of any major litigation, either current or potential, being undertaken by the company or against the company.
- Treasury issues:
  - Funding position and arrangements;
  - Dividend policy.
- The corporate brochure, mission statement and any other reports issued by the company such as an environmental report, with a summary of the main events (such as mergers, divestments, introductions of new products, diversification into new areas, restructuring, etc.) over the last three years.

Board Issues

- Up to date copy of the company's Memorandum and Articles of Association/Constitution, with a summary of the most important provisions.
- Minutes of the last 3–6 board meetings.
- Schedule of dates of future board meetings and board subcommittees if appropriate.
- Description of board procedures covering details such as when papers are sent out, the normal location of meetings, how long they last and an indication of the routine business transacted.

- Brief biographical and contact details of all directors of the company, the company secretary and other key executives. This should include any executive responsibilities of directors, their dates of appointment and any board committees upon which individual directors sit.
- Details of board subcommittees together with terms of reference and, where the director will be joining a committee, copies of the minutes of meetings of that committee during the previous 12 months.

Additional material to be provided during the first few months

The following information is crucial to assist the director to develop his/her knowledge of the company, its operations and staff, but is not necessary for him/her to commence his/her involvement. It is suggested, however, that a detailed schedule of the information available is provided to him/her, and the information is supplied either on request or within three months of appointment. It would also be appropriate to involve senior members of staff in the induction programme, for example the Investor Relations Manager could give a presentation on the IR programme, so that the non-executive director begins to get a view of the depth of management available and the executive director is exposed to areas of the business he/she has less previous knowledge of.

- Copies of the company's main product/service brochures.
- Copies of recent press cuttings, reports and articles concerning the company.
- Details of the company's advisers (lawyers, bankers, auditors, registrars etc.), both internal and external, with the name of the partner dealing with the company's affairs.
- The company's risk management procedures and relevant disaster recovery plans.
- An outline of the provisions of the Combined Code as appended to the UK Listing Rules together with details of the company's corporate governance guidelines and any investor's corporate governance guidelines which the company seeks to follow.
- Brief history of the company including when it was incorporated and any significant events during its history.
- Notices of any general meetings held in the last 3 years, and accompanying circulars as appropriate.
- Company organisation chart and management succession plans.
- Copy of all management accounts prepared since the company's last audited accounts.
- The company's investor relations policy and details of the major shareholders.
- Details of the five largest customers with the level of business done over the last five years.
- Details of the five largest suppliers to the company.
- Policies as regards:
  - Health & Safety;
  - Environment;
  - Ethics and Whistleblowing;
  - Charitable & Political Donations.
- Internal company telephone directory (including any overseas contact numbers and names).

Additional information which the company secretary might consider making the director aware of

The final section includes information which will differ for all companies depending on the sector and the company secretary will need to use his/her experience and knowledge to pass on information to allow the director to feel accustomed to the business as soon as possible.

- Protocol, procedures and dress code for:
  - Board meetings;
  - General meetings;
  - Formal dinners, staff social events, site visits etc. including the involvement of partners where appropriate.
- Procedures for:
  - Accounts sign off;
  - Results announcements;
  - Items requiring approval outside of board meetings.
- Expenses policy and method of reimbursement.

Appendix 12
ICSA Guidance Note: Directors' and Officers' Insurance

In 2002, at the request of the Secretary of State, Derek Higgs undertook a review of the role and effectiveness of non-executive directors. One point identified as causing concern related to the perceived inadequacies and high costs of Directors' and Officers' Liability cover (D & O). Following publication of the Report,[1] and at the request of the Higgs team, ICSA convened a meeting of representatives of:

- City of London Law Society;
- ICSA;
- The Association of British Insurers;
- British Insurance Brokers Association; and
- The ICSA Company Secretaries Forum

to produce guidance on this topic.

It was agreed that, given the wide variety of organisations, the range of industries in which they operate and the differing everyday business risks, it would not be practical to draft a 'specimen policy'. This note is therefore:

- a check-list of just some of the major issues that prospective directors (whether executive or non-executive) should consider, both to help them understand D & O insurance and also to evaluate the cover provided by companies they are considering joining; and
- a useful aide-mémoire for existing directors and for organisations when considering their own requirements for such cover.

The Guidance is not intended to be a comprehensive summary of the topic and should not be considered a substitute for specific advice from a good broker or legal adviser.

It should be remembered that D & O insurance is only one of the methods by which risk is transferred from directors. They may also, for example, have an indemnity from the company, but this will undoubtedly be restricted, either by its specific terms or by law.

D & O insurance is not compulsory. Although Section 137 of the Companies Act(1985) permits companies to take out insurance on behalf of their directors and to pay the premiums, it is not mandatory. However the newly published Combined Code2 includes a provision (A.1.5) that "The company should arrange appropriate insurance cover in respect of legal action against its directors".

D & O insurance is normally taken out in one of three formats:

- A policy which is taken out by the company (and most usually the policy schedule will be in the name of that company) and which provides cover for indemnifiable risks under one section and non-indemnifiable risks under another – commonly referred to as sections A and B;

- A policy which is taken out by the company (again most usually the policy schedule will be in the name of that company) and which provides cover only for non-indemnifiable risks. This type of policy is particularly popular for companies that wish to provide significant limits of indemnity for directors and officers when the company does not, cannot or will not indemnify. Particular care and attention must be paid to the wording of the operative clause in such policies (i.e. regarding when indemnity can be provided);
- A policy covering an individual named person, e.g. Mr David Smith, who may have one and/or a number of directorships, executive and/or non-executive positions which he wishes to insure under his "own personal policy".

From this it is clear that individuals may find themselves covered by more than one policy which can cause major difficulties between parties. It is therefore important that due cognisance is made of potential overlap and/or gaps in cover.

The headings in this note are for general guidance; many of the issues raised overlap between areas.

Who does it cover?

Unless written as an 'individual' policy, the company itself, parent and/or subsidiary companies may be covered to the extent that they in turn have to indemnify their directors and officers. Associated companies[3] may not be included at all.

The policy normally covers the directors, the company secretary(ies) and any other nominated officers of the insured company(ies).

Those seeking to join a company as a director or officer should seek written confirmation that they will be included in the company's D & O insurance and notified of any changes in cover that might affect them. This may be particularly important when considering the sufficiency of the amount of cover provided – see section headed "Amount of cover".

From the individual's point of view it is also important to check that the policy covers 'past and present directors' to ensure that cover continues after 'retirement'[4] – at least in respect of situations occurring during their period of office. There are examples where those who ceased to be directors prior to the inception of the policy were not covered, even where the claim arose after the policy's inception, – see section headed "Automatic conversion to run-off".

Outside Directors

Standard policies will not automatically cover directors and officers sitting on unconnected boards, i.e. boards outside the insured group, where the director sits at the request of the group. In such cases, 'Outside Directors' cover will be required. This will often only be available on different, more restricted terms, than the basic D & O cover. Typical wording of such an inclusion may read:

> "a past, present or future director of an outside entity who has become or became a director of the entity at the specific request of the company"

Care will be needed to ensure that the particular needs of the company and individual are correctly catered for, e.g. **directors or officers seconded to, or given an additional role in, an associated or unrelated company should check that they will be covered either under the main or the associated/unrelated company's policies.**

Acquisitions

As with many issues in D & O insurance different insurers deal with acquisitions in differing ways. Some will cover acquisitions automatically, but this could be on any one of a number of different bases. It is essential to check. A typical clause may read:

> "The benefit of the insurance cover provided by this policy shall extend automatically to all newly acquired or created subsidiaries of the company, other than those which have or have had a listing of any of its securities on any exchange in the USA or Canada; such extension to apply solely in respect of WRONGFUL ACTS alleged to have been committed whilst the newly acquired or created company was a subsidiary of the company."

Note the exclusion of US and Canadian listed companies. If such an organisation is involved, the insurer would undoubtedly seek to clarify the risk involved and quote specific terms and conditions for such an inclusion.

Period of cover

Cover will normally start from the date of appointment, but there may be a requirement to notify the insurer of the appointment. Frequently, the only obligation is to update the list of directors and officers at annual renewal.

Directors should ask the company to confirm that the appropriate notifications have been or will be made. In any event, companies would be wise to play safe and notify the insurer/broker of changes – especially in circumstances such as the appointment of a new US based director which may fundamentally alter the risk.

Care should be taken to ensure that the insurer will be or has been notified of the appointment within any prevailing time limits.

Basis of cover

D & O policies are almost exclusively written on a 'claims made' basis. Cover will normally cease when the appointment comes to an end, but an individual's liability may continue for some time in respect of actions or inactions occurring during the period of appointment. To cover this a policy can be extended to include 'run-off' cover.

Directors should obtain clear guidance on the extent of 'run-off' cover that is provided under the policy and what, if any, action is required to ensure that they are/will be included under such provision. Although there are examples of run-off cover being provided for up to six years, there are also examples where it has been restricted to just six months. This can pose particular problems for 'retiring' directors and officers or where divisions or parts of businesses are disposed of, and the continuity of cover is broken.

Automatic conversion to run-off

Some policies have an 'automatic run-off' option. More often, this will come under the condition of "Extended Discovery Period". Either approach usually involves payment of an additional premium, which varies in amount. It can be as little as 25% or up to 100% of the most recent annual premium, depending on the duration of the run-off period and the insurer's willingness to extend the policy on this basis.

It is vital to remember that indemnity contracts do not have any automatic extensions or "periods of grace". If renewal is required, the insurer must be advised long before the expiry of the existing contract otherwise continuity[5] of cover will be broken and then backdating the start of the cover can become a serious issue.

What is a 'claim'?

A 'claim' is usually defined quite narrowly e.g. "a demand made in writing". Anything else, such as a threat of legal action, has to be notified as a 'Circumstance' (which may give rise to a claim). As a 'Circumstance', if accepted by the insurer, will lodge in the year it is registered regardless of when the eventual claim may materialise, insurers are generally reluctant to accept them.

Duty of disclosure

As with all insurances, the policy will incorporate a duty of disclosure whether or not specifically mentioned. **A director will therefore be obliged to disclose to the insurer any claims or circumstances which may give rise to a claim.**

Some policies contain clauses which can be quite helpful to the insured e.g. severability clauses whereby one insured's knowledge, or facts pertaining to one insured, are not ascribed to other insureds. In addition, insurers will sometimes agree not to void a policy for non-disclosure or misrepresentation if the insured can establish that such non-disclosure or misrepresentation was entirely innocent.

Extent of cover

Policy wording, and the extent of cover, can vary widely and care should be taken to understand what is (and – more importantly – what is not) covered, and any areas of risk that may remain.

It is usual and/or highly desirable to include the following:

- Damages awarded against an insured person;
- Out-of-court settlements – care should be taken to ensure that these are also specifically included;
- Costs, including fees, professional costs and expenses resulting from the investigation and/or defence or settlement of a claim will normally be covered. However, material or information may come to light during a claim which causes the insurer to cease paying the defence costs half-way through. In such cases the insurer may also seek to recover costs already paid out;
- Libel and slander – may be included, but not always;
- Wrongful Acts which can be defined as any error, misstatement, misleading statement, act, omission, neglect or breach of duty committed or attempted or any matter claimed against

the individual **solely by reason of their serving in a capacity as a director or officer of the company**. Whilst the definition of Wrongful Acts can vary and be very widely construed it is of vital importance to recognise that the act must be something done in the capacity of director or officer.

The following are common restrictions and/or exclusions:

- Fines, penalties and punitive damages levied by regulators or criminal courts. (Note that the Financial Services Authority has recently suggested that it will, in any event, ban insurance cover for regulatory fines.)
- Criminal defence costs can apply in respect of criminal proceedings, but only to the point of conviction/release. No cover is given for appeal costs in the event of a conviction – the premise of innocent until proven guilty applies only to a limited extent;
- Loss of earnings or expenses incurred by the insured themselves, such as PR expenses to preserve reputations;
- Personal injury or property damage are also frequently excluded (this will typically be covered elsewhere – see below);
- Fraudulent, dishonest or illegal acts. Cover will not extend to deliberate dishonesty or the deliberate committing of fraudulent or illegal acts as to do so would be against the public interest;
- Legal jurisdiction. Some policies may restrict cover to certain geographical areas or exclude specific jurisdictions, e.g. the highly litigious USA. Directors and potential directors should consider carefully the possibility of a claim arising in any area excluded under the policy;
- Taxes are rarely covered. It should also be noted that premiums may not be tax deductible by the insuring company but, if structured properly, they may not be taxable as a benefit in kind to the director or officer. Directors and potential directors should obtain confirmation of the tax treatment in relation to the policy and their personal position. Premiums paid by an individual where cover is taken out personally will, on the other hand, usually be tax deductible;
- Existing conditions. Cover will normally exclude any loss or liability arising from an action or inaction occurring prior to the commencement of the cover. Careful attention should be paid to 'Conditions precedent' clauses which can be quite onerous;
- Liabilities covered elsewhere – e.g. liabilities normally covered under Employer's or Public Liability policies or Prospectus Liability policies. Those who may find themselves covered by more than one policy should make a point of clarifying the precise position. Some policies, for example, will cover executive directors in non-executive positions of other companies who may also have their own cover;
- Insured v insured. Some policies will not cover actions between parties covered by the same policy, often now described as the 'Equitable Life Claim scenario'. This might be an action taken by the company against a director or one director against another covered by the same policy. This can be particularly complicated when one policy covers a Group of companies including directors and officers of the parent and various subsidiary companies. Policies differ widely in the wording here but it is critical that directors and potential directors

recognise whether the policy would cover them against claims from the company itself and/or another director covered by the same policy;

- Additional services. D & O policies are designed to cover liabilities arising from the insured services as a director or officer and will not extend to services, e.g. professional services, outside the scope of their role as directors or officers of the company. Similarly D & O cover will not normally extend to personal guarantees and undertakings given by directors and officers. Although they may be given in connection with the role, e.g. personal guarantees to lenders, they do not arise out of the role itself;
- Service Companies. Additional complications can arise where a director may provide his/her services through a service company. If a director intends to act through a service company, care should be taken to clarify the position.

"Basis of Contract" clause

The proposal form for the policy may include a "basis of contract" clause. This seemingly innocuous phrase can have far-reaching consequences – its legal effect is to give every statement in the proposal form the status of a warranty so that a trivial error can be used by the insurer to avoid the policy. This has been upheld by UK courts despite criticism of the potentially severe consequences it can have for the insured – while the Statement of General Insurance Practice issued by the ABI recommends that personal lines insurance is not written on this basis, Directors & Officers Liability cover is treated as corporate insurance and may still include a "basis of contract" clause. Companies should therefore seek to have this removed in renewal negotiations and a director who hopes to benefit from cover under a D & O policy should establish whether the policy contains this clause, given its potential to negate the cover provided by the policy.

Amount of cover

Policies are usually written with a specific monetary limit but how this limit is applied may vary:

- Per claim – the policy will normally have a limit per claim or incident and may have sub-limits for different heads of claim;
- Per year – cover will frequently have an overall limit per year, often including defence costs. This can be particularly problematic where a number of companies or individuals are covered by the same policy. If the overall limit is exhausted by one or two claims, the unfortunate subject of a third claim may find they have no cover at all. This situation is often exacerbated when policy cover for one area is extended without due consideration to the impact on the overall or other parts of the policy.

Directors and potential directors should clarify the amount of cover provided.

Automatic re-instatement of sums insured

This extension, if available, can be particularly useful in guarding against the using up of cover. Clauses vary between insurers. Many take the position that they would seek a higher initial sum insured – for example, several hundreds of millions. In the UK, the tendency has been to err on the side of caution, which sees the vast majority of limits in the tens of millions. More recently, many new companies coming into the market have found it difficult to obtain this type of extension. Insurers are becoming more concerned over the complications of providing a "top up" of sums insured – but existing policies with this cover built in may still be able to renew with the extension. In the current market, the availability of cover has been restricted – but the hope is that it will become easier as the liability market settles down in the coming months.

Deductibles

Any deductible will be a matter of commercial negotiation, and can vary from nil to quite a high "excess". Different deductibles will apply to different sections of a policy and **directors should be clear when or whether a deductible applies and, if so, in which circumstances this will be paid by the company and when it might be for their own account**. If, for example, deductibles apply 'per event' it is essential to be clear on what constitutes a single event. For example, was 9/11 a single act of terrorism or a series of separate hijackings?

Conditions

All D & O policies will have fairly strict conditions attached. These may cover such things as:

- notification of appointments or other changes in the list of insured persons;
- notification of potential or actual claims;
- what actually constitutes a 'claim' in the terms of the policy;
- admission of liability;
- the actual conduct of any claims; and
- an obligation to make oneself available to defend a claim;

most of which are dealt with individually within this Guidance Note.

The general point, however, is that the exact wording in some of these clauses can be critical. For example, where there is an obligation to 'notify', the language might refer to circumstances which 'may' or 'are likely' to give rise to a claim. Clearly the two situations are significantly different. It can however be a double-edged sword; if the duty is to notify 'promptly' or within a specified time limit then there is a greater risk of breaching the 'may' condition than there is if the threshold is 'likely to'.

If there is simply an obligation to notify (without a time limit) then 'may' reduces the prospect of insurers alleging that a claim is not sufficiently probable. Further difficulties can then arise because, in the ordinary way, the matter giving rise to concern would have to be disclosed to the next insurer for the following period and the new insurer might insist on an exclusion in respect of that particular matter.

As with all insurance policies, it is a contract of "utmost good faith". Additionally there will be a requirement to mitigate losses wherever possible. It may, for example, be financially beneficial to settle a claim out of court rather than bear the costs of a protracted and complicated defence, especially if advice is that the defence is unlikely to succeed – even though this may be damaging to the reputation of the individual concerned.

Right of litigation

The insurer will almost invariably have the right to act on behalf of the insured although, unlike most insurance policies, with D & O insurance it is the duty of the company/director actually to defend a claim. This can be an extremely onerous experience for the individual.

Whilst the choice of legal adviser might be agreed between the insured and insurer there will be a tendency to appoint a legal firm who will have a good degree of insurance knowledge – which is all well and good in major centres like London, Birmingham etc. but might raise problems in more remote areas.

Summary

The (July 2003) Combined Code contains a specimen appointment letter for new non-executive directors and suggests that a copy of the D & O policy is provided. Clearly this is a pragmatic and reasonable practice. Potential directors should make every effort to understand the D & O policy, what it does and does not cover and the manner in which cover operates when joining, serving or leaving the company. It may also be prudent to understand the company's procedures for renewing or amending the cover to ensure that the cover cannot be diluted without the knowledge of those affected. If anything is unclear, clarification should be sought from the company secretary.

Given the complexity of the topic we make no apologies for repeating the earlier warning. The purpose of this Guidance Note is to alert, particularly new, directors to some of the issues involved with D & O insurance. It is not intended to be, nor in just a few pages can it be, a comprehensive guide. For those requiring more detailed information there are some authoritative books available on the subject. The risks and extent of cover available are however changing all the time and anyone contemplating taking out D & O insurance is advised to seek good professional advice.

It has been suggested that a short guide such as this is likely to raise more questions than it answers. If that is what happens then it may be that this Guide has served its purpose.

Notes

1 Review of the Role and Effectiveness of Non-Executive Directors, DTI January 2003.

2 The Combined Code on Corporate Governance issued by the Financial Reporting Council, July 2003.

3 Whilst different insurers may define "associated companies" differently, the Financial Reporting Standard FRS9 defines it as "An entity (other than a subsidiary) in which another entity (the investor) has a participating interest and over whose operating and financial policies the investor exercises significant influence."

4 "Retirement" is used here in its broadest sense and covers a director leaving the company for whatever reason.

5 We understand that the word 'continuity' may have a specific meaning within the realms of D & O insurance, however in this text the word is used in its everyday sense.

Appendix 13

Performance Evaluation Guidance (Higgs Guidance)

Guidance on performance evaluation

The [Combined] Code provides that the board should undertake a formal and rigorous annual evaluation of its own performance and that of its committees and individual directors. Individual evaluation should aim to show whether each director continues to contribute effectively and to demonstrate commitment to the role (including commitment of time for board and committee meetings and any other duties). The chairman should act on the results of the performance evaluation by recognising the strengths and addressing the weaknesses of the board and, where appropriate, proposing new members be appointed to the board or seeking the resignation of directors. The board should state in the annual report how such performance evaluation has been conducted.

It is the responsibility of the chairman to select an effective process and to act on its outcome. The use of an external third party to conduct the evaluation will bring objectivity to the process.

The non-executive directors, led by the senior independent director, should be responsible for performance evaluation of the chairman, taking into account the views of executive directors.

The evaluation process will be used constructively as a mechanism to improve board effectiveness, maximise strengths and tackle weaknesses. The results of board evaluation should be shared with the board as a whole while the results of individual assessments should remain confidential between the chairman and the non-executive director concerned.

The following are some of the questions that should be considered in a performance evaluation. They are, however, by no means definitive or exhaustive and companies will wish to tailor the questions to suit their own needs and circumstances.

The responses to these questions and others should enable boards to assess how they are performing and to identify how certain elements of their performance areas might be improved.

Performance evaluation of the board

- How well has the board performed against any performance objectives that have been set?
- What has been the board's contribution to the testing and development of strategy?
- What has been the board's contribution to ensuring robust and effective risk management?
- Is the composition of the board and its committees appropriate, with the right mix of knowledge and skills to maximise performance in the light of future strategy? Are inside and outside the board relationships working effectively?
- How has the board responded to any problems or crises that have emerged and could or should these have been foreseen?
- Are the matters specifically reserved for the board the right ones?

- How well does the board communicate with the management team, company employees and others? How effectively does it use mechanisms such as the AGM and the annual report?
- Is the board as a whole up to date with latest developments in the regulatory environment and the market?
- How effective are the board's committees? [Specific questions on the performance of each committee should be included such as, for example, their role, their composition and their interaction with the board.]

The processes that help underpin the board's effectiveness should also be evaluated e.g.:

- Is appropriate, timely information of the right length and quality provided to the board and is management responsive to requests for clarification or amplification? Does the board provide helpful feedback to management on its requirements?
- Are sufficient board and committee meetings of appropriate length held to enable proper consideration of issues? Is time used effectively?
- Are board procedures conducive to effective performance and flexible enough to deal with all eventualities?

In addition, there are some specific issues relating to the chairman which should be included as part of an evaluation of the board's performance e.g.:

- Is the chairman demonstrating effective leadership of the board?
- Are relationships and communications with shareholders well managed?
- Are relationships and communications within the board constructive?
- Are the processes for setting the agenda working? Do they enable board members to raise issues and concerns?
- Is the company secretary being used appropriately and to maximum value?

Performance evaluation of the non-executive director

The chairman and other board members should consider the following issues and the individual concerned should also be asked to assess themselves. For each non-executive director:

- How well prepared and informed are they for board meetings and is their meeting attendance satisfactory?
- Do they demonstrate a willingness to devote time and effort to understand the company and its business and a readiness to participate in events outside the boardroom such as site visits?
- What has been the quality and value of their contributions at board meetings?
- What has been their contribution to development of strategy and to risk management?
- How successfully have they brought their knowledge and experience to bear in the consideration of strategy?
- How effectively have they probed to test information and assumptions? Where necessary, how resolute are they in maintaining their own views and resisting pressure from others?
- How effectively and proactively have they followed up their areas of concern?

- How effective and successful are their relationships with fellow board members, the company secretary and senior management?
- Does their performance and behaviour engender mutual trust and respect within the board?
- How actively and successfully do they refresh their knowledge and skills and are they up to date with:
  - the latest developments in areas such as corporate governance framework and financial reporting?
  - the industry and market conditions?
- How well do they communicate with fellow board members, senior management and others, for example shareholders? Are they able to present their views convincingly yet diplomatically and do they listen and take on board the views of others?

Appendix 14

Summary of the Principal Duties of the Remuneration Committee (Higgs Guidance)

The Code provides that the remuneration committee should consist exclusively of independent non-executive directors and should comprise at least three or, in the case of smaller companies,[1] two such directors.

Duties

The committee should:

- determine and agree with the board the framework or broad policy for the remuneration of the chief executive, the chairman of the company and such other members of the executive management as it is designated to consider.[2] At a minimum, the committee should have delegated responsibility for setting remuneration for all executive directors, the chairman and, to maintain and assure their independence, the company secretary. The remuneration of non-executive directors shall be a matter for the chairman and executive members of the board. No director or manager should be involved in any decisions as to their own remuneration;
- determine targets for any performance-related pay schemes operated by the company;
- determine the policy for and scope of pension arrangements for each executive director;
- ensure that contractual terms on termination, and any payments made, are fair to the individual and the company, that failure is not rewarded and that the duty to mitigate loss is fully recognised;[3]
- within the terms of the agreed policy, determine the total individual remuneration package of each executive director including, where appropriate, bonuses, incentive payments and share options;
- in determining such packages and arrangements, give due regard to the contents of the Code as well as the UK Listing Authority's Listing Rules and associated guidance;
- be aware of and advise on any major changes in employee benefit structures throughout the company or group;
- agree the policy for authorising claims for expenses from the chief executive and chairman;
- ensure that provisions regarding disclosure of remuneration, including pensions, as set out in the Directors' Remuneration Report Regulations 2002 and the Code, are fulfilled;
- be exclusively responsible for establishing the selection criteria, selecting, appointing and setting the terms of reference for any remuneration consultants who advise the committee;
- report the frequency of, and attendance by members at, remuneration committee meetings in the annual reports; and

- make available the committee's terms of reference. These should set out the committee's delegated responsibilities and be reviewed and, where necessary, updated annually.

Notes

1 A smaller company is one that is below the FTSE 350 throughout the year immediately prior to the reporting year.

2 Some companies require the remuneration committee to consider the packages of all executives at or above a specified level such as those reporting to a main board director whilst others require the committee to deal with all packages above a certain figure.

3 Remuneration committees should consider reviewing and agreeing a standard form of contract for their executive directors, and ensuring that new appointees are offered and accept terms within the previously agreed level.

This guidance has been compiled with the assistance of ICSA who have kindly agreed to produce updated guidance on their website www.icsa.org.uk in the future.

Appendix 15
ABI Principles on Executive Remuneration (December 2004)

Introduction

The ABI Guidelines on remuneration are designed to provide a practical framework and reference point for both shareholders in reaching voting decisions and for companies in deciding upon their remuneration policy.

In conjunction with these Guidelines, institutional shareholders continue to expect companies to follow good practice under the Combined Code by establishing Remuneration Committees of independent non-executive directors. They will also expect companies to demonstrate best practice as regards disclosure as well as compliance with statutory regulation.

Shareholders believe that the key determinant for assessing remuneration is performance in the creation of shareholder value. The overall quantum of the remuneration package and the employment costs to companies must be weighed against the company's ability to recruit, retain and incentivise individuals.

Remuneration Reports should provide a full and clear explanation of the policy, establishing a clear link between reward and performance. Effective consultation by companies when formulating policy can help to avoid inappropriate outcomes. Companies should ensure that an appropriate policy is in place and followed, rather than to risk controversy when remuneration outcomes are disclosed in the Annual Report. Appropriate disclosures on remuneration for executives at below board level can be best achieved on a banded basis in order to illustrate the coherence of the company's remuneration policy.

During the transition to international accounting standards, shareholders would expect to see in the next Remuneration Committee Report a clear statement of the approach to achieving consistent measurement of performance. We are also encouraging disclosure of any structural changes in remuneration that may be recognised as appropriate in the context of impending changes to pensions taxation.

Other revisions include a preference for Remuneration Committees to structure Long Term Incentive Plans (LTIPs) so that dividends can accrue on shares which vest. We believe this better aligns management's interests with those of shareholders.

REMUNERATION – PRINCIPLES

1 Remuneration Committees should maintain a constructive and timely dialogue with their major institutional shareholders and the ABI on matters relating to remuneration such as contemplated changes to remuneration policy and practice, including issues relating to share-based incentive schemes. Any proposed departure from the stated remuneration policy should be subject to prior approval by shareholders.

2 Companies should ensure that Remuneration Committees are properly established and constituted to exercise independent judgment with appropriate powers of authority delegated from Company Boards.

3 Boards should demonstrate that performance based remuneration arrangements are clearly aligned with business strategy and objectives and are regularly reviewed. They should ensure that overall arrangements are prudent, well communicated, incentivise effectively and accord with current best practice. The description of the arrangements should be clear and accessible.

4 Remuneration Committees must guard against the possibility of unjustified windfall gains when designing and implementing share-based incentives and other associated entitlements. They must also ensure that variable and share-based remuneration is not payable unless the performance measurement governing this is robust. They should satisfy themselves as to the accuracy of recorded performance measures that govern vesting of such remuneration. They should work with audit committees in evaluating performance criteria.

5 Remuneration Committees should have regard to pay and conditions throughout the company. They should use external comparisons with caution, in view of the risk of an upward ratchet of remuneration levels with no corresponding improvement in performance and should avoid paying more than is necessary.

6 Remuneration Committees should pay particular attention to arrangements for senior executives who are not board members but have a significant influence over the company's ability to meet its strategic objectives.

7 All new share-based incentive schemes should be subject to approval by shareholders by means of a separate and binding resolution. Furthermore where the rules of share-based incentive schemes, or the basis on which the scheme was approved by shareholders, permit some degree of latitude as regards quantum of grant or performance criteria it is expected that any changes will be detailed in the Remuneration Report. Any substantive changes in practical operation of schemes resulting from policy changes or modifications of scheme rules as previously approved should be subject to prior shareholder approval.

8 Where there is any type of matching arrangement or performance-linked enhancement in respect of shares awarded under deferred bonus arrangements, there should be a separate shareholder vote. (See paragraphs 6.6 and 13.4.)

9 There should be transparency on all components of remuneration of present and past directors and where appropriate other senior executives. Shareholders' attention should be drawn to any special arrangements and significant changes since the previous Remuneration Report.

10 Shareholders consider it inappropriate for chairmen and independent directors to be in receipt of incentive awards geared to the share price or performance, as this could impair their ability to provide impartial oversight and advice.

11 Awards should be structured to promote as close an alignment as possible of participants with the risks and rewards faced by shareholders. It is undesirable for directors to seek out leveraged arrangements on the price of the company's securities.

GUIDELINES FOR THE STRUCTURE OF REMUNERATION

1 Remuneration Committees should look at overall remuneration, at whether there is an appropriate balance between fixed and variable remuneration and between short and long-term variable components of long-term remuneration, and, if not, how the remuneration package should be rebalanced in order to accommodate new elements.

2 When setting salary levels Remuneration Committees should take into consideration the requirements of the market, bearing in mind competitive forces applicable to the sector in which the company operates and to the particular challenges facing the company. Disclosure of policy in this regard is helpful to shareholders. Remuneration Committees should be able to satisfy shareholders that the company is not paying more than is necessary to attract and retain the directors needed to run the company successfully. It is also appropriate to evaluate other elements of the overall remuneration package, which are usually expressed by reference to base salary. Simple structures assist with motivation and enhance the prospects of successful communication with the employees involved and with shareholders.

3 A policy of setting salary levels below the comparator group median can provide more scope for increasing the amount of variable performance based pay and incentive scheme participation. Where a company seeks to pay salaries at above median, justification is required.

4 Annual bonuses, normally payable in cash, can provide a useful means of short-term incentivisation, but should be related to performance. Both individual and corporate performance targets are relevant and should be tailored to the requirements of the business and reviewed regularly to ensure they remain appropriate.

5 The performance targets should generally be disclosed in the Remuneration Report. Shareholders understand that considerations of commercial confidentiality may prevent disclosure of specific short-term targets, but they expect to be informed about the basic parameters adopted in the financial year being reported on. When the bonus has been paid, shareholders expect to see analysis in the Remuneration Report of the extent to which the relevant targets were actually met. The maximum participation levels should be disclosed, and any increases in the maximum from one year to the next should be explicitly justified. As provided for under the Combined Code, annual bonuses should not be pensionable.

6 Shareholders are not supportive of transaction bonuses which reward directors and other executives for effecting transactions irrespective of their future financial consequences. Any material payments that may be viewed as being ex-gratia in nature should be fully explained, justified and subject to shareholder approval prior to payment.

7 Boards should review regularly the potential liabilities associated with all elements of remuneration including share incentive participation and pension arrangements and should make appropriate disclosures to shareholders.

8 Institutional shareholders recognise that pension entitlements accruing to directors represent a significant, and potentially costly, item of remuneration. There should be informative disclosure identifying incremental value accruing to pension scheme participation or from any other superannuation arrangements, relating to service during the

year in question. Pension costs should be clearly explained, any disproportionate costs and values identified, and the extent to which liabilities are funded and aggregate outstanding unfunded liabilities disclosed.

9 With impending changes to pensions taxation, Remuneration Committees should carefully consider what role will be continued to be played by additional pension accrual as against other forms of remuneration that might more clearly align with shareholder value creation. Companies are not responsible for compensating individuals for changes in personal tax liabilities.

Changes to transfer values should be fully explained. Where there are discretionary increases in pension entitlement, beyond those arising from the published base pay such as those resulting from significant changes in actuarial assumption or from ex-gratia awards or contributions, these should be fully explained and justified.

10 Remuneration Committees should scrutinise all other benefits, including benefits in kind and other financial arrangements to ensure they are justified, appropriately valued and suitably disclosed.

11 Remuneration Committees should have regard to outstanding dilution in accordance with Guideline limits (see Section 20) and where appropriate available dilution capacity should be disclosed so that this can be compared with previous years.

12 Institutional shareholders encourage companies to require their senior executives to build up meaningful shareholdings in the companies for which they work. Consistent with this approach, consideration should be given to incorporating provisions in the rules of incentive schemes to require retention of a proportion of shares to which participants become entitled until such times as shareholding guidelines are met.

13 The chairman and non-executive directors should be appropriately remunerated either in cash or in shares bought or allocated at market price. The granting of incentives linked to the share price or performance is not appropriate as this could impair the ability of chairmen and independent directors to provide impartial oversight and advice.

Where, in exceptional circumstances, specific reasons arise for wishing togrant share incentives to a chairman, these should be fully discussed and approved by shareholders in advance. Recipients would be expected to hold all shares awarded under such schemes for the duration of their term of office.

GUIDELINES FOR SHARE INCENTIVE SCHEMES

1.1 Institutional shareholders generally support share incentive schemes that link remuneration to performance and align the interests of participating directors and senior executives with those of shareholders.

1.2 The implementation of such schemes involves either the commitment of shareholder funds or the dilution of shareholders' equity. It is important, therefore, that they be objectively costed, well-designed and form a coherent part of the overall remuneration package.

1.3 Shareholders expect all share incentive schemes to follow the spirit of the Guidelines.

2 General Principles

2.1 Share incentive schemes should emphasise the importance of linking remuneration to performance, limits on dilution and individual participation, and a structure that effectively aligns the long-term interests of management with those of shareholders, having due regard to the cost of the schemes, which should be disclosed.

2.2 Shareholders strongly encourage the adoption of phased grants and welcome the trend towards awards being applied on a sliding scale in relation to the achievement of demanding and stretching financial performance against a target group or other relevant benchmark

2.3 Dilution is a matter of particular concern to investors. These Guidelines reaffirm the basic principle that overall dilution under all schemes should not exceed 10% in any 10-year period with the further limitations of 5% in any 10-year period on discretionary schemes (see Section 20).

3 Scope

3.1 These Guidelines apply to all share incentive schemes or arrangements sponsored by UK listed companies whether option-based or involving conditional awards of shares, and including arrangements whereby awards on vesting or exercise are made in cash, or the transfer of shares to the value of the imputed gain at vesting date. Other companies should have regard for them, whenever possible.

4 Remuneration Committees

4.1 Remuneration Committees should:

- regularly review share incentive schemes to ensure their continued effectiveness, compliance with current Guidelines and contribution to shareholder value
- obtain prior shareholder authorisation for any substantive or exceptional amendments to scheme rules and practice including changes to limits and changes which make it easier to achieve performance targets, also where significant exercise of discretion is proposed by the Remuneration Committee.

5 Disclosure

5.1 Companies must make full and relevant disclosure in their Remuneration Reports and in new proposals regarding share incentive schemes. Their rationale should be fully explained in order to enable shareholders to make informed decisions. In the absence of clear disclosure, shareholders may not be able to take the informed decision that will enable them to give their support.

5.2 Scheme and individual participation limits must be fully disclosed in share incentive schemes. Disclosure should, *inter alia*, cover performance conditions and related costs and dilution limits as set out in the relevant sections below. The reasons for selecting the performance conditions and target levels, together with the overall policy for granting conditional share or option awards, should be fully explained to shareholders.

6 Performance Conditions

6.1 It is now widely recognised that the desired alignment of interests is best achieved through the vesting of awards under share incentive schemes being conditional on satisfaction of performance criteria. These should demonstrate the achievement of demanding and stretching financial performance over the incentivisation period.

6.2 Challenging performance conditions should govern the vesting of awards or the exercise of options under any form of long term share-based incentive scheme. These should:

- relate to overall corporate performance
- demonstrate the achievement of a level of performance which is demanding in the context of the prospects for the company and the prevailing economic environment in which it operates
- be measured relative to an appropriate defined peer group or other relevant benchmark
- be disclosed and transparent.

The reasons for selecting the performance condition(s), together with the overall policy for granting conditional share or share option incentive awards, should be fully explained to shareholders.

6.3 Share-based performance awards should not be made for less than median performance. Initial vesting levels should not be significant in relation to annual salary.

6.4 The greater the level of potential reward to individual participants the more stretching and demanding the performance conditions should be.

Companies should explain clearly how this is achieved, especially when annual grants of options in excess of one times salary, or equivalent long term share incentive awards, are made.

6.5 Sliding scales that correlate the reward potential with a performance scale that incorporates the provisions of these Guidelines are a useful way of ensuring that performance conditions are genuinely stretching. They generally provide a better motivator for improving corporate performance than a "single hurdle".

6.6 When Share Schemes provide for awards of matching shares in respect of annual bonuses, such awards should be kept within reasonable limits and further performance conditions should be satisfied before the matching shares are permitted to vest (see Paragraph 13.4).

7 Performance Criteria

7.1 All types of performance measures should be fully explained. It should be demonstrated that they are robust and demanding, and linked clearly to the achievement of enhanced shareholder value.

7.2 Total shareholder return (TSR) relative to a relevant index or peer group is one of a number of generally acceptable performance criteria. However, the Remuneration Committee should satisfy itself prior to vesting that the recorded TSR or other criterion is a genuine reflection of the company's underlying financial performance, and explain its reasoning.

7.3 Shareholders need to have sufficient data to judge the appropriate size of the award for any given performance level. They also expect a maximum level of grant to be disclosed.

7.4 Other than in exceptional circumstances, the setting of a premium exercise price is not of itself a substitute for the adoption of relative performance conditions in accordance with these Guidelines.

8 Retesting of Performance Conditions

8.1 It is increasingly recognised that retesting of performance conditions for all share-based incentive schemes is unnecessary and unjustified as is clearly the case for Long Term Incentive Plans (LTIPs) and similar nilpriced option schemes. The stipulated performance conditions should never combine a fixed performance hurdle with measurement from a variable base date.

9 Vesting of Awards

9.1 Performance conditions should be measured over a period of three or more years. Strong encouragement is given to use of longer performance measurement periods of more than 3 years and deferred vesting schedules, in order to motivate the achievement of sustained improvements in financial performance.

9.2 Where LTIP awards are made over whole shares,[1] a better alignment of interest with shareholders will be achieved if, in respect of those shares that do vest, equivalent value to that which has accrued to shareholders by way of dividends during the period from date of grant also vests in the hands of LTIP recipients. To the extent that the shares conditionally awarded do not vest then nor should any scrip or cash amounts representing the rolled-up dividends.

Remuneration Committees should also be mindful to ensure that the size of grants made on this basis takes into account reasonable expectations as to the value of the dividend stream on the company's shares over the period to vesting. Where the facility for rolled-up dividends is introduced a smaller initial grant size is required in order to target a similar level of value in the conditional share award.

10 Performance on Grant

10.1 Where competitive factors genuinely make awards of performance-linked grants impossible then shareholders will consider alternative proposals carefully and only in the most exceptional circumstances approve them. For example, Remuneration Committees may consider the application of challenging performance conditions to govern the grant instead of the vesting of options. However shareholders are likely only to consider such proposals in certain specific and exceptional circumstances, and in particular that the company has clearly demonstrated to the satisfaction of shareholders that it is operating in a global environment which genuinely requires it to pay attention to global remuneration practices. Shareholders will expect that at least the conditions (see Appendix A) have been met.

11 Change of Control Provisions

11.1 Scheme rules should state that there will be no automatic waiving of performance conditions either in the event of a change of control or where subsisting options and awards are "rolled-over" in the event of a capital reconstruction, and/or the early termination of the participant's employment. Remuneration Committees should use best endeavours to provide meaningful disclosure that quantifies the aggregate payments arising on a change of control.

11.2 Shareholders expect that the underlying financial performance of a company that is subject to a change of control should be a key determinant of what share-based awards, if any, should vest for participants. Remuneration Committees should satisfy themselves that the performance criterion genuinely reflects a robust measure of underlying financial achievement over any shorter time period. They should explain their reasoning in the Remuneration Report or other relevant documentation sent to shareholders.

11.3 In the event of change of control, share incentive awards should vest on a time pro-rata basis i.e. taking into account the vesting period that has elapsed at the time of change of control.

12 Cost

12.1 The cost of share incentive schemes (and any amendments to existing schemes) should be disclosed at the time shareholder approval is sought in order that shareholders can assess the benefits of the proposal against the total costs and award justification. The following information should be disclosed:

- The total cost of all incentive arrangements.
- The potential value of awards (see Appendix B Note 1) due to individual scheme participants on full vesting. This should be expressed by reference to the face value of shares or shares under option at point of grant, and expressed as a multiple of base salary.
- The expected value (see Appendix B Note 2) of the award at the outset, bearing in mind the probability of achieving the stipulated performance criteria.
- The maximum dilution which may arise through the issue of shares to satisfy entitlements.

12.2 There should be prudent and appropriate arrangements governing acquisition of shares, and financing thereof, to meet contingent obligations under share-based incentive schemes.

12.3 The use of phased grants of share options and restricted shares, and utilisation of both new and purchased shares to satisfy the vesting of awards, requires a comprehensive approach to valuation. Assessment should focus on expected value, which should be disclosed, and it should take account of the performance vesting schedule which is adopted as well as the existence of any "retesting" and "replacement option" facilities such as have been prevalent under traditional schemes. Shareholders are helped in this task by disclosure of face value of any share award or option grant as well as of expected value.

13 Participation

13.1 Participation in share incentive schemes should be restricted to bona-fide employees and executive directors, and be subject to appropriate limits for individual participation which should be disclosed.

13.2 There should be no absolute right of participation in share incentive schemes. Grant policy should be disclosed and consistently applied and, within the limits approved by shareholders, reflect changing commercial and competitive conditions. In the event of declining share price levels it is particularly important to avoid unjustified increases in the actual number of shares or options awarded.

13.3 Participation in more than one share incentive scheme must form part of a well-considered remuneration policy, and should not be part of a multiple arrangement designed to raise the prospects of payout.

13.4 Institutional shareholders are not supportive of arrangements whereby shares or options may, in effect, be granted at a discount. This principle applies in circumstances where Remuneration Committees provide for awards of matching shares in respect of annual bonuses payable in the form of shares where these are then held for a qualifying period of, say, 3 years. In these cases, institutional shareholders will generally expect that satisfaction of further performance criteria will be required in order for the matching element to vest (see Paragraph 6.6).

14 Phasing of Awards and Grants

14.1 The regular phasing of share incentive awards and option grants, generally on an annual basis, is encouraged because:

- It reduces the risk of unanticipated outcomes that arise out of share price volatility and cyclical factors.
- It eliminates the perceived problem that a limit on subsisting options encourages early exercise.
- It allows the adoption of a single performance measurement period.
- It lessens the possible incidence of "underwater" options, where the share price falls below the exercise price.

The phased vesting of awards in specific tranches following the minimum three year performance measurement period is not an alternative to phased grants. However, it can help to enhance the linking of vesting of awards to sustained performance and maintain incentivisation.

15 Pricing of Options and Shares

15.1 The price at which shares are issued under a scheme should not be less than the mid-market price (or similar formula) immediately preceding grant of the shares under the scheme.

15.2 Options granted under executive (discretionary) schemes should not be granted at a discount to the prevailing mid-market price.

15.3 Repricing or surrender and regrant of awards or "underwater" share options is not appropriate.

16 Timing of Grant

16.1 The rules of a scheme should provide that share or option awards normally be granted only within a 42 day period following the publication of the company's results.

17 Life of Schemes and Incentive Awards

17.1 No awards should be made beyond the life of the scheme approved on adoption by shareholders, which should not exceed 10 years.

17.2 Shares and options should not vest or be exercisable within three years from the date of grant. In addition, options should not be exercisable more than 10 years from the date of grant.

17.3 Where a company is taken over (except where arrangements are made for a switch to options of the offeror company) or in the event of the death or cessation of employment of the option holder, outstanding options may be exercised (or lapse) within 12 months. Any performance conditions attaching to the exercise of options should normally be fulfilled prior to exercise.

17.4 Any shares or options that a company may grant in exchange for those released under the schemes of acquired companies should normally be taken into account for the purposes of dilution and individual participation limits determined in accordance with these Guidelines.

18 Retirement

18.1 Options or other conditional share awards should not be granted within 6 months of a participant's anticipated retirement date. In determining the size and other terms of a grant made within 3 years of the anticipated retirement date, Remuneration Committees should have regard to the executive's ability to contribute to the achievement of the performance conditions.

18.2 Any unvested options or other conditional share awards which are outstanding at a participant's retirement date should be subject to performance measurement over the original stipulated period. Where the rules of the scheme require early exercise on retirement, performance should be pro-rated over the shorter period. In any event options should vest no later than the end of the initial performance measurement period, and should be finally exercisable no later than 12 months following the date of vesting.

19 Subsidiary Companies and Joint Venture Companies

19.1 It is generally undesirable for options to be granted over the share capital in a joint venture company.

19.2 In normal circumstances grants over the shares in a subsidiary company should not be made. However shareholders may consider exceptions where the condition of exercise is subject to flotation or sale of the subsidiary company. In such circumstances, grants should be conditional so that vesting is dependent on a return on investment that exceeds the cost of capital and that the market value of the shares at date of grant is subject to external validation. Exceptions will apply in the case of an overseas subsidiary where required by local legislation, or in circumstances where at least 25% of the ordinary share capital of the subsidiary is listed and held outside the group.

20 Dilution Limits

20.1 Where the terms of any incentive scheme provide that entitlements may be satisfied through the issue of new shares or utilisation of treasury shares, then the rules of that scheme must provide that, when aggregated with awards under all of the company's other schemes, commitments to issue new shares or re-issue treasury shares must not exceed 10% of the issued ordinary share capital (adjusted for scrip/bonus and rights issues) in any rolling 10 year period. Remuneration Committees should ensure that appropriate policies regarding flow-rates exist in order to spread the potential issue of new shares over the life of relevant schemes in order to ensure the limit is not breached.

20.2 Commitments to issue new shares or re-issue treasury shares under executive (discretionary) schemes should not exceed 5% of the issued ordinary share capital of the company (adjusted for scrip/bonus and rights issues) in any rolling 10 year period. This may be exceeded where vesting is dependent on the achievement of significantly more stretching performance criteria, with full vesting threshold at top quartile or above.

20.3 For small companies, up to 10% of the ordinary share capital may be utilised for executive (discretionary) schemes, provided that the total market value of the capital utilised for the scheme at the time of grant does not exceed £500,000.

21 Employee Share Ownership Trusts – ESOTs

21.1 ESOTs should not hold more shares at any one time than would be required in practice to match their outstanding liabilities, nor should they be used as an anti-takeover or similar device. Furthermore an ESOT's deed should provide that any unvested shares held in the ESOT shall not be voted at shareholder meetings. The prior approval of shareholders should be obtained before 5% or more of a company's share capital at any one time may be held within ESOTs.

21.2 Where companies have provided for an ESOT to be used to meet scheme requirements, they should disclose the number of shares held by the ESOT in order to assist shareholders with their evaluation of the overall use of shares for remuneration purposes. The company should explain its strategy in this regard.

22 All-Employee Schemes

22.1 All-Employee schemes, such as SAYE schemes and Share Incentive Plans (SIPs) – (formerly known as AESOPs), should operate within an appropriate best practice framework. If newly issued shares are utilised, the overall dilution limits for share schemes should be complied with. Guidelines relating to timing of grants (except for pre-determined regular appropriation of shares under SIPs) apply.

Appendix A

The following are the minimum criteria that shareholders will expect to be satisfied in respect of any share incentive scheme adopting performance at point of grant instead of performance criteria governing the vesting of awards or exercise of options (see Paragraph 10.1).

- The scheme should be tailored to executives who are exposed to global remuneration practices and the approach should not be applied automatically to UK based participants. Comparisons with overseas companies should take account of the different practices for setting remuneration, including pension provision, when compared with UK practices.
- Performance conditions covering the grant should refer to overall corporate performance as a reference, not just individual performance of the grantee.
- The basis of performance criteria should be fully disclosed and explained.
- Performance-linking at grant does not alter the requirement that the minimum period for exercise of options should be three years from the date of grant.
- The dilution limits set out in Section 20 are adhered to.
- Participants in schemes are expected by the Board to build up a significant and disclosed shareholding through retention of awards that vest. Holding share options is not a substitute for share ownership in meeting ownership targets.
- Disclosure concerning the scheme should comply with the highest standards relevant to the other jurisdictions in which the company operates e.g. those applied by the US Securities and Exchange Commission.

Appendix B

Note 1

Potential Value of the Award

Shareholders are likely to have regard to the potential value of the award assuming full vesting. This should be expressed on the basis that a conditional award is made of shares, or options over shares, with a face value, at current prices, equal to a given percentage of base salary. However the potential value will also be a function of share price at the time of vesting and of illustrative disclosures of potential outcomes may also be helpful. Full vesting of awards of higher potential value should require the achievement of commensurately greater performance.

Note 2

Expected Value

The concept of expected value (EV) should be central to assessment of share incentive schemes.

Essentially, EV will be the present value of the sum of all the various possible outcomes at vesting or exercise of awards. This will reflect the probabilities of achieving these outcomes and also the future value implicit in these outcomes. The calculation of the EV of share schemes is often complex and relies on a range of assumptions, and reliance on this concept by Remuneration Committees will require a sufficient measure of disclosure to enable shareholders to make informed judgments about such arrangements.

The nature of performance hurdles governing exercise is also crucial to calculations of EV and it must also be recognised that any facility for "retesting" will also increase the EV of the award whereas in contrast if the exercise price is set at a premium to the share price at the outset, this will reduce the value of the EV of the instrument.

Institutional investors welcome efforts towards ensuring that accounting for share options and other share-based payment awarded under incentive schemes fully reflects the true cost to shareholders.

BEST PRACTICE ON EXECUTIVE CONTRACTS AND SEVERANCE – A JOINT STATEMENT BY THE ASSOCIATION OF BRITISH INSURERS AND THE NATIONAL ASSOCIATION OF PENSION FUNDS

1 Introduction

1.1 Institutional shareholders believe top executives of listed companies should be appropriately rewarded for the value they generate. However, they are also concerned to avoid situations where departing executives are rewarded for failure or under-performance. This is a matter of good governance, about which the ABI and NAPF have been concerned for many years.

1.2 It is unacceptable that failure, which detracts from the value of an enterprise and which can threaten the livelihood of employees, can result in large payments to its departing leaders. Executives, whose remuneration is already at a level which allows for the risk inherent in their role, should show leadership in aligning their financial interests with those of their shareholders.

1.3 Our two organisations, whose members are leading institutional investors in UK markets, are therefore publishing this statement of best practice, which sets out the expectations of shareholders that boards will give careful consideration to the risk that negotiation of inappropriate executive contracts can lead to situations where failure is rewarded.

1.4 If companies are to recruit executives of sufficient calibre, Boards must bear in mind the basic demands of the market. These require them to offer incoming executives a degree of protection against downside risk. Contract law also provides employees with certain rights that must be respected.

1.5 However, shareholders also believe it is the duty of Boards to develop and implement recruitment and remuneration policies which will prevent them being required to make payments that are not strictly merited. When companies recruit senior executives, they do so in a mood of optimism and expectation of success. They may therefore tend to overlook the consequences of failure, which is clearly inappropriate.

1.6 At the outset, Boards should calculate the potential cost of termination in monetary terms. This should cover all elements of the severance package, including any property liabilities the company may be required to assume on behalf of the departing executive. They must also consider and avoid the serious reputational risk of being obliged to make and disclose large payments to executives who have failed to perform.

1.7 Shareholders will hold Boards accountable for the design and implementation of appropriate contracts. The primary responsibility resides, however, with Remuneration Committees.

1.8 Remuneration Committees should have the leeway to design a policy appropriate to the needs and objectives of the company, but they must also have a clear understanding of their responsibility to negotiate suitable contracts and be able to justify severance payments to shareholders.

1.9 This statement provides a reference point, both to make companies aware of the reasonable expectations of shareholders and to inform voting decisions under the new legislation giving shareholders an annual vote on the remuneration report. We expect that this guidance will be reviewed periodically and refreshed as necessary to take account of changing market circumstances.

2 Basic Principles

2.1 The design of contracts should not commit companies to payment for failure. Shareholders expect Boards to pay attention to minimising this risk when drawing up contracts. They should bear in mind that it may be in the interest of incoming executives and their personal advisers to exaggerate their potential loss on dismissal. Boards should resist consequent pressure to concede overly generous severance conditions.

2.2 Choices made when the contract is agreed have an important bearing on subsequent developments. Companies should have a clear, considered policy on directors' contracts which should be clearly stated in the remuneration report. Boards should calculate and take account of all the material commitments which the company would face in the event of severance for failure or underperformance. The Nomination Committee needs to see through the process of appointment by working with the Remuneration Committee to ensure that the contract is fair to all parties.

2.3 Objectives set for executives by the Board should be clear. The more transparent the objectives, the easier it is to determine whether an executive has failed to perform and therefore to prevent payment for failure. Wherever possible, objectives against which performance will be measured should be made public.

2.4 It should be clearly understood that investors do not expect executives to be automatically entitled to cash or share-based payments other than basic pay. Bonuses should be cut or eliminated when individual performance is poor. From the outset, Boards should therefore establish a clear link between performance and bonus as well as other aspects of variable pay.

2.5 Compensation for risks run by senior executives is already implicit in the absolute level of remuneration. Boards should ensure that there is an appropriate balance between contractual protection and total remuneration and be able to justify their policies to shareholders. Shareholders prefer short contracts of one year or less, and Boards must be able to justify the length agreed. The one-year period provided for under the Combined Code best practice should thus not be seen as a floor. Shorter periods would be appropriate if other remuneration conditions would mean that a one-year contract period would lead to excessive severance payment.

2.6 In highly exceptional circumstances – for example, where a new chief executive is being recruited to a troubled company – a longer initial notice period may be appropriate. These cases should be justified to shareholders and the longer notice period should apply to the initial term only with reversion to best practice at the earliest opportunity.

2.7 Experience suggests that courts take account of some elements of variable pay, such as bonuses, when making awards to departing executives. This can be limited through the attachment of clear performance conditions to variable pay. Boards may also wish to specify that a proportion of the bonus is for retaining the executive and this should fall away in the event of severance. A remuneration policy that favours relatively low base pay and a higher proportion of variable pay is a good way of linking remuneration to performance.

3 Contract Setting

3.1 There is no standard form of contract that can apply in all circumstances. Companies have taken a number of different approaches to severance in the past. These include phased payments, liquidated damages, and reliance on mitigation. It is important that Boards consider the relative merits of different approaches as they apply to their own company's situation, follow their chosen approach consequentially and are able to justify it to shareholders.

3.2 A welcome recent innovation has been the use of **phased payments**, which involve continued payment, eg on a normal monthly basis to the departing executive for the outstanding term of his or her contract. Payments cease when and if the executive finds fresh employment. Shareholders believe this approach has considerable advantages, which deserve the active consideration of Boards, but this approach does need to be specifically provided for in the contract and specific reference made to the legal obligation to mitigate. It does not involve payment of large lump sums, which cannot be recovered. In many cases, executives will wish to seek further employment rather than remain idle till the monthly payments lapse. Allowing the contract to run off may also obviate the need for pension enhancement (see below).

3.3 The **liquidated damages** approach involves agreement at the outset on the amount that will be paid in the event of severance. It is clear from the beginning how much will be paid, but the amount cannot be varied to reflect under-performance. Shareholders do not believe the liquidated damages approach is generally desirable. Boards which adopt this should justify their decision, and should therefore consider a modified approach. This would involve reaching agreement in advance that, in the event of severance, the parties would go to arbitration to decide how much should be paid. This approach needs to take account of the likely cost of arbitration.

3.4 The concept of **mitigation** refers to the legal obligation on the part of the outgoing director to mitigate the loss incurred through severance, for example by seeking other employment and reducing the need for compensation. Where this is the sole approach, shareholders expect reassurance that the Board has taken steps to ensure that the full benefit is obtained. As with liquidated damages, boards need to have considered at the outset what the cost of severance would be under the proposed contract as well as the relative merits of arbitration as opposed to litigation.

3.5 An essential problem is that it is not normally possible for underperformance to be established as a ground for **summary dismissal** without compensation. Under the Employment Act 2002, however, a statutory disciplinary procedure will be implied into every employment contract, including those of executive directors. Boards should be aware of this and be prepared to use disciplinary procedures if warranted.

3.6 In the wake of this legislation contracts should also make clear that, if a director is dismissed in the wake of a disciplinary procedure, a shorter notice period than that given in the contract would apply. A reasonable period would be the statutory period, comprising one week for each year's service up to a maximum of 12 weeks. Without such a provision the full notice period would continue to apply even after dismissal following a disciplinary procedure.

3.7 Companies should also consider including in contracts a safeguard for more extreme cases, for example, that compensation would not be payable in case of dismissal for financial failure such as a very significant fall of the share price relative to the sector.

3.8 Other than in highly exceptional circumstances, such as the recruitment of a new chief executive of a troubled company, contracts should not provide additional protection in the form of compensation for severance as a result of **change of control**. Where exceptional circumstances apply, any additional protection should relate to the initial contract term only and not be a rolling provision.

3.9 Companies may consider other options, including a provision for **compensation to be paid by reference to shares** with the amount of shares set at the outset of employment. Where such an option is proposed it should, however, be clearly explained both as to purpose and to the details of its operation. Remuneration committees should satisfy themselves that it is workable and will yield advantages greater than the phased payment and other approaches outlined above. Compensation paid by reference to shares should be paid in cash rather than directly in shares to prevent unmerited windfall gains.

3.10 The use of **shareholding targets** for senior executives and directors is likely to be a powerful and therefore more effective means of aligning the financial interests of executives with those of shareholders.

4 Pension Arrangements and Other Remuneration Issues

4.1 Pension enhancements can represent a large element of severance pay and involve heavy cost to shareholders, the full extent of which may not be immediately evident. It is important that Boards state the full cost for pension enhancement at the earliest opportunity. Boards should not support enhanced pension payments without making themselves fully aware of the costs

4.2 A large liability looms in the future where companies choose not to fund an enhanced pension liability but to pay it as it arises. In all cases, whether the pension is funded or not, Boards must disclose the cost, justify their choice to shareholders and demonstrate that they have chosen a route that involves the least overall cost to the company.

4.3 An important principle with regard to pensions is that Boards should distinguish between the amount that is a contractual entitlement and the amount of discretionary enhancement agreed as part of a severance package. Contracts should state clearly that the pension would not be enhanced in the event of early retirement unless the board was satisfied that the objectives set for the executive had been met or that the enhancement was merited. Shareholders are likely to question enhancement decisions when they are doubtful of the merit and, if not satisfied with the board's justification, they may vote against the remuneration report.

5 General Considerations and Conclusion

5.1 Boards should have a clear and explicit policy on contracts and on how Remuneration Committees will play a primary role. It should include calculation of the cost of severance at the time the contract is drawn up and an approach to implementation which ensures that all payments made on severance take account of performance in relation to objectives set for the departing executive by the board.

5.2 Companies should fulfil their legal obligations to make contracts readily available for shareholders to inspect, together with any side letters relating to severance terms and pension arrangements. Shareholders will take account of contracts and the way they are implemented in considering their vote on the remuneration report.

Note

1 This term covers awards structured in the form of either 'restricted shares' or 'nil-cost options'.

Appendix 16

Institutional Shareholders' Committee: The Responsibilities of Institutional Shareholders and Agents – Statement of Principles (2002)

1 Introduction and Scope

This Statement of Principles has been drawn up by the Institutional Shareholders' Committee.[1] It develops the principles set out in its 1991 statement "The Responsibilities of Institutional Shareholders in the UK" and expands on the Combined Code on Corporate Governance of June 1998. It sets out best practice for institutional shareholders and/or agents in relation to their responsibilities in respect of investee companies in that they will:

- set out their policy on how they will discharge their responsibilities – clarifying the priorities attached to particular issues and when they will take action – see 2 below;
- monitor the performance of, and establish, where necessary, a regular dialogue with investee companies – see 3 below;
- intervene where necessary – see 4 below;
- evaluate the impact of their activism – see 5 below; and
- report back to clients/beneficial owners – see 5 below.

In this statement the term "institutional shareholder" includes pension funds, insurance companies, and investment trusts and other collective investment vehicles. Frequently, agents such as investment managers are appointed by institutional shareholders to invest on their behalf.

This statement covers the activities of both institutional shareholders and those that invest as agents, including reporting by the latter to their institutional shareholder clients. The actions described in this statement in general apply only in the case of UK listed companies. They can be applied to any such UK company, irrespective of market capitalisation, although institutional shareholders' and agents' policies may indicate de minimis limits for reasons of cost-effectiveness or practicability. Institutional shareholders and agents should keep under review how far the principles in this statement can be applied to other equity investments.

The policies of activism set out below do not constitute an obligation to micro-manage the affairs of investee companies, but rather relate to procedures designed to ensure that shareholders derive value from their investments by dealing effectively with concerns over under-performance. Nor do they preclude a decision to sell a holding, where this is the most effective response to such concerns. Fulfilling fiduciary obligations to end-beneficiaries in accordance with the spirit of this statement may have implications for institutional shareholders' and agents' resources. They should devote appropriate resources, but these should be commensurate with the benefits for beneficiaries. The duty of institutional shareholders and agents is to the end beneficiaries and not to the wider public.

2 Setting out their policy on how they will discharge their responsibilities

Both institutional shareholders and agents will have a clear statement of their policy on activism and on how they will discharge the responsibilities they assume. This policy statement will be a public document. The responsibilities addressed will include each of the matters set out below.

- How investee companies will be monitored. In order for monitoring to be effective, where necessary, an active dialogue may need to be entered into with the investee company's board and senior management.
- The policy for requiring investee companies' compliance with the core standards in the Combined Code.
- The policy for meeting with an investee company's board and senior management.
- How situations where institutional shareholders and/or agents have a conflict of interest will be minimised or dealt with.
- The strategy on intervention.
- An indication of the type of circumstances when further action will be taken and details of the types of action that may be taken.
- The policy on voting.

Agents and their institutional shareholder clients should agree by whom these responsibilities are to be discharged and the arrangements for agents reporting back.

3 Monitoring performance

Institutional shareholders and/or agents, either directly or through contracted research providers, will review Annual Reports and Accounts, other circulars, and general meeting resolutions. They may attend company meetings where they may raise questions about investee companies' affairs. Also investee companies will be monitored to determine when it is necessary to enter into an active dialogue with the investee company's board and senior management. This monitoring needs to be regular, and the process needs to be clearly communicable and checked periodically for its effectiveness. Monitoring may require sharing information with other shareholders or agents and agreeing a common course of action.

As part of this monitoring, institutional shareholders and/or agents will:

- seek to satisfy themselves, to the extent possible, that the investee company's board and sub-committee structures are effective, and that independent directors provide adequate oversight; and
- maintain a clear audit trail, for example, records of private meetings held with companies, of votes cast, and of reasons for voting against the investee company's management, for abstaining, or for voting with management in a contentious situation.

In summary, institutional shareholders and/or agents will endeavour to identify problems at an early stage to minimise any loss of shareholder value. If they have concerns and do not propose to sell their holdings, they will seek to ensure that the appropriate members of the investee company's board are made aware of them. It may not be sufficient just to inform the Chairman and/or Chief Executive. However, institutional shareholders and/or agents may not wish to be made insiders.

Institutional shareholders and/or agents will expect investee companies and their advisers to ensure that information that could affect their ability to deal in the shares of the company concerned is not conveyed to them without their agreement.

4 Intervening when necessary

Institutional shareholders' primary duty is to those on whose behalf they invest, for example, the beneficiaries of a pension scheme or the policyholders in an insurance company, and they must act in their best financial interests. Similarly, agents must act in the best interests of their clients. Effective monitoring will enable institutional shareholders and/or agents to exercise their votes and, where necessary, intervene objectively and in an informed way. Where it would make intervention more effective, they should seek to engage with other shareholders. Many issues could give rise to concerns about shareholder value. Institutional shareholders and/or agents should set out the circumstances when they will actively intervene and how they propose to measure the effectiveness of doing so. Intervention should be considered by institutional shareholders and/or agents regardless of whether an active or passive investment policy is followed. In addition, being underweight is not, of itself, a reason for not intervening. Instances when institutional shareholders and/or agents may want to intervene include when they have concerns about:

- the company's strategy;
- the company's operational performance;
- the company's acquisition/disposal strategy;
- independent directors failing to hold executive management properly to account;
- internal controls failing;
- inadequate succession planning;
- an unjustifiable failure to comply with the Combined Code;
- inappropriate remuneration levels/incentive packages/severance packages; and
- the company's approach to corporate social responsibility.

If boards do not respond constructively when institutional shareholders and/or agents intervene, then institutional shareholders and/or agents will consider on a case-by-case basis whether to escalate their action, for example, by:

- holding additional meetings with management specifically to discuss concerns;
- expressing concern through the company's advisers;
- meeting with the Chairman, senior independent director, or with all independent directors;
- intervening jointly with other institutions on particular issues;
- making a public statement in advance of the AGM or an EGM;
- submitting resolutions at shareholders' meetings; and
- requisitioning an EGM, possibly to change the board.

Institutional shareholders and/or agents should vote all shares held directly or on behalf of clients wherever practicable to do so. They will not automatically support the board; if they have been unable to reach a satisfactory outcome through active dialogue then they will register an abstention or vote against the resolution. In both instances it is good practice to inform the company in advance of their intention and the reasons why.

5 Evaluating and reporting

Institutional shareholders and agents have a responsibility for monitoring and assessing the effectiveness of their activism. Those that act as agents will regularly report to their clients details on how they have discharged their responsibilities. This should include a judgement on the impact and effectiveness of their activism. Such reports will be likely to comprise both qualitative as well as quantitative information. The particular information reported, including the format in which details of how votes have been cast will be presented, will be a matter for agreement between agents and their principals as clients.

Transparency is an important feature of effective shareholder activism. Institutional shareholders and agents should not however be expected to make disclosures that might be counterproductive. Confidentiality in specific situations may well be crucial to achieving a positive outcome.

6 Conclusion

The Institutional Shareholders' Committee believes that adoption of these principles will significantly enhance how effectively institutional shareholders and/or agents discharge their responsibilities in relation to the companies in which they invest. To ensure that this is the case, the Institutional Shareholders' Committee will monitor the impact of this statement with a view to reviewing and refreshing it, if needs be, within two years in the light of experience and market developments.

Note

1 In 1991 the members of the Institutional Shareholders' Committee were: the Association of British Insurers; the Association of Investment Trust Companies; the British Merchant Banking and Securities Houses Association; the National Association of Pension Funds; and the Unit Trust Association. In 2002, the members are: the Association of British Insurers; the Association of Investment Trust Companies; the National Association of Pension Funds; and the Investment Management Association.

Appendix 17

National Association of Pension Funds: Corporate Governance Policy 2005

Statement of Underlying Principles

1 The welfare of pension fund investors is an economic and social benefit from which society as a whole derives value.

2 The welfare of pension fund investors is no different from the welfare of other long-term investors and this alignment of interest is beneficial to wealth-creation for all participants in society.

3 The interests of management should be aligned with the long-term interests of investors. This principle dictates that managers should hold shares in the business for which they are responsible.

4 It should be clearly recognised that shareholders in aggregate are the owners of Companies and that Boards are their agents.

5 It is essential that shareholders as owners recognise that they have responsibilities to monitor and normally to support the work of the management of the Companies in which they invest. Good corporate governance is about dialogue and the promotion of success. Confrontation is a sign of failure by owners or Boards or, sometimes, both.

6 One of the duties of owners is to allow Company Boards to manage the businesses which have been entrusted to their care without excessive interference. The NAPF robustly supports the Combined Code in its entirety and wishes to add minimal requirements to that body of work. The NAPF will keep this under review.

7 It is the duty of Boards, as the agents of the owners of the Companies they manage, to set out their interpretation of the objectives, aspirations and culture of the Company in order that the shareholders, as owners, can let it be known whether they share and accept these views.

8 At all times the Board and management should be mindful of the wider perception of the Company in society, bearing in mind that maximization of short-term gain in a manner which is deemed unacceptable by society as a whole, can seriously damage the longer-term prospects of a Company.

9 The NAPF considers the ownership rights of shareholders to be a principle of fundamental importance. For that reason the NAPF supports the principle underlying pre-emption rights and will not countenance any material erosion of this principle unless a clear case is made for it in the context of the best interests of the owners of the Company concerned. For the same reason the NAPF will generally oppose the creation of any "poison pill" provisions.

The above principles, together with the principles and detail of the Combined Code, set the framework for the bulk of the NAPF's detailed policies and voting guidelines.

Additional Issues

There are additional Issues which the NAPF would wish readers to bear in mind.

a The NAPF considers that the informed use of votes is an obligation (although not a legal duty) of owners and an implicit fiduciary duty of Trustees and of Investment Managers to whom Trustees may delegate this function. In recognition of this, the NAPF policy will recommend active voting, in support of management wherever possible, but will recommend a vote against where appropriate. Recommendations of abstention will rarely be made and, whenever such a recommendation occurs, it will be carefully explained why the NAPF considers that this is the appropriate course of action.

b Engagement with Companies is a necessary part of good ownership. The NAPF and its associates will engage with Companies at various levels on routine and more serious matters. In addition the NAPF is prepared to facilitate confidential Case Committees for members who have concerns about particular issues and/or about the strategic direction of Companies. Equally, Companies should take great care to ensure that their messages are clearly understood by shareholders and that the concerns of the shareholders are clearly understood by the Board. The roles of the Chairman and the Senior Independent Director in these regards are of the greatest importance.

c The NAPF expects Boards to show that they accept the terms of the Combined Code by observing its requirements wherever appropriate. Non-compliance must be accompanied by clear and valid explanation. The NAPF policy will be to recommend to its members whenever appropriate that they should not accept "boiler-plate" explanations which provide no valid insights into the reason for a Board choosing to ignore the clearly argued case for the provisions of the Code. Nonacceptance by the NAPF of the reasons for non-compliance will frequently result in the recommendation of a vote against. Notwithstanding this, the NAPF recognises that special circumstances dictate special actions and will go to great lengths to listen to Boards which believe it is appropriate not to comply. Good corporate governance is a matter of principle and nuance, not dogma. Similarly the NAPF expects Boards to listen to the NAPF and its members in their wish to achieve Good Practice.

d In all the key areas of Good Practice (as opposed to explicit requirements) identified by the Combined Code the NAPF expects Boards to state unequivocally in the Annual Report that they have met the standard and how they have done so. If they have not done so, clear and valid explanations should be set out which will allow shareholders to determine whether or not they accept the reasoning. The absence of adequate information to reach an informed judgement will lead the NAPF to conclude that the required standards are not being met and could lead to a recommendation of a vote against the Board, where appropriate.

e The status of Independent Non-Executive Directors is a bastion of security for shareholders. This has been NAPF policy for some time and more recently has been reinforced by the Higgs report. The NAPF will not accept a dilution of this principle and will monitor the position carefully.

f Whenever a significant change is made (for example, between the roles of Executive and Non-Executive Director or to an element of remuneration policy) the NAPF expects the matter to be brought before shareholders for a vote of approval at the first possible AGM or

EGM. Failure to do this could result in a recommendation of a vote against the Board on a comparable issue.

g The balance and structure of the Board are of crucial importance to the NAPF and its members. The NAPF has consistently supported the concept of the unitary Board with a healthy balance of Executive Directors and independent Non-Executive Directors. The NAPF sees no contradiction in this statement. All the Directors in a unitary Board are responsible for the strategy and governance of the Company. The Executive Directors are responsible and accountable for the successful implementation of that strategy. The independent Non- Executive Directors have a special responsibility for the oversight of the performance of the Executive Directors and have a key role in managing conflicts in certain of the Board Committees as set out in the Combined Code.

h The balance and structure of the Board and the role of the Company Secretary in serving the Board as defined in the Combined Code are crucial issues. The NAPF does not believe that the role of Company Secretary can normally be effectively fulfilled by an Executive Director with another role. Furthermore the NAPF expects the resignation of a Non-Executive Director or of a Company Secretary to be announced on a regulatory information service together with a full explanation, at the earliest opportunity.

i The NAPF expects Nomination Committees to anticipate change by ensuring the proper planning of succession. This is part of the process of refreshing the Board to which reference is made in the Combined Code. Inadequate succession planning could lead the NAPF to recommend a vote against the Chairman of the Nomination Committee or another member of that Committee.

j The Remuneration Committee has a particular responsibility to ensure that Executive Directors and senior management are appropriately rewarded. This is a complex area which, unfortunately, tends to attract a great deal of adverse and, often, uninformed comment. The NAPF supports the principle that the remuneration of Executive Directors should be set at a level which makes it possible to recruit, retain and motivate the right individuals. As a corollary, it should be clear that shareholders' funds should not be squandered by paying more than is deemed necessary to achieve these objectives. Furthermore, the Remuneration Committee must be mindful of the reputational damage which can be caused both externally and within the ranks of the employees of the Company if apparently unjustifiable payments, particularly 'payments for failure', are made to Executive Directors. A system of remuneration should be established which clearly aligns the interests of Executive Directors with those of shareholders. Such a system should be readily explicable and transparent. This can best be achieved by establishing a system of incentives which are harmonised with the stated objectives of the Company as set out in Principle 7 above.

December 2003

Appendix 18

ICSA Recommended Best Practice on Electronic Communications with Shareholders

The Companies Act 1985 (Electronic Communications) Order 2000 allows documents which the Companies Act had previously required a company to send out in writing to be sent to shareholders electronically e.g. by e-mail or placed on a website, where shareholders agree. The Order also makes appropriate amendments to Table A of CA 1985, one of which, an amendment to Regulation 115 (when notices given) reads:

After the words 'notice was given' insert

> '*Proof that a notice contained in an electronic communication was sent in accordance with guidance issued by the Institute of Chartered Secretaries and Administrators shall be conclusive evidence that notice was given*'.

The guidance referred to is contained in ICSA's publication *Electronic Communications with Shareholders – A Guide to Recommended Best Practice*: this includes 25 points of recommended best practice (set out below), together with other points that companies should consider before offering the facility to shareholders and a specimen invitation to shareholders to use electronic communications. Detailed guidance on such issues as:

- Offering the facility to shareholders and maintaining an appropriate register
- What to do if electronic communications obviously fail
- Records necessary to establish 'proof of sending'
- Security, use of a unique identifier, encryption, etc.
- Identification of audited material on a web-site
- Electronic delivery of proxy form

The ICSA's 25 Points of Recommended Best Practice

It is recommended best practice that:

1 a company takes steps to amend its Articles specifically to facilitate the use of electronic communications as soon as is practical. (para 2.2)

2 the invitation to shareholders to use electronic communications includes full details of any particular software or equipment specifications which will be required to enable the shareholder to take advantage of the options being made available. (para 3.10)

3 shareholders electing to use computer based electronic communications are warned that any electronic communication, including the filing of an electronic proxy form, found to contain a computer virus will not be accepted by the company. (para 3.15)

4 the offer and provision of a facility to communicate with shareholders electronically should not discriminate between shareholders of the same class and should include a statement reassuring shareholders of that fact. The invitation to participate and provision of the

facility should be made available to all shareholders on equal terms and in such a way as to make it as simple as possible for shareholders to participate. (para 4.3)

5 the initial invitation to use electronic means of communications should be sent by post to each member of the company. The invitation should detail which documents will be available by which means and explain the procedures that will be adopted in each case. (para 4.4)

6 the list of alternative delivery mechanisms offered by the company should specifically include an option to continue to receive all material in hard copy by post. (para 4.5)

7 the company should, at least once each year, repeat the invitation to use electronic communications to those shareholders who continue to receive hard copy material. Such an offer should be included at the latest with the Notice of the Annual General Meeting unless the company has elected not to hold an AGM. (para 4.8)

8 the invitation to opt to use electronic communications should include clear advice on how to register an election. This should include any dedicated telephone number, fax number or e-mail address provided for the purpose and/or the address of an Internet web-site page where the election form may be completed on-line. (para 5.1)

9 where a company is offering shareholders the opportunity to use electronic communications all newly registered shareholders should, within 3 months of registration, be provided with a statement as to the company's policy on electronic shareholder communications together with a copy of the facility letter providing the shareholder with the opportunity to register his/her choice. (para 5.3)

10 the company's web-site should include fax and telephone numbers and an 'on-line' facility to enable shareholders to notify the company of any change in their choice of communication medium or contact details. (para 6.2)

11 where the information being made available on a web-site includes a notice of a general meeting, the 'notification of availability' should:

- Draw specific attention to that fact;
- Indicate the date, time and place of the meeting;
- Highlight any applicable deadlines e.g. for the return of proxy forms; and
- include any special or non-routine business (such as proposed amendments to the Articles or Members' (s.376) resolutions) that may be on the Agenda (para 7.2)

12 an e-mail notifying a shareholder that information is being made available on a web-site should contain a hyperlink direct to the appropriate pages of the web-site to enable the information to be accessed as simply as possible. (para 7.3)

13 when notices are delivered by telephone, the company should compile and retain a suitable evidential record of all those contacted with the date and time of the call. (para 8.6)

14 when information or notifications of availability are sent by fax a comprehensive transaction report or log generated by the fax machine should be suitably certified and retained by or on behalf of the company as 'proof of sending'. (para 8.7)

15 when information or notifications of availability are sent by e-mail the company should ensure that it uses a system which produces either confirmation of the total number of

recipients sent to or, preferably, a record of each recipient to whom the message has been sent. A copy of such record and any notices of any failed transmissions and subsequent resending, suitably certified, should be retained by or on behalf of the company as 'proof of sending'. (para 8.8)

16 the company should alert those shareholders electing to receive communications electronically that the company's obligation is satisfied when it transmits an electronic message and that it cannot be held responsible for a failure in transmission beyond its control. (para 8.9)

17 the company should where it is aware of the failure in delivery of an electronic communication (and subsequent attempts do not remedy the situation) revert to sending a hard copy of the communication by mail to the recipient's last known postal address. This should be done within 48 hours of the original attempt. The company should include a standard notice advising the shareholder why he/she is being sent a copy by post and should take the opportunity of asking him/her to confirm his contact details. (para 8.10)

18 electronic proxy forms should contain:

- Clear instructions as to the address to which the proxy form should be returned;
- Warning that a proxy lodged electronically will only be valid if lodged at the address supplied by the company; and
- Where applicable, a notice that proxy appointments may, subject to a specified verification procedure, be made by telephone (para 10.2)

19 each shareholder is allocated a discrete identifier which should be required to be entered on the proxy form, used when logging on to the company's website to complete a proxy 'on-line' or as part of the verification procedure in the case of proxy appointments lodged by telephone. (para 10.4)

20 where no poll is demanded, electronically lodged proxy forms should be retained until one month after the meeting. Where a poll is held records should be retained for a period of one year after the meeting. (para 14.3)

21 any e-mail or other electronic address provided by the shareholder for the purposes of electronic communication should not be recorded as part of the publicly available part of the company's register of members. (para 14.4)

22 the company liaises closely with and obtain clearance from its auditors prior to the display of audited information and the Audit Report on a company web-site. (para 15.3)

23 the company should clearly identify 'statutory' information on its web-site and to indicate when the information being viewed forms part of the audited accounts. (para 15.4)

24 the company establishes a routine system of checking that statutory or audited information made available via a web-site has not been tampered with and that the home page of the statutory section of the web-site contains a message indicating the time and date when the contents of that section of the site were last verified. (para 15.8)

25 the company gives serious thought to arranging a form of back up facility for its own web-site. (para 19.6)

Appendix 19

Accounting Standards Board: [Draft] Reporting Standard: Operating and Financial Review

Paragraphs in bold type state the Main Principles and elements of the disclosure framework.

SUMMARY

a The [draft] Reporting Standard applies to all entities that prepare an OFR.

b The [draft] Reporting Standard requires directors to prepare an OFR addressed to investors, setting out their analysis of the business, with a forward-looking orientation in order to assist investors to assess the strategies adopted by the entity and the potential for those strategies to succeed. The information disclosed in the OFR will also be of relevance to other stakeholders.

c The [draft] Reporting Standard sets out a number of other principles regarded as essential to the preparation of an OFR, namely that the review shall: both complement and supplement the financial statements; be comprehensive and understandable; be balanced and neutral; and be comparable over time.

d The [draft] Reporting Standard sets out the key elements of the disclosure framework that directors are required to apply in preparing an OFR, together with requirements to include details on particular matters to the extent necessary to meet the objective of the OFR and the general disclosure requirements.

e Those Key Performance Indicators (KPIs) judged by the directors to be the most effective to use in measuring the delivery of their strategies and in managing their business shall be disclosed, together with information that will enable investors to understand and evaluate each KPI.

f The [draft] Reporting Standard encourages the inclusion of other measures and evidence to support the information included in the OFR.

g The [draft] Reporting Standard is accompanied by [draft] Implementation Guidance that provides illustrative examples of KPIs that might be disclosed in an OFR, as well as further guidance as to what is envisaged with regard to particular matters.

OBJECTIVE

1 The objective of this [draft] Reporting Standard is to specify the requirements for an OFR, which shall be a balanced and comprehensive analysis of:

   a the development and performance of the business of the entity during the financial year;

   b the position of the entity at the end of the year;

   c the main trends and factors underlying the development, performance and position of the business of the entity during the financial year; and d the main trends and factors which are likely to affect their future development, performance and position, prepared so as to assist investors to assess the strategies adopted by the entity and the potential for those strategies to succeed.

COMPLIANCE WITH COMPANIES ACT 1985 (OFR)

2 Compliance with this [draft] Reporting Standard will be presumed to constitute compliance with the requirements of the Companies Act 1985 (Operating and Financial Review and Directors Report) Regulations 2004.

SCOPE

3 The [draft] Reporting Standard applies to all entities that prepare an OFR.

DEFINITIONS

4 The following terms are used in this [draft] Reporting Standard with the meanings specified:

Directors

Reference to either "directors" or "board of directors" within the Reporting Standard is taken to be the entity's governing body where the entity is not a company.

Key Performance Indicators (KPIs)

KPIs are quantified measurements that reflect the critical success factors of an entity and disclose progress towards achieving a particular objective or objectives.

Operating and Financial Review (OFR)

An OFR is a narrative explanation, provided in the annual report, of the main trends and factors underlying the development, performance and position of an entity during the period covered by the financial statements, and which are likely to affect the entity's future development, performance and position.

PRINCIPLES

5 **The OFR shall set out an analysis of the business through the eyes of the board of directors.**

6 The OFR shall reflect the directors' view of the business and accordingly, the entity shall disclose appropriate elements of information used in managing the entity, including its subsidiary undertakings. Where appropriate, the review may give greater emphasis to those matters which are significant to the entity and its subsidiary undertakings taken as a whole.

7 **The OFR shall focus on matters that are relevant to the interests of investors.**

8 Investors' needs are paramount when directors consider what information shall be contained in the OFR. Information in the OFR will also be of interest to users other than investors, for example customers, suppliers, employees and society more widely. The directors will need to consider the extent to which they shall report on issues relevant to those other users where,

because of their influence on the performance of the business and its value, they are also of significance to investors.

9 The OFR shall have a forward-looking orientation, identifying those trends and factors relevant to the investors' assessment of the current and future performance of the business and the progress towards the achievement of long-term business objectives.

10 The particular factors discussed shall be those that have affected performance in the period and those that are expected to have an effect on the future performance and financial position of the business.

11 The OFR shall comment on the impact on future operations of significant events after the balance sheet date.

12 The OFR shall also discuss predictive comments made in previous statements where these have not been borne out by events.

13 The OFR shall complement as well as supplement the financial statements, in order to enhance the overall corporate disclosure.

14 In complementing the financial statements, the OFR shall provide useful financial and non-financial information about the business and its performance that is not reported in financial statements but which is relevant to the investors' evaluation of past results and assessment of future prospects.

15 In supplementing the financial statements, the OFR shall where relevant:

- provide additional explanations of amounts recorded in the financial statements;
- explain the conditions and events that shaped the information contained in the financial statements.

Where amounts from the financial statements have been adjusted for inclusion in the OFR, that fact shall be highlighted and a reconciliation provided.

16 The OFR shall be comprehensive and understandable.

17 Directors shall consider whether the omission of information might reasonably be expected to influence significantly the assessment made by investors.

18 The requirement for the OFR to be comprehensive does not mean that the OFR shall cover all possible matters: the objective is quality, not quantity of content. It is neither possible nor desirable for a [draft] Reporting Standard to list all the elements that might need to be included, since these will vary depending on the nature and circumstances of the particular business and how the business is run.

19 Directors will need to consider the key issues to include in the OFR that will provide investors with focused and relevant information. The inclusion of too much information may obscure judgements and will not promote understanding. Where additional information is discussed elsewhere in the annual report, or in other reports, cross-referencing to those sources will assist investors.

20 The OFR shall be written in a clear and readily understandable style.

21 The OFR shall be balanced and neutral, dealing even-handedly with both good and bad aspects.

22 Directors shall consider the evidence underpinning the information to be included in the OFR. The directors shall ensure that the OFR retains balance and that investors are not misled as a result of the omission of any information on unfavourable aspects.

23 **The OFR shall be comparable over time.**

24 Disclosure shall be sufficient for the investor to be able to compare the information presented with similar information about the entity for previous periods. Comparability enables identification of the main trends and factors, and their analysis, over successive time periods. Directors shall also consider the extent to which the OFR is comparable with reviews prepared by other entities in the same industry or sector.

DISCLOSURE FRAMEWORK

25 Paragraphs 26 to 72 below set out a framework for the disclosures to be provided by directors in an OFR. It is for directors to consider how best to use the framework to structure the OFR and the precise content, including the level of detail to be disclosed, under each heading given the particular circumstances of the entity. These circumstances may include:

- a the industry or industries in which it operates;
- b the range of products, services or processes it offers;
- c the number of markets it serves.

26 **The OFR shall provide information to assist investors to assess the strategies adopted by the entity and the potential for those strategies to succeed. The key elements of the disclosure framework necessary to achieve this are:**

- a **the nature, objectives and strategies of the business;**
- b **the development and performance of the business, both in the period under review and in the future;**
- c **the resources, risks and uncertainties and relationships that may affect the entity's long-term value; and**
- d **position of the business including a description of the capital structure, treasury policies and objectives and liquidity of the entity, both in the period under review and the future.**

27 **To the extent necessary to meet the requirements set out in paragraph 26 above, the OFR shall include information about:**

- a **market and competitive environment;**
- b **regulatory environment;**
- c **technological change;**
- d **persons with whom the entity has relations, such as customers and suppliers;**
- e **employees;**
- f **environmental matters;**
- g **social and community issues;**

h **receipts from, and returns to, shareholders; and**

i **all other relevant matters.**

Note: Items (d) to (h) above reflect the wording in the OFR Regulations of "particular matters"

The nature, objectives and strategies of the business

28 **The OFR shall include a description of the business and the external environment in which it operates as context for the directors' discussion and analysis of performance and financial position.**

29 A description of the business is necessary to provide investors with an understanding of the industry or industries in which the entity operates, its main products and services, business processes and distribution methods, the structure of the business, and its economic model, including an overview of the main operating facilities and their location.

30 Every entity is affected by its external environment. Depending on the nature of the business, the OFR shall include discussion of matters such as the entity's major markets and competitive position within those markets and the significant features of the legal, regulatory, macroeconomic and social environment that influence the business. For example, an entity may disclose the fact that it has significant operations in a number of different countries, which could have an impact on the future development and performance of the business.

31 **The OFR shall discuss the objectives of the business to generate or preserve value over the longer term.**

32 Objectives will often be defined in terms of financial performance; however, objectives in non-financial areas shall also be discussed where appropriate.

33 The nature of the industry will affect the directors' determination of an appropriate time perspective for reporting in the OFR. For example, a business that focuses on large long-term projects must carry out its strategic planning over the full project lifecycle, which may be 20 years or more. Furthermore, where a project has a long-term impact on the environment, this is likely to affect long-term value and shall therefore determine the time perspective for reporting in the OFR. By contrast, a service industry with few physical assets and depending on the supply of particular employee skills for its source of competitive advantage, will plan over a period consistent with its ability to recruit, train and develop its staff, which may be much shorter.

34 **The OFR shall set out the directors' strategies for achieving the objectives of the business.**

35 Disclosure of the directors' strategies is necessary for investors to assess the current and past action undertaken by directors in respect of the stated objectives. The OFR shall provide the information that an investor would want to know in making an investment decision regarding value accruing over time.

36 **To the extent necessary to meet the requirements set out in paragraph 26 above, the OFR shall include the key performance indicators, both financial and non-financial, used by the directors to assess progress against their stated objectives.**

37 The KPIs disclosed shall be those that the directors judge are the most effective to use in measuring the delivery of their strategies and managing their business. Regular

measurement using KPIs will enable an entity to set and communicate its performance targets and to measure whether it is achieving them.

38 Comparability will be enhanced if the KPIs disclosed are accepted and widely used, either within the industry sector or more generally.

39 Directors shall also consider the extent to which other measures and evidence shall be included in the OFR.

40 These could be narrative evidence describing how the directors manage the business or quantified measures used to monitor the entity's external environment and/or progress towards the achievement of its objectives.

Current and future development and performance

41 The OFR shall describe the significant features of the development and performance of the business in the period covered by the financial statements, focusing on those business segments that are relevant to an understanding of the performance as a whole.

42 Trends and factors in development and performance suggested by an analysis of the current and previous periods shall be highlighted. Development and performance shall be described in the context of the strategic objectives of the business.

43 The OFR shall cover significant aspects of the statements of financial performance and where appropriate shall be linked to other aspects of performance.

44 The OFR shall set out the directors' analysis of the effect on current development and performance of changes during the period in the industry or the external environment in which the business operates and of developments within the business. For example, changes in market conditions could have an impact on the development and performance of the entity during the period, as could the introduction, or announcement, of new products and services.

45 The OFR shall analyse the main trends and factors that directors consider likely to impact future prospects.

46 The main trends and factors likely to affect the future development and performance will vary according to the nature of the business, but could include the development of known new products and services or the benefits expected from capital investment. The OFR shall discuss the current level of investment expenditure together with planned future expenditure and shall explain how that investment is directed to assist the achievement of business objectives. Any assumptions underlying the main trends and factors shall be disclosed.

47 Directors will need to consider the potential future significance of issues in deciding whether or not to include an analysis of them in the OFR.

Resources

48 The OFR shall include a description of the resources available to the entity and how they are managed.

49 The OFR shall set out the key strengths and resources, tangible and intangible, available to the business, which will assist it in the pursuit of its objectives and, in particular, those items

that are not reflected in the balance sheet. Depending on the nature of the business, these may include: corporate reputation and brand strength; natural resources; employees; research and development; intellectual capital; licences, patents, copyright and trademarks; and market position.

Risks and uncertainties

50 **The OFR shall include a description of the principal risks and uncertainties facing the entity, together with a commentary on the directors' approach to them.**

51 While different industries and entities use different risk models or approaches for identifying and managing risk, all entities face and shall disclose strategic, operational and financial risks where these may significantly affect the entity's strategies and development of the entity's value.

52 The risks and uncertainties facing entities will vary according to the nature of the business, although it is expected that some risks, such as reputational risk, will be common to all.

53 The description of the risks and uncertainties shall cover both the exposure to negative consequences as well as potential opportunities. The directors' policy for managing risks shall be disclosed.

54 The OFR shall cover risks and uncertainties necessary for an understanding of the objectives and strategies of the business, both where they constitute a significant external risk to the entity, and where the entity's impact on other parties through its activities, products or services, affects its performance. Directors will need to consider the full range of business risks.

Relationships

55 **To the extent necessary to meet the requirements set out in paragraph 26 above, the OFR shall include information about significant relationships with stakeholders other than investors, which are likely, directly or indirectly, to influence the performance of the business and its value.**

56 Directors, in deciding what shall be included in the OFR, will need to take a broad view in considering the extent to which the actions of stakeholders other than investors can affect an entity's performance and thus its value. For example, for many entities, relationships with customers, suppliers, employees, contractors, lenders, creditors and regulators will be important, as will the entity's broader impact on society and the communities affected by its activities. Strategic alliances with other entities can also affect the performance of the entity and its value.

57 **Where necessary for an understanding of the business, the OFR shall describe receipts from, and returns to, shareholders in relation to shares held by them. This shall include a description of any distributions, capital raising and share repurchases.**

Financial position

58 **The OFR shall contain an analysis of the financial position of the entity.**

59 The analysis, whilst based upon the financial statements, shall comment on the events that have impacted the financial position of the entity during the period, and future factors that

are likely to affect the financial position going forward. The analysis shall supplement the disclosures in particular required by FRS 25 (IAS 32) 'Financial Instruments: Disclosure and Presentation' or [draft] FRS 'Financial Instruments: Disclosure'.

60 The OFR shall highlight accounting policies that are critical to an understanding of the performance and financial position of the entity, focusing on those which have required the particular exercise of judgement in their application and to which the results are most sensitive. In addition, it shall draw attention to the accounting policies which have changed during the year.

61 The OFR shall contain a discussion of the capital structure of the business.

62 This could include the balance between equity and debt, the maturity profile of debt, type of capital instruments used, currency, regulatory capital and interest rate structure. The discussion shall include comments on short and longer-term funding plans to support the directors' strategies to achieve the entity's objectives. In addition, the discussion shall comment on why the entity has adopted its particular capital structure.

63 The OFR shall set out the entity's treasury policies and objectives.

64 The OFR shall also discuss the implementation of these policies in the period under review.

65 The purpose and effect of major financing transactions undertaken up to the date of approval of the financial statements shall be explained. The effect of interest costs on profits and the potential impact of interest rate changes shall also be discussed.

Cash flows

66 The OFR shall discuss the cash inflows and outflows during the period under review, along with the entity's ability to generate cash, to meet known or probable cash requirements and to fund growth.

67 Any discussion shall supplement the information provided in the financial statements by, for example, commenting on any special factors that have influenced cash flows in the current period and those that may have a significant effect on future cash flows. This could include, for example, the existence and timing of commitments for capital expenditures and other known or probable cash requirements. Where entities have cash that is surplus to future operating requirements and current levels of distribution, the discussion shall include future plans for making use of the excess cash.

68 Although segmental analysis of profit may be indicative of the cash flow generated by each segment, this will not always be so – for example, because of fluctuations in capital expenditure and depreciation. Where segmental cash flows are significantly out of line with segmental revenues or profits, this shall be indicated and explained.

Liquidity

69 The OFR shall discuss the entity's current and prospective liquidity. Where relevant, this shall include commentary on the level of borrowings, the seasonality of borrowing requirements (indicated by the peak level of borrowings during that period) and the maturity profile of both borrowings and undrawn committed borrowing facilities.

70 The discussion on liquidity shall discuss the ability of the entity to meet its payment commitments. Where appropriate, reference shall be made to the funding requirements for investment commitments and authorisations.

71 The discussion shall cover internal sources of liquidity, referring to any restrictions on the ability to transfer funds from one part of the group to meet the obligations of another part of the group, where these represent, or might foreseeably come to represent, a significant restraint on the group. Such constraints would include exchange controls and taxation consequences of transfers.

72 Where the entity has entered into covenants with lenders which could have the effect of restricting the use of credit facilities, and negotiations with the lenders on the operation of these covenants are taking place or are expected to take place, this fact shall be indicated in the OFR. Where a breach of a covenant has occurred or is expected to occur, the OFR shall give details of the measures taken or proposed to remedy the situation.

KEY PERFORMANCE INDICATORS

73 An entity shall provide information that enables investors to understand each KPI disclosed in the OFR.

74 For each KPI disclosed in the OFR:

- **the definition and its calculation method shall be explained;**
- **its purpose shall be explained;**
- **the source of underlying data shall be disclosed and, where relevant, assumptions explained;**
- **quantification or commentary on future targets shall be provided;**
- **where information from the financial statements has been adjusted for inclusion in the OFR, that fact shall be highlighted and a reconciliation provided;**
- **where available, corresponding amount for the financial year immediately preceding the current year shall be disclosed; and**
- **any changes to KPIs shall be disclosed and the calculation method used compared to previous periods, including significant changes in the underlying accounting policies adopted in the financial statements, shall be identified and explained.**

OTHER MEASURES

75 Where a quantified measure, other than a KPI, is included, the OFR shall disclose:

- **the definition and its calculation method; and**
- **where available, corresponding amount for the financial year immediately preceding the current year.**

EFFECTIVE DATE

76 The reporting practices set out in this [draft] Reporting Standard shall be regarded as standard in respect of OFRs relating to accounting periods beginning on or after 1 April 2005.

STATEMENT OF COMPLIANCE

77 The OFR shall include a statement as to whether it has been prepared in accordance with this [draft] Reporting Standard and contain particulars of, and reasons for, any departure.

APPENDIX A

NOTE ON LEGAL REQUIREMENTS GREAT BRITAIN

A1 The Companies Act 1985 (Operating and Financial Review and Directors' Report) Regulations 2004, which will shortly be laid before Parliament, require the directors of a quoted company to prepare an OFR for financial years beginning on or after 1 April 2005. The specific requirements for the objective and contents of the OFR are contained in Schedule 7ZA of the Companies Act 1985. The requirements of that Schedule that are relevant to the [draft] Reporting Standard are set out below.

A2 A quoted company is defined in Section 262 of the Companies Act 1985 as "a company whose equity share capital:

(a) has been included in the official list in accordance with the provisions of Part VI of the Financial Services and Markets Act 2000; or

(b) is officially listed in an EEA state; or

(c) is admitted to dealing on either the New York Stock Exchange or the exchange known as Nasdaq".

The objective of the OFR

A3 Schedule 7ZA (the Schedule) requires that the OFR shall be a "balanced and comprehensive analysis" of:

a the development and performance of the business of the company and its subsidiary undertakings during the financial year;

b the position of the company and its subsidiary undertakings at the end of the year;

c the main trends and factors underlying the development, performance and position of the business of the company and its subsidiary undertakings during the financial year; and

d the main trends and factors which are likely to affect their future development, performance and position; prepared so as to assist the members of the company to assess the strategies adopted by the company and its subsidiary undertakings and the potential for those strategies to succeed.

Other general requirements

A4 The Schedule requires that information on certain matters shall always be included in an OFR:

a a statement of the business, objectives and strategies of the company and its subsidiary undertakings;

b a description of the resources available to the company and its subsidiary undertakings;

c a description of the principal risks and uncertainties facing the company and its subsidiary undertakings; and

d a description of the capital structure, treasury policies and objectives and liquidity of the company and its subsidiary undertakings.

Details of particular matters... "to the extent necessary"

A5 The Schedule also sets out details of "particular matters" which must be reported on "to the extent necessary" to comply with the objective of the OFR and the other general requirements outlined in paragraph A4 above. The wording "to the extent necessary" derives from the EU Accounts Modernisation Directive (see Note below), which requires an enhanced review of a company's business in the directors' report to be prepared and published for financial years beginning on or after 1 January 2005.

Note: Directive 2003/51/EC of the European Parliament and the Council of 18 June 2003 amending Directives 78/660/EEC, 83/349/EEC, 86/635/EEC and 91/674/EEC on the annual and consolidated accounts of certain types of companies, banks and other financial institutions and insurance undertakings.

A6 The Schedule sets out a non-exhaustive list of particular matters that directors must consider for inclusion in their OFR to the extent necessary.

A7 The review shall include information about:

a the employees of the company and its subsidiary undertakings;

b environmental matters; and

c social and community issues.

A8 The review shall also include information about:

a the persons with whom the company or its subsidiary undertakings have relations (whether contractual or otherwise) which are essential to the business of the company and its subsidiary undertakings; and

b receipts from, and returns to members of the company and its subsidiary undertakings in relation to shares held by them.

A9 The Schedule also specifies that – to the extent necessary – the review shall include analysis using financial and other key performance indicators, including information relating to environmental matters and employee matters. Key performance indicators are defined as "the factors by which the development, performance and position of the business of the company and its subsidiary undertakings can be measured most effectively".

A10 The OFR shall also, where appropriate, include references to, and additional explanations of, amounts included in the company's annual accounts.

Parent companies

A11 The Schedule permits an OFR prepared and published by a parent company, where appropriate, to give greater emphasis to those matters which are significant to the company and its subsidiary undertakings taken as a whole.

Reporting standards and compliance with them

A12 The Regulations insert into the Companies Act 1985 a new section 256A, a definition of "reporting standards" as meaning statements of standard reporting practice which relate to OFRs and which are issued by a body or bodies specified in an order made by the Secretary of State. By complying with those standards, directors shall be presumed (unless proved to the contrary) to have complied with the statutory requirements to prepare an OFR.

A13 Clause 13 of the Companies (Audit, Investigations and Community Enterprise) Act 2004 establishes a system to specify a body to issue reporting standards. The Government has said that it intends to specify in a Regulation the ASB as that body.

A14 The Schedule requires that an OFR must:

- a state whether it has been prepared in accordance with relevant reporting standards; and
- b contain particulars of, and reasons for, any departure from those standards.

NORTHERN IRELAND

A15 There are no legal requirements in Northern Ireland relating to the preparation and publication of an OFR.

REPUBLIC OF IRELAND

A16 There are no legal requirements in the Republic of Ireland relating to the preparation and publication of an OFR.

Appendix 20

Audit Committees – Combined Code Guidance (the Smith Guidance)

1 Introduction

1.1. This guidance is designed to assist company boards in making suitable arrangements for their audit committees, and to assist directors serving on audit committees in carrying out their role.

1.2. The paragraphs in bold are taken from the Combined Code (Section C3). Listed companies that do not comply with those provisions should include an explanation as to why they have not complied in the statement required by the Listing Rules.

1.3. Best practice requires that every board should consider in detail what arrangements for its audit committee are best suited for its particular circumstances. Audit committee arrangements need to be proportionate to the task, and will vary according to the size, complexity and risk profile of the company.

1.4. While all directors have a duty to act in the interests of the company the audit committee has a particular role, acting independently from the executive, to ensure that the interests of shareholders are properly protected in relation to financial reporting and internal control.

1.5. Nothing in the guidance should be interpreted as a departure from the principle of the unitary board. All directors remain equally responsible for the company's affairs as a matter of law. The audit committee, like other committees to which particular responsibilities are delegated (such as the remuneration committee), remains a committee of the board. Any disagreement within the board, including disagreement between the audit committee's members and the rest of the board, should be resolved at board level.

1.6. The Code provides that a separate section of the annual report should describe the work of the committee. This deliberately puts the spotlight on the audit committee and gives it an authority that it might otherwise lack. This is not incompatible with the principle of the unitary board.

1.7. The guidance contains recommendations about the conduct of the audit committee's relationship with the board, with the executive management and with internal and external auditors. However, the most important features of this relationship cannot be drafted as guidance or put into a code of practice: a frank, open working relationship and a high level of mutual respect are essential, particularly between the audit committee chairman and the board chairman, the chief executive and the finance director. The audit committee must be prepared to take a robust stand, and all parties must be prepared to make information freely available to the audit committee, to listen to their views and to talk through the issues openly.

1.8. In particular, the management is under an obligation to ensure the audit committee is kept properly informed, and should take the initiative in supplying information rather than waiting to be asked. The board should make it clear to all directors and staff that they must cooperate with the audit committee and provide it with any information it requires. In addition, executive board members will have regard to their common law duty to provide all directors, including those on the audit committee, with all the information they need to discharge their responsibilities as directors of the company.

1.9. Many of the core functions of audit committees set out in this guidance are expressed in terms of 'oversight', 'assessment' and 'review' of a particular function. It is not the duty of audit committees to carry out functions that properly belong to others, such as the company's management in the preparation of the financial statements or the auditors in the planning or conducting of audits. To do so could undermine the responsibility of management and auditors. Audit committees should, for example, satisfy themselves that there is a proper system and allocation of responsibilities for the day-to-day monitoring of financial controls but they should not seek to do the monitoring themselves.

1.10. However, the high-level oversight function may lead to detailed work. The audit committee must intervene if there are signs that something may be seriously amiss. For example, if the audit committee is uneasy about the explanations of management and auditors about a particular financial reporting policy decision, there may be no alternative but to grapple with the detail and perhaps to seek independent advice.

1.11. Under this guidance, audit committees have wide-ranging, time-consuming and sometimes intensive work to do. Companies need to make the necessary resources available. This includes suitable payment for the members of audit committees themselves. They – and particularly the audit committee chairman – bear a significant responsibility and they need to commit a significant extra amount of time to the job. Companies also need to make provision for induction and training for new audit committee members and continuing training as may be required.

1.12 This guidance applies to all companies to which the Code applies – i.e. UK listed companies. For groups, it will usually be necessary for the audit committee of the parent company to review issues that relate to particular subsidiaries or activities carried on by the group. Consequently, the board of a UK-listed parent company should ensure that there is adequate cooperation within the group (and with internal and external auditors of individual companies within the group) to enable the parent company audit committee to discharge its responsibilities effectively.

2 Establishment and role of the audit committee; membership, procedures and resources

Establishment and role

2.1 The board should establish an audit committee of at least three, or in the case of smaller companies two, members.

2.2 The main role and responsibilities of the audit committee should be set out in written terms of reference and should include:

- **to monitor the integrity of the financial statements of the company and any formal announcements relating to the company's financial performance, reviewing significant financial reporting judgements contained in them;**
- **to review the company's internal financial controls and, unless expressly addressed by a separate board risk committee composed of independent directors or by the board itself, the company's internal control and risk management systems;**
- **to monitor and review the effectiveness of the company's internal audit function;**
- **to make recommendations to the board, for it to put to the shareholders for their approval in general meeting, in relation to the appointment of the external auditor and to approve the remuneration and terms of engagement of the external auditor;**
- **to review and monitor the external auditor's independence and objectivity and the effectiveness of the audit process, taking into consideration relevant UK professional and regulatory requirements;**
- **to develop and implement policy on the engagement of the external auditor to supply non-audit services, taking into account relevant ethical guidance regarding the provision of non-audit services by the external audit firm;**
- **and to report to the Board, identifying any matters in respect of which it considers that action or improvement is needed, and making recommendations as to the steps to be taken.**

Membership and appointment

2.3 **All members of the committee should be independent non-executive directors. The board should satisfy itself that at least one member of the audit committee has recent and relevant financial experience.**

2.4 The chairman of the company should not be an audit committee member.

2.5 Appointments to the audit committee should be made by the board on the recommendation of the nomination committee (where there is one), in consultation with the audit committee chairman.

2.6 Appointments should be for a period of up to three years, extendable by no more than two additional three-year periods, so long as members continue to be independent.

Meetings of the audit committee

2.7 It is for the audit committee chairman, in consultation with the company secretary, to decide the frequency and timing of its meetings. There should be as many meetings as the audit committee's role and responsibilities require. It is recommended there should be not fewer than three meetings during the year, held to coincide with key dates within the financial reporting and audit cycle.[1] However, most audit committee chairmen will wish to call more frequent meetings.

2.8 No one other than the audit committee's chairman and members is entitled to be present at a meeting of the audit committee. It is for the audit committee to decide if non-members should attend for a particular meeting or a particular agenda item. It is to be expected that the external audit lead partner will be invited regularly to attend meetings as well as the finance director. Others may be invited to attend.

2.9 Sufficient time should be allowed to enable the audit committee to undertake as full a discussion as may be required. A sufficient interval should be allowed between audit committee meetings and main board meetings to allow any work arising from the audit committee meeting to be carried out and reported to the board as appropriate.

2.10 The audit committee should, at least annually, meet the external and internal auditors, without management, to discuss matters relating to its remit and any issues arising from the audit.

2.11 Formal meetings of the audit committee are the heart of its work. However, they will rarely be sufficient. It is expected that the audit committee chairman, and to a lesser extent the other members, will wish to keep in touch on a continuing basis with the key people involved in the company's governance, including the board chairman, the chief executive, the finance director, the external audit lead partner and the head of internal audit.

Resources

2.12 The audit committee should be provided with sufficient resources to undertake its duties.

2.13 The audit committee should have access to the services of the company secretariat on all audit committee matters including: assisting the chairman in planning the audit committee's work, drawing up meeting agendas, maintenance of minutes, drafting of material about its activities for the annual report, collection and distribution of information and provision of any necessary practical support.

2.14 The company secretary should ensure that the audit committee receives information and papers in a timely manner to enable full and proper consideration to be given to the issues.

2.15 The board should make funds available to the audit committee to enable it to take independent legal, accounting or other advice when the audit committee reasonably believes it necessary to do so.

Remuneration

2.16 In addition to the remuneration paid to all non-executive directors, each company should consider the further remuneration that should be paid to members of the audit committee to recompense them for the additional responsibilities of membership. Consideration should be given to the time members are required to give to audit committee business, the skills they bring to bear and the onerous duties they take on, as well as the value of their work to the company. The level of remuneration paid to the members of the audit committee should take into account the level of fees paid to other members of the board. The chairman's responsibilities and time demands will generally be heavier than the other members of the audit committee and this should be reflected in his or her remuneration.

Skills, experience and training

2.17 It is desirable that the committee member whom the board considers to have recent and relevant financial experience should have a professional qualification from one of the professional accountancy bodies. The need for a degree of financial literacy among the other members will vary according to the nature of the company, but experience of corporate financial matters will normally be required. The availability of appropriate financial expertise will be particularly important where the company's activities involve specialised financial activities.

2.18 The company should provide an induction programme for new audit committee members. This should cover the role of the audit committee, including its terms of reference and expected time commitment by members; and an overview of the company's business, identifying the main business and financial dynamics and risks. It could also include meeting some of the company staff.

2.19 Training should also be provided to members of the audit committee on an ongoing and timely basis and should include an understanding of the principles of and developments in financial reporting and related company law. In appropriate cases, it may also include, for example, understanding financial statements, applicable accounting standards and recommended practice; the regulatory framework for the company's business; the role of internal and external auditing and risk management.

2.20 The induction programme and ongoing training may take various forms, including attendance at formal courses and conferences, internal company talks and seminars, and briefings by external advisers.

3 Relationship with the board

3.1 The role of the audit committee is for the board to decide and to the extent that the audit committee undertakes tasks on behalf of the board, the results should be reported to, and considered by, the board. In doing so it should identify any matters in respect of which it considers that action or improvement is needed, and make recommendations as to the steps to be taken.

3.2 The terms of reference should be tailored to the particular circumstances of the company.

3.3 The audit committee should review annually its terms of reference and its own effectiveness and recommend any necessary changes to the board.

3.4 The board should review the audit committee's effectiveness annually.

3.5 Where there is disagreement between the audit committee and the board, adequate time should be made available for discussion of the issue with a view to resolving the disagreement. Where any such disagreements cannot be resolved, the audit committee should have the right to report the issue to the shareholders as part of the report on its activities in the annual report.

4 Role and responsibilities

Financial reporting

4.1 The audit committee should review the significant financial reporting issues and judgements made in connection with the preparation of the company's financial statements, interim reports, preliminary announcements and related formal statements.

4.2 It is management's, not the audit committee's, responsibility to prepare complete and accurate financial statements and disclosures in accordance with financial reporting standards and applicable rules and regulations. However the audit committee should consider significant accounting policies, any changes to them and any significant estimates and judgements. The management should inform the audit committee of the methods used to account for significant or unusual transactions where the accounting treatment is open to different approaches. Taking into account the external auditor's view, the audit committee should consider whether the company has adopted appropriate accounting policies and, where necessary, made appropriate estimates and judgements. The audit committee should review the clarity and completeness of disclosures in the financial statements and consider whether the disclosures made are set properly in context.

4.3 Where, following its review, the audit committee is not satisfied with any aspect of the proposed financial reporting by the company, it shall report its views to the board.

4.4 The audit committee should review related information presented with the financial statements, including the operating and financial review, and corporate governance statements relating to the audit and to risk management. Similarly, where board approval is required for other statements containing financial information (for example, summary financial statements, significant financial returns to regulators and release of price sensitive information), whenever practicable (without being inconsistent with any requirement for prompt reporting under the Listing Rules) the audit committee should review such statements first.

Internal controls and risk management systems

4.5 The audit committee should review the company's internal financial controls (that is, the systems established to identify, assess, manage and monitor financial risks); and unless expressly addressed by a separate board risk committee comprised of independent directors or by the board itself, the company's internal control and risk management systems.

4.6 The company's management is responsible for the identification, assessment, management and monitoring of risk, for developing, operating and monitoring the system of internal control and for providing assurance to the board that it has done so. Except where the board or a risk committee is expressly responsible for reviewing the effectiveness of the internal control and risk management systems, the audit committee should receive reports from management on the effectiveness of the systems they have established and the conclusions of any testing carried out by internal and external auditors.

4.7 Except to the extent that this is expressly dealt with by the board or risk committee, the audit committee should review and approve the statements included in the annual report in relation to internal control and the management of risk.

Whistleblowing

4.8 **The audit committee should review arrangements by which staff of the company may, in confidence, raise concerns about possible improprieties in matters of financial reporting or other matters. The audit committee's objective should be to ensure that arrangements are in place for the proportionate and independent investigation of such matters and for appropriate follow-up action.**

The internal audit process

4.9 **The audit committee should monitor and review the effectiveness of the company's internal audit function. Where there is no internal audit function, the audit committee should consider annually whether there is a need for an internal audit function and make a recommendation to the board, and the reasons for the absence of such a function should be explained in the relevant section of the annual report.**

4.10 The audit committee should review and approve the internal audit function's remit, having regard to the complementary roles of the internal and external audit functions. The audit committee should ensure that the function has the necessary resources and access to information to enable it to fulfil its mandate, and is equipped to perform in accordance with appropriate professional standards for internal auditors.[2]

4.11 The audit committee should approve the appointment or termination of appointment of the head of internal audit.

4.12 In its review of the work of the internal audit function, the audit committee should, inter alia:

- ensure that the internal auditor has direct access to the board chairman and to the audit committee and is accountable to the audit committee;
- review and assess the annual internal audit work plan;
- receive a report on the results of the internal auditors' work on a periodic basis;
- review and monitor management's responsiveness to the internal auditor's findings and recommendations;
- meet with the head of internal audit at least once a year without the presence of management; and
- monitor and assess the role and effectiveness of the internal audit function in the overall context of the company's risk management system.

The external audit process

4.13 The audit committee is the body responsible for overseeing the company's relations with the external auditor.

Appointment

4.14 **The audit committee should have primary responsibility for making a recommendation on the appointment, reappointment and removal of the external auditors. If the board does not accept the audit committee's recommendation, it should include in the annual report, and in any papers recommending appointment or reappointment, a statement from the audit committee explaining its recommendation and should set out reasons why the board has taken a different position.**

4.15 The audit committee's recommendation to the board should be based on the assessments referred to below. If the audit committee recommends considering the selection of possible new appointees as external auditors, it should oversee the selection process.

4.16 The audit committee should assess annually the qualification, expertise and resources, and independence (see below) of the external auditors and the effectiveness of the audit process. The assessment should cover all aspects of the audit service provided by the audit firm, and include obtaining a report on the audit firm's own internal quality control procedures.

4.17 If the external auditor resigns, the audit committee should investigate the issues giving rise to such resignation and consider whether any action is required.

Terms and Remuneration

4.18 The audit committee should approve the terms of engagement and the remuneration to be paid to the external auditor in respect of audit services provided.

4.19 The audit committee should review and agree the engagement letter issued by the external auditor at the start of each audit, ensuring that it has been updated to reflect changes in circumstances arising since the previous year. The scope of the external audit should be reviewed by the audit committee with the auditor. If the audit committee is not satisfied as to its adequacy it should arrange for additional work to be undertaken.

4.20 The audit committee should satisfy itself that the level of fee payable in respect of the audit services provided is appropriate and that an effective audit can be conducted for such a fee.

Independence, including the provision of non-audit services

4.21 The audit committee should have procedures to ensure the independence and objectivity of the external auditor annually, taking into consideration relevant UK professional and regulatory requirements. This assessment should involve a consideration of all relationships between the company and the audit firm (including the provision of non-audit services). The audit committee should consider whether, taken as a whole and having regard to the views, as appropriate, of the external auditor, management and internal audit, those relationships appear to impair the auditor's judgement or independence.

4.22 The audit committee should seek reassurance that the auditors and their staff have no family, financial, employment, investment or business relationship with the company (other than in the normal course of business). The audit committee should seek from the audit firm, on an annual basis, information about policies and processes for maintaining independence and monitoring compliance with relevant requirements, including current requirements regarding the rotation of audit partners and staff.

4.23 The audit committee should agree with the board the company's policy for the employment of former employees of the external auditor, paying particular attention to the policy regarding former employees of the audit firm who were part of the audit team and moved directly to the company. This should be drafted taking into account the relevant ethical guidelines governing the accounting profession. The audit committee should monitor application of the policy, including the number of former employees of the external auditor currently employed in senior positions in the company, and consider whether in the light of this there has been any impairment, or appearance of impairment, of the auditor's judgement or independence in respect of the audit.

4.24 The audit committee should monitor the external audit firm's compliance with applicable United Kingdom ethical guidance relating to the rotation of audit partners, the level of fees that the company pays in proportion to the overall fee income of the firm, office and partner, and other related regulatory requirements.

4.25 The audit committee should develop and recommend to the board the company's policy in relation to the provision of non-audit services by the auditor. The audit committee's objective should be to ensure that the provision of such services does not impair the external auditor's independence or objectivity. In this context, the audit committee should consider:

- whether the skills and experience of the audit firm make it a suitable supplier of the non audit service;
- whether there are safeguards in place to ensure that there is no threat to objectivity and independence in the conduct of the audit resulting from the provision of such services by the external auditor;
- the nature of the non-audit services, the related fee levels and the fee levels individually and in aggregate relative to the audit fee; and the criteria which govern the compensation of the individuals performing the audit.

4.26 The audit committee should set and apply a formal policy specifying the types of non-audit work:

- from which the external auditors are excluded;
- for which the external auditors can be engaged without referral to the audit committee; and
- for which a case-by-case decision is necessary.

In addition, the policy may set fee limits generally or for particular classes of work.

4.27 In the third category, if it is not practicable to give approval to individual items in advance, it may be appropriate to give a general pre-approval for certain classes for work, subject to a fee limit determined by the audit committee and ratified by the board. The subsequent provision of any service by the auditor should be ratified at the next meeting of the audit committee.

4.28 In determining the policy, the audit committee should take into account relevant ethical guidance regarding the provision of non-audit services by the external audit firm, and in principle should not agree to the auditor providing a service if, having regard to the ethical guidance, the result is that:

- the external auditor audits its own firm's work;
- the external auditor makes management decisions for the company;
- a mutuality of interest is created; or
- the external auditor is put in the role of advocate for the company.

The audit committee should satisfy itself that any safeguards required by ethical guidance are implemented.

4.29 The annual report should explain to shareholders how, if the auditor provides non-audit services, auditor objectivity and independence is safeguarded.

Annual audit cycle

4.30 At the start of each annual audit cycle, the audit committee should ensure that appropriate plans are in place for the audit.

4.31 The audit committee should consider whether the auditor's overall work plan, including planned levels of materiality, and proposed resources to execute the audit plan appears consistent with the scope of the audit engagement, having regard also to the seniority, expertise and experience of the audit team.

4.32 The audit committee should review, with the external auditors, the findings of their work. In the course of its review, the audit committee should:

- discuss with the external auditor major issues that arose during the course of the audit and have subsequently been resolved and those issues that have been left unresolved;
- review key accounting and audit judgements; and
- review levels of errors identified during the audit, obtaining explanations from management and, where necessary the external auditors, as to why certain errors might remain unadjusted.

4.33 The audit committee should also review the audit representation letters before signature by management and give particular consideration to matters where representation has been requested that relate to non-standard issues.[3] The audit committee should consider whether the information provided is complete and appropriate based on its own knowledge.

4.34 As part of the ongoing monitoring process, the audit committee should review the management letter (or equivalent). The audit committee should review and monitor management's responsiveness to the external auditor's findings and recommendations.

4.35 At the end of the annual audit cycle, the audit committee should assess the effectiveness of the audit process. In the course of doing so, the audit committee should:

- review whether the auditor has met the agreed audit plan and understand the reasons for any changes, including changes in perceived audit risks and the work undertaken by the external auditors to address those risks;

- consider the robustness and perceptiveness of the auditors in their handling of the key accounting and audit judgements identified and in responding to questions from the audit committees, and in their commentary where appropriate on the systems of internal control;
- obtain feedback about the conduct of the audit from key people involved, e.g. the finance director and the head of internal audit; and
- review and monitor the content of the external auditor's management letter, in order to assess whether it is based on a good understanding of the company's business and establish whether recommendations have been acted upon and, if not, the reasons why they have not been acted upon.

5 Communication with shareholders

5.1 The terms of reference of the audit committee, including its role and the authority delegated to it by the board, should be made available. A separate section in the annual report should describe the work of the committee in discharging those responsibilities.

5.2 The audit committee section should include, inter alia:

- a summary of the role of the audit committee;
- the names and qualifications of all members of the audit committee during the period;
- the number of audit committee meetings;
- a report on the way the audit committee has discharged its responsibilities; and
- the explanation provided for in paragraph 4.29 above.

5.3 The chairman of the audit committee should be present at the AGM to answer questions, through the chairman of the board, on the report on the audit committee's activities and matters within the scope of the audit committee's responsibilities.

Notes

1 For example, when the audit plans (internal and external) are available for review and when interim statements, preliminary announcements and the full annual report are near completion.

2 Further guidance can be found in the Institute of Internal Auditors' Code of Ethics and the International Standards for the Professional Practice of Internal Auditing Standards.

3 Further guidance can by found in the Auditing Practices Board's Statement of Auditing Standard 440 'Management Representations'.

Appendix 21

The Smith Report: Specimen Terms of Reference for an Audit Committee

Constitution

1 The board hereby resolves to establish a committee of the board to be known as the Audit [and Risk] Committee.

Membership

2 The committee shall be appointed by the board. All members of the committee shall be independent non-executive directors of the company. The committee shall consist of not less than three members. A quorum shall be two members.

3 The chairman of the committee shall be appointed by the board from amongst the independent non-executive directors.

Attendance at meetings

4 The finance director, head of internal audit and a representative of the external auditors shall attend meetings at the invitation of the committee.

5 The chairman of the board, the CEO and other board members shall attend if invited by the committee.

6 There should be at least one meeting a year, or part thereof, where the external auditors attend without management present.

7 The company secretary shall be secretary of the committee.

Frequency of meetings

8 Meetings shall be held not less than [three]times a year, and where appropriate should coincide with key dates in the company's financial reporting cycle.

9 External auditors or internal auditors may request a meeting if they consider that one is necessary.

Authority

10 The committee is authorised by the board to:

- a investigate any activity within its terms of reference;
- b seek any information that it requires from any employee of the company and all employees are directed to cooperate with any request made by the committee; and
- c obtain outside legal or independent professional advice and such advisors may attend meetings as necessary.

Responsibilities

11 The responsibilities of the committee shall be:

a to consider the appointment of the external auditor and assess independence of the external auditor, ensuring that key partners are rotated at appropriate intervals;

b to recommend the audit fee to the board and preapprove any fees in respect of non audit services provided by the external auditor and to ensure that the provision of non audit services does not impair the external auditors' independence or objectivity;

c to discuss with the external auditor, before the audit commences, the nature and scope of the audit and to review the auditors' quality control procedures and steps taken by the auditor to respond to changes in regulatory and other requirements;

d to oversee the process for selecting the external auditor and make appropriate recommendations through the board to the shareholders to consider at the AGM ;

e to review the external auditor's management letter and management's response;

f to review the internal audit programme and ensure that the internal audit function is adequately resourced and has appropriate standing within the company;

g to consider management's response to any major external or internal audit recommendations;

h to approve the appointment or dismissal of the head of internal audit;

i to review the company's procedures for handling allegations from whistleblowers;

j to review management's and the internal auditor's reports on the effectiveness of systems for internal financial control, financial reporting and risk management;

k to review, and challenge where necessary, the actions and judgements of management, in relation to the interim and annual financial statements before submission to the board, paying particular attention to:

- i critical accounting policies and practices, and any changes in them
- ii decisions requiring a major element of judgement
- iii the extent to which the financial statements are affected by any unusual transactions in the year and how they are disclosed
- iv the clarity of disclosures
- v significant adjustments resulting from the audit
- vi the going concern assumption
- vii compliance with accounting standards
- viii compliance with stock exchange and other legal requirements
- ix reviewing the company's statement on internal control systems prior to endorsement by the board and to review the policies and process for identifying and assessing business risks and the management of those risks by the company

l to consider other topics, as defined by the board.

Reporting procedures

12 The secretary shall circulate the minutes of meetings of the committee to all members of the board, and the chairman of the committee or, as a minimum, another member of the committee, shall attend the board meeting at which the accounts are approved.

13 The committee members shall conduct an annual review of their work and these terms of reference and make recommendations to the board.

The committee's duties and activities during the year shall be disclosed in the annual financial statements.

The chairman shall attend the AGM and shall answer questions, through the chairman of the board, on the audit committee's activities and their responsibilities.

Appendix 22
Guidance on Internal Control (the Turnbull Guidance)

INTRODUCTION

Internal control requirements of the Combined Code

1 When the Combined Code of the Committee on Corporate Governance (the Code) was published, the Institute of Chartered Accountants in England & Wales agreed with the London Stock Exchange that it would provide guidance to assist listed companies to implement the requirements in the Code relating to internal control.

2 Principle D.2 of the Code states that 'The board should maintain a sound system of internal control to safeguard shareholders' investment and the company's assets'.

3 Provision D.2.1 states that 'The directors should, at least annually, conduct a review of the effectiveness of the group's system of internal control and should report to shareholders that they have done so. The review should cover all controls, including financial, operational and compliance controls and risk management'.

4 Provision D.2.2 states that 'Companies which do not have an internal audit function should from time to time review the need for one'.

5 Paragraph 12.43A of the London Stock Exchange Listing Rules states that 'in the case of a company incorporated in the United Kingdom, the following additional items must be included in its annual report and accounts:

(a) a narrative statement of how it has applied the principles set out in Section 1 of the Combined Code, providing explanation which enables its shareholders to evaluate how the principles have been applied;

(b) a statement as to whether or not it has complied throughout the accounting period with the Code provisions set out in Section 1 of the Combined Code. A company that has not complied with the Code provisions, or complied with only some of the Code provisions or (in the case of provisions whose requirements are of a continuing nature) complied for only part of an accounting period, must specify the Code provisions with which it has not complied, and (where relevant) for what part of the period such non-compliance continued, and give reasons for any non-compliance.

6 The Preamble to the Code, which is appended to the Listing Rules, makes it clear that there is no prescribed form or content for the statement setting out how the various principles in the Code have been applied. The intention is that companies should have a free hand to explain their governance policies in the light of the principles, including any special circumstances which have led to them adopting a particular approach.

7 The guidance in this document should be followed by boards of listed companies in:

- assessing how the company has applied Code principle D.2;
- implementing the requirements of Code provisions D.2.1 and D.2.2; and

- reporting on these matters to shareholders in the annual report and accounts.

Objectives of the guidance

8 This guidance is intended to:

- reflect sound business practice whereby internal control is embedded in the business processes by which a company pursues its objectives;
- remain relevant over time in the continually evolving business environment; and
- enable each company to apply it in a manner which takes account of its particular circumstances.

The guidance requires directors to exercise judgement in reviewing how the company has implemented the requirements of the Code relating to internal control and reporting to shareholders thereon.

9 The guidance is based on the adoption by a company's board of a risk-based approach to establishing a sound system of internal control and reviewing its effectiveness. This should be incorporated by the company within its normal management and governance processes. It should not be treated as a separate exercise undertaken to meet regulatory requirements.

The importance of internal control and risk management

10 A company's system of internal control has a key role in the management of risks that are significant to the fulfilment of its business objectives. A sound system of internal control contributes to safeguarding the shareholders' investment and the company's assets.

11 Internal control (as referred to in paragraph 20) facilitates the effectiveness and efficiency of operations, helps ensure the reliability of internal and external reporting and assists compliance with laws and regulations.

12 Effective financial controls, including the maintenance of proper accounting records, are an important element of internal control. They help ensure that the company is not unnecessarily exposed to avoidable financial risks and that financial information used within the business and for publication is reliable. They also contribute to the safeguarding of assets, including the prevention and detection of fraud.

13 A company's objectives, its internal organisation and the environment in which it operates are continually evolving and, as a result, the risks it faces are continually changing. A sound system of internal control therefore depends on a thorough and regular evaluation of the nature and extent of the risks to which the company is exposed. Since profits are, in part, the reward for successful risk- taking in business, the purpose of internal control is to help manage and control risk appropriately rather than to eliminate it.

Groups of companies

14 Throughout this guidance, where reference is made to 'company' it should be taken, where applicable, as referring to the group of which the reporting company is the parent company. For groups of companies, the review of effectiveness of internal control and the report to the shareholders should be from the perspective of the group as a whole.

The Appendix

15 The Appendix to this document contains questions which boards may wish to consider in applying this guidance.

MAINTAINING A SOUND SYSTEM OF INTERNAL CONTROL

Responsibilities

16 The board of directors is responsible for the company's system of internal control. It should set appropriate policies on internal control and seek regular assurance that will enable it to satisfy itself that the system is functioning effectively. The board must further ensure that the system of internal control is effective in managing risks in the manner which it has approved.

17 In determining its policies with regard to internal control, and thereby assessing what constitutes a sound system of internal control in the particular circumstances of the company, the board's deliberations should include consideration of the following factors:

- the nature and extent of the risks facing the company;
- the extent and categories of risk which it regards as acceptable for the company to bear;
- the likelihood of the risks concerned materialising;
- the company's ability to reduce the incidence and impact on the business of risks that do materialise; and
- the costs of operating particular controls relative to the benefit thereby obtained in managing the related risks.

18 It is the role of management to implement board policies on risk and control. In fulfilling its responsibilities, management should identify and evaluate the risks faced by the company for consideration by the board and design, operate and monitor a suitable system of internal control which implements the policies adopted by the board.

19 All employees have some responsibility for internal control as part of their accountability for achieving objectives. They, collectively, should have the necessary knowledge, skills, information and authority to establish, operate and monitor the system of internal control. This will require an understanding of the company, its objectives, the industries and markets in which it operates, and the risks it faces.

Elements of a sound system of internal control

20 An internal control system encompasses the policies, processes, tasks, behaviours and other aspects of a company that, taken together:

- facilitate its effective and efficient operation by enabling it to respond appropriately to significant business, operational, financial, compliance and other risks to achieving the company's objectives. This includes the safeguarding of assets from inappropriate use or from loss and fraud, and ensuring that liabilities are identified and managed;
- help ensure the quality of internal and external reporting. This requires the maintenance of proper records and processes that generate a flow of timely, relevant and reliable information from within and outside the organisation;

- help ensure compliance with applicable laws and regulations, and also with internal policies with respect to the conduct of business.

21 A company's system of internal control will reflect its control environment which encompasses its organisational structure. The system will include:

- control activities;
- information and communications processes; and
- processes for monitoring the continuing effectiveness of the system of internal control.

22 The system of internal control should:

- be embedded in the operations of the company and form part of its culture;
- be capable of responding quickly to evolving risks to the business arising from factors within the company and to changes in the business environment; and
- include procedures for reporting immediately to appropriate levels of management any significant control failings or weaknesses that are identified together with details of corrective action being undertaken.

23 A sound system of internal control reduces, but cannot eliminate, the possibility of poor judgement in decision-making; human error; control processes being deliberately circumvented by employees and others; management overriding controls; and the occurrence of unforeseeable circumstances.

24 A sound system of internal control therefore provides reasonable, but not absolute, assurance that a company will not be hindered in achieving its business objectives, or in the orderly and legitimate conduct of its business, by circumstances which may reasonably be foreseen. A system of internal control cannot, however, provide protection with certainty against a company failing to meet its business objectives or all material errors, losses, fraud, or breaches of laws or regulations.

REVIEWING THE EFFECTIVENESS OF INTERNAL CONTROL

Responsibilities

25 Reviewing the effectiveness of internal control is an essential part of the board's responsibilities. The board will need to form its own view on effectiveness after due and careful enquiry based on the information and assurances provided to it. Management is accountable to the board for monitoring the system of internal control and for providing assurance to the board that it has done so.

26 The role of board committees in the review process, including that of the audit committee, is for the board to decide and will depend upon factors such as the size and composition of the board; the scale, diversity and complexity of the company's operations; and the nature of the significant risks that the company faces. To the extent that designated board committees carry out, on behalf of the board, tasks that are attributed in this guidance document to the board, the results of the relevant committees' work should be reported to, and considered by, the board. The board takes responsibility for the disclosures on internal control in the annual report and accounts.

The process for reviewing effectiveness

27 Effective monitoring on a continuous basis is an essential component of a sound system of internal control. The board cannot, however, rely solely on the embedded monitoring processes within the company to discharge its responsibilities. It should regularly receive and review reports on internal control. In addition, the board should undertake an annual assessment for the purposes of making its public statement on internal control to ensure that it has considered all significant aspects of internal control for the company for the year under review and up to the date of approval of the annual report and accounts.

28 The reference to 'all controls' in Code Provision D.2.1 should not be taken to mean that the effectiveness of every internal control (including controls designed to manage immaterial risks) should be subject to review by the board. Rather it means that, for the purposes of this guidance, internal controls considered by the board should include all types of controls including those of an operational and compliance nature, as well as internal financial controls.

29 The board should define the process to be adopted for its review of the effectiveness of internal control. This should encompass both the scope and frequency of the reports it receives and reviews during the year, and also the process for its annual assessment, such that it will be provided with sound, appropriately documented, support for its statement on internal control in the company's annual report and accounts.

30 The reports from management to the board should, in relation to the areas covered by them, provide a balanced assessment of the significant risks and the effectiveness of the system of internal control in managing those risks. Any significant control failings or weaknesses identified should be discussed in the reports, including the impact that they have had, could have had, or may have, on the company and the actions being taken to rectify them. It is essential that there be openness of communication by management with the board on matters relating to risk and control.

31 When reviewing reports during the year, the board should:

- consider what are the significant risks and assess how they have been identified, evaluated and managed;
- assess the effectiveness of the related system of internal control in managing the significant risks, having regard, in particular, to any significant failings or weaknesses in internal control that have been reported;
- consider whether necessary actions are being taken promptly to remedy any significant failings or weaknesses; and
- consider whether the findings indicate a need for more extensive monitoring of the system of internal control.

32 Additionally, the board should undertake an annual assessment for the purpose of making its public statement on internal control. The assessment should consider issues dealt with in reports reviewed by it during the year together with any additional information necessary to ensure that the board has taken account of all significant aspects of internal control for the company for the year under review and up to the date of approval of the annual report and accounts.

33 The board's annual assessment should, in particular, consider:

- the changes since the last annual assessment in the nature and extent of significant risks, and the company's ability to respond to changes in its business and the external environment;
- the scope and quality of management's ongoing monitoring of risks and of the system of internal control, and, where applicable, the work of its internal audit function and other providers of assurance;
- the extent and frequency of the communication of the results of the monitoring to the board (or board committee(s)) which enables it to build up a cumulative assessment of the state of control in the company and the effectiveness with which risk is being managed;
- the incidence of significant control failings or weaknesses that have been identified at any time during the period and the extent to which they have resulted in unforeseen outcomes or contingencies that have had, could have had, or may in the future have, a material impact on the company's financial performance or condition;
- and the effectiveness of the company's public reporting processes.

34 Should the board become aware at any time of a significant failing or weakness in internal control, it should determine how the failing or weakness arose and re-assess the effectiveness of management's ongoing processes for designing, operating and monitoring the system of internal control.

THE BOARD'S STATEMENT ON INTERNAL CONTROL

35 In its narrative statement of how the company has applied Code principle D.2, the board should, as a minimum, disclose that there is an ongoing process for identifying, evaluating and managing the significant risks faced by the company, that it has been in place for the year under review and up to the date of approval of the annual report and accounts, that it is regularly reviewed by the board and accords with the guidance in this document.

36 The board may wish to provide additional information in the annual report and accounts to assist understanding of the company's risk management processes and system of internal control.

37 The disclosures relating to the application of principle D.2 should include an acknowledgement by the board that it is responsible for the company's system of internal control and for reviewing its effectiveness. It should also explain that such a system is designed to manage rather than eliminate the risk of failure to achieve business objectives, and can only provide reasonable and not absolute assurance against material misstatement or loss.

38 In relation to Code provision D.2.1, the board should summarise the process it (where applicable, through its committees) has applied in reviewing the effectiveness of the system of internal control. It should also disclose the process it has applied to deal with material internal control aspects of any significant problems disclosed in the annual report and accounts.

39 Where a board cannot make one or more of the disclosures in paragraphs 35 and 38, it should state this fact and provide an explanation. The Listing Rules require the board to disclose if it has failed to conduct a review of the effectiveness of the company's system of internal control.

40 The board should ensure that its disclosures provide meaningful, high-level information and do not give a misleading impression.

41 Where material joint ventures and associates have not been dealt with as part of the group for the purposes of applying this guidance, this should be disclosed.

INTERNAL AUDIT

42 Provision D.2.2 of the Code states that companies which do not have an internal audit function should from time to time review the need for one.

43 The need for an internal audit function will vary depending on company-specific factors including the scale, diversity and complexity of the company's activities and the number of employees, as well as cost/benefit considerations. Senior management and the board may desire objective assurance and advice on risk and control. An adequately resourced internal audit function (or its equivalent where, for example, a third party is contracted to perform some or all of the work concerned) may provide such assurance and advice. There may be other functions within the company that also provide assurance and advice covering specialist areas such as health and safety, regulatory and legal compliance and environmental issues.

44 In the absence of an internal audit function, management needs to apply other monitoring processes in order to assure itself and the board that the system of internal control is functioning as intended. In these circumstances, the board will need to assess whether such processes provide sufficient and objective assurance.

45 When undertaking its assessment of the need for an internal audit function, the board should also consider whether there are any trends or current factors relevant to the company's activities, markets or other aspects of its external environment, that have increased, or are expected to increase, the risks faced by the company. Such an increase in risk may also arise from internal factors such as organisational restructuring or from changes in reporting processes or underlying information systems. Other matters to be taken into account may include adverse trends evident from the monitoring of internal control systems or an increased incidence of unexpected occurrences.

46 The board of a company that does not have an internal audit function should assess the need for such a function annually having regard to the factors referred to in paragraphs 43 and 45 above. Where there is an internal audit function, the board should annually review its scope of work, authority and resources, again having regard to those factors.

47 If the company does not have an internal audit function and the board has not reviewed the need for one, the Listing Rules require the board to disclose these facts.

APPENDIX

Assessing the effectiveness of the company's risk and control processes

Some questions which the board may wish to consider and discuss with management when regularly reviewing reports on internal control and carrying out its annual assessment are set out below. The questions are not intended to be exhaustive and will need to be tailored to the particular circumstances of the company.

This Appendix should be read in conjunction with the guidance set out in this document.

1 Risk assessment

- Does the company have clear objectives and have they been communicated so as to provide effective direction to employees on risk assessment and control issues? For example, do objectives and related plans include measurable performance targets and indicators?
- Are the significant internal and external operational, financial, compliance and other risks identified and assessed on an ongoing basis? (Significant risks may, for example, include those related to market, credit, liquidity, technological, legal, health, safety and environmental, reputation, and business probity issues.)
- Is there a clear understanding by management and others within the company of what risks are acceptable to the board?

2 Control environment and control activities

- Does the board have clear strategies for dealing with the significant risks that have been identified? Is there a policy on how to manage these risks?
- Do the company's culture, code of conduct, human resource policies and performance reward systems support the business objectives and risk management and internal control system?
- Does senior management demonstrate, through its actions as well as its policies, the necessary commitment to competence, integrity and fostering a climate of trust within the company?
- Are authority, responsibility and accountability defined clearly such that decisions are made and actions taken by the appropriate people? Are the decisions and actions of different parts of the company appropriately co-ordinated?
- Does the company communicate to its employees what is expected of them and the scope of their freedom to act? This may apply to areas such as customer relations; service levels for both internal and outsourced activities; health, safety and environmental protection; security of tangible and intangible assets; business continuity issues; expenditure matters; accounting; and financial and other reporting.
- Do people in the company (and in its providers of outsourced services) have the knowledge, skills and tools to support the achievement of the company's objectives and to manage effectively risks to their achievement?
- How are processes/controls adjusted to reflect new or changing risks, or operational deficiencies?

3 Information and communication

- Do management and the board receive timely, relevant and reliable reports on progress against business objectives and the related risks that provide them with the information, from inside and outside the company, needed for decision-making and management review purposes? This could include performance reports and indicators of change, together with qualitative information such as on customer satisfaction, employee attitudes etc.
- Are information needs and related information systems reassessed as objectives and related risks change or as reporting deficiencies are identified?
- Are periodic reporting procedures, including half-yearly and annual reporting, effective in communicating a balanced and understandable account of the company's position and prospects?
- Are there established channels of communication for individuals to report suspected breaches of laws or regulations or other improprieties?

4 Monitoring

- Are there ongoing processes embedded within the company's overall business operations, and addressed by senior management, which monitor the effective application of the policies, processes and activities related to internal control and risk management? (Such processes may include control self-assessment, confirmation by personnel of compliance with policies and codes of conduct, internal audit reviews or other management reviews.)
- Do these processes monitor the company's ability to re-evaluate risks and adjust controls effectively in response to changes in its objectives, its business, and its external environment?
- Are there effective follow-up procedures to ensure that appropriate change or action occurs in response to changes in risk and control assessments?
- Is there appropriate communication to the board (or board committees) on the effectiveness of the ongoing monitoring processes on risk and control matters? This should include reporting any significant failings or weaknesses on a timely basis.
- Are there specific arrangements for management monitoring and reporting to the board on risk and control matters of particular importance? These could include, for example, actual or suspected fraud and other illegal or irregular acts, or matters that could adversely affect the company's reputation or financial position?

Appendix 23

Association of British Insurers: Disclosure Guidelines on Socially Responsible Investment

1 Background and introduction

Public interest in corporate social responsibility has grown to the point where it seems helpful for institutional shareholders to set out basic disclosure principles, which will guide them in seeking to engage with companies in which they invest.

In drawing up guidelines for this purpose they are mindful of statements made at multilateral level through the Guidelines for Multinational Corporations published in 2000 by the Organisation for Economic Cooperation and Development, as well as by the European Union and UK Government. These, coupled with legal disclosure obligations on UK pension funds and local authority investments, point to clear responsibilities both for companies and for institutions that invest in them.

Institutional shareholders are also anxious to avoid unnecessary prescription or the imposition of costly burdens, which can unnecessarily restrict the ability of companies to generate returns. Indeed, by focusing on the need to identify and manage risks to the short- and long-term value of the business from social, environmental and ethical matters, the guidelines highlight an opportunity to enhance value through appropriate response to these risks.

It is not the intention of these guidelines to set a limit on the amount of information companies should provide on their response to social, environmental and ethical matters. Some shareholders with specific ethical investment objectives may seek more specific information. Some companies may choose to make additional information available in order to enhance their appeal to investors.

The ABI hopes that in elaborating these guidelines it will provide a helpful basic benchmark for companies seeking to develop best practice in this area.

2 The Disclosure Guidelines

The guidelines take the form of disclosures, which institutions would expect to see included in the annual report of listed companies. Specifically they refer to disclosures relating to Board responsibilities and to policies, procedures and verification.

With regard to the board, the company should state in its annual report whether:

1.1 The Board takes regular account of the significance of social, environmental and ethical (SEE) matters to the business of the company.

1.2 The Board has identified and assessed the significant risks to the company's short- and long-term value arising from SEE matters, as well as the opportunities to enhance value that may arise from an appropriate response.

1.3 The Board has received adequate information to make this assessment and that account is taken of SEE matters in the training of directors.

1.4 The Board has ensured that the company has in place effective systems for managing significant risks, which, where relevant, incorporate performance management systems and appropriate remuneration incentives.

With regard to policies, procedures and verification, the annual report should:

2.1 Include information on SEE-related risks and opportunities that may significantly affect the company's short- and long-term value, and how they might impact on the business.

2.2 Describe the company's policies and procedures for managing risks to short- and long-term value arising from SEE matters. If the annual report and accounts states that the company has no such policies and procedures, the Board should provide reasons for their absence.

2.3 Include information about the extent to which the company has complied with its policies and procedures for managing risks arising from SEE matters.

2.4 Describe the procedures for verification of SEE disclosures. The verification procedure should be such as to achieve a reasonable level of credibility.

3 Towards best practice

Institutional shareholders consider that adherence to the principles outlined above will help companies to develop appropriate policies on corporate social responsibility. The principles should also provide a constructive basis for engagement between companies and their shareholders. Over time this will allow both parties jointly to develop a clear joint understanding of best practice in the handling of social, environmental and ethical matters which will help preserve and enhance value. It is the intention of the ABI to continue regular contact with companies and stakeholders with a view to refining the concept of best practice.

Current understanding of best practice leads to the following conclusions and indications as to how the guidelines should operate:

1 The guidelines are intended to apply to all companies, including small and medium companies. Shareholders recognise both that it may take time for smaller companies to put the appropriate procedures in place, and that even larger companies may not be in an immediate position to comply fully with the principles set out in the guidelines. In the first instance, though, and while the guidelines are still new, they would welcome a statement of intent to comply in the annual report.

2 The cost of managing risks should be proportionate to their significance. Ideally, procedures should be integrated into existing management structures and systems.

3 Statements relating to the guidelines should be made in the annual report, and not separately as part of the summary accounts or on a web site dedicated to social responsibility. In view of the close philosophical linkage between these guidelines and Turnbull reporting, it would make sense to include a brief statement in the Internal Control section of the annual report, although this would not preclude a cross reference to other parts of the report where more detailed disclosure of the type of risks involved and systems for managing those risks may also fit with other content.

4 With regard to the implementation, shareholders are anxious to leave leeway for companies to establish their own systems best suited to their business. However, they believe that, with regard to clause 1.1, best practice would require the full Board to consider the issues on a regular basis, although some on-going detailed work might be delegated to a committee.

5 Examples of initiatives for reducing and managing risks (see 1.4 and 2.2) include regular contact with stakeholders and mechanisms to ensure that appropriate standards are maintained in the supply chain. Evidence of such initiatives would be viewed positively by shareholders.

6 Independent external verification of SEE disclosures would be regarded by shareholders as a highly significant advantage. Credible verification may also be achieved by other means, including internal audit. It would assist shareholders in their assessment of SEE policies if the reason for choosing a particular method of verification were explained in the annual report.

Appendix 1 Questions on social, environmental and ethical matters

In assessing compliance, investors are likely to seek from the annual report answers to the following questions:

1 Has the company made any reference to social, environmental and ethical matters? If so, does the board take these regularly into account?

2 Has the company identified and assessed significant risks and opportunities affecting its short- and long-term value arising from its handling of SEE matters?

3 Does the company state that it has adequate information for identification and assessment?

4 Are systems in place to manage the SEE risks?

5 Are any remuneration incentives relating to the handling of SEE risks included in risk management systems?

6 Does Directors' training include SEE matters?

7 Does the company disclose significant short- and long-term risks and opportunities arising from SEE issues? If so, how many different risks/opportunities are identified?

8 Are policies for managing risks to the company's value described?

9 Are procedures for managing risk described? If not, are reasons for non-disclosure given?

10 Does the Company report on the extent of its compliance with its policies and procedures?

11 Are verification procedures described?

Appendix 2 Questions for investment trusts

1 Is the voting policy of the trust publicly available?

2 Does the voting policy make reference to SEE matters?

3 Is the manager encouraged actively to engage with companies to promote better SEE practice?

Appendix 24
ICSA Model Internal Whistleblowing Procedure

Our assurances to you

The Board and Chief Executive of [Organisation name] are committed to maintaining the highest standards of honesty, openness and accountability and recognises that you have an important role to play in achieving this goal.

Employees will usually be the first to know when someone inside or connected with an organisation is doing something illegal or improper, but often they feel apprehensive about voicing their concerns. This may be because they feel that speaking up would be disloyal to their colleagues or the organisation itself. Or it may be because they do not think that their concerns will be taken seriously because, they are afraid that they will be bullied or dismissed. However, [Organisation name] does not believe that it is in anyone's interests for employees with knowledge of wrongdoing to remain silent.

[Organisation name] takes all malpractice very seriously, whether it is committed by senior managers, staff, suppliers or contractors; this document sets out a procedure by which you can report your concerns to us.

This procedure has been [drawn up in consultation with/endorsed by] [name of trade union/employees' representatives].

What sort of activities should I report using this procedure?

It is impossible to give an exhaustive list of the activities that constitute misconduct or malpractice but, broadly speaking, [organisation name] would expect you to report the following:

- Criminal offences;
- Failure to comply with legal obligations;
- Miscarriages of justice;
- Actions which endanger the health or safety of staff or the public;
- Actions which cause damage to the environment;
- Actions which are intended to conceal any of the above.

It will not always be clear that a particular action falls within one of these categories and you will need to use your own judgement. However, [organisation name] would prefer you to report your concerns rather than keep them to yourself. If you make a report in good faith then, even if it is not confirmed by an investigation, your concern will be valued and appreciated and you will not be liable to disciplinary action. However if you make a false report, maliciously or for personal gain, then you may face disciplinary action.

How do I make a report?

You can make a report orally or in writing (standard report forms are enclosed with this document). [Organisation name] would normally expect you to raise your concerns internally to either:

- your line manager (or his or her superior), or
- [designated senior manager]

Which of these individuals is the more appropriate will depend on the serious of the malpractice and who you think is involved in it. If, under the circumstances, you do not feel comfortable about making a report directly to management, then you can report instead to:

- [name and contact details of designated "independent" person]

Please say if you want to raise the matter in confidence so that appropriate arrangements can be made.

Independent advice

If you are unsure whether to use this procedure or you want independent advice at any stage, you may contact the independent charity Public Concern at Work (see Directory).

External contacts

While we hope that this policy gives you the reassurance you need to raise such matters internally, [organisation name] recognises that there may be circumstances (for example, where the wrongdoing is extremely serious) where it may be appropriate for you to report your concerns to an outside body, such as the police. Public Concern at Work will be able to advise you on such an option and the circumstances in which you may be able to contact an outside body safely.

Do I need proof of wrongdoing to make my report?

[Organisation name] does not expect you to have absolute proof of any misconduct or malpractice that you report. However, you will need to be able to show the reasons for your concern.

Will [Organisation name] protect my identity if I make a report?

[Organisation name] will do everything possible to keep your identity secret, if you so wish. However, there may be circumstances (for example, if your report becomes the subject of a criminal investigation) wherein you may be needed as a witness. Should this be the case we will discuss the matter with you at the earliest opportunity.

How will my report be investigated?

Once you have made a report [Organisation name] will acknowledge receipt of it within [5] working days.

There are, of course, two sides to every story and [organisation name] will need to make preliminary enquiries to decide whether a full investigation is necessary. If such an investigation is necessary then, depending on the nature of the misconduct, your concerns will be either:

- investigated internally (by management, internal audit, personnel) or
- referred to the appropriate external person (for example our external auditors or the police) for investigation.

Subject to any legal constraints, [Organisation name] will inform you of the outcome of the preliminary enquiries, full investigation and any further action that has been taken.

What can I do if I am unhappy with the way [Organisation name] has dealt with my report?

If you are unhappy with the outcome of an investigation [Organisation name] would prefer that you submit another report explaining why this is the case. Your concern will be investigated again if there is good reason to do so.

However, it may be that you do not think that this is appropriate and wish to raise your concern with an external organisation, such as a regulator. It is, of course, open for you to do so provided you have sufficient evidence to support your concern.

[Organisation name] strongly advises that before reporting your concern externally, you seek advice from one of the following:

- [Contact details of employees' representatives];
- Public Concern at Work
  Suite 306
  16 Baldwins Gardens
  London EC1N 7RJ

  Telephone (general enquiries and helpline): 020 7404 6609

  Fax: 020 7404 6576

  E-mail: UK enquiries: whistle@pcaw.co.uk
  UK helpline: helpline@pcaw.co.uk
  UK services: services@pcaw.co.uk

Scottish office

Public Concern at Work
The Nerv Centre
80 Johnstone Avenue
Hillington Business Park
Glasgow, G52 4NZ

Telephone (general): 0141 883 6761

E-mail: ht@pcaw.co.uk

Website: www.pcaw.co.uk

While [Organisation name] cannot guarantee that we will respond to your report in the way that you might wish, we will try to handle the matter fairly and properly. By using this procedure, you will help us to achieve this.

Appendix 25

The Linklaters Matrix: An Overview of Corporate Governance

Note: This matrix has been updated to 9 December 2004.

This matrix is intended merely to highlight issues and not to be comprehensive, nor to provide legal advice.

To receive the latest version as it is published, please email gemma.bishop@linklaters.com or see the link at www.icsapublishing.co.uk/briefings.

Glossary

United Kingdom

ABI Association of British Insurers

APB Auditing Practices Board

ASB Accounting Standards Board

CA 85 Companies Act 1985

CA 85 (IAS) Regulations 2004 Companies Act 1985 (International Accounting Standards and Other Accounting Amendments) Regulations 2004

C(AICE)A Companies (Audit, Investigations and Community Enterprise) Act 2004

CB Draft Companies Bill (July 2002)

CGAA Co-ordinating Group on Audit and Accounting Issues

CGAA Report Final Report of the CGAA (January 2003)

Combined Code Revised version of Combined Code on Corporate Governance dated July 2003 and effective for financial periods beginning on or after 1 November 2003

CP 04/16 Consultation Paper 04/16, "The Listing Review and Implementation of the Prospectus Directive", published by the FSA in October 2004

CP 203 Consultation Paper 203, "Review of the Listing Regime", published by the FSA in October 2003

CSR Corporate social responsibility

DRRR Directors' Remuneration Report Regulations 2002

DTI Department of Trade and Industry

ED/FRED Exposure Draft

FMLC Financial Markets Law Committee, a body established by the Bank of England to identify issues of legal uncertainty affecting the wholesale financial markets and to consider how such issues should be addressed

FRC Financial Reporting Council

FRRP Financial Reporting Review Panel

FRS Financial Reporting Standard

FSA Financial Services Authority

Higgs Review "Review of the role and effectiveness of non-executive directors" by Derek Higgs (January 2003)

ICAEW Institute of Chartered Accountants in England and Wales

ICSA Institute of Chartered Secretaries and Administrators

ISC Institutional Shareholders' Committee

NAPF National Association of Pension Funds

NEDs Non-executive directors

OFR Operating and Financial Review

PIRC Pensions & Investment Research Consultants

Smith Guidance "Guidance on Audit Committees", based on Sir Robert Smith's report and proposed guidance published in January 2003, and appended to the Combined Code

Trade and Industry Committee Report House of Commons Trade and Industry Committee Sixth Report (April 2003)

Turnbull Guidance Guidance on internal control systems published by the ICAEW in September 1999, and appended to the Combined Code

UKLA UK Listing Authority

WP White Paper "Modernising Company Law" CM 5553 (July 2002)

European Union

ARC Accounting Regulatory Committee of EU Member States

CESR Committee of European Securities Regulators

Company Law Action Plan EC Communication entitled "Modernising Company Law and Enhancing Corporate Governance in the European Union" setting out an action plan (May 2003)

EC European Commission

EU European Union

Fair Value Directive Directive 2001/65/EC amending, among others, the Fourth and Seventh Directives as regards the valuation rules for annual and consolidated accounts

Fourth and Seventh Directives Directives 78/660/EEC on the annual accounts of certain types of company and 83/349/EEC on consolidated accounts

IAS International Accounting Standards

IASB International Accounting Standards Board

IFAC International Federation of Accountants

IFRS International Financial Reporting Standards (also comprising IAS)

IOSCO International Organization of Securities Commissions

Modernisation Directive Directive 2003/51/EC amending, among others, the Fourth and Seventh Directives

OECD Organisation for Economic Co-operation and Development

Statutory Audit Directive Proposed directive on statutory audit of annual accounts and consolidated accounts adopted by the Council (December 2004) and referred to the European Parliament under the co-decision procedure

TOD Directive on the harmonisation of transparency requirements for information about issuers with securities admitted to trading on a regulated market (known as the "Transparency Obligations Directive")

United States of America

CERES Coalition for Environmentally Responsible Economies

CII Council of Institutional Investors

Conference Board Conference Board's Commission on Public Trust and Private Enterprise (a committee of the US non-profit research and business membership organisation)

FASB Financial Accounting Standards Board

Nasdaq Nasdaq Stock Market, Inc.

Nasdaq Amendments Nasdaq amendments to corporate governance listing standards approved by the SEC in November 2003

NYSE New York Stock Exchange

NYSE Amendments NYSE amendments to corporate governance listing standards approved by the SEC in November 2003

PCAOB The Public Company Accounting Oversight Board

SEC Securities and Exchange Commission

SOX Sarbanes–Oxley Act of 2002

Directors *Directors' general duties*

United Kingdom	European Union	United States of America
Directors' duties are largely embedded in common law, with some statutory overlay. Statutory codification of directors' duties, applicable to all directors, was proposed in WP. Schedule 2 of CB set out a statutory statement of general principles. Duties would be owed to the company "in place of corresponding equitable and common law rules". It is not yet clear what the consequences of breach would be. Duties of directors to creditors or on insolvency would not be covered. DTI consultative document "Company Law. Flexibility and Accessibility" (May 2004) indicates that these proposals will be revived in a new Companies Bill expected to be tabled in 2005. The Combined Code refers to the need for companies to arrange appropriate insurance cover in respect of legal action against directors (Provision A1.5). ICSA published a guidance note on directors' and officers' insurance (September 2003). Sections 19 and 20 C(AICE)A amend CA 85 to permit companies to indemnify directors in respect of proceedings brought by third parties and to permit companies to pay directors' legal costs as they are incurred. This follows concerns about the restricted nature of the indemnity permitted under Section 310 CA 85, the inadequacy of some directors' and officers' insurance policies and cases such as *Equitable Life Assurance Society v Roger Bowley and others* (October 2003) which demonstrated that it would be very difficult for directors to obtain relief from liability from the courts under Section 727 CA 85 without their case proceeding to a full trial. The amendments are expected to come into force on 1 April 2005.	The Company Law Action Plan sets out a proposal for a directive in the medium term (2006–8) which would include a wrongful trading rule whereby directors would be held personally accountable for the consequences of a company's failure if it was foreseeable that the company could not continue to pay its debts and the directors did not decide either to rescue the company and ensure payment or to put it into liquidation. TOD requires EU Member States to make directors of issuers of securities traded on an EU regulated market liable for annual reports, half yearly reports and interim financial statements they publish in the EU. Since the purpose of the Directive seems to be that published reports should inform the investment decisions of the public, there is considerable concern that the Directive may overturn existing principles of English law, making directors liable not just to shareholders (as at present) but also to potential investors. FMLC has asked the DTI to clarify how it proposes to implement the Directive. EC's proposed directive to amend the Fourth and Seventh Directives (October 2004) confirms the collective responsibility of board members towards the company for the financial and other key information that they publish in their annual report and accounts. The proposals apply to all types of company incorporated in the EU, not just listed ones. For both TOD and the proposed directive to amend the Fourth and Seventh Directives, Member States are required to have appropriate sanctions and liability rules for failure to comply with accounting rules. The proposed directive to amend the Fourth and Seventh Directives adds further confusion to the question of who is liable for financial information and to whom.	Directors' duties are generally governed by the laws of a company's state of incorporation. No general federal codification of directors' duties exists. Under Delaware law, companies may limit or exclude the liability of directors for breach of duty or due care. In addition, case law has evolved to provide relief for directors from personal liability if they had addressed their minds to the issues involved, were free from personal conflicts and had acted in good faith in what they saw as being the best commercial interests of the company at the time (the so-called "business judgement rule").

Directors *Non-executive directors*

United Kingdom	European Union	United States of America
Provisions of Combined Code relevant to NEDs include: • except for smaller companies (i.e. companies below the FTSE 350 throughout the previous reporting year), at least half the board, excluding the chairman, should comprise NEDs determined by the board to be independent. Smaller companies should have at least two independent NEDs (A3.2) • a new, more detailed definition of independence (A3.1) • the chairman must meet the criteria for independence on appointment (A2.2) • the roles of the chairman and chief executive should be separate and documented (A2.1) • a chief executive should not go on to become chairman of the same company. If "exceptionally" the board decides otherwise, it should consult major shareholders in advance and set out its reasons at the time of appointment and in the next annual report (A2.2) • no individual should be appointed to a second chairmanship of a FTSE 100 company (A4.3) • the board should not agree to a full-time executive director taking on more than one non-executive directorship in a FTSE 100 company nor the chairmanship of such a company (A4.5) • any term beyond six years for a NED should be subject to "particularly rigorous review" and should take into account the need for progressive refreshing of the board. NEDs may serve longer than nine years, subject to annual re-election, although this could be relevant to the board's determination of whether the NED is independent (A7.2) • an explanation should be given in the annual report if neither an external search consultancy nor open	EC adopted a Recommendation on independent directors and board committees (October 2004). Among other things it sets out a general statement of independence (freedom from business, family or other relationship that creates a conflict of interest such as to jeopardise the exercise of free judgement). Minimum criteria for independence and the suggestion that independent directors should undertake to maintain their independence of judgement, remain free of conflicts and clearly express their opposition if they believe that a decision of the board may harm the company are included as guidance and contained in an annex of the Recommendation. In most respects the measures set out in the Recommendation are similar to, or slightly less onerous than, the Combined Code. For example: • no proportion of independent NEDs is specified although this should be "sufficient" to ensure that any material conflict of interest involving directors is properly dealt with • there is no requirement to separate the roles of the chairman and the chief executive (the separation of roles is just "one of the possible ways" to ensure that the executive responsibilities of the chairman do not stand in the way of his ability to exercise executive oversight). However, the measures appear to go beyond the Combined Code in the following respects: • the Recommendation is expressed to apply to all companies with securities admitted to a regulated market, including non-EU companies with a primary listing. The Combined Code only applies to companies incorporated in the UK	NYSE/Nasdaq Amendments promote greater independence at board level: • a majority of the board of directors must consist of independent directors within the meaning of a tightened definition of "independence" • non-management or independent directors must meet on a regular basis without management or non-independent directors present. The Conference Board recommended: • the separation of the roles of chairman and CEO, or at least a lead or presiding independent director • maintaining a substantial majority of independent directors on the board (this goes beyond NYSE/Nasdaq Amendments, although the Conference Board has not specified what "substantial" means). Nasdaq requires listed companies to certify that they have adopted a formal written charter or board resolution addressing the nomination process and is considering whether to require continuing education for all directors. NYSE requires listed companies to adopt and disclose formal corporate governance guidelines which address director qualification standards, director orientation and continuing education as well as board evaluation. Accommodations/exemptions to the NYSE/Nasdaq Amendments are available to non-US companies – see Corporate governance codes below.

Directors *Non-executive directors (continued)*

United Kingdom	European Union	United States of America
advertising has been used in the appointment of a chairman or NED (A4.6) • the nomination committee should prepare a job specification for the appointment of a chairman, including an assessment of the time commitment expected. A chairman's other significant commitments should be disclosed to the board before appointment and in the annual report (A4.3) • the chairman should ensure that new directors receive a full, formal and tailored induction on joining the board. As part of this, the company should offer to major shareholders the opportunity to meet a new NED (A5.1). The company secretary is responsible for facilitating induction and assisting with professional development, under the direction of the chairman (Supporting Principle A5) • the board should state in the annual report how performance evaluation of the board, its committees and individual directors, including NEDs, has been conducted (A6.1) (this procedure should be "formal and rigorous" and conducted annually (Main Principle A6)). See also Corporate governance committees below.	• the detail of disclosure about directors' other time commitments and the requirement for a director to undertake to limit the number of any professional commitments, including directorships held in other companies, to the extent that the proper performance of his duties is assured. The Recommendation is non-binding but Member States are invited to take the necessary measures, either through a "comply or explain" approach or by legislation, to promote its application by 30 June 2006 and to notify the EC of any such measures taken. The EC will closely monitor the situation to determine the need for additional measures.	
Guidance on liability of NEDs contained in Schedule B of the Combined Code sets out matters relevant in assessing the knowledge, skill and diligence that a NED may be expected to exercise. ICSA published a Guidance Note on the induction of directors (February 2003) and a Guidance Note on due diligence for prospective directors (July 2003) to support the induction checklist and due diligence checklist appended to the Combined Code.		

Directors *Non-executive directors (continued)*

United Kingdom	European Union	United States of America
ICSA has also published a Guidance Note on the roles of the chairman, chief executive and senior independent director (September 2004) to clarify the Combined Code. It includes specimen descriptions of roles for each, an alternative statement on the division of responsibilities between the chairman and the chief executive and a draft board responsibilities statement. Unsurprisingly, PIRC's Shareholder Voting Guidelines (February 2004) demand tougher policies than the Combined Code in some respects, e.g. PIRC's definition of independence includes additional factors and it wants board nomination committees to be made up solely of independent directors (i.e. excluding the chairman). At the invitation of the DTI, Laura D'Andrea Tyson chaired a group to investigate widening the pool of candidates for NED appointments. Its findings are set out in "The Tyson Report on the Recruitment and Development of Non-Executive Directors" (June 2003). This recommended: • a more rigorous and transparent selection process • more and better training and evaluation • research and management to encourage greater board diversity, including an annual census to measure diversity and encourage progress. The first two recommendations are addressed in part by the Combined Code.		
Notwithstanding the desire to increase diversity, there is some evidence from surveys (e.g. Taylor Wessing June 2003, Ernst & Young January 2004) to suggest a reluctance to take on NED roles because of increasing regulation and concerns about liability.		Korn/Ferry survey of directors worldwide (November 2004) shows that the percentage of American respondents declining board invitations because of increased liability has doubled from 13% in 2002 to 29% in 2004.

Directors *Non-executive directors (continued)*

United Kingdom	European Union	United States of America
Against this background, changes to the CA 85 to permit companies to indemnify directors in respect of proceedings brought by third parties and to permit companies to pay directors' legal costs as they are incurred have been enacted by Sections 19 and 20 C(AICE)A and are expected to come into force on 1 April 2005. See Directors' general duties above. DTI published "Building Better Boards" (December 2004) building on the recommendations of the Higgs Review and the Tyson Report. It sets out the business case for diversity and better practice in the boardroom, cites evidence of companies that have benefited from boardroom diversity and outlines Government and business-led initiatives to develop the talent pool.		
Directors' remuneration		
DRRR (now in Schedule 7A CA 85) came into force on 1 August 2002 and apply to quoted companies (i.e. UK incorporated companies that are UK, EU or Nasdaq/NYSE listed but not AIM listed companies) with financial years ended on or after 31 December 2002. They require quoted companies to publish a report on directors' pay as part of the annual reporting cycle on which shareholders will vote at each AGM. The vote of shareholders is advisory only. Report to include: • details of individual director's pay packages • justification for any compensation packages given in preceding year • details of the board's consideration of directors' pay • membership of the remuneration committee • the name of any remuneration consultants used	EC adopted a Recommendation on remuneration for directors of listed companies (October 2004). The Recommendation advises that shareholders be kept informed about a company's policy on directors' remuneration as well as how much individual directors are earning and in what form; and that they should have adequate control over these matters and over share-based remuneration schemes. It invites Member States to adopt measures in four areas: • an annual statement in relation to remuneration policy should be released by all listed companies containing information about the breakdown of remuneration (fixed and variable), performance criteria and the parameters for bonus schemes and/or non-cash benefits. Commercially sensitive information need not be disclosed	NYSE/Nasdaq Amendments require independent committees to play a greater role in remuneration policies: • compensation and nominating/corporate governance committees must consist solely of independent directors (NYSE) or committee functions must be carried out by a majority of independent directors meeting in "executive sessions" (Nasdaq) • independent directors must determine, or recommend to the board for determination, executive officer compensation and must select, or recommend to the board for selection, director nominees (Nasdaq) • compensation committee must determine and approve the CEO's compensation, make

Directors *Directors' remuneration (continued)*

United Kingdom	European Union	United States of America
• a performance graph on the company's performance in comparison with an appropriate share market index • a forward-looking statement of policy on directors' pay, including details of any incentive and share option schemes. The ABI published revised guidelines on executive remuneration (December 2004). Among other things, these recommend that companies publish in advance the approach they will take to adjusting performance hurdles in the transition to IFRS. They also include the ABI/NAPF joint best practice guidelines on contracts and severance pay, last revised in December 2003. The NAPF published its 2004 Corporate Governance Policy (December 2003) setting out good practice principles and voting guidelines on a number of issues, including remuneration policy and committee. Provisions of the Combined Code relevant to directors' remuneration include: • remuneration committee should carefully consider what compensation commitments their directors' terms of appointment would entail in the event of early termination to avoid rewarding poor performance (B1.5). See also Corporate governance committees below • notice or general contract periods should be one year or less. If it is necessary to offer longer periods to new directors recruited from outside, such periods should reduce to one year or less after the initial period (B1.6) • shareholder approval for all long-term incentive schemes (as defined in the Listing Rules) and significant changes to existing schemes, save as permitted by the Listing Rules (B2.4).	• directors' remuneration should be on the agenda at the shareholders' general meeting and, to increase accountability, should be the subject of a vote (either binding or advisory) • disclosure of the remuneration of individual directors should include detailed information such as remuneration and/or emoluments, shares or rights to share options, contributions to supplementary pension schemes and any loans, advances or guarantees to each director • shares and share option schemes for directors should be subject to prior approval of shareholders at the AGM. The Recommendation is expressed to apply to all companies with securities admitted to a regulated market, including non-EU companies with a primary listing. The Recommendation is non-binding but Member States are invited to take the necessary measures, either through a "comply or explain" approach or by legislation, to promote its application by 30 June 2006 and to notify the EC of any such measures taken. The EC will closely monitor the situation to determine the need for additional measures. In many respects, the measures contained in the Recommendation will be familiar to UK companies and it is unlikely that the Government will suggest changes to UK practice.	recommendations to the board with respect to non-CEO compensation, incentive compensation plans and equity-based plans, produce a compensation committee report to be included in the company's annual proxy statement or annual report and evaluate its performance annually (NYSE). NYSE/Nasdaq rules call for additional shareholder involvement. Equity compensation plans, with minor exemptions, are now subject to a shareholder approval requirement. Accommodations/exemptions are available to non-US companies. The CII adopted a revised executive compensation policy in October 2004. The policy emphasises compensation for performance over the long term and goes beyond what the SEC currently requires in terms of disclosure. Specifically, the CII calls for more transparent disclosure in relation to benchmarking, executive salaries, annual as well as long-term incentive compensation, dilution, stock options, perquisites, employment contracts, retirement arrangements and stock ownership requirements. Staff at the SEC have also recently called for more transparency with respect to the disclosure of executive compensation (October 2004).

Directors *Directors' remuneration (continued)*

United Kingdom	European Union	United States of America
DTI consultation paper "Rewards for Failure" Directors' Remuneration – Contracts, Performance and Severance (June 2003) published to deal with concerns about directors who receive excessive compensation when they depart a company even though the company has performed poorly. Following the consultation, Patricia Hewitt, the Secretary of State for Trade and Industry, confirmed by a written statement to Parliament (February 2004) that there would be no immediate change to company law. Instead, the DTI commissioned a detailed assessment of compliance with the DRRR in the course of the 2004 AGM season and an assessment of changes in remuneration practices. While the Secretary of State indicated that the best way forward would be through the application and development of best practice in negotiating contracts which deal with performance issues effectively, action would be taken if the 2004 AGM season demonstrated that further changes of law were required.		

Corporate governance codes

United Kingdom	European Union	United States of America
The Combined Code is the cornerstone of corporate governance in the UK. The "comply or explain" principle applies to UK incorporated listed companies and is embedded in paragraph 12.43A of the UKLA's Listing Rules. The DTI has stated that it intends that the Combined Code will remain non-statutory (WP 5.12).	In the Company Law Action Plan, the EC rejected the creation of a single European code of corporate governance but proposed that the EU should adopt a common approach covering a few essential rules and ensure adequate co-ordination and convergence of national corporate governance codes. It has now established the European Corporate Governance Forum	There is no unitary corporate governance code. Corporate governance is covered by state law, federal law and regulation and exchange listing requirements. Also, NYSE Amendments require companies to: • adopt and disclose a code of business conduct and ethics (see Corporate social responsibility below)

Corporate governance codes *(continued)*

United Kingdom	European Union	United States of America
The FRC is responsible for the Combined Code and for fostering high standards of corporate governance generally. It established a corporate governance committee (March 2004) to keep corporate governance developments under review, monitor the operation of the Combined Code and consider the case for issuing any clarifications, where appropriate. In CP 04/16 (October 2004), the UKLA indicates that it will not be extending the obligation to "comply or explain" against the Combined Code to non-UK incorporated companies with a primary listing. It had previously considered doing this in CP 203 (October 2003). The Combined Code was revised by the FRC in 2003 following the Higgs Review and Sir Robert Smith's report and proposed guidance on audit committees. The revised version of the Combined Code is effective for accounting periods beginning on or after 1 November 2003. It has been restructured to comprise: • Main and Supporting Principles (a UK incorporated listed company will have to state in its annual report how it has applied these) • Provisions (with which a UK incorporated listed company must either comply or explain non-compliance in its annual report). Appended to the Combined Code are related guidance and good practice suggestions, including the Turnbull Guidance, the Smith Guidance, guidance for the chairman and for NEDs and various checklists. The FRC announced (June 2004) that it intends to undertake a regular review of the Combined Code to ensure that it is working effectively and identify if any amendments are needed. A formal review is planned for the second half of 2006.	(October 2004) comprising 15 experts to take this forward. The Forum will meet two to three times a year and will present an annual report to the EC. The EC has indicated that this is not a precursor to a European-wide corporate governance code. The EC has published a proposal to amend the Fourth and Seventh Directives to require EU-incorporated listed companies to include a statement on corporate governance in their annual report and accounts. The amendments will also make unlisted companies' transactions with related parties more transparent and ensure that all companies provide full information about off-balance sheet arrangements. The EC adopted a Recommendation on independent directors and board committees (October 2004). It is generally similar to, or slightly less onerous than, the Combined Code (see Non-executive directors above and Corporate governance committees below). The governments of 30 OECD countries have approved a revised version of the OECD's Principles of Corporate Governance (April 2004). The principles advocate, among other things, facilitation of the exercise of shareholder rights, an effective role for shareholders in executive compensation and improved transparency and disclosure requirements to counter conflicts of interest.	• adopt and disclose formal corporate governance guidelines that include, inter alia, director qualification standards, director responsibilities, director access to management and outside advisers, director compensation and management succession • establish an internal audit function • certify annually as to compliance with NYSE corporate governance listing standards. Nasdaq Amendments also require the adoption and disclosure of a code of conduct, which must be applicable to all directors, officers and employees and must comply with the definition of a "code of ethics" under SOX § 406. Current rules permit the NYSE and Nasdaq to exempt non-US companies listed on NYSE/Nasdaq from corporate governance requirements. However, NYSE/Nasdaq Amendments impose the following additional requirements:

Corporate governance codes *(continued)*

United Kingdom	European Union	United States of America
The FRC established a committee (July 2004) under the chairmanship of Douglas Flint to review the Turnbull Guidance. The committee published a consultation paper seeking views on the effectiveness of the Turnbull Guidance (December 2004) and plans to issue a further consultation on draft revised guidance in mid-2005. The intention is that any revised guidance will take effect for accounting periods commencing on or after 1 January 2006. The FRC has published for comment a draft guide to UK and Irish companies registered with the SEC on the use of the Turnbull Guidance to comply with the SEC requirements to report on internal controls over financial reporting (October 2004). It hopes to publish the guide in final form in December 2004. UK and other foreign registrant companies need to comply with the SEC requirements for reporting years ending on or after 15 July 2005. Minor, largely consequential, changes have been made to paragraph 12.43A of the Listing Rules in relation to the provisions of the Combined Code that auditors are required to review to reflect the new Combined Code. The changes took effect on 1 November 2004. Notwithstanding the Government's statement about the non-statutory nature of the Combined Code, there has been some trend towards statutory codification (e.g. the DRRR). There also continues to be an overlay by institutional investors (e.g. the ISC Statement of Principles and PIRC's Shareholder Voting Guidelines). However, there remains a helpful focus on the Combined Code (e.g. the inclusion of a cross-reference to the ISC Statement of Principles in the Combined Code).		• annual disclosure of any significant ways in which a non-US company's corporate governance practices differ from NYSE/Nasdaq listing standards (NYSE/Nasdaq) • exemption from corporate governance requirements upon establishment of home country practice (NYSE) or showing that a listing standard is contrary to a law, rule, regulation or generally accepted business practice in the non-US company's home country (Nasdaq).

Corporate governance committees

United Kingdom	European Union	United States of America
Standing committees to address particular concerns have been a feature of UK corporate governance since the Cadbury Report (1992). Recent developments: Audit committees See Audit committees below. Remuneration committees Provisions of the Combined Code relevant to remuneration committees include: • the board should establish a remuneration committee of at least three (or, in the case of smaller companies below the FTSE 350 throughout the previous reporting year, two) members who should all be independent NEDs (B2.1) • the remuneration committee should recommend and monitor the level and structure of remuneration for senior management in addition to the remuneration for all executive directors and the chairman. "Senior management" should be determined by the board but should normally include the first layer of management below board level (B2.2) • the remuneration committee should carefully consider what compensation commitments their directors' terms of appointment would entail in the event of early termination to avoid rewarding poor performance. They should also take a robust line on reducing compensation to reflect the departing directors' obligations to mitigate loss (B1.5).	The EC has adopted a Recommendation to reinforce the presence and role of independent NEDs on listed company boards (October 2004). It focuses on the role of independent directors in areas where executive directors may have conflicts of interest and recommends standards for the qualifications, commitment and independence of NEDs. The measures contained in the Recommendation tend to be similar or slightly less onerous than the Combined Code. However the scope is wider in that the Recommendation is expressed to apply to all companies with securities admitted to a regulated market, including non-EU companies with a primary listing. The Combined Code only applies to companies incorporated in the UK. EC invites Member States to take the necessary measures to promote the Recommendation by 30 June 2006 and notify the EC of any such measures taken. The EC will closely monitor the situation to determine the need for additional measures. Although the Recommendation is non-binding, audit committees will be made mandatory for certain companies once the Statutory Audit Directive comes into force. See Audit committees below.	Compensation and nomination committees Under NYSE/Nasdaq Amendments, the compensation committee and nominating/corporate governance committee must: • consist solely of independent directors (NYSE) or committee functions must be carried out by a majority of independent directors meeting in "executive sessions" (Nasdaq) • adopt and disclose formal charters (NYSE) or certification of adoption of charter or board resolution addressing nominations process (Nasdaq). Accommodations/exemptions to the NYSE/Nasdaq Amendments are available to non-US companies. The Conference Board also recommended that the nominating/corporate governance committee should consist solely of independent directors and should be responsible for: • nominating qualified candidates to stand for election to the board • monitoring all matters involving corporate governance • making recommendations to the full board for action in governance matters. Although non-US issuers are exempt, SEC Rules adopted in November 2003 require US listed companies to provide more robust disclosure of nominating committee processes in their annual proxy statements to shareholders, including: • whether the company has a separate nominating committee and, if not, why not • whether members of the nominating committee satisfy independence requirements

Corporate governance committees *(continued)*

United Kingdom	European Union	United States of America
Nomination committees Provisions of the Combined Code relevant to nomination committees include: • the nomination committee should consist of a majority of independent NEDs (A4.1) • the chairman should be allowed to chair the nomination committee but should stand down when the committee discusses appointment of a new chairman (A4.1) • the nomination committee should evaluate the balance of skills, knowledge and experience on the board and prepare a description of the role and capabilities required for a particular appointment in light of this (A4.2). Guidance prepared by ICSA on the principal duties of the nomination and remuneration committees has been appended to the Combined Code as a suggestion for good practice. Terms of reference to support this guidance have been updated by ICSA (October 2003). Other committees include risk committees which were established by some companies following the Turnbull Guidance. UK companies generally do not have US-style disclosure committees although the UKLA's guidance on price-sensitive information suggests the maintenance of procedures for the identification and dissemination of such information. In practice, the audit committee may fulfil the role of a disclosure committee. Provision C3.2 of the Combined Code provides that the audit committee should monitor the integrity of a company's financial statements and any formal announcements relating to financial performance, reviewing significant financial reporting judgements contained in them. ICSA provides guidance (September 2004) on terms of reference for an executive committee, intended as a forum where the chief executive can consider major operational decisions.	The EC had originally proposed that the nomination committee should be composed mainly of executive directors because they were best placed to know the qualities required for a board position. The EC changed its view following feedback on the Company Law Action Plan, and its Recommendation to reinforce the presence and role of independent NEDs provides that the nomination committee should be composed of a majority of independent NEDs or supervisory directors. The chief executive must be adequately consulted by, and entitled to submit proposals to, the nomination committee and can be a member of the committee if non-independent members are permitted by national law.	• the company's process for identifying and evaluating candidates to be nominated as directors (including the involvement of third parties and minimum qualifications and standards for director nominees) • whether a company considers director nominees put forward by shareholders and, if so, its process • whether the company has rejected candidates put forward by large, long-term shareholders or groups of shareholders. Disclosure committees SEC Rules addressing SOX certification requirements extend to "disclosure controls and procedures", i.e. procedures to ensure that required information is recorded, processed, summarised and reported on a timely basis. CEOs/CFOs must certify as to their evaluation of disclosure controls and procedures and the inclusion in the filing of their conclusions about the effectiveness of such controls. The SEC has recommended establishing a disclosure committee to assist in establishing controls and procedures as well as to oversee the preparation of disclosure. Members might include the general counsel, heads of major subsidiaries, the head of investor relations and risk management staff. Qualified legal compliance committees The SEC has provided that issuers may establish qualified legal compliance committees ("QLCCs") as an alternative means of addressing "reporting requirements" for attorneys mandated by SOX. Attorneys obliged to report evidence of a material violation of US securities laws or a breach of fiduciary duty or similar violation by a client, or by any officer, director, employee or agent of that client, may report to the QLCC. A QLCC would be composed of at least one member of the audit committee and two or more additional independent board members.

Shareholder activism

United Kingdom	European Union	United States of America
The Myners Report, "Institutional Investment in the UK: A Review" (March 2001), recommended that those responsible for pension scheme investment should: • actively monitor and communicate with the management of investee companies • exercise shareholder votes where these would enhance the value of an investment. The Government accepted the report recommendations and proposed an express statutory duty to use shareholder powers to intervene in investee companies where this was in a pension scheme's best interests (Joint HM Treasury and Department for Work and Pensions consultation paper, "Encouraging Shareholder Activism" (February 2002)). However, in October 2002, ISC published a "Statement of Principles" setting out strengthened responsibilities of institutional shareholders and agents and outlining best practice. Institutional investors are expected to: • maintain and publish policies of active engagement in companies in which they invest • monitor performance of and maintain appropriate dialogue with those companies • intervene when necessary • evaluate the impact of their policies and report back to clients/beneficial owners. The Government stated that it would review the impact of the ISC Statement of Principles after two years to determine whether a non-legislative approach has been successful in delivering change. Also in October 2002, Hermes published its own set of principles, "What shareholders expect of public	As part of its plans to implement the Company Law Action Plan, the EC has published a consultation paper (September 2004) seeking views on key elements of a future directive on shareholders' rights. The main issues on which the EC is seeking responses are: • whether the directive should apply only to listed companies, with Member States being invited to extend the measures to non-listed companies • how to ensure that investors in shares who are not recognised as shareholders (e.g. because they hold their shares through one or more intermediaries) can control the voting rights over the shares • the dissemination of information before the general meeting and the possible need for minimum standards to ensure that all shareholders, irrespective of where they live, get information in time • the criteria for participation in general meetings and the removal of overly cumbersome criteria, such as share blocking requirements • possible minimum standards for the right to ask questions and table resolutions • possible measures to enable shareholders to vote by post, electronically or by proxy • the dissemination of information following the general meeting and the possible need for confirmation that votes have been cast as instructed. The Company Law Action Plan rejected a requirement for institutional investors to exercise voting rights but proposes to require institutional investors to disclose their investment and voting policies and, at the request of beneficiaries, their voting records in individual cases. Proposals are expected in 2005.	Regulations under the Employment Retirement Income Security Act of 1974 state that the fiduciary responsibility of managing employee benefit plan assets consisting of equity securities extends to the exercise of voting rights attaching to those securities. SEC Rules (January 2003) require SEC-registered investment advisers with authority over client proxies to: • adopt voting policies and procedures designed to ensure that the adviser votes in the best interest of clients • disclose voting policies and procedures to clients. SEC-registered management investment companies are also required to disclose proxy voting policies and procedures, as well as voting records (SEC Rules adopted January 2003). The SEC has proposed rules (October 2003) which would make it easier for shareholders to nominate candidates to corporate boards by getting their names on the corporate proxy ballots. Final action has not yet been taken on those rules. SEC Rules (November 2003) require enhanced disclosure regarding shareholder communications with directors, including whether a company has a process for communications by shareholders to directors, and if not, why not and disclosure of director attendance at annual meetings. Non-US issuers are exempt from these rules. There was evidence of increased shareholder activism in terms of the numbers of (and the profile of) "vote-no" compaigns and shareholder proposals during the 2004 proxy season.

Shareholder activism *(continued)*

United Kingdom	European Union	United States of America
companies – and what companies should expect of their investors". The Combined Code encourages closer relations between major shareholders and NEDs, e.g.: • the chairman should discuss governance and strategy with major shareholders (Provision D1.1) • the senior independent director should attend sufficient meetings with a range of major shareholders to help develop a balanced understanding of their concerns (Provision D1.1) • the chairman should ensure the views of shareholders are communicated to the board as a whole (Provision D1.1) • the board should state in the annual report the steps taken to ensure that members of the board, especially NEDs, develop an understanding of the views of major shareholders e.g. through face to face contact, analysts' or brokers' briefings and surveys of shareholder opinion (Provision D1.2) • the company should offer to major shareholders the opportunity to meet a new NED (Provision A5.1). The Combined Code also endorses more active engagement by institutional investors: • institutional shareholders should apply the ISC Statement of Principles (Supporting Principle E1) • institutional shareholders should consider carefully explanations for departure from the Combined Code. They should give an explanation to the company, in writing where appropriate, and be prepared to enter into a dialogue if they do not accept the company's position (Supporting Principle E2).		

Shareholder activism *(continued)*

United Kingdom	European Union	United States of America
ICSA has published guidance notes on: • voting at general meetings which sets out the pros and cons of voting on a show of hands and voting on a poll (December 2003) • corporate representation at general meetings (March 2004) which outlines the differences between proxies and corporate representatives and attempts to clarify the law and practice relating to corporate representation. Paul Myners published a review of the impediments to voting UK shares for the Shareholder Voting Working Group (which includes, among others, the ABI, DTI, ICSA, NAPF and PIRC) (January 2004). The recommendations include: • issuers in the FTSE 350, investment managers, custodians and proxy voting agencies should introduce the necessary system changes so that electronic voting capabilities are universally available as soon as practicable • institutional investors should report to clients how they have voted but there should be no mandatory public disclosure • best practice should be to call a poll on all resolutions at company meetings • the FSA should make it a listing requirement for the results of polls to be disclosed. ICSA has updated the following guidance notes to reflect Paul Myners' review: • Disclosing Proxy Votes (August 2004) which sets out best practice on how companies should publish proxy votes and recommends that voting figures should be provided for resolutions decided on a poll as well as on a show of hands		

Shareholder activism *(continued)*

United Kingdom	European Union	United States of America
• Proxy Voting – Abstentions (August 2004) which recommends that proxy forms should include a vote withheld option. DTI consultative document "Company Law. Flexibility and Accessibility" (May 2004) indicates that a new Companies Bill will contain reforms to the rules governing company meetings, e.g. to enhance the rights of proxies. FTSE and Institutional Shareholder Services have announced their intention to launch the first corporate governance index (March 2004). This is expected to be launched in phases beginning in the fourth quarter of 2004.		

Corporate social responsibility

United Kingdom	European Union	United States of America
Initiatives in CSR include: • appointment by the Government of a minister for CSR (March 2000) (currently Nigel Griffiths MP) and the launch of the "Business and Society" initiative (March 2001), publicising examples of good business practice and giving advice and information on CSR • launch of FTSE4Good (July 2001) – a share index with selection criteria which cover working towards environmental sustainability, developing positive relationships with stakeholders and upholding and supporting human rights. There is a consultation on changes to the criteria (December 2004)	EC Green Paper "Promoting a European framework for corporate social responsibility" (July 2001) fell short of proposing legislation but promised active consideration of future legislative action. EC Recommendation (May 2001) (non-binding) outlined how firms can report on their environmental performance, costs, risks and liabilities. EC Communication (July 2002) set out key principles and strategy for the promotion of CSR in the EU. The EC launched the European Multi-Stakeholder Forum on Corporate Social Responsibility in October 2002 to bring together companies and other stakeholders to exchange good practices and assess the appropriateness of establishing common guiding principles.	Litigation Cases have been brought under the Alien Tort Claims Act of 1789 calling for corporations to adopt minimum international standards throughout their operations. The Alien Tort Claims Act gives US courts jurisdiction to hear cases of human rights abuses including slave labour, genocide, torture and extra-judicial murder occurring across the globe so long as the court has personal jurisdiction over the defendant. For example: • in September 2000, a Federal Appeals Court ruled that Shell could be sued in the US for human rights violations in Nigeria

Corporate social responsibility *(continued)*

United Kingdom	European Union	United States of America
• publication by Business in the Community (a movement of over 700 member companies committed to improving their impact on society) of the second edition of the Corporate Responsibility Index (March 2004) • the publication of a draft global framework setting out the Government's approach to CSR at the international level (March 2004) • the launch by the DTI of a new website on CSR which refers to key projects and initiatives which the Government is supporting and the publication by the DTI of a report "Corporate Social Responsibility: A Government Update" which outlines progress towards the Government's goal of seeing CSR become part of mainstream business practice (June 2004) • the launch, sponsored by the Government, of a CSR academy to provide advice and support to companies to enable them to develop CSR education and training programmes (July 2004). Business in the Community's "Awards for Excellence" given to companies who have demonstrated outstanding examples of best business practice (most recent awards July 2004).	EU Council Resolution (February 2003) called upon Member States to promote CSR at national level and to integrate CSR into national policies and their own management. European Parliament Report (April 2003) on EC Communication called on the EC to submit a White Paper and recommended that the European Multi-Stakeholder Forum should address small and medium-sized companies and that environmental, development, enterprise and social aspects of CSR should be treated with equal emphasis. Modernisation Directive (June 2003) requires large and medium-sized companies to provide an analysis of the development and performance of their business in their annual reports, describing the principal risks and uncertainties they face and providing financial and non-financial performance indicators such as environmental and employee information. Member States may exempt medium-sized companies from certain non-financial requirements. The European Multi-Stakeholder Forum presented its final report to the EC (June 2004). The EC is expected to produce a Communication on CSR in early 2005.	• in cases brought against Gap and Chevron the plaintiffs have alleged that working conditions violated employees' human rights • claims against Texaco were brought based on the environmental impact of operations in Ecuador.
Government policy is to encourage companies to report on topics such as CSR and sustainability on a voluntary basis. There are a growing number of disclosure guidelines, including: • ABI "Disclosure Guidelines on Social Responsibility" (February 2003) call on companies to disclose in their annual reports that their boards have	Other international initiatives include: • the Global Reporting Initiative, an independent body, which aims to develop and disseminate globally applicable Sustainability Reporting Guidelines. These Guidelines are for voluntary use by organisations for reporting on the economic, environmental and social dimensions of their activities, products and services. GRI is an official	Reporting Initiatives CERES, a coalition of social investors, shareholder proxy activists and environmental organisations, aims to encourage corporations to achieve specified environmental goals by persuading companies to report to CERES on a company's environmental impact in a standard form. The CERES principles

Corporate social responsibility *(continued)*

United Kingdom	European Union	United States of America
assessed the business and reputational risks arising from the way they manage social, ethical and environmental issues, and that these risks are being managed appropriately • FORGE Guidance on Corporate Social Responsibility Management and Reporting for the Financial Services Sector launched by the ABI, British Bankers' Association and eight leading financial institutions (known as the FORGE Group) in November 2002 • General Guidelines on Environmental Reporting (November 2001) published by the Department of the Environment, Food and Rural Affairs • PIRC's environmental reporting guidelines contained in its annual Shareholder Voting Guidelines (latest edition February 2004) • Business in the Community's "Indicators that count", a report on indicators found useful and measurable as a starting point for measuring and reporting social and environmental impact, published July 2003. Disclosure requirements have also been imposed on investors. The Occupational Pension Schemes (Investment and Assignment, Forfeiture, Bankruptcy etc.) Amendment Regulations 1999 require pension funds to disclose in their Statement of Investment Principles the extent to which they take social, ethical or environmental issues into account in their investment decisions. There is a need for harmonisation and rationalisation. Investors criticise the type of reporting resulting from the different guidelines as inconsistent and ineffective and companies question the demands placed on them by the detailed and overlapping questionnaires they are	collaborating centre of the United Nations Environment Programme (UNEP) and works in co-operation with UN Secretary-General Kofi Annan's Global Compact • the OECD Guidelines for Multinational Enterprises, recommendations addressed by governments to multinational enterprises. They provide voluntary principles and standards for responsible business conduct in areas including employment and industrial relations, human rights, environment, information disclosure, combating bribery, consumer interests, science and technology, competition, and taxation.	require that companies commit to and report their compliance with the following environmental issues: • protection of the biosphere • sustainable use of natural resources • reduction and disposal of waste • energy conservation • risk reduction • safe products and services • environmental restoration. Companies that adopt the principles are expected to keep the public informed of their stance on environmental matters and conduct regular environmental audits of their practices. Codes of ethics Developments in the US have accelerated moves to create regulatory codes of ethics for directors which overlay corporate governance codes and impose overriding standards of behaviour. For example, the SEC has issued rules under SOX § 406 requiring companies to disclose whether they have adopted a code of ethics for senior financial and chief executive officers and if not, the reasons why not (SEC Rules adopted January 2003). While the terms of codes of ethics are not prescribed, they must be reasonably designed to deter wrongdoing and promote honest and ethical conduct, full and fair disclosure, compliance, prompt internal reporting and accountability for adherence to the code. Both the NYSE Amendments and the Nasdaq Amendments require companies to adopt codes of business conduct and ethics.

Corporate social responsibility *(continued)*

United Kingdom	European Union	United States of America
asked to complete. There may be scope for standardisation in the OFR which quoted companies (i.e. UK incorporated companies that are UK, EU or Nasdaq/NYSE listed but not AIM listed companies) will be required to publish for financial years commencing on or after 1 April 2005. See OFR below. The London Stock Exchange has launched an online service, the Corporate Responsibility Exchange (August 2004), which allows companies to fill out one questionnaire instead of many and gives investors a single site where they can locate and analyse data. Proposed statutory codification of directors' duties in Schedule 2 of CB requires directors to act to promote the success of the company for the benefit of its members as a whole. In deciding what would be most likely to promote that success, the directors are required to take account of factors such as the impact of their company's operations on the communities affected and on the environment and the need to maintain a reputation for high standards of business conduct. DTI consultative document "Company Law: Flexibility and Accessibility" (May 2004) indicates that these proposals will be revived in a new Companies Bill. ABI-commissioned research, "Risk, returns and responsibility" (February 2004), showed that 80 of the top 100 FTSE 100 companies provide at least moderate disclosure of social, ethical and environmental issues in accordance with ABI disclosure guidelines on social responsibility but that half of the FTSE 250 fail to make moderate disclosure and one in six of the FT All-Share companies fail to disclose anything at all.		

Accounting standards *IFRS*

United Kingdom	European Union	United States of America
IAS Regulation (July 2002) has the force of law in the UK without the need for further legislative action. It will require UK publicly traded companies to prepare consolidated accounts on the basis of IFRS for financial years commencing on or after 1 January 2005. CA 85 (IAS) Regulations 2004 implement certain options in the IAS Regulation and will permit UK publicly traded companies to use IFRS in their individual accounts and other UK companies and limited liability partnerships to use IFRS in their individual and consolidated accounts, from the same date. There will be no mandatory extension of the IAS Regulation but the DTI will review the position in 2008. CA 85 (IAS) Regulations 2004 also implement the Fair Value Directive and, in part, the Modernisation Directive. The DTI has issued guidance on the amendments made by the CA 85 (IAS) Regulations 2004 (October 2004). Listing Rule 12.42 already allows annual reports to be prepared in accordance with IAS (as an alternative to UK or US GAAP). The AIM Rules were amended with effect from 7 October 2004 and provide that AIM companies will be required to use IFRS adopted by the EC for accounting periods commencing on or after 1 January 2007. Until then, AIM companies may use UK or US GAAP or IFRS. ICAEW technical release, "Auditing Implications of IFRS Transition" (July 2004) gives guidance on what auditors should expect the management and audit committees of their audit clients to be doing to manage the transition to IFRS and sets out good practice on what auditors should be doing in the run up to the first audit under IFRS.	IAS Regulation (July 2002) requires "publicly traded companies" (i.e. companies governed by the law of a Member State whose securities are admitted to trading on an EU regulated market) to prepare their consolidated accounts on the basis of IFRS for financial years commencing on or after 1 January 2005. It does not cover companies incorporated outside the EU. Significant non-EU countries are moving towards adoption of IFRS (Australia, New Zealand, Canada). Modernisation Directive (June 2003) removes conflicts with IFRS in the Fourth and Seventh Directives. To apply for the purposes of the IAS Regulation, individual standards must be endorsed by the ARC and adopted by the EC. The status of the adoption process in relation to IFRS can be viewed on the Financial Reporting section of the EC's website. Following opposition from some banks and insurance undertakings to IAS 39 "Financial Instruments: Recognition and Measurement" and ARC's failure to endorse the standard, EC has adopted an amended version minus the controversial provisions on the fair value option for liabilities and the ban on portfolio hedging of core deposits (November 2004). This means that EU companies with securities admitted to trading on an EU regulated market will have to produce their consolidated accounts using the version of IAS 39 adopted by the EC. Although the EC has confirmed that Member States may require compliance in full with IAS 39's ban on portfolio hedging of core deposits, Member States and companies will not be able to apply the fair value option for liabilities as this will be inconsistent with EU accounting legislation.	Memorandum of Understanding issued by IASB and FASB in the US (October 2002) formalised a commitment to the convergence of US and international accounting standards. Joint or co-operative projects underway include business combinations, measuring financial performance, stock-based compensation and revenue recognition. Both Boards have also agreed to undertake a short-term convergence project aimed at removing certain differences between US GAAP and IFRS. FASB issued four exposure drafts (December 2003) and IASB issued IFRS 3 "Business Combinations" and IFRS 5 "Non-current Assets held for Sale and Discontinued Operations" (March 2004) pursuant to this initiative In March 2004 the SEC proposed rules that would allow eligible non-US companies adopting IFRS to file two years', rather than three years', of financial statements in a registration statement or annual report during the year in which IFRS are first adopted.

Accounting standards *IFRS (continued)*

United Kingdom	European Union	United States of America
ASB discussion paper on converging UK accounting standards with IFRS (March 2004) proposed a phased approach to convergence, including new standards effective in 2005 and 2006 and thereafter, a series of step changes replacing one or more existing UK accounting standards with standards based on IFRS, as prospective IASB projects are completed. Standards on share options and events after the balance sheet date were issued in April and May 2004, respectively. Further standards were issued in December 2004, including one on the measurement of financial instruments. Notwithstanding the EC's adoption of an amended version of IAS 39, the UK standard implements in full the measurement and hedge accounting requirements of the IASB's standard. The ASB also published amendments to FRS 2 "Accounting for Subsidiary Undertakings" in December 2004. This reflects changes to UK company law arising from the implementation of the Modernisation Directive. In particular, the circumstances in which a parent/subsidiary relationship exists are being expanded by the removal of the requirement for a parent undertaking to hold a participating interest in a subsidiary undertaking for the purposes of Section 258 CA 85. The ASB has issued a statement on the implications for UK financial reporting of the modified version of IAS 39 adopted by the EC (October 2004). The ASB strongly supports the view that all UK companies should comply as far as possible with the full hedging requirements of the standard and will issue guidance on this and the amended fair value option as soon as possible. The FSA has written to all listed companies allowing them 120 days (rather than the 90 days under the Listing Rules) to prepare their first interim accounts under IFRS.	There is uncertainty as to whether a company that produces accounts using the EC's adopted version of IAS 39 is eligible as a "first time adopter" for the purposes of reliefs in IFRS 1 (and IAS 1 and IAS 8). This status is intended only to apply to someone who adopts IFRS in full, although the EC regulation to adopt the amended version of IAS 39 purports to modify IFRS 1 so that it is construed as referring to IFRS as adopted by the EC. Only IFRS issued by IASB before the end of March 2004 will come into effect in 2005. A flurry of IFRS were issued before the deadline, including IFRS 2 "Share Based Payment", IFRS 3 "Business Combinations" and IFRS 5 "Non-current Assets held for Sale and Discontinued Operations". CESR published its recommendation to regulators on how listed companies can effectively manage the communication of the financial impact of the transition to IFRS (December 2003). Companies will have to restate their accounts for 2004 to make comparisons with 2005 meaningful although they won't be required to restate their accounts for prior years.	

Accounting standards *Domestic accounting standards*

United Kingdom	European Union	United States of America
Companies that are not required to prepare their accounts on the basis of IFRS, or who choose not to do so (see IFRS above), will continue to prepare their accounts in accordance with domestic accounting standards. WP contained a number of proposals for a new domestic accounting regime e.g. merging the rules in CA 85 with accounting standards to create a single coherent set of accounting standards, including EU requirements (WP 5.9). The proposal to devolve power to a new Standards Board (WP 5.7 et seq) to deal with accounting standards, the form and content of financial statements for companies not subject to IFRS, the Combined Code and other disclosure requirements has been abandoned following the reorganisation of the FRC and its subsidiary bodies. The FRC is responsible for the Combined Code and the ASB is responsible for accounting standards, the form and content of financial statements and the OFR (see OFR below). C(AICE)A gives the FRC and its subsidiaries new powers to exercise their statutory functions in relation to accounts and audit.		SEC study, mandated by SOX, recommends the adoption of a principles-based accounting system (SOX § 108). The SEC staff have labelled this approach "objectives-oriented", whereby the standards would clearly establish the objectives and the accounting model for the class of transaction, while providing companies and auditors with a framework that is sufficiently detailed.
Enforcement		
Administrative enforcement (where the Secretary of State or FRRP can apply to the court for a declaration that the accounts do not comply with CA 85 or for an order requiring directors to produce revised accounts) will be extended to cover the OFR for financial years commencing on or after 1 April 2006, i.e. a one-year delay (see OFR below).	CESR issued Standard No. 1 on Financial Information, "Enforcement of standards on financial information in Europe" in March 2003. It is based on general principles with a view to harmonising institutional oversight systems in Europe. It issued Standard No. 2 on Financial Information "Co-ordination of enforcement activities" in April 2004 to contribute to the creation within the EU of robust and consistent enforcement of IFRS.	SOX provisions include: • SEC review of periodic reports, including financial statements, for SEC reporting companies every three years (SOX § 408) • SEC review of its enforcement initiatives for the five years preceding SOX (SOX § 704)

Accounting standards *Enforcement (continued)*

United Kingdom	European Union	United States of America
The CGAA recommended that the FRRP should develop a more pro-active role for the enforcement of accounting standards and that the FSA should also play an active part (paras 4.22-25 of CGAA Report). The FRRP and the FSA have agreed a Memorandum of Understanding to facilitate co-operation and co-ordination. The new pro-active approach is summarised in the FRRP Chairman's Statement in the FRC Annual Report 2003. Broadly, the FRRP will adopt a risk-based approach founded on the probability of mis-statement occurring within a set of annual financial statements and the potential impact on the confidence and economic decisions of the investing and broader stakeholder community. Resources will be focused on the financial information of those companies with a greater potential for market impact. The FRC has established (August 2004) the FRRP Standing Advisory Group on Proactivity to advise the FRRP on the selection of financial statements for review and drawing to the FRRP's attention risk factors which should inform its approach. C(AICE)A contains provisions to strengthen the enforcement of accounting and reporting requirements by: • extending the remit of the FRRP so it can look at interim as well as annual accounts of issuers of listed securities (this would also cover non-UK companies) • giving the FRRP power to require information from companies it is investigating • allowing the Inland Revenue to pass information on defective accounts to the FRRP	TOD will require directors of issuers of securities traded on an EU regulated market to give a responsibility statement for information contained in annual reports, half yearly reports and interim financial statements they publish in the EU. EC's proposal for a directive to amend the Fourth and Seventh Directives (October 2004) applicable to all EU-incorporated companies confirms the collective responsibility of board members towards the company for the financial and other key information that they publish in their annual report and accounts. For both TOD and the EC's proposal for a directive to amend the Fourth and Seventh Directives, Member States would be required to apply their liability regimes to the givers of such statements.There are concerns about the possible extension of directors' liability – see Directors' general duties. Statutory Audit Directive seeks to strengthen the regulatory framework applicable to auditors and enforcement matters. It includes common criteria for public oversight systems, lays out a concept for a model of co-operation between Member States and establishes procedures for the exchange of information between oversight bodies of Member States in investigations. It also allows reciprocal co-operation with third countries. CESR paper published for comment (June 2004) on proposed guidance for implementation of co-ordination of enforcement of financial information. The guidance deals mainly with the organisational aspects of meetings at which national enforcers will discuss enforcement decisions and provides practical guidance on the functioning of the database of enforcement decisions that national enforcers will feed and use.	• CEOs and CFOs to certify that the financial information included in periodic reports fairly presents in all material respects the financial condition and results of operations of the company. There are two overlapping certification requirements with civil and criminal penalties (SOX §§ 302 and 906) (SEC Rules adopted August 2002) • new criminal sanctions for securities fraud involving a public company and tampering with records (SOX §§ 802, 807 and 1102) • prohibition on officers and directors taking any action that improperly or fraudulently influences or misleads auditors (SOX § 303) (SEC Rules adopted May 2003) • CEOs and CFOs to forfeit equity-based compensation and trading profits if their company has had to restate financial statements as a result of misconduct (SOX § 304).

Accounting standards *Enforcement (continued)*

United Kingdom	European Union	United States of America
• giving additional powers to auditors to obtain information from companies and other persons • requiring directors to state that they have not withheld information from auditors • requiring any person to provide relevant information to DTI investigators • giving DTI investigators the right to require entry and remain on the premises of a company under investigation • providing protection from breach of confidence claims for people who voluntarily provide information in certain circumstances. The extension to the FRRP's remit to look at interim accounts is expected to come into force in January 2005. The remaining provisions are expected to come into force on 1 April 2005.		

Financial statements *Changes to financial statements*

United Kingdom	European Union	United States of America
The Companies Act 1985 (Accounts of Small and Medium-Sized Enterprises and Audit Exemption) (Amendment) Regulations 2004 (January 2004) increased: • the thresholds, below which most small companies are exempt from the requirements of an independent financial audit, to £5.6 million turnover or £2.8 million balance sheet total, in each case the maximum permitted under EU law	Directive amending Fourth Directive (May 2003) raised the thresholds for turnover and balance sheet by about 17% under which Member States can exempt small- and medium-sized enterprises from certain accounting requirements, e.g. permitting them to publish an abridged balance sheet, abridged notes to the accounts and an abridged profit and loss account. Member States may also exempt small companies from publishing a profit and loss account or annual report or from having their accounts audited.	Additional disclosure requirements under SOX for financial statements of all companies filing or about to file reports with the SEC: • material off-balance sheet arrangements and known contractual commitments must be disclosed (SOX § 401(a)) (SEC Rules adopted January 2003) • pro forma figures must be reconciled to GAAP figures and not be misleading (SOX § 401(b)) (SEC Rules adopted January 2003)

Financial statements *Changes to financial statements (continued)*

United Kingdom	European Union	United States of America
• the small and medium-sized company turnover thresholds in relation to accounting requirements to £5.6 million and £22.8 million, respectively, also the maximum permitted by EU law. The changes will allow more companies to take advantage of less onerous accounting disclosure requirements. The new thresholds for small and medium-sized companies came into effect for financial years ended on or after 30 January 2004. The audit exemption threshold came into effect in relation to financial years ended on or after 30 March 2004. CA 85 (IAS) Regulations 2004 amend the accounting and reporting provisions of CA 85 to give effect to certain options in the IAS Regulation and to implement the Modernisation Directive and the Fair Value Directive. The DTI has issued guidance on the amendments (October 2004). Changes arising from the implementation of the Modernisation Directive and the Fair Value Directive include: • changes to the requirements and options on consolidation for parent companies • changes to the audit report • changes to the presentation of items in the balance sheet and profit and loss account • changes to the disclosure of proposed dividends in the accounts • changes to the disclosure of information on derivatives. There is also an accounting option to use fair value accounting for financial instruments and investment property.		• management must report on internal control over financial reporting, including the effectiveness of those controls, and auditors must issue an attestation report on management's assessment (SOX § 404) (SEC Rules adopted June 2003 and February 2004). The additional requirements apply to financial years commencing on or after 15 November 2004 (certain US companies) and 15 July 2005 (non-US companies). The FRC is consulting on draft guidance for US and Irish companies – see Corporate governance codes above.

Financial statements *Changes to financial statements (continued)*

United Kingdom	European Union	United States of America
For changes arising from the IAS Regulation, see IFRS above. The Modernisation Directive also requires an enhanced review of a company's business in the directors' report. There is an overlap with the OFR (which quoted companies will be required to prepare) but the DTI has indicated that unnecessary duplication will be avoided – see OFR below.		
Performance statement or P&L?		
Government supports a "single performance statement" (recording gains and losses such as asset revaluations in addition to income and expenses) but will not pre-empt changes in accounting standards or IFRS (WP 4.12). ASB FRED 22 (December 2000) proposes a single performance statement, to replace FRS 3. This is being taken forward as a joint project on reporting performance with the IASB. Since it is unclear when the IASB will publish an accounting standard on reporting financial performance, the Government indicated, in its consultation on the switch to IFRS and the modernisation of accounting directives (March 2004), that it would not be exercising the option (given to Member States in the Modernisation Directive) to permit or require companies to present a statement of performance.	IASB (in partnership with ASB) is reviewing presentation of financial performance. Final standard will not be mandatory until after 2005. Modernisation Directive (June 2003) removes conflicts with IFRS and allows for future developments, e.g. performance statement.	

Financial statements *OFR*

United Kingdom	European Union	United States of America
The DTI has announced (November 2004) how it proposes to proceed with regulations to require quoted companies to publish an OFR. The DTI confirmed that the scope of the regulations will be as set out in its consultation paper on draft regulations (May 2004) and no changes of substance will be made to the objectives and content of the OFR. UK incorporated companies that are UK, EU or Nasdaq/NYSE listed (but not AIM listed) will be required to publish an OFR for financial years commencing on or after 1 April 2005. The OFR should give a balanced and comprehensive analysis of a company's development and performance, position at the end of the year and the main trends and factors governing past and future development, performance and position to enable shareholders to assess the strategies adopted by the company and the potential for those strategies to succeed. The directors will need to consider including information on employees, environmental matters, social and community issues, customers and suppliers, significant relationships with stakeholders and key performance indicators. Key points contained in the DTI's announcement: • the FRRP's role in administrative enforcement of the OFR has been put back one year to financial years commencing on or after 1 April 2006 • the DTI has dropped the proposal to require auditors to give an opinion on whether the directors have used "due and careful enquiry" in preparing the OFR. Also, there will be no requirement for the auditors to review the process for producing the OFR • unnecessary duplication of reporting requirements will be avoided so that quoted companies who produce an OFR will not have to report separately on matters specified in the Modernisation Directive	Modernisation Directive (June 2003) requires large- and medium-sized companies to provide an analysis of the development and performance of their business in their annual reports, describing the principal risks and uncertainties they face and providing financial and non-financial performance indicators such as environmental and employee information. Member States may exempt medium-sized companies from certain non-financial requirements. IOSCO (the forum for securities regulators that promotes co-operation and high standards of regulation to maintain fair, efficient and sound markets) published a report (February 2003), "General Principles Regarding Disclosure of Management's Discussion and Analysis of Financial Condition and Results of Operations".	Registration statements and annual reports (Form 20-F for most non-US companies) required to include "Operating and Financial Review and Prospects" (previously, "Management's Discussion and Analysis of Financial Condition and Results of Operations" or "MD&A"). Management discusses company's "financial condition, changes in financial condition and results of operations" for the historical period covered by the financial statements and management's assessment of factors, trends and uncertainties which are anticipated to have a material effect. Additional disclosure regarding liquidity and capital resources and critical accounting policies and estimates is typically included (SEC Rules proposed May 2002 and interpretive guidance issued December 2003). New rules under SOX require disclosure of non-GAAP financial information (SEC Rules adopted January 2003) and off-balance sheet arrangements (SOX § 401) (SEC Rules adopted January 2003).

Financial statements *OFR (continued)*

United Kingdom	European Union	United States of America
• there is no safe harbour from litigation for forward-looking statements although the DTI will give guidance on the inclusion of health warnings regarding the directors' good faith judgements as to future events or prospects. It will also be made clear that there will be no obligation to disclose specific information about impending developments or matters in the course of negotiation • there will be no obligation to circulate the OFR to shareholders who have opted to receive summary financial statements. The DTI intends to lay regulations before Parliament to implement the OFR by the end of January 2005. Guidance will also be issued on the OFR and the new requirements for the directors' report arising from the introduction of the Modernisation Directive. The Secretary of State for Trade and Industry has specified the ASB to issue standards for the OFR, using powers contained in Section 13 of C(AICE)A. The ASB consulted on draft standards (November 2004) which build on the DTI's forthcoming regulations and the ASB's existing best practice guidance (on a non-statutory OFR, last revised in 2003). Other guidance includes: • "Practical Guidance for Directors" (May 2004) produced by the OFR working group set up by the DTI. An updated version will be published once the regulations are finalised • report of the Accounting for People Task Force on measuring and evaluating the workforce (November 2003) • ICAEW interim process guidance for UK directors "Preparing an Operating and Financial Review"		

Audit committees *Constitution of audit committees*

United Kingdom	European Union	United States of America
Provisions of the Combined Code relevant to the constitution of audit committees include: • the audit committee should have a minimum of three (or, in the case of smaller companies below the FTSE 350 throughout the previous reporting year, two) members, all of whom should be independent NEDs (C3.1) • the board should satisfy itself that at least one member should have recent and relevant financial experience (C3.1) (there is no detailed definition equivalent to "audit committee financial expert" in the US). The Smith Guidance provides guidance on how to comply with the provisions relating to audit committees and auditors in the Combined Code. The CGAA Report (para 2.31) recommended that a legal requirement for listed companies to have an audit committee should be considered again if the best practice approach of the Combined Code proves ineffective. Higgs Review (para 17.11) recommended that the Government and FRC review progress after two years.	Statutory Audit Directive contains a requirement for all "public interest entities" to have an audit committee. Public interest entities include EU-incorporated companies listed on an EU regulated market, credit institutions and insurance undertakings (although Member States may exempt non-listed credit institutions and non-listed insurance undertakings). The audit committee should be composed of non-executive members of the administrative body and/or members of the supervisory body, i.e. NEDs, and/or members appointed by the shareholders in general meeting, with at least one independent member with competence in accounting and/or auditing. The EC's Recommendation on independent directors and board committees (October 2004) also covers audit committees partly because the EC hopes that it will encourage listed companies to set up audit committees pending the approval of the Statutory Audit Directive and its incorporation into national laws. The Recommendation provides more detailed provisions to supplement the general principles of the Statutory Audit Directive. The Recommendation sets out broad qualifications for audit committee membership but these are weaker than in the Statutory Audit Directive or in the UK or US. Although recent and relevant experience of finance and accounting must be present, it can be provided collectively from the audit committee members' backgrounds and experience. The Recommendation is non-binding but Member States are encouraged to take measures to implement it by 30 June 2006 and notify the EC of any such measures taken. The EC will closely monitor the situation to determine the need for additional measures.	The NYSE and Nasdaq have promulgated rules under SOX which prohibit listing of companies not meeting the following requirements: • each company must have an audit committee • each member of the audit committee must be "independent" (SOX § 301). The SEC Rules make significant accommodations for non-US issuers (SEC Rules adopted April 2003 and NYSE/Nasdaq Amendments approved November 2003). Each audit committee must either designate an "audit committee financial expert" or explain why such an expert has not been appointed. To qualify as an "audit committee financial expert", an individual must have all of the following attributes: • an understanding of GAAP and financial statements • an ability to assess the general application of GAAP in connection with the accounting for estimates, accruals and reserves • experience preparing, auditing, analysing or evaluating financial statements that present a breadth and level of complexity of accounting issues that are generally comparable to the breadth and complexity of issues that can reasonably be expected to be raised by the company's financial statements, or experience actively supervising one or more persons engaged in such activities • an understanding of internal controls and procedures for financial reporting and • an understanding of audit committee functions.

Audit committees *Constitution of audit committees (continued)*

United Kingdom	European Union	United States of America
		A person can acquire such attributes through any one or more of the following means: • education and experience as a principal financial officer, principal accounting officer, controller, public accountant or auditor or experience in one or more positions that involve the performance of similar functions • experience actively supervising a principal financial officer, principal accounting officer, controller, public accountant, auditor or person performing similar functions • experience overseeing or assessing the performance of companies or public accountants with respect to the preparation, auditing or evaluation of financial statements or • other relevant experience. (SOX § 407) (SEC Rules adopted January 2003).
Role of audit committees		
Provision C3.2 of the Combined Code sets out the main role and responsibilities of the audit committee. The audit committee should, among other things: • monitor the integrity of the financial statements of the company and any formal announcements relating to the company's financial performance, reviewing significant financial reporting judgements contained in them • review the company's internal financial controls and, unless expressly addressed by a separate risk committee of independent directors or by the board	IOSCO (the worldwide forum for securities regulators that promotes co-operation and high standards of regulation to maintain fair, efficient and sound markets) published its statement (October 2002) "Principles of Auditor Independence and the Role of Corporate Governance in Monitoring an Auditor's Independence". EC Recommendation on Auditor Independence (May 2002) proposes that auditors should consider whether the governance structure of the audited entity provides safeguards to mitigate threats to independence. The	SOX specifies certain audit committee responsibilities including (SOX §§ 202, 204 and 301): • pre-approval of non-prohibited non-audit services • receiving reports of critical accounting policies and practices as well as alternative accounting treatments • oversight of accounting firm (including payment of compensation) • whistleblowing procedures • authority and funding to engage outside advisers. (SEC Rules adopted January and April 2003)

Audit committees *Role of audit committees (continued)*

United Kingdom	European Union	United States of America
itself, review the company's internal control and risk management systems • monitor and review the effectiveness of the company's internal audit function • make recommendations to the board in relation to the appointment, reappointment and removal of the external auditor and approve the remuneration and terms of engagement of the external auditor • review and monitor the external auditor's independence and objectivity and the effectiveness of the audit process, taking into consideration relevant UK professional and regulatory requirements • develop and implement policy on the engagement of the external auditor to supply non-audit services, taking into account relevant ethical guidance, and report to the board, identifying any matters in which it considers that action or improvement is needed and making recommendations as to the steps to be taken.	involvement of the governance body of listed entities in an auditor's appointment or in commissioning non-audit services is a factor to be considered in determining the significance of a threat to independence (para A 4.1.1 and Annex para 4.1.1). Statutory Audit Directive provides that the audit committee shall, *inter alia*: • monitor the financial reporting process • monitor the effectiveness of the company's internal control, internal audit and risk management systems • oversee the statutory audit of the annual and consolidated accounts • review and monitor the independence of the statutory auditor or audit firm and in particular the provision of additional services to the audited entity. Also, the appointment of the statutory auditor of a public interest entity shall be based on a recommendation of the audit committee. These roles are also discussed and elaborated in the guidance appended to the EC's Recommendation on independent directors and board committees (October 2004). The Recommendation is non-binding but Member States are encouraged to take measures to implement it by 30 June 2006. The EC will closely monitor the situation to determine the need for additional measures.	Also, pursuant to SOX § 307 and SEC Rules, audit committees may receive and take action on attorneys' reports of "evidence of material violations of securities law…". NYSE/Nasdaq Amendments require/authorise audit committees to, *inter alia*: • hire and fire independent auditors; approve non-audit services; review their work; obtain advice from outside legal or accounting advisers if necessary (NYSE and Nasdaq) • consider annual/quarterly financial statements and MD&A; discuss earnings press releases, guidance provided to analysts and rating agencies and risk management policies; meet regularly with management, internal auditors and independent auditors (NYSE) • review and approve all related party transactions (Nasdaq).
Other provisions of the Combined Code relating to the role of audit committees include: • the audit committee should review arrangements by which staff of the company may, in confidence, raise concerns about possible improprieties in financial reporting or other matters, to ensure that		NYSE/Nasdaq Amendments are largely consistent with SOX, although they allow for the exemption of non-US issuers where such exemptions would not be contrary to US securities laws. However, audit committee rules under SOX § 301 apply to non-US issuers, albeit with significant accommodations.

Audit committees *Role of audit committees (continued)*

United Kingdom	European Union	United States of America
arrangements are in place for the proportionate and independent investigation of such matters and for appropriate follow up action (C3.4) • if the board does not accept the audit committee's recommendation on the appointment, reappointment or removal of the external auditors, it should include in the annual report, and in any papers recommending appointment or reappointment, a statement from the audit committee explaining its recommendation and the reasons why the board has taken a different position (C3.6) • the annual report should explain to shareholders how, if the auditor provides non-auditor services, auditor objectivity and independence are safeguarded (C3.7). ICSA's terms of reference for audit committees have been updated following the Combined Code (October 2003). ICAEW published guidance for audit committees (May 2003 and March 2004) designed to help NEDs understand the provisions of the Combined Code relating to audit committees and auditors and the Smith Guidance. An APB research study was published (September 2003) summarising the results of research into the practical application of Statement of Auditing Standard 610 "Communication of audit matters to those charged with governance".		

Auditor independence *Non-audit services*

United Kingdom	European Union	United States of America
Auditors' ethical guidance in relation to non-audit services is based on a threats and safeguards approach. Non-audit services are generally allowed, provided there is no involvement in management function or decision making and threats to objectivity are reduced to acceptable levels by safeguards. CGAA did not call for a blanket ban on provision of non-audit services but recommended a further strengthening of the requirements: • there should be a strong presumption against providing internal audit services other than in exceptional circumstances • a new standard-setting body under the FRC (now identified as the APB) should review the circumstances in which it is possible to provide valuation services (in particular, actuarial services and litigation support services), taxation services and the design and supply of IT and financial information technology systems, (paras 1.41-48 CGAA Report). Trade and Industry Committee agreed with CGAA that there should not be a ban on non-audit services but recommended a strengthening of requirements in relation to the supply of financial control systems and internal audit systems (para 92 Trade and Industry Committee Report). Following the DTI's review of the regulatory regime of the accountancy profession (January 2003), the APB has taken over the responsibilities of ICAEW and the other professional accountancy bodies for setting standards for independence. It published five Ethical Standards (October 2004), including one on non-audit services provided to audit clients, ES 5. This retains a	EC Recommendation on Auditor Independence (May 2002) adopted a principles-based approach (whereby auditors cannot provide non-audit services that would compromise their independence or be involved in management decisions) and set out specific instances where provision of non-audit services caused too high a risk to an auditor's independence. It also recommended full disclosure at least annually of fees for audit and non-audit services. Statutory Audit Directive follows the basic principles laid down in the EC Recommendation but sets out additional measures, such as requiring the auditor to document in the audit working papers significant threats to its independence and safeguards to mitigate those threats. IOSCO's "Statement of Principles of Auditor Independence and Role of Corporate Governance in Monitoring an Auditor's Independence" (October 2002) recommends that the audit committee should oversee policies governing circumstances in which contracts for non-audit services can be entered into with the company's external auditors. Code of Ethics for Professional Accountants of IFAC (November 2001) analyses potential threats to auditor independence under five headings: self-interest, self-review, advocacy, familiarity and intimidation. An ED (July 2003) proposes that the Code of Ethics be elevated from a model code on which to base national requirements to a standard requiring member body compliance. It also expands the guidance in a number of areas, including integrity, objectivity, professional competence, confidentiality and professional behaviour. A further ED was published (October 2004) to clarify	Pursuant to SOX: • the PCAOB has authority to issue standards for auditor independence (SOX § 103) • prohibition of eight specified types of non-audit services (SOX § 201) • audit committee must approve non-prohibited non-audit services (SOX § 301). (SEC Rules adopted January 2003.)

Auditor independence *Non-audit services (continued)*

United Kingdom	European Union	United States of America
threats and safeguards approach and provides guidance on particular services which may create threats to an auditor's objectivity or perceived loss of independence. These include internal audit, IT services, valuation, tax, litigation support, remuneration and recruitment and corporate finance services. ES 5 also sets out a number of situations where the APB believes safeguards are insufficient and where audit firms should not provide non-audit services. Concerns have been expressed about the application of ES 5 to smaller entities. The Ethical Standards are effective for audits of financial statements for periods commencing on or after 15 December 2004. The Combined Code contains a provision that the annual report should explain to shareholders how, if the auditor provides non-audit services, auditor objectivity and independence are safeguarded (C3.7). Existing regulations require remuneration for non-audit services to be disclosed by companies (Companies Act 1985 (Disclosure of Remuneration for Non-Audit Work) Regulations 1991). C(AICE)A will increase these requirements with effect from 1 April 2005 so that companies have to disclose, in addition, the different types of non-audit services they buy from their auditors and a breakdown of the cost of each. ICAEW published a statement of guidance to directors on the disclosure of the nature and value of services provided by auditors (ICAEW Technical Release 24/03 (July 2003)).	the independence requirements for professional accountants in public practice who perform assurance engagements. A final version of the revised Code of Ethics is expected in February 2005 and to take effect in December 2005.	

Auditor independence *Rotation of audit firm*

United Kingdom	European Union	United States of America
The CGAA recommended that there should not be a requirement for mandatory rotation of audit firms or for the mandatory retendering for the audit engagement (paras 1.23-30 CGAA Report). House of Commons Trade and Industry Committee did not recommend mandatory rotation of audit firms but thought that it should not be ruled out altogether if other measures to restore confidence in objectivity of auditors prove insufficient (para 102 Trade and Industry Committee Report). DTI indicated in its consultation on EC's proposal for Statutory Audit Directive (September 2004) that is has no plans to implement mandatory audit firm rotation in the UK.	Mandatory auditor rotation provisions are included in the Statutory Audit Directive. Member States will have the option of requiring a change of key audit partner(s) or of the audit firm every seven years.	Study of mandatory audit firm rotation required (SOX § 207). NYSE has asked audit committees to consider, where appropriate, audit firm rotation.
Rotation of audit partner		
APB published five Ethical Standards (October 2004), including one on long association with the audit engagement, ES 3: • no one should act as audit engagement partner or as independent partner for a continuous period longer than five years • no one should act as key audit partner for a continuous period longer than seven years • anyone who has acted as an audit engagement partner or independent partner, or held a combination of such positions for a particular audit client for a period of five years, whether continuously or in aggregate, should not hold any position of responsibility in relation to audit engagement until a further period of five years has elapsed.	EC Recommendation on Auditor Independence (May 2002) that "Key Audit Partners" (broadly those responsible for reporting on significant matters) should rotate within seven years. IFAC approved a revision to its Code of Ethics for Professional Accountants (June 2004) to make it clear that an individual who has completed a pre-defined period in the role of lead engagement partner for an audit of a listed entity should not participate in the audit engagement until a further period, normally two years, has elapsed. A further ED (October 2004) proposes to extend the rotation requirements applicable to the engagement partner to the individual responsible for the engagement quality review in the audit of a listed entity. A final version of the revised Code of	Mandatory audit partner rotation every five fiscal years (lead and concurring audit partners) or seven years (other key audit partners) (SOX § 203) (SEC Rules adopted January 2003).

Auditor independence *Rotation of audit partner(continued)*

United Kingdom	European Union	United States of America
The Ethical Standards are effective for audits of financial statements for periods commencing on or after 15 December 2004 and replace the guidance of the ICAEW and other professional accountancy bodies.	Ethics is expected in February 2005 and to take effect in December 2005. Mandatory auditor rotation provisions are included in the Statutory Audit Directive. Member States will have the option of requiring a change of key audit partner(s) or of the audit firm every seven years.	
Regulation of auditors and accountants		
Following the DTI's review of the regulatory regime of the accountancy profession (January 2003), the FRC has assumed (March 2004) the functions of the Accountancy Foundation with responsibility for setting accounting and auditing standards, their enforcement or monitoring and the oversight of the major professional accountancy bodies. Two existing boards from the Accountancy Foundation, the APB and the Accountancy Investigation and Discipline Board have come under the FRC umbrella and a new Professional Oversight Board for Accountancy has been established. One of its functions will be to monitor the quality of audit of economically significant entities, initially focusing on FTSE 350 companies. C(AICE)A: • requires professional accountancy bodies that supervise auditors to sign up to independent auditing standards, monitoring and disciplinary procedures • makes those bodies subject to a more independent regulatory regime in setting, monitoring and enforcement of auditing standards • allows the Government to contribute to the funding of the FRC's new functions and allows a levy to be imposed if voluntary arrangements break down.	EC Recommendation on Quality Assurance for the Statutory Audit in the EU (November 2000). IOSCO statement (October 2002) "Principles for Auditor Oversight" sets out principles of oversight for auditors of listed companies. Statutory Audit Directive: • requires use of International Standards of Auditing as endorsed by the EC for all EU statutory audits • establishes common criteria for public oversight systems at Member State level • establishes an audit regulatory committee of Member State representatives at EU level to implement detailed measures of the directive and allow for continuous monitoring • creates a co-operative model between regulatory authorities of Member States on the basis of "home country control" (i.e. audit firms principally regulated by authorities in the Member State where they are established). This model of co-operation is also extended to third countries on the basis of reciprocity • contains rules on approval of third country auditors on condition that the country concerned offers reciprocity to EU auditors	SOX mandates the creation of the PCAOB to register, inspect, investigate and discipline public accounting firms that prepare audit reports for companies. PCAOB is responsible for establishing audit, quality control and ethics standards for registered accounting firms (SOX §§ 101 et seq). PCAOB "determined" (i.e. established) by the SEC on 25 April 2003. US accounting firms must have registered with the PCAOB by 22 October 2003. Non-US accounting firms must have registered with the PCAOB by 19 July 2004.

Auditor independence *Regulation of auditors and accountants (continued)*

United Kingdom	European Union	United States of America
These provisions are expected to come into force on 1 April 2005. The APB announced (May 2004) that it is proposing to adopt International Standards of Auditing from 2005, with the addition of some material from existing UK standards. It issued (June 2004) exposure drafts of 29 new standards. The Government has decided (September 2004) against introducing a cap on auditor liability following a report by the Office of Fair Trading (August 2004) that this would not significantly enhance competition.	• introduces public oversight by Member State authorities on third country auditors if the latters' oversight system is not considered equivalent • allows for derogation from registration, oversight, quality assurance and investigations and sanctions if audit firms from third countries are subject to equivalent systems of registration and oversight.	

Directory

Further Reading

General

Bingham, K. *Corporate Governance Handbook* (Gee Publishing). A looseleaf subscription service dedicated to corporate governance issues.

Chambers, A., *Tolley's Corporate Governance Handbook*, 2nd edition (Tolley's, 2004).

Charkham, J., *Keeping Good Company: A Study of Corporate Governance in Five Countries* (Oxford University Press, 1995).

Mallin, C., *Corporate Governance* (Oxford University Press, 2004).

Monks, A. G. and Minow, N. (eds), *Corporate Governance* (Blackwell, 2001).

Tricker, R. I., *Corporate Governance* (Gower, 1984).

Directors and Boards

Bingham, K., *The Professional Board* (Gee Publishing, 2001).

Bruce, M., *Tolley's Rights and Duties of Directors* (5th edition, Tolley's, 2002).

Bruce, M., *The ICSA Director's Guide*, 2nd edition (ICSA Publishing, 20034).

Cadbury, A., *Corporate Governance and Chairmanship: A Personal View* (Oxford University Press, 2002).

Cooper, B. *The ICSA Handbook of Good Boardroom Practice* (ICSA Publishing, 2004).

ICSA, *The Appointment and Induction of Directors* (ICSA, 1998).

ICSA *Matters Reserved for the Board.* Available at www.icsa.org.uk/news/guidance.php.

ICSA *Terms of Reference – Board Committees.* Available at www.icsa.org.uk/news/guidance.php.

Stiles, P. and Taylor, B., *Boards at Work* (Oxford University Press, 2001).

UK Listing Authority, *The Model Code (Appendix to The UK Listing Rules)* (FSA, updated annually).

Audit Committees

Copnell, T., *The ICSA Guide to Audit Committees* (ICSA Publishing/KPMG, 2005).

A series of booklets aimed at directors who do not regard themselves as financial experts. See www.icaew.co.uk.

Shareholder relations

Charkham, J. and Simpson, A., *Fair Shares: The Future of Shareholder Power and Responsibility* (Oxford University Press, 1999).

ICSA, *Electronic Communications with Shareholders: A Guide to Best Practice* (ICSA, 2000), updated at . An update to this guide is available at www.icsa.org.uk/news/guidance.php.

Corporate Social Responsibility

Hoskins, T., *The ICSA Handbook of Corporate Social Responsibility* (ICSA Publishing, 2005).

OECD guidelines for multinational companies. See www.oecd.org.

Smith, D., *Demonstrating Corporate Values* (Institute of Business Ethics, 2002).

Whistleblowing

ICSA, *Establishing a Whistleblowing Procedure* (ICSA, 1999).

Reports and Codes of Practice

ABI (2001) *Disclosure Guidelines on Socially Responsible Investment*. Available at www.abi.org.uk.

ABI (2004) *Principles and Guidelines on on Long-Term Remuneration for Senior Executives (ABI, 1996)Executive Remuneration*. See www.abi.org.uk.

ABI, Statement of Principles on Share Incentive Schemes (ABI, 1999)

ABI/NAPF (1999) Statement on Responsible Voting.

Accounting Standards Board (2003 Statement on the Operating and Financial Review.

Accounting Standards Board (2004) [*Draft*] *Reporting Standard: Operating and Financial Review (RED 1, including draft Implementation Guidelines)*. Available at: www.frc.org.uk/asb)

Cadbury Committee on the Financial Aspects of Corporate Governance, *Report of the Committee on the Financial Aspects of Corporate Governance: The Code of Best Practice (Cadbury Code)* (Gee Publishing, 1992).

The Combined Code on Corporate Governance (2003). Includes the Turnbull and Smith Guidance and Suggestions for Good Practice from the Higgs Report. Available at www.frc.org.uk.

Commonwealth Association for Corporate Governance (1999), *Principles for Corporate Governance in the Commonwealth: Towards Global Competitiveness and Economic Accountability*.

European Commission (2003) *Action Plan for Company Law and Corporate Governance*.

Greenbury Study Group (1995) *Directors' Remuneration: Report of a Study Group chaired by Sir Richard Greenbury (Greenbury Committee Report)*, (Gee Publishing).

Hampel Committee on Corporate Governance (1998) *Committee of Corporate Governance Final Report (Hampel Committee report)*,(Gee Publishing).

Hermes Pensions Management (1998, updated 2001) *Statement on Corporate Governance and Voting Policy*. Available at www.hermes.co.uk.

Hermes Pensions Management (2002) *The Hermes Principles*. Available at www.hermes.co.uk).

Higgs Review (2003) *The Role and Effectiveness of Non-Executive Directors*, The Department of Trade and Industry. Available at www.dti.gov.uk.

Institutional Shareholders' Committee (ISC) (2002) *Responsibilities of Institutional Shareholders and Agents – Statement of Principles*. Available at www.abi.org.uk.

Myners, P. (2001) *Institutional Investment in the UK: A Review*, HM Treasury.

NAPF (2005) *Corporate Governance Policy*. Available at www.napf.co.uk.

OECD (1999, updated 2004) *Principles of Corporate Governance*. Available at www.oecd.org.

PIRC, *Shareholder Voting Guidelines* (PIRC, 1994, 2003).

Sarbanes–Oxley Act of 2002, H.R. 3763.

Smith Review Panel (2003) *Audit Committees: Combined Code Guidance (The Smith Report) (Financial Reporting Council)*. Available at www.frc.org.uk.

South African Institute of Directors (2002) *King II Report on Corporate Governance for South Africa 2002*.

Turnbull Working Party, *The Combined Code (Financial Services Authority, current edition 2000). Available at www.fsa.gov.uk.*

(The Turnbull report) Internal Control: Guidance for Directors on the Combined Code (Croner CCH, 1999). Also available at www.icaew.co.uk.

Tyson, L. (2003) *The Tyson Report on the Recruitment and Development of Non-Executive Directors*. Available at www.london.edu/tysonreport.

Updates and analysis

This is an area informed by regular statistical reports and analysis. Some recent examples of these include:

PIRC's Annual Survey of Corporate Governance Trends and Structures in the FTSE All Share Index

Corporate Governance: the opinions of UK Asset Managers, KPMG Survey 2002

ICSA Guidance Notes

The ICSA Policy Unit produces a range of Guidance Notes on corporate governance topics. These are available at www.icsa.org.uk/news/guiodance.php. This area of the site also offers an e-mail alert service for new Guidance Notes.

Magazines, journals and newsletters

Chartered Secretary

The ICSA monthly magazine carries regular updates and articles on a variety of corporate governance topics and issues. The magazine's companion website, www.charteredsecretary.net has a searchable archive of recent features and regular news updates.

Corporate Governance: An International Review
Blackwell Publishing
108 Cowley Road
Oxford OX4 1JF
An academic research journal with particular emphasis on international issues.

Global Proxy Watch
Monthly e-mail or fax newsletter from Davis Global Advisors (see below).

Governance
An independent monthly newsletter, which is particularly strong on international developments. Available in print, electronically or both.
Governance Publications
www.governance.co.uk

Investor Relations
Cross-Border Publishing Ltd
111–113 Great Titchfield Street
London W1W 6RY
Monthly review with strong international coverage.

Professional bodies and useful organisations

Association of British Insurers
51 Gresham Street
London
EC2V 7HQ
Tel: 020-7600 3333
Fax: 020-7696 8999
www.abi.org.uk

The Corporate Library
www.thecorporatelibrary.com

The Department of Trade and Industry
1 Victoria Street
London SW1H 0ET
Tel: 020-7215 5000
DTI Publications order line: 0870 1502 500
www.dti.gov.uk

Financial Reporting Council
4th Floor
117 Houndsditch
London EC3A 7BT
Tel: 020-7404 8818
www.frc.org.uk

Financial Services Authority
25 The North Colonnade
Canary Wharf
London E14 5HS
Tel: 020-7676 1000
www.fsa.gov.uk

The Institute of Chartered Secretaries and Administrators
16 Park Crescent
London W1B 1AH
Tel: 020-7580 4741
www.icsa.org.uk

ICSA Corporate Services Limited
Board Performance Evaluation Unit
16 Park Crescent
London W1B 1AH
Telephone: 020 7580 4741
E-mail: boardperformance@icsa.co.uk

The Institute of Directors
116 Pall Mall
London SW1Y 5ED
Tel: 020-7839 1233
www.iod.co.uk

International Corporate Governance Network
ICGN Secretariat
Caroline J. Phillips FCIS
ICSA
16 Park Crescent
London W1B 1AH
England
Tel: (44 20) 7580 4741
www.icgn.org

National Association of Pension Funds (NAPF)
NIOC House
4 Victoria Street
London SW1H 0NE
Tel: 020-7808 1300
Fax: 020-7222 7585
www.napf.co.uk
www.votingissues.com

Pensions and Investment Research Consultants Limited
4th Floor
Cityside
40 Adler Street
London E1 1EE
Tel: 020-7247 2323
Fax: 020-7247 2457
www.pirc.co.uk/

Other web resources

Accounting Standards Board
www.frc.org.uk/asb

Audit Committee Institute
www.kpmg.co.uk/aci

Business for Social Responsibility
www.bsr.org

Business in the Community
www.bitc.org.uk

CalPERS
www.calpers.org

Committee on Standards in Public Life, UK
www.public-standards.gov.uk

Company Law Review
www.dti.gov.uk/cld/

Council of Institutional Investors, USA
www.cii.org

Davis Global Advisors
www.davisglobal.com

Deminor (scorecards)
www.deminor.com

Department of Trade and Industry (CSR)
www.csr.gov.uk

EIRIS (Ethical Investment Research Service)
www.eiris.org

Global Corporate Governance Forum
www.gcgf.org

Hermes Pensions Management
www.hermes.co.uk

The Institute of Business Ethics
www.ibe.org.uk

Institutional Shareholder Services (ISS)
www.issproxy.com

Investor Relations Society
www.ir-soc.org.uk

The Investor Responsibility Research Centre
www.irrc.org

London Stock Exchange
www.stockex.co.uk

The National Association of Corporate Directors, USA
www.nacdonline.org

New York Stock Exchange
www.nyse.com

OECD Principles of Corporate Governance
www.oecd.org

Public Concern at Work (Whistleblowing)
www.pcaw.co.uk

Standard and Poors (ratings)
www.standardand poors.com

Tyson Report
(www.london.edu/tysonreport).

US Securities and Exchange Commission
www.sec.gov

Table of Combined Code Provisions

Index